CIVILIZATION

Readings from
SCIENTIFIC AMERICAN

CIVILIZATION

With Introductions by
Brian M. Fagan
University of California, Santa Barbara

W. H. Freeman and Company
San Francisco

Some of the SCIENTIFIC AMERICAN articles in
CIVILIZATION are available as separate Offprints. For
a complete list of articles now available as Offprints,
write to W. H. Freeman and Company, 660 Market
Street, San Francisco, California 94104.

Library of Congress Cataloging in Publication Data

Main entry under title:

Civilization: readings from Scientific American.

   CONTENTS: Adams. The origin of cities.—Kramer. The
Sumerians.—Lamberg-Karlovsky and Lamberg-Karlovsky.
An early city in Iran.—Millon. [etc.]

  Bibliography: p.
  Includes index.
  1. Civilization, Ancient—Addresses, essays, lectures.
2. Cities and towns, Ancient—Addresses, essays, lectures.
I. Fagan, Brian M.   II. Scientific American.
CB311.C68   909   78-15780
ISBN 0-7167-1024-2
ISBN 0-7167-1023-4 pbk.

Copyright © 1957, 1960, 1965, 1967, 1968, 1970, 1971,
1972, 1974, 1977, 1978, 1979 by Scientific American, Inc.

No part of this book may be reproduced by any
mechanical, photographic, or electronic process, or in
the form of a phonographic recording, nor may it be
stored in a retrieval system, transmitted, or otherwise
copied for public or private use, without written
permission from the publisher.

Printed in the United States of America

9 8 7 6 5 4 3 2 1

PREFACE

Civilization brings together a series of articles from SCIENTIFIC AMERICAN dealing with one of the critical issues of history and prehistory: the growth and long-term human consequences of urban civilization. "Civilization" is a truly human concept—a notion of "behavior proper to the intercourse of civilized people," as the Oxford Dictionary rather quaintly puts it. We Westerners think of ourselves as refined people who behave in a "civilized" manner, with a proper legal sense of right and wrong. We have well-developed tastes in art, literature, music, and culture that reflect cultural behavior acquired through generations of our distinctive civilization. A century ago, our civilization tended to look down on other societies, to denigrate the institutions of other cultures considered "uncivilized." But the vastly improved communications of this century, among other factors, have led to a much better understanding of other societies, and so to a realization that humans have many different definitions of "civilization."

This book will introduce the reader to the meaning, origins, and evolution of civilization. It is intended for students of anthropology and for anyone interested in the origins and development of human society.

June 1978   Brian M. Fagan

CONTENTS

General Introduction   1

I   EARLY CIVILIZATION

                   Introduction   6
ADAMS   1   The Origin of Cities   10
KRAMER   2   The Sumerians   18
LAMBERG-KARLOVSKY AND LAMBERG-KARLOVSKY   3   An Early City in Iran   31
MILLON   4   Teotihuacán   41

II   INVENTIONS AND THE URBAN TRADITION

                   Introduction   54
MADDIN, MUHLY, AND WHEELER   5   How the Iron Age Began   57
PIGGOTT   6   The Beginnings of Wheeled Transport   65
HUMPHREY AND PEDLEY   7   Roman Carthage   75
BIDDLE   8   The Archaeology of Winchester   83
HAMMOND   9   The Planning of a Maya Ceremonial Center   95

III   CONSEQUENCES

                   Introduction   106
SJOBERG   10   The Origin and Evolution of Cities   109
BROWN   11   Human Food Production as a Process in the Biosphere   119
NEF   12   An Early Energy Crisis and Its Consequences   129
DAVIS   13   The Migrations of Human Populations   137

                   Bibliographies   151
                   Index   155

Note on cross-references: References to articles included in this book are noted by the title of the article and the page on which it begins; references to articles that are available as Offprints, but are not included here, are noted by the article's title and Offprint number; references to articles published by SCIENTIFIC AMERICAN, but which are not available as Offprints, are noted by the title of the article and the month and year of its publication.

GENERAL INTRODUCTION

The emergence of civilization was, along with the beginnings of food production, one of the most significant events in human history and prehistory. Only the emergence of humanity from the nonhuman primates was a more profound development. But what forces shaped civilization? Can there be such a thing as a uniform definition of civilization? Anthropologists and historians have long tried to define civilization in uniform terms. Historians such as Arnold Toynbee have tried to explain the origins of civilization in terms of successful responses to challenging difficulties. Toynbee thought in terms not only of challenges but also of at least 21 civilizations, each a species of the "genus human society." The distinguished Orientalist Henri Frankfort spoke of the "form" of a civilization—the style that shaped its political and judicial institutions and its art, literature, religion, and morals. The form of a civilization changes through time, he wrote, as a result both of continuous internal change and of external forces. And the anthropologist Robert Redfield made a sharp distinction between the folk society of prehistoric and later times and the literate civilization. Folk societies were based on the notion that the moral order is more important than the technological order. Technology in these societies is simple; no formal religion or state regulations control the behavior of the members of a folk society. Redfield regards civilization as the exact opposite of the folk society with respect to its relations between technology and morality. He defines civilization as a single state (rather than 21)—a state of society in which the community is much larger and less self-sufficient. The simple division of labor between males and females is replaced by more complex, much more impersonal relationships. Family and kin relationships are replaced by the larger affiliations of social class or religious belief. Social thinking has generally become more systematic, as its dominant attitudes and philosophies result from more reflective postures about the human condition. Civilizations usually want to justify their existence and their place in the world; folk societies are more concerned with a state of equilibrium, with simply "being."

Civilization is, of course, mostly things added to society: writing, public works, cities, markets, long-distance trading, and so on. A whole new and elaborate social structure comes into being, based on a state organized into social or economic classes, with power in the hands of an aristocratic elite and, often, a divine ruler or a group of military leaders and priests. To study the origins of civilization is to trace the evolution of human societies away from folk societies. Not all civilizations depart completely from the norms of folk society. Chinese civilization, for example, retained much of the social organization of earlier times, but Chinese art and philosophy underwent dramatic refinement.

Redfield's way of looking at civilization involves study of both the technological and intangible aspects of human society. Archaeologists must, perforce, work with the material remains of ancient civilizations—with artifacts and houses, food remains and art objects. As a result, archaeologists have defined civilization in technological terms, in the context of such phenomena as the city. Archaeologist V. Gordon Childe referred to an Urban Revolution, a revolution in human history that coincided with the emergence of the city and urban life. Cities are a truly human product; the first city dwellers in Mesopotamia some 5,000 years ago had behind them a long cultural and technological evolution. Archaeological students of early civilization tend to study the remains of early cities, for those represent the most conspicuous surviving remains of early civilization. Thus it is no coincidence that the archaeological articles in this Reader are concerned mainly with the evolution and nature of the city and of urban life. Archaeologists have paid too little attention to the phenomenon of civilization itself, although today's prehistorian is as much concerned with the intangibles of human society as with the technological achievements of the past. Focusing on the new challenges involved in urban life—much higher population densities in teeming urban communities, without the tribal ties of the village and countryside—offers a means of understanding how cities and civilizations arose. The leaders of the new cities had to create new organizational structures to feed more mouths and handle the increased political and economic complexities of the city-state. Scribes created archives as they recorded the process of government. Even more complex societies emerged, with political, economic, and military leadership overshadowing kin and clan ties. The distinctive cultural styles of such early civilizations developed either from thousands of years of earlier cultural evolution or from contacts with other civilizations. The Maya of Mesoamerica acquired many culture traits from the people of Teotihuacán, for example, the Mycenaeans from the Minoans, and so on. And human cultural evolution did not cease with the emergence of urban civilization.

After 5,000 years, we can contemplate the awesome achievements of the people who developed and evolved human civilization in its many diverse forms. Today we live in an environment controlled to a great extent by our own technology. Our taxes support a bewildering range of services and thousands of salaried officials who organize our lives and deal with the complex problems of contemporary civilization. The achievements of modern civilization surround us with remarkable technologies and new opportunities for self-enrichment. American civilization has become the civilization of the impersonal and utilitarian institution, and of anonymous, lonely individuals among thousands of strangers. Today's industrial civilization has created massive problems that few Americans fully appreciate: overpopulation, urban poverty, and overexploitation of the global environment. Few of us realize how massive the population movements of recent centuries have been. These movements have diluted human diversity and made it harder and harder to think of the world's problems in anything but global terms.

Above all, we live in a world run by politicians, whose presence is truly the mark of all civilizations. For in the final analysis, civilization is not the society of tribal leaders or powerful military or religious figures; rather, it is the creation of *Homo politicus*—the human entrepreneur.

This short volume examines, through the pages of *Scientific American*, some of the issues involved in the study of early civilizations and some of the consequences of the trend toward urban dwelling and literate civilization. The earlier articles are vital to students of world prehistory concerned with the broad sweep of human cultural evolution. Later articles enter the realm of students of Western Civilization and of the history of technology. To what extent did the early civilizations contribute to the development of new technologies and to the development of the industrial civilization?

For most of the past 5,000 years, human civilization was a tentative and often fragile experiment, supported by relatively simple technologies and abundant cheap labor. In many areas where early civilizations flourished and empires waxed and waned, large and prosperous settlements vanished forever: the fragile pioneer civilizations could not survive the collapse of the political and economic structure that begat them. More permanent traditions of civilized life began to emerge with Roman cities and military camps, with the rebuilding of Carthage by its new masters only a short time after they destroyed it, and with the survival of Roman provincial towns after the collapse of the empire. But not until Medieval times did the explosion of city building begin that has continued unabated ever since. This explosion led to demands for goods, materials, and services on such a large scale that only major technological innovation could satisfy them. The *preindustrial civilization*, with its many innovations coming from repeated experimentation and craftspeople's accumulated experience with new technologies, was the ancestor of the *industrial civilization* and its mechanized technologies and almost infinite capacity for expansion and production.

The industrial civilization emerged with the Industrial Revolution of the eighteenth and nineteenth centuries. Mechanized technologies powered by fossil fuels, scientific experimentation, and vastly expanded commercial activity were among the factors that led to a quantum jump in the global population, worldwide trade, scientific knowledge, and large-scale migration. Today most Americans—and an increasing proportion of the world's population—live in an industrial civilization, in economic, political, and social contexts that were unimagined even 500 years ago. The pace of cultural evolution is now so rapid that one can measure change in terms of months and years instead of centuries and millennia.

The perceptive student of world prehistory and early civilization will follow the cultural evolution of civilization to its present global perspective. Everyone can see that, for the millions of people who enjoy a higher standard of living because of it, the industrial civilization has made enormous achievements. For many other people, its consequences have been unfortunate.

Especially obvious are the results of industrial civilization and its expanding consumption of natural resources. Most of the earliest civilizations were organized on a local scale, with territories that covered a few thousand square miles. The industrial civilization of today has a worldwide impact: our industrial cities affect not only the local environment but the global one as well. Through their technological developments, modern cities have created migrations of human populations on a greater scale than ever before. The Industrial Revolution exacerbated some long-term human problems that first arose at the time of the earliest civilizations, for famine and overpopulation are nothing new. But the industrial civilization has extended them around the world.

The closing articles in this book address the problems of the global implications of civilization. These contributions shed light on the central problem of our future cultural evolution, for worldwide industrial civilization affects not only city dwellers but societies living in the remotest corners of the earth. Problems of energy, food supplies, inflation, and poverty confront civilization on all sides, to such an extent that doomsday prophets worry about our long-term chances of survival. Is twentieth-century civilization the last chapter in human history? Will we simply run out of essential resources? People have been predicting civilization's demise ever since its beginning. I believe the essays in this anthology should be required reading—not only for archaeologists and anthropologists concerned with cultural evolution and civilization, but also for demographers, ecologists, and biologists. The articles should help them realize that humankind has faced serious food and energy shortages before, and has weathered major economic crises. Although today we face similar problems on an unprecedented scale, the articles in this volume give us every chance to believe that we will solve them.

The emergence of urban civilization began a process whereby the minds of people living in small communities were no longer shaped exclusively by local moral orders. The advent of writing furthered the spread of faiths, reformist ideas, and universal philosophies that were preached in thousands of villages, towns, and cities. Only civilization could bring about the moral conflict that enabled new ideas to arise and spread over large areas of the world. And the development of these ideas through debate and reflection was a whole new dimension in human experience. Robert Redfield wrote of great ideas developing in troubled minds and becoming agents of cultural and social change. Such ideas shape the moral order in human civilization. There is no reason to believe that humanity is running short of great ideas. The lessons of history, and of the articles in this Reader, give us hope for the future

EARLY CIVILIZATION

I

I   EARLY CIVILIZATION

INTRODUCTION

The city is truly a human creation—one that has only a 5,000 year history, beginning in Mesopotamia and extending to the present. City dwelling is now the dominant human settlement pattern—so dominant that the demands of the urban environment have torn apart in a few centuries the old social and cultural patterns that people followed for millennia. The industrial and technological innovations that resulted from city life have enabled us to exercise almost complete control over our environment. Nearly 70 percent of all Americans live in cities, and the proportions elsewhere in the world are rising rapidly. Urban dwellers' rapacious demands on the environment—for food and energy, for building land and water—have led to chronic strains on the natural environment and to catastrophic diminution of the earth's natural resources. The articles in this section examine some of the underlying issues in the origin and development of urban civilization.

As mentioned in the General Introduction, intense academic debate surrounds the origin of cities and civilization. Archaeologists tend to center their research on the origin of the city, for its remains are a tangible record of early civilization. Civilization itself is a concept that corresponds to changes in human society and in the moral order. Civilization also produces many tangible things: cities, writing, monumental architecture, and so on. Research into the origins of civilization has concentrated on technology and architecture to the virtual exclusion of intangible factors. It is no coincidence that the articles in this section are primarily concerned with the city and the denser settlement patterns of the early civilizations.

Although nineteenth-century scholars argued that humanity had progressed from a state of unsophisticated savagery to a pinnacle of achievement represented by literate civilization, serious research into the causes of urban civilization began only in this century. European archaeologist V. Gordon Childe believed that a great Urban Revolution occurred in the Near East about 5,000 years ago. Childe based his definition of the Urban Revolution on the development of densely populated settlements whose farmers supported a small army of craftspeople, priests, and traders by producing massive food supplies. Metallurgical industries developed, and wheeled and water-borne transport aided the development of long-distance trade routes and city industries. A class society of priests, administrators, soldiers, and full-time specialists emerged. Writing was used essentially for record keeping and the development of exact sciences and astronomy. "A unifying religious form" dominated urban life, argued Childe, as priests and despots rose to power over huge populations of peasants and craftspeople.

Childe's bold concept became a popular hypothesis, widely quoted in world histories and other popular works about the past. His Urban Revolution, thought to be a critical turning point in human cultural, economic, and social changes, dominated archaeological thinking for years. But unfortunately, some of Childe's criteria for cities and civilization are far from universal. Some early civilizations, such as those of the Maya and Mycenaeans, had no cities. Others, such as the Inca of Peru, never developed writing. The only features common to all civilizations seem to be a degree of craft specialization and a well-formulated religious structure.

Subsequent debate about the origin of cities and civilization has included both critiques of Childe's Urban Revolution hypothesis and attempts to understand some of the actual processes that led to the emergence of the city. Robert Adams's article "The Origin of Cities" discusses some of the issues that confront archaeologists and historians concerned with the beginnings of urban civilization. Adams emphasizes the importance of the development of social organization and craft specialization during the Urban Revolution. He describes the rise of cities as a reflection of changes rather in people's ways of interacting with each other than in their ways of interacting with their environment. The essential elements were a whole series of new institutions and vastly more complex social units. Urban civilization arose from interacting political, social, and economic forces. Because of these forces, the kin groups of peasant societies were gradually supplanted by a class society with political and religious officials to rule the state. This state involved military establishments, craftspeople, slaves, and bureaucrats.

In spite of many efforts, no one has yet succeeded in satisfactorily defining civilization itself. Archaeologists and historians have developed many different working definitions. One of the most widely accepted is that of anthropologist Clyde Kluckhohn, who delineated three criteria for civilization: towns with a population of more than 5,000 persons; writing; and monumental ceremonial architecture, including ceremonial centers. Archaeologists continue to search for the intangible causes of the earliest civilizations—the reasons why humans decided to congregate in large cities. These reasons are still imperfectly understood, partly because of the difficulty of reconstructing from archaeological evidence the complex system of interacting processes and factors that influenced the evolution of early civilization.

More recently, archaeologists have been considering systems models, regarding human society as one class of living system. Such models view the early urban-based civilization as a very complex system in which many different subsystems—such as technology, social organization, religious beliefs, and trade—interact with each other. Although such subsystems are found in hunter-gatherer and other less complex societies as well, their number and complexity multiplies with the more elaborate organization of the urban civilization. Complex mechanisms involving both decision-making and society's policies keep the whole system in equilibrium, a process analogous to the "checks and balances" in the U.S. Constitution. University of Michigan archaeologist Kent Flannery, among others, has studied systems models of early civilization in Mesoamerica and the Near East that suggest that the emergence of early civilization has no single overriding cause. He has tried to isolate a series of rules by which the origins of an urban civilization might be simulated. Investigating these mechanisms of decision-making lies at the center of systems modeling efforts, which are still in their infancy. Research of this type requires large quantities of field data; no comprehensive examples have yet been published.

The earliest urban civilization, that of the Sumerians, developed in the hot, low-lying Tigris-Euphrates plain of Iraq. This preindustrial urban civilization generated an abundant food surplus that permitted labor specialization and the development of a class structure capable of organizing irrigation schemes and other large-scale public works. Writing was the key to simple accounting and record keeping. But the Sumerians, like the Egyptians, Chinese, Greeks, Romans, and other preindustrial civilizations, had few energy sources. They relied heavily on human labor for manufacturing their basic industrial needs and on wood for heating. Samuel Kramer's description of the Sumerian civilization provides an insight into the earliest preindustrial urban civilization. The Sumerians used the natural resources of their environment intensively; they were the first to divert the great rivers of Mesopotamia for agricultural purposes. Kramer describes the innovations developed by the Sumerians—writing, new crafts, massive temples, and a remarkably free society. One has a sense that here society began by being democratic, then gradually evolved into a despotic state ruled by a divine king. As Kramer points out, Sumerian history is a record of bitter conflicts and increasing interrecine warfare. City-state after city-state rose to domination in a debilitating power struggle that gradually exhausted the Sumerians. After a series of powerful royal dynasties rose and fell, the Sumerians were submerged by Semitic peoples and vanished from history until archaeologists found their remains in the nineteenth century. But the political, religious, social, and economic innovations of their preindustrial civilization survived and became an essential part of the heritage of later, far larger empires.

Trade was a critical lifeline for early Mesopotamian civilizations. The trading connections of the Sumerians and their successors extended into the Nile Valley, to the Persian Gulf, onto the Iranian highlands, and to the Indus. Regular long-distance trade routes and barter networks, expanded from earlier times, were controlled by city rulers and organized by an emerging merchant class. Prosperous towns and cities sprang up far from the bustling delta, in places where essential raw materials could be mined for distant markets. One such site is Tepe Yahya in southeastern Iran. Tepe Yahya owed its importance to the manufacture of soapstone (steatite) vessels, which were traded to the Mesopotamian Delta as well as into the Indus Valley. Mesopotamia was deficient in metals and other commodities vital for an urban state dependent on resident craftspeople. So the Sumerians traded with the mineral-rich highlands, obtaining copper, silver, tin, and lead, as well as more prosaic commodities such as timber and obsidian, from the Elamites who lived at Tepe Yahya and elsewhere in highland Iran. This trade flourished more than 5,000 years ago. Places like Tepe Yahya were focal points in the long-distance trade that spread urban civilization to areas outside the narrow confines of Mesopotamia and the Nile Valley.

After 3000 B.C., literate, urban civilizations emerged in many parts of the world. The cities of Mohenjodaro and Harappa were flourishing in the Indus Valley by about 2500 B.C.; the first Chinese urban communities were certainly in existence in the Yellow River area about 1500 B.C., but they may have developed centuries earlier. Although the classic Near Eastern city form, with its narrow streets and dense urban populations, was widespread, it was by no means universal. Chinese urban centers housed priests, nobles, and rulers, while craftspeople and peasants lived in villages scattered over the countryside. But even as late as Medieval times, a relatively small proportion of the world's population lived in cities, although political and economic power lay in the hands of city rulers.

The peoples of Mesoamerica—notably the Maya, Zapotecs, Mixtecs, and Aztecs—developed large urban communities. Ceremonial centers were supported by a scattered rural population of lesser towns and small villages. But the most famous pre-Columbian city of all was Teotihuacán.

Today Teotihuacán is an international tourist attraction, and rightly so, for it was a religious and economic center of great importance during its heyday in the first millennium A.D. At the height of its prosperity Teotihuacán covered an area of 8 square miles and probably supported a population between 50,000 and 100,000, more than twice the population of Roman London. The top strata of society included religious leaders, bureaucrats, and soldiers. Their fine houses lined the great avenues in the center of the city, dwarfed by the huge pyramids and temples that formed the nucleus of Teotihuacán. The city's markets displayed merchandise from all over Mesoamerica as well as the products of local craftspeople. Teeming *barrio* apartment complexes housed an enormous and tightly controlled urban population fed by agricultural settlements near the city, many of them controlled by Teotihuacán's rulers. René Millon has spent many years in a comprehensive study of this huge preindustrial city. His article shows how Teotihuacán rose to remarkable prosperity within a few centuries and then just as suddenly collapsed. Millon looks closely at the mechanisms involved in the rise, prosperity, and fall of Teotihuacán. He concludes that "Teotihuacán was as influential in its collapse as in its long and brilliant flowering."

One striking aspect of the history of early civilizations is the rapidity with which many city-states rose and fell. Even the Roman Empire collapsed in a few centuries, as alien peoples usurped much of its power by manipulating its own administrative system. But for all their instability, most of the early civilizations left behind them an urban legacy: a tradition of cultural continuity, innovation, and basic religious and social institutions that have survived into modern times.

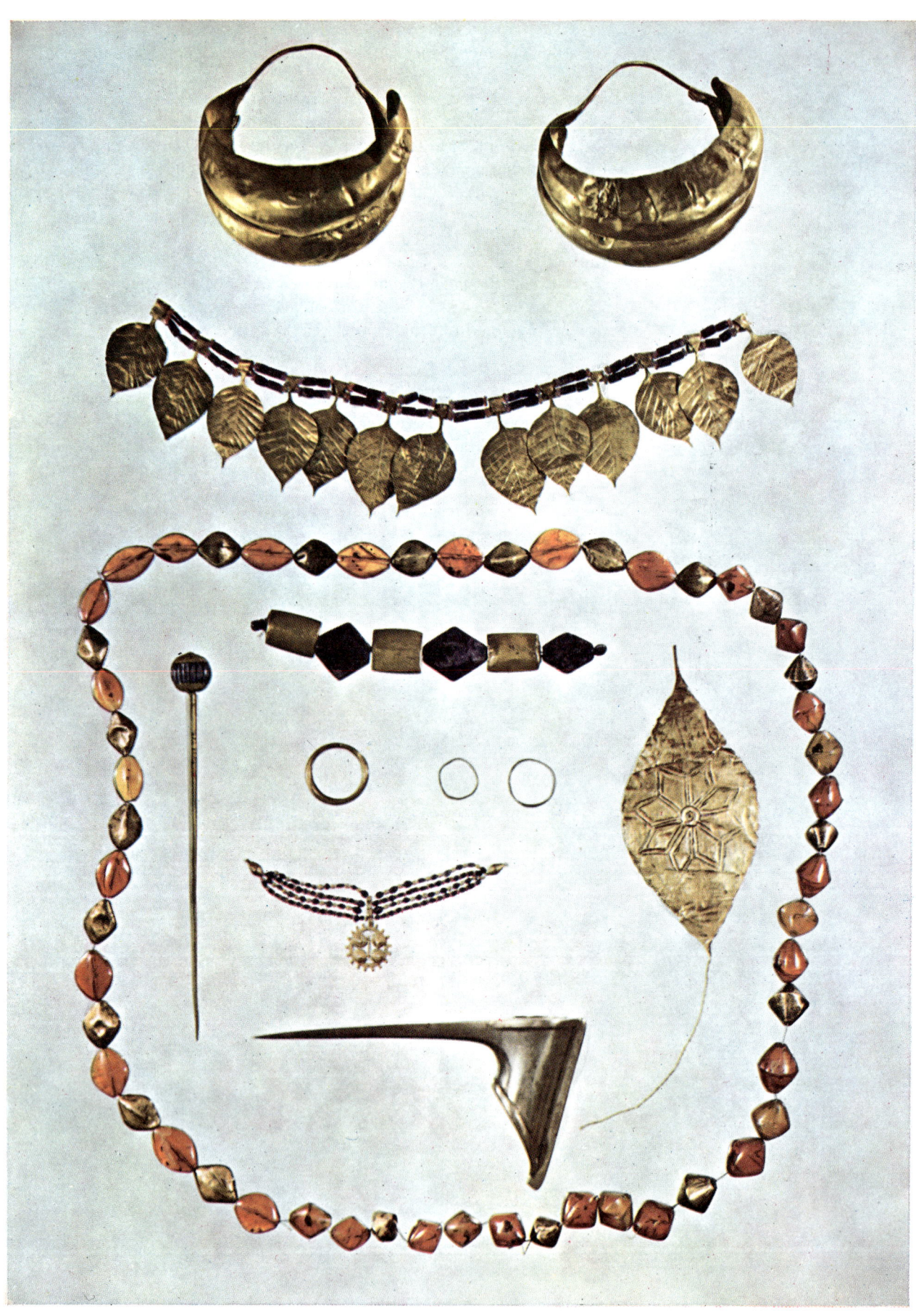

ROYAL GRAVE OFFERINGS from later tombs at Ur indicate the concentration of wealth that accompanied the emergence of a kingly class. Dated at about 2500 B.C., the objects include large gold earrings (*top*); a headdress with gold leaves; beads of gold, lapis and carnelian; gold rings; a gold leaf; a hairpin of gold and lapis; an ornament with a gold pendant; an adz head of electrum.

The Origin of Cities

by Robert M. Adams
September 1960

The agricultural revolution ultimately made it possible for men to congregate in large communities, and to take up specialized tasks. The first cities almost certainly arose in Mesopotamia

The rise of cities, the second great "revolution" in human culture, was pre-eminently a social process, an expression more of changes in man's interaction with his fellows than in his interaction with his environment. For this reason it marks not only a turning but also a branching point in the history of the human species.

Earlier steps are closely identified with an increasing breadth or intensity in the exploitation of the environment. Their distinguishing features are new tools and techniques and the discovery of new and more dependable resources for subsistence. Even in so advanced an achievement as the invention of agriculture, much of the variation from region to region was simply a reflection of local differences in subsistence potential.

In contrast the urban revolution was

MAP OF NIPPUR on a clay tablet dates from about 1500 B.C. Two lines at far left trace the course of Euphrates River; adjacent lines show one wall of the city. Square structures at far right are temples; the two vertical lines at right center represent a canal.

EARLY GRAVE OFFERINGS from Mesopotamian tombs of about 3900 B.C. consist mainly of painted pottery such as two vessels at left. Vessels of diorite (*center and right center*) and alabaster (*far right*), found in tombs of about 3500 B.C. and later, reflect growth of trade with other regions and increasing specialization of crafts. These vessels and objects on opposite page are in the University Museum of the University of Pennsylvania.

a decisive cultural and social change that was less directly linked to changes in the exploitation of the environment. To be sure, it rested ultimately on food surpluses obtained by agricultural producers above their own requirements and somehow made available to city dwellers engaged in other activities. But its essential element was a whole series of new institutions and the vastly greater size and complexity of the social unit, rather than basic innovations in subsistence. In short, the different forms that early urban societies assumed are essentially the products of differently interacting political and economic—human —forces. And the interpretive skills required to understand them are correspondingly rooted more in the social sciences and humanities than in the natural sciences.

Even the term urban needs qualification. Many of the qualities we think of as civilized have been attained by societies that failed to organize cities. At least some Egyptologists believe that civilization advanced for almost 2,000 years under the Pharaohs before true cities appeared in Egypt. The period was marked by the development of monumental public works, a formal state superstructure, written records and the beginnings of exact science. In the New World, too, scholars are still searching the jungles around Maya temple centers in Guatemala and Yucatán for recognizably urban agglomerations of dwellings. For all its temple architecture and high art, and the intellectual achievement represented by its hieroglyphic writing and accurate long-count calendar, classic Maya civilization apparently was not based on the city.

These facts do not detract from the fundamental importance of the urban revolution, but underline its complex character. Every high civilization other than possibly the Mayan did ultimately produce cities. And in most civilizations urbanization began early.

There is little doubt that this was the case for the oldest civilization and the earliest cities: those of ancient Mesopotamia. The story of their development, which we will sketch here, is still a very tentative one. In large part the uncertainties are due to the state of the archeological record, which is as yet both scanty and unrepresentative. The archeologist's preoccupation with early temple-furnishings and architecture, for example, has probably exaggerated their importance, and has certainly given us little information about contemporary secular life in neighboring precincts of the same towns.

Eventually written records help overcome these deficiencies. However, 500 or more years elapsed between the onset of the first trends toward urbanism and the earliest known examples of cuneiform script. And then for the succeeding 700 or 800 years the available texts are laconic, few in number and poorly understood. To a degree, they can be supplemented by cautious inferences drawn from later documents. But the earliest chapters rest primarily on archeological data.

Let us pick up the narrative where Robert J. Braidwood left it in *The Agricultural Revolution*, with the emergence of a fully agricultural people, many of them grouped together in villages of perhaps 200 to 500 individuals. Until almost the end of our own story, dating finds little corroboration in written records. Moreover, few dates based on the decay of radioactive carbon are yet available in Mesopotamia for this crucial period. But by 5500 B.C., or even earlier, it appears that the village-farming community had fully matured in southwestern Asia. As a way of life it then stabilized internally for 1,500 years or more, although it continued to spread downward from the hills and piedmont where it had first crystallized in the great river valleys.

Then came a sharp increase in tempo. In the next 1,000 years some of the small agricultural communities on the alluvial plain between the Tigris and Euphrates rivers not only increased greatly in size, but changed decisively in structure. They culminated in the Sumerian city-state with tens of thousands of inhabitants, elaborate religious, political and military establishments, stratified social classes, advanced technology and widely extended trading contacts [see "The Sumerians," by Samuel Noah Kramer; SCIENTIFIC AMERICAN, October, 1957]. The river-valley agriculture on which the early Mesopotamian cities were established differed considerably from that of the uplands where domestication had begun. Wheat and barley remained the staple crops, but they were supplemented by dates. The date palm yielded not only prodigious and dependable supplies of fruit but also wood. Marshes and estuaries teemed with fish, and their reeds provided another building material. There was almost no stone, however; before the establishment of trade with surrounding areas, hard-fired clay served for such necessary agricultural tools as sickles.

The domestic animals—sheep, goats, donkeys, cattle and pigs by the time of the first textual evidence—may have differed little from those known earlier in the foothills and northern plains. But they were harder to keep, particularly the cattle and the donkeys which were needed as draft animals for plowing. During the hot summers all vegetation withered except for narrow strips along the watercourses. Fodder had to be cultivated and distributed, and pastureland was at a premium. These problems of management may help explain why the herds rapidly became a responsibility of people associated with the temples. And control of the herds in turn may have provided the stimulus that led temple officials frequently to assume broader control over the economy and agriculture.

Most important, agriculture in the alluvium depended on irrigation, which had not been necessary in the uplands. For a long time the farmers made do with small-scale systems, involving breaches in the natural embankments of the streams and uncontrolled local flooding. The beginnings of large-scale canal networks seem clearly later than the advent of fully established cities.

In short, the immediately pre-urban society of southern Mesopotamia consisted of small communities scattered along natural watercourses. Flocks had to forage widely, but cultivation was confined to narrow enclaves of irrigated plots along swamp margins and stream banks. In general the swamps and rivers provided an important part of the raw materials and diet.

Where in this pattern were the inducements, perhaps even preconditions, for urbanization that explain the precocity of the Mesopotamian achievement? First, there was the productivity of irrigation agriculture. In spite of chronic water-shortage during the earlier part of the growing season and periodic floods around the time of the harvest, in spite of a debilitating summer climate and the ever present danger of salinity in flooded or over-irrigated fields, farming yielded a clear and dependable surplus of food.

Second, the very practice of irrigation must have helped induce the growth of cities. It is sometimes maintained that the inducement lay in a need for centralized control over the building and maintaining of elaborate irrigation systems, but this does not seem to have been the case. As we have seen, such systems came after the cities themselves. However, by engendering inequalities in access to productive land, irrigation contributed to the formation of a stratified society. And by furnishing a reason for border disputes between neighboring communities, it surely promoted a warlike atmosphere that drew people together in offensive and defensive concentrations.

Finally, the complexity of subsistence pursuits on the flood plains may have indirectly aided the movement toward cities. Institutions were needed to medi-

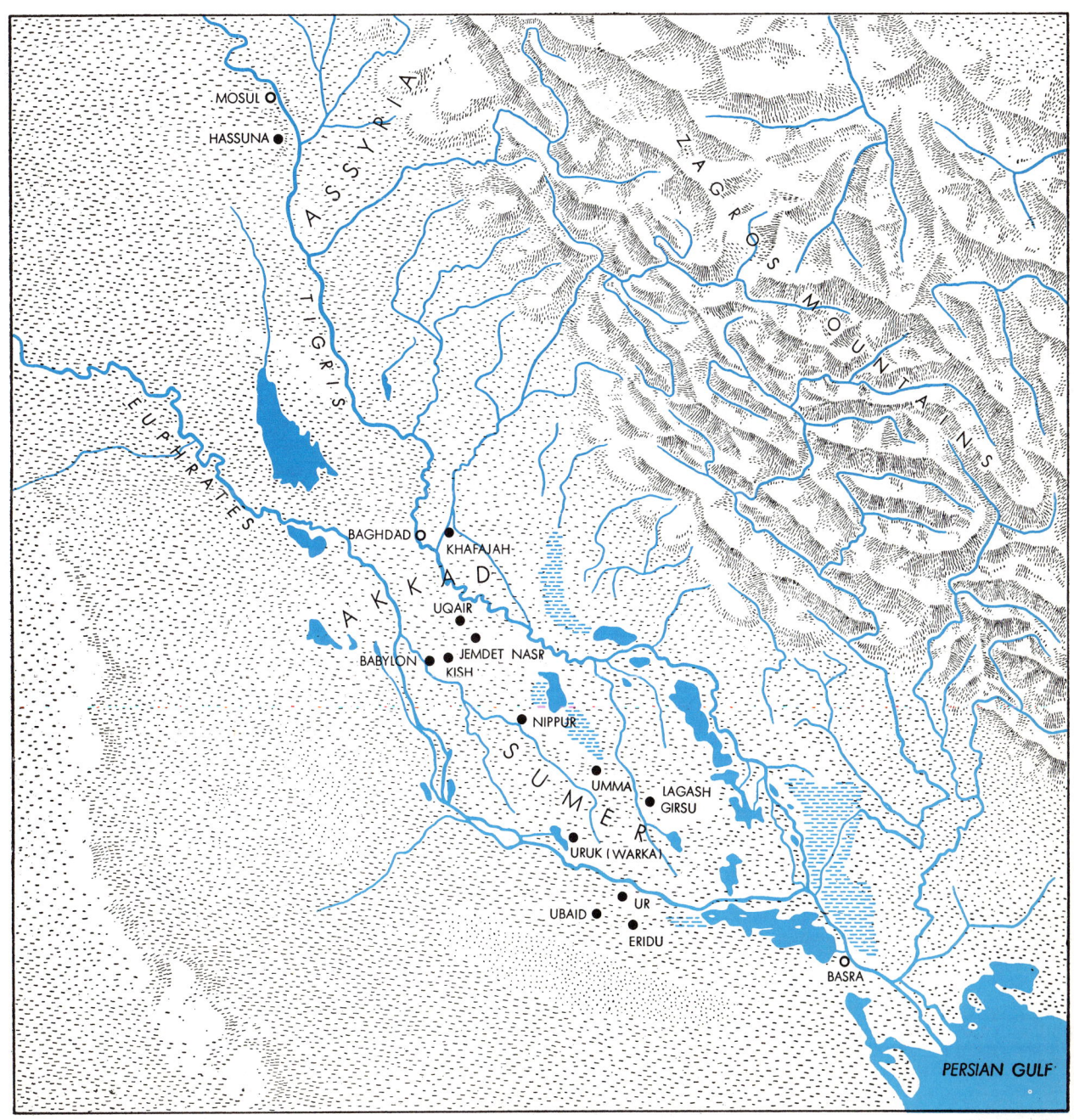

ANCIENT CITIES of Mesopotamia (*black dots*) were located mainly along Tigris and Euphrates rivers and their tributaries. In ancient times these rivers followed different courses from those shown on this modern map. Modern cities are shown as open dots.

CITY OF ERBIL in northern Iraq is built on the site of ancient city of Arbela. This aerial view suggests the character and appearance of Mesopotamian cities of thousands of years ago, with streets and houses closely packed around central public buildings.

ate between herdsman and cultivator; between fisherman and sailor; between plowmaker and plowman. Whether through a system of rationing, palace largesse or a market that would be recognizable to us, the city provided a logical and necessary setting for storage, exchange and redistribution. Not surprisingly, one of the recurrent themes in early myths is a rather didactic demonstration that the welfare of the city goddess is founded upon the harmonious interdependence of the shepherd and the farmer.

In any case the gathering forces for urbanization first become evident around 4000 B.C. Which of them furnished the initial impetus is impossible to say, if indeed any single factor was responsible. We do not even know as yet whether the onset of the process was signaled by a growth in the size of settlements. And of course mere increase in size would not necessarily imply technological or economic advance beyond the level of the village-farming community. In our own time we have seen primitive agricultural peoples, such as the Yoruba of western Nigeria, who maintained sizable cities that were in fact little more than overgrown village-farming settlements. They were largely self-sustaining because most of the productive inhabitants were full-time farmers.

The evidence suggests that at the beginning the same was true of Mesopotamian urbanization: immediate economic change was not its central characteristic. As we shall see shortly, the first clear-cut trend to appear in the archeological record is the rise of temples. Conceivably new patterns of thought and social organization crystallizing within the temples served as the primary force in bringing people together and setting the process in motion.

Whatever the initial stimulus to growth and reorganization, the process itself clearly involved the interaction of many different factors. Certainly the institutions of the city evolved in different directions and at different rates, rather than as a smoothly emerging totality. Considering the present fragmentary state of knowledge, it is more reasonable here to follow some of these trends individually rather than to speculate from the shreds (or, rather, sherds!) and patches of data about how the complete organizational pattern developed.

Four archeological periods can be distinguished in the tentative chronology of the rise of the Mesopotamian city-state. The earliest is the Ubaid, named for the first site where remains of this period were uncovered [see map on page 13]. At little more than a guess, it may have lasted for a century or two past 4000 B.C., giving way to the relatively brief Warka period. Following this the first written records appeared during the Protoliterate period, which spanned the remainder of the fourth millennium. The final part of our story is the Early Dynastic period, which saw the full flowering of independent city-states between about 3000 and 2500 B.C.

Of all the currents that run through the whole interval, we know most about religious institutions. Small shrines existed in the early villages of the northern plains and were included in the cultural inventory of the earliest known agriculturalists in the alluvium. Before the end of the Ubaid period the free-standing shrine had lost its original fluidity of plan and adopted architectural features that afterward permanently characterized Mesopotamian temples. The development continued into the Early Dynastic period, when we see a complex of workshops and storehouses surrounding a greatly enlarged but rigidly traditional arrangement of cult chambers. No known contemporary structures were remotely comparable in size or complexity to these establishments until almost the end of the Protoliterate period.

At some point specialized priests appeared, probably the first persons released from direct subsistence labor. Their ritual activities are depicted in Protoliterate seals and stone carvings. If not immediately, then quite early, the priests also assumed the role of economic administrators, as attested by ration or wage lists found in temple premises among the earliest known examples of writing. The priestly hierarchies continued to supervise a multitude of economic as well as ritual activities into (and beyond) the Early Dynastic period, although by then more explicitly political forms of organization had perhaps become dominant. For a long time, however, temples seem to have been the

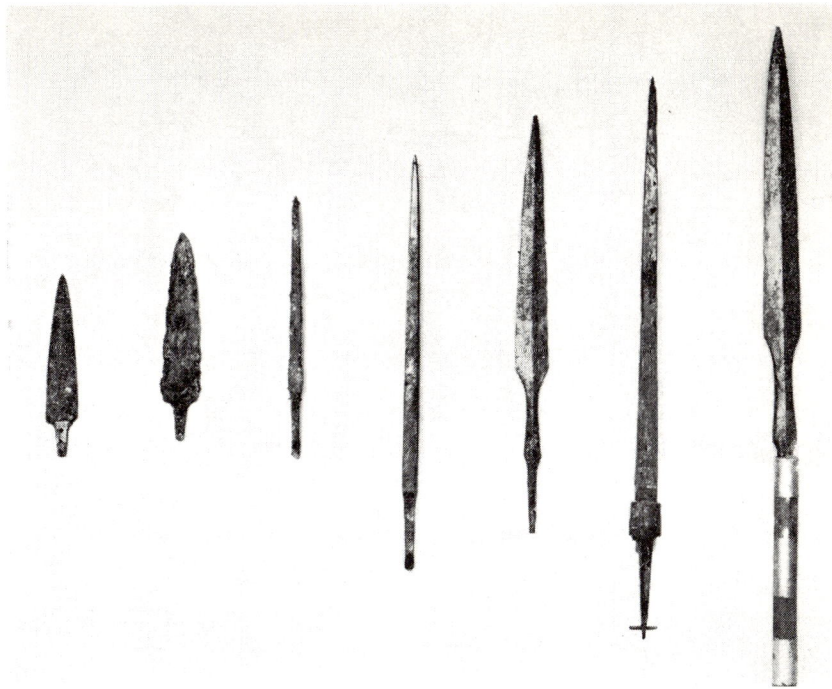

SPEARHEADS of copper and bronze from the royal cemetery at Ur date back to the third millennium B.C. The workmanship of these weapons matches that of the jewelry shown on page 10.

largest and most complex institutions that existed in the communities growing up around them.

The beginnings of dynastic political regimes are much harder to trace. Monumental palaces, rivaling the temples in size, appear in the Early Dynastic period, but not earlier. The term for "king" has not yet been found in Protoliterate texts. Even so-called royal tombs apparently began only in the Early Dynastic period.

Lacking contemporary historical or archeological evidence, we must seek the origins of dynastic institutions primarily in later written versions of traditional myths. Thorkild Jacobsen of the University of Chicago has argued persuasively that Sumerian myths describing the world of the gods reflect political institutions as they existed in human society just prior to the rise of dynastic authority. If so, they show that political authority in the Protoliterate period rested in an assembly of the adult male members of the community. Convoked only to meet sporadic external threat, the assembly's task was merely to select a short-term war leader.

Eventually, as the myths themselves suggest, successful war leaders were retained even in times of peace. Herein lies the apparent origin of kingship. At times springing up outside the priestly corporations, at times coming from them,

ROYAL WAR-CHARIOT carved on limestone plaque from city of Ur reflects increasing concern of Mesopotamian cities about methods of warfare in middle of third millennium B.C.

RELIGIONS of ancient Mesopotamia were dominated by the idea that man was fashioned to serve the gods. Here a worshipper followed by figure with pail brings a goat as an offering to goddess seated at right. A divine attendant kneels before her. This impression and the one below were made from stone cylinder-seals of Akkadian period (about 2400 B.C.).

new leaders emerged who were preoccupied with, and committed to, both defensive and offensive warfare against neighboring city-states.

The traditional concerns of the temples were not immediately affected by the new political leadership. Palace officials acquired great landed estates of their own, but the palace itself was occupied chiefly with such novel activities as raising and supplying its army, maintaining a large retinue of servants and entertainers and constructing a defensive wall around the city.

These undertakings took a heavy toll of the resources of the young city-states, perhaps too heavy to exact by the old "democratic" processes. Hence it is not surprising that as permanent, hereditary royal authority became established, the position of the assembly declined. In the famous epic of Gilgamesh, an Early Dynastic king of Uruk, the story opens with the protests of the citizenry over their forced labor on the city walls. Another episode shows Gilgamesh manipulating the assembly, obviously no longer depending on its approval for his power. Rooted in war, the institution of kingship intensified a pattern of predatory expansionism and shifting military rivalries. The early Mesopotamian king could trace his origin to the need for military leadership. But the increasingly militaristic flavor of the Early Dynastic period also can be traced at least in part to the interests and activities of kings and their retinues as they proceeded to consolidate their power.

As society shifted its central focus from temple to palace it also separated into classes. Archeologically, the process can best be followed through the increasing differentiation in grave offerings in successively later cemeteries. Graves of the Ubaid period, at the time when monumental temples were first appearing, hold little more than a variable number of pottery vessels. Those in the cemetery at Ur, dating from the latter part of the Early Dynastic period, show a great disparity in the wealth they contain. A small proportion, the royal tombs (not all of whose principal occupants may have belonged to royal families), are richly furnished with beautifully wrought weapons, ornaments and utensils of gold and lapis lazuli. A larger number contain a few copper vessels or an occasional bead of precious metal, but the majority have only pottery vessels or even nothing at all. Both texts and archeological evidence indicate that copper and bronze agricultural tools were beyond the reach of the ordinary peasant until after the Early Dynastic period, while graves of the well-to-do show "conspicuous consumption" of copper in the form of superfluous stands for pottery vessels even from the beginning of the period.

Early Dynastic texts likewise record social and economic stratification. Records from the main archive of the Baba Temple in Girsu, for example, show substantial differences in the allotments from that temple's lands to its parishioners. Other texts describe the sale of houseplots or fields, often to form great estates held by palace officials and worked by communities of dependent clients who may originally have owned the land. Still others record the sale of slaves, and the rations allotted to slaves producing textiles under the supervision of temple officials. As a group, however, slaves constituted only a small minority of the population until long after the Early Dynastic period.

Turning to the development of technology, we find a major creative burst in early Protoliterate times, involving very rapid stylistic and technical advance in the manufacture of seals, statuary and ornate vessels of carved stone, cast copper or precious metals. But the number of craft specialists apparently was very small, and the bulk of their products seems to have been intended only for cult purposes. In contrast the Early Dynastic period saw a great increase in production of nonagricultural commodities, and almost certainly a corresponding increase in the proportion of the population that was freed from the tasks of primary subsistence to pursue their craft on a full-time basis. Both stylistically and technologically, however, this expansion was rooted in the accomplishments of the previous period and produced few innovations of its own.

Production was largely stimulated by three new classes of demand. First, the burgeoning military establishment of the palace required armaments, including not only metal weapons and armor but also more elaborate equipment such as chariots. Second, a considerable vol-

GILGAMESH, early Mesopotamian king and hero of legend, may be figure attacking water buffalo (right center). Figure stabbing lion may be his companion, the bull-man Enkidu.

ume of luxury goods was commissioned for the palace retinue. And third, a moderate private demand for these goods seems to have developed also. The mass production of pottery, the prevalence of such articles as cylinder seals and metal utensils, the existence of a few vendors' stalls and the hoards of objects in some of the more substantial houses all imply at least a small middle class. Most of these commodities, it is clear, were fabricated in the major Mesopotamian towns from raw materials brought from considerable distance. Copper, for example, came from Oman and the Anatolian plateau, more than 1,000 miles from the Sumerian cities. The need for imports stimulated the manufacture of such articles as textiles, which could be offered in exchange, and also motivated the expansion of territorial control by conquest.

Some authorities have considered that technological advance, which they usually equate with the development of metallurgy, was a major stimulant or even a precondition of urban growth. Yet, in southern Mesopotamia at least, the major quantitative expansion of metallurgy, and of specialized crafts in general, came only after dynastic city-states were well advanced. While the spread of technology probably contributed further to the development of militarism and social stratification, it was less a cause than a consequence of city growth. The same situation is found in New World civilizations. Particularly in aboriginal Middle America the technological level remained very nearly static before and after the urban period.

Finally we come to the general forms of the developing cities, perhaps the most obscure aspect of the whole process of urbanization. Unhappily even Early Dynastic accounts do not oblige us with extensive descriptions of the towns where they were written, nor even with useful estimates of population. Contemporary maps also are unknown; if they were made, they still elude us. References to towns in the myths and epics are at best vague and allegorical. Ultimately archeological studies can supply most of these deficiencies, but at present we have little to go on.

The farming villages of the pre-urban era covered at most a few acres. Whether the villages scattered over the alluvial plain in Ubaid times were much different from the earlier ones in the north is unclear; certainly most were no larger, but the superficial appearance of one largely unexcavated site indicates that they may have been more densely built up and more formally laid out along a regular grid of streets or lanes. By the end of the Ubaid period the temples had begun to expand; a continuation of this trend is about all that the remains of Warka and early Protoliterate periods can tell us thus far. Substantial growth seems to have begun toward the end of the Protoliterate period and to have continued through several centuries of the Early Dynastic. During this time the first battlemented ring-walls were built around at least the larger towns.

A few Early Dynastic sites have been excavated sufficiently to give a fairly full picture of their general layout. Radiating out from the massive public buildings of these cities, toward the outer gates, were streets, unpaved and dusty, but straight and wide enough for the passage of solid-wheeled carts or chariots. Along the streets lay the residences of the well-to-do citizenry, usually arranged around spacious courts and sometimes provided with latrines draining into sewage conduits below the streets. The houses of the city's poorer inhabitants were located behind or between the large multiroomed dwellings. They were approached by tortuous, narrow alleys, were more haphazard in plan, were less well built and very much smaller. Mercantile activities were probably concentrated along the quays of the adjoining river or at the city gates. The marketplace or bazaar devoted to private commerce had not yet appeared.

Around every important urban center rose the massive fortifications that guarded the city against nomadic raids and the usually more formidable campaigns of neighboring rulers. Outside the walls clustered sheepfolds and irrigated tracts, interspersed with subsidiary villages and ultimately disappearing into the desert. And in the desert dwelt only the nomad, an object of mixed fear and scorn to the sophisticated court poet. By the latter part of the Early Dynastic period several of the important capitals of lower Mesopotamia included more than 250 acres within their fortifications. The city of Uruk extended over 1,100 acres and contained possibly 50,000 people.

For these later cities there are written records from which the make-up of the population can be estimated. The overwhelming majority of the able-bodied adults still were engaged in primary agricultural production on their own holdings, on allotments of land received from the temples or as dependent retainers on large estates. But many who were engaged in subsistence agriculture also had other roles. One temple archive, for example, records that 90 herdsmen, 80 soldier-laborers, 100 fishermen, 125 sailors, pilots and oarsmen, 25 scribes, 20 or 25 craftsmen (carpenters, smiths, potters, leather-workers, stonecutters, and mat- or basket-weavers) and probably 250 to 300 slaves were numbered among its parish of around 1,200 persons. In addition to providing for its own subsistence and engaging in a variety of specialized pursuits, most of this group was expected to serve in the army in time of crisis.

Earlier figures can only be guessed at from such data as the size of temple establishments and the quantity of craft-produced articles. Toward the end of the Protoliterate period probably less than a fifth of the labor force was substantially occupied with economic activities outside of subsistence pursuits; in Ubaid times a likely figure is 5 per cent.

It is not easy to say at what stage in the whole progression the word "city" becomes applicable. By any standard Uruk and its contemporaries were cities. Yet they still lacked some of the urban characteristics of later eras. In particular, the development of municipal politics, of a self-conscious corporate body with at least partially autonomous, secular institutions for its own administration, was not consummated until classical times.

Many of the currents we have traced must have flowed repeatedly in urban civilizations. But not necessarily all of them. The growth of the Mesopotamian city was closely related to the rising tempo of warfare. For their own protection people must have tended to congregate under powerful rulers and behind strong fortifications; moreover, they may have been consciously and forcibly drawn together by the elite in the towns in order to centralize political and economic controls. On the other hand, both in aboriginal Central America and in the Indus Valley (in what is now Pakistan) great population centers grew up without comprehensive systems of fortification, and with relatively little emphasis on weapons or on warlike motifs in art.

There is not one origin of cities, but as many as there are independent cultural traditions with an urban way of life. Southern Mesopotamia merely provides the earliest example of a process that, with refinements introduced by the industrial revolution and the rise of national states, is still going on today.

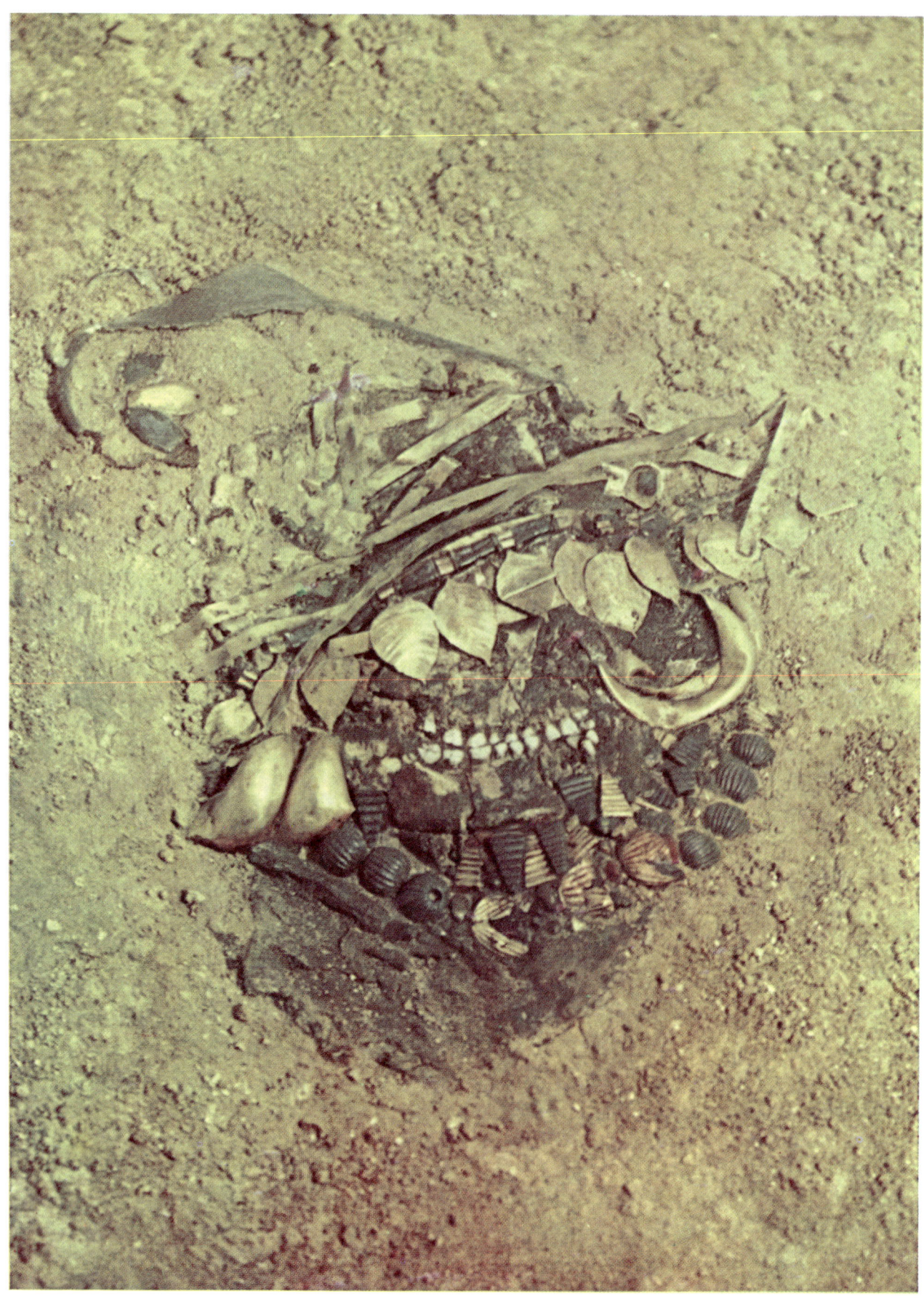

PARTLY EXCAVATED BURIAL of a lady-in-waiting to a Sumerian royal family of 2500 B.C. was moved intact from Ur to the University Museum of the University of Pennsylvania. Amid the rich ornaments of gold may be seen the teeth of their wearer.

The Sumerians

by Samuel Noah Kramer
October 1957

This gifted people lived at the head of the Persian Gulf roughly between 5,000 and 3,000 years ago. Their brilliant technological and social inventions laid the foundation of modern civilization

The Tigris-Euphrates plain is a hot, arid land. Six thousand years ago it was a wind-swept barren. It had no minerals, almost no stone, no trees, practically no building material of any kind. It has been described as a land with "the hand of God against it." Yet it was in this desolate region that man built what was probably the first high civilization. Here were born the inventions of writing, farming technology, architecture, the first codes of law, the first cities. Perhaps the very poverty of the land provided the stimulus that mothered these inventions. But the main credit must go to the people who created them—a most remarkable people called the Sumerians.

These Sumerians, as now revealed by long archaeological research, were a surprisingly modern folk. In many ways they were like the pioneers who built the U. S.—practical, ambitious, enterprising, jealous of their personal rights, technologically inventive. Having no stone or timber, they built with marsh reeds and river mud, invented the brick mold and erected cities of baked clay. They canalled the waters of the Tigris and Euphrates rivers into the arid fields and turned Sumer into a veritable Garden of Eden. To manage their irrigation systems they originated regional government, thus emerging from the petty social order of the family and village to the city-state. They created a written language and committed it to permanent clay tablets. They traded their grain surpluses to distant peoples for metals and other materials they lacked. By the third millennium B.C. the culture and civilization of Sumer, a country about the size of the state of Massachusetts, had spread its influence over the whole Middle East, from India to the Mediterranean. And there is hardly an area of our culture today—in mathematics or philosophy, literature or architecture, finance or education, law or politics, religion or folklore—that does not owe some of its origins to the Sumerians.

One might suppose that the story of the Sumerians and their accomplishments would be one of the most celebrated in history. But the astonishing fact is that until about a century ago the modern world had no idea that Sumer or its people had ever existed. For more than 2,000 years they had simply vanished from the human record. Babylonia and ancient Egypt were known to every history student, but the earlier Sumerians were buried and forgotten. Now, thanks to a century of archaeological labor and to the Sumerians' own cuneiform tablets, we have come to know them intimately—as well as or better than any other people of the early history of mankind. The story of how the lost Sumerian civilization was discovered is itself a remarkable chapter. This article will review briefly how the history of the Sumerians was resurrected and what we have learned about them.

The Cuneiform Tablets

Modern archaeologists began to dig in Mesopotamia for its ancient civilizations around a century ago. They were looking for the cities of the Assyrians and Babylonians, who of course were well known from Biblical and Greek literature. As the world knows, the diggers soon came upon incredibly rich finds. At the sites of Nineveh and other ancient Assyrian cities they unearthed many clay tablets inscribed with the wedge-shaped writing called cuneiform. This script was taken to be the invention of the Assyrians. Since the Assyrians were apparently a Semitic people, the language was assumed to be Semitic. But few clues were available for decipherment of the strange cuneiform script.

Then came a development which was to be as important a key to discovery in Mesopotamia as the famous Rosetta Stone in Egypt. In western Persia, notably on the Rock of Behistun, European scholars found some cuneiform inscriptions in three languages. They identified one of the languages as Old Persian, another as Elamite, and the third as the language of the Assyrian tablets. The way was now open to decipher the cuneiform writing—first the Old Persian, then the Assyrian, of which it was apparently a translation.

When scholars finally deciphered the "Assyrian" script, they discovered that the cuneiform writing could not have been originated by the Assyrian Semites. Its symbols, which were not alphabetic but syllabic and ideographic, apparently were derived from non-Semitic rather than Semitic words. And many of the cuneiform tablets turned out to be written in a language without any Semitic characteristics whatever. The archaeologists had to conclude, therefore, that the Assyrians had taken over the cuneiform script from a people who had lived in the region before them.

Who were this people? Jules Oppert, a leading 19th-century investigator of ancient Mesopotamia, found a clue to their name in certain inscriptions which referred to the "King of Sumer and Akkad." He concluded that Akkad was the northern part of the country (indeed, the Assyrians and Babylonians are now called Akkadians), and that Sumer was the southern part, inhabited by the people who spoke the non-Semitic language and had invented cuneiform writing.

So it was that the Sumerians were rediscovered after 2,000 years of oblivion. Oppert resurrected their name in 1869. In the following decades French, American, Anglo-American and German expeditions uncovered the buried Sumerian cities—Lagash, Nippur, Shuruppak, Kish, Ur (Ur of the Chaldees in the Bible), Erech, Asmar and so on. The excavation of ancient Sumer has proceeded almost continuously for three quarters of a century; even during World War II the Iraqi went on digging at a few sites. These historic explorations have recovered hundreds of thousands of Sumerian tablets, great temples, monuments, tombs, sculptures, paintings, tools, irrigation systems and remnants of almost every aspect of the Sumerian culture. As a result we have a fairly complete picture of what life in Sumer was like 5,000 years ago. We know something about how the Sumerians looked (from their statues); we know a good deal about their houses and palaces, their tools and weapons, their art and musical instruments, their jewels and ornaments, their skills and crafts, their industry and commerce, their *belles lettres* and government, their schools and temples, their loves and hates, their kings and history.

The Peoples of Sumer

Let us run quickly over the history. The area where the Sumerians lived is lower Mesopotamia, from Baghdad down to the Persian Gulf [*see the map at the right*]. It is reasonably certain that the Sumerians themselves were not the first settlers in this region. Just as the Indian names Mississippi, Massachusetts, etc., show that North America was inhabited before the English-speaking settlers came, so we know that the Sumerians were preceded in Mesopotamia by another people because the ancient names of the Tigris and Euphrates rivers (*Idigna* and *Buranun*), and even the names of the Sumerian cities (Nippur, Ur, Kish, etc.), are not Sumerian words. The city names must be derived from villages inhabited by the earlier people.

The same kind of clue—words that turn up in the Sumerian writing but are plainly not Sumerian in origin—tells us something about those first settlers in Sumer. As Benno Landsberger of the University of Chicago, one of the keenest minds in cuneiform research, has shown, among these pre-Sumerian words are those for farmer, herdsman, fisherman, plow, metal smith, carpenter, weaver, potter, mason and perhaps even merchant. It follows that the predecessors of the Sumerians must already have developed a fairly advanced civilization. This is confirmed by excavations of their stone implements and pottery.

The dates of Sumer's early history have always been surrounded with uncertainty, and they have not been satisfactorily settled by tests with the new method of radiocarbon dating. According to the best present estimates, the first settlers occupied the area some time before 4000 B.C.; new geological evidence indicates that the lower Tigris-Euphrates Valley, once covered by the Persian Gulf, became an inhabitable land well before that date. Be that as it may, it seems that the people called Sumerians did not arrive in the region until nearly 3000 B.C. Just where they came from is in doubt, but there is some reason to believe that their original home had been in the neighborhood of a city called Aratta, which may have been near the Caspian Sea: Sumerian epic poets sang glowingly of Aratta, and its people were said to speak the Sumerian language.

Wherever the Sumerians came from, they brought a creative spirit and an extraordinary surge of progress to the land of Sumer. Uniting with the people who already inhabited it, they developed a rich and powerful civilization. Not long after they arrived, a king called Etana became the ruler of all Sumer: he is described in Sumerian literature as "the man who stabilized all the lands," and he may therefore be the first empire builder in human history. Sumer reached its fullest flowering around 2500 B.C., when its people had developed the cuneiform symbols and thereby originated their finest gift to civilization—the gift of written communication and history. Their own history came to an end some 800 years later: about 1720 B.C. In that year Hammurabi of Babylon won control of the country, and Sumer disappeared in a Babylonian kingdom.

Life in Sumer

The Sumerians' writings and disinterred cities, as I have said, make it possible to reconstruct their life in great detail. Their civilization rested on agriculture and fishing. Among their inventions were the wagon wheel, the plow and the sailboat, but their science and engineering went far beyond these elementary tools. For irrigation the Sumerians built intricate systems of canals, dikes, weirs and reservoirs. They developed measuring and surveying instru-

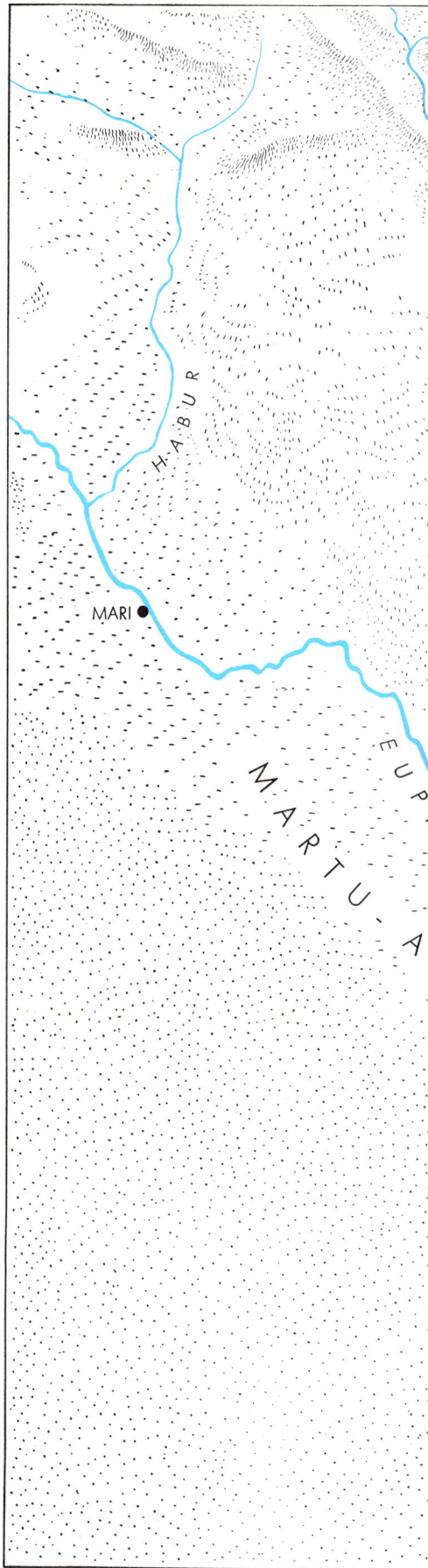

SUMER and its neighbors are located on this map of the area between modern

Turkey and the Persian Gulf. Ancient cities are indicated by black dots; modern cities, by open dots. Cities and areas whose exact location is not known are marked by asterisks. In Sumerian times a large fresh-water lake lay beyond the head of the Persian Gulf.

SUMERIAN TABLETS are inscribed with cuneiform signs. At upper left is the medical tablet of which a section is shown on the cover (about 2000 B.C.). At upper right is a fragment of the epic poem "Enmerkar and the Lord of Aratta" (about 1800 B.C.). At lower left is part of the law code of Hammurabi (about 1700 B.C.). At lower right is a textile inventory (about 1950 B.C.).

ments, and a sexagesimal number system (*i.e.*, based on the number 60) with a place notation device not unlike our decimal system. Their farming was highly sophisticated: among their tablets is a veritable farmer's almanac of instructions in agriculture.

In the crafts, the Sumerians' inventions included the potter's wheel, metal casting (of copper and bronze), riveting, soldering, engraving, cloth fulling, bleaching and dyeing. They manufactured paints, leather, cosmetics, perfumes and drugs. Prescriptions recorded on some of their tablets show that the Sumerian physician had command of a large assortment of *materia medica*, prepared from plants, animals and inorganic sources.

Although the Sumerians' economy was primarily agricultural, their life was centered mainly in the cities. Here lived many of the farmers, herdsmen and fishermen, as well as merchants, craftsmen, architects, doctors, scribes, soldiers and priests. Artisans and traveling merchants sold their products in the central town market, and were paid in kind or in money—usually silver coin in the form of a disk or ring. The dozen or so cities in Sumer probably ranged from 10,000 to 50,000 in population. Each was enclosed by a wall and surrounded with suburban villages and hamlets.

The dominant feature of every Sumerian city was a massive temple mounted on a high terrace. It usually had the form of a ziggurat, Sumer's most distinctive contribution to religious architecture. This is a pyramidal tower with a series of ascending terraces winding around the outside. To break the unattractive blankness of the temple's mud-brick walls, the Sumerian architects introduced buttresses and recesses, and they also beautified the building with columns decorated in colored mosaics. Inside the temple were rooms for the priests and a central shrine with a niche for the statue of the god. Each city in Sumer had a different tutelary god, and the Sumerians considered the city the god's property. Thus the city of Nippur, for example, belonged to Enlil, the god of the air. Nippur became Sumer's chief religious and cultural center, and Enlil was elevated to the highest rank as father of all the gods.

Originally the cities were governed by the citizens themselves, presided over by a governor of their selection. On all important decisions the citizens met in an assembly divided into two chambers —the "elders" and the "men." But for military reasons they gradually relinquished this democratic system. Each city acquired a ruler—at first elected, later hereditary—who organized its defense against the other cities and against foreign invaders. In the course of time the king rivaled the city's religious leaders in wealth and influence. The rulers of Sumer's dozen or so city-states also contended with one another for control of the whole country, and the history of Sumer is largely a record of bitter conflicts among its cities, which eventually led to its downfall.

TWO SUMERIAN CYLINDER SEALS are shown at left. Impressions were made with the seals by rolling them over wet clay. At right are two impressions made by this method.

The life of the individual citizen in a Sumerian city was remarkably free and prosperous. The poorest citizen managed to own a farm and cattle or a house and garden. To be sure, slavery was permitted, and a man could sell his children or his entire family to pay off his debts. But even slaves had certain legal rights: they could engage in business, borrow money and buy their freedom. (The average price for an adult slave was 10 shekels— less than the price of an ass.) The great majority of Sumerians were free citizens, going about their business and the pursuit of happiness with a minimum of restrictions. This did not, however, apply to children, who were under the absolute authority of their parents, could be disinherited or sold into slavery, and had to marry mates chosen by the parents. But in the normal course of events Sumerian families cherished their children and were knit closely together by love and mutual obligations. Women had many legal rights, including the right to hold property and engage in business. A man could divorce his wife on comparatively slender grounds, or, if they had no children, he was allowed to take a second wife.

Most Sumerian families lived in a one-story, mud-brick house consisting of several rooms grouped around an open court. The well-to-do had two-story houses of about a dozen rooms, plastered and whitewashed inside and out; these houses boasted servants' rooms and sometimes even a private chapel. Often the house had a mausoleum in the basement where the family buried its dead. The Sumerians believed that the souls of the dead traveled to a nether world where existence continued more or less as on earth. They therefore buried pots, tools, weapons and jewels with the dead. When a king died, the palace sometimes buried with him some of his courtiers and servants and even his chariot and animals.

Sumerian men were often clean-shaven, but many of them wore a long beard and had long hair parted in the middle. In early times their usual dress was a flounced skirt and felt cloak; later these were replaced by a long shirt and a big fringed shawl draped over the left shoulder, leaving the right arm bare. The common dress for women was a long shawl covering the body from head to foot, except for the right shoulder. Women usually braided their hair into a heavy pigtail and wound it around the head, but on important occasions they wore elaborate headdresses consisting of ribbons, beads and pendants.

Music apparently occupied a large place in the life of the Sumerians—at home, in school and in the temple. Beautifully constructed harps and lyres were found in the royal tombs at Ur. Research has also turned up references to drums, tambourines, reed and metal pipes, and hymns written on tablets. Some of the important personages in the palaces and temples of the Sumerian cities were musicians.

The Sumerians cannot be said to have produced any great art, but they did show considerable skill in carving and sculpture. Perhaps their most original contribution to the graphic arts was the cylinder seal—a stone cylinder with a carved design which was impressed in clay by rolling the cylinder over it. These designs, or seals, appear on clay tablets, jar covers and so on. They depict scenes such as a king on the battlefield, a shepherd defending his flock from wild beasts, heraldic arrangements of animals. Eventually the Sumerians settled on one favorite seal design which became almost their trademark—a scene showing a worshipper being presented to a god by his personal good angel.

Religion

The Sumerians lived by a simple, fatalistic theology. They believed that the universe and their personal lives were ruled by living gods, invisible to mortal

EARLIEST PICTOGRAPHS (3000 B.C.)	DENOTATION OF PICTOGRAPHS	PICTOGRAPHS IN ROTATED POSITION	CUNEIFORM SIGNS CA. 1900 B.C.	BASIC LOGOGRAPHIC VALUES		ADDITIONAL LOGOGRAPHIC VALUES		SYLLABARY (PHONETIC VALUES)
				READING	MEANING	READING	MEANING	
	HEAD AND BODY OF A MAN			LÚ	MAN			
	HEAD WITH MOUTH INDICATED			KA	MOUTH	KIRI$_3$ ZÚ GÙ DUG$_4$ INIM	NOSE TEETH VOICE TO SPEAK WORD	KA ZÚ
	BOWL OF FOOD			NINDA	FOOD, BREAD	NÍG GAR	THING TO PLACE	
	MOUTH + FOOD			KÚ	TO EAT	ŠAGAR	HUNGER	
	STREAM OF WATER			A	WATER	DURU$_5$	MOIST	A
	MOUTH + WATER			NAG	TO DRINK	EMMEN	THIRST	
	FISH			KUA	FISH			KU$_6$ HA
	BIRD			MUŠEN	BIRD			HU PAG
	HEAD OF AN ASS			ANŠE	ASS			
	EAR OF BARLEY			ŠE	BARLEY			ŠE

EVOLUTION OF SUMERIAN WRITING is outlined in the chart at left. The earliest pictographs were inscribed vertically on tablets. Around 2800 B.C. the direction of this writing was changed from vertical to horizontal, with a corresponding rotation of the pictographs. The pictographs were now reduced to collections of linear strokes made by a stylus which had a triangular point. Some of these cuneiform signs are logographic, i.e., each sign represents a spoken word. Some of the signs represent more than one word;

eyes. The chief gods were those of water, earth, air and heaven, named respectively Enki, Ki, Enlil and An. From a primeval sea were created the earth, the atmosphere, the gods and sky, the sun, moon, planets and stars, and finally life. There were gods in charge of the sun, moon and planets, of winds and storms, of rivers and mountains, of cities and states, of farms and irrigation ditches, of the pickax, brick mold and plow. The major gods established a set of unchangeable laws which must be obeyed willy-nilly by everything and everybody.

Thus the Sumerians were untroubled by any question of free will. Man existed to please and serve the gods, and his life followed their divine orders. Because the great gods were far away in the distant sky and had more important matters to attend to, each person appealed to a particular personal god, a "good angel," through whom he sought salvation. Not that the people neglected regular public devotions to the gods. In the Sumerian temples a court of professionals, including priests, priestesses, musicians and eunuchs, offered daily libations and sacrifices of animal and vegetable fats. There were also periodic feasts and celebrations, of which the most important was a royal ceremony ushering in each new year.

This ceremony is traceable to the cycle of nature in Mesopotamia. Every summer, in the hot, parched months, all vegetation died and animal life languished. In the autumn the land began to revive and bloom again. The Sumerian theology explained these events by supposing that the god of vegetation retired to the nether world in the summer and returned to the earth around the time of the new year; his sexual reunion with his wife Inanna, the goddess of love and procreation, then restored fertility to the land. To celebrate this revival and ensure fecundity, the Sumerians each year staged a marriage ceremony between their king, as the risen god, and a priestess representing the goddess Inanna. The marriage was made an occasion of prolonged festival, ritual, music and rejoicing.

The Sumerians considered themselves to be a chosen people, in more intimate contact with the gods than was the rest of mankind. Nevertheless they had a moving vision of all mankind living in peace and security, united by a universal faith and perhaps even by a universal language. Curiously, they projected this vision into the past, into a long-gone golden age, rather than into the future. As a Sumerian poet put it:

Once upon a time there was no snake, there was no scorpion,
There was no hyena, there was no lion,
There was no wild dog, no wolf
There was no fear, no terror,
Man had no rival.

Once upon a time . . .
The whole universe, the people in unison,
To Enlil in one tongue gave praise.

To students of the ancient religions of the Near East, much of the Sumerian cosmology and theology is easily recognizable. The order of the universe's creation, the Job-like resignation of sinful and mortal man to the will of the gods, the mystic tale of the dying god and his triumphant resurrection, the Aphrodite-like goddess Inanna, the ideals of "humaneness"—these and many other features of the Sumerian creed survive without much change in the later religions of the ancient world. Indeed, the very name of the Sumerian dying god, Dumuzi, endures as Biblical Tammuz, whose descent to the nether regions was still

CUNEIFORM SIGNS	TRANSLITERATION	TRANSLATION
	AMA-AR-GI$_4$	FREEDOM
	ARHUŠ	COMPASSION
	DINGIR	GOD, GODDESS
	DUB-SAR	SCRIBE
	É-DUB-BA	SCHOOL, ACADEMY
	HÉ-GÁL	PLENTY, PROSPERITY
	ME	DIVINE LAWS
	NAM-LÚ-LU$_7$	HUMANITY, HUMANENESS
	NAM-LUGAL	KINGSHIP
	NAM-TAR	FATE, DESTINY
	NÍG-GA	PROPERTY
	NÍG-GE-NA	TRUTH
	NÍG-SI-SÁ	JUSTICE
	SAG-GÍG	BLACK-HEADED ONES, THE SUMERIAN PEOPLE
	UKKIN	ASSEMBLY

some are syllabic, *i.e.*, they also represent syllables. The accents and subscript numbers on the modern transliteration of the cuneiform signs are used by modern scholars to distinguish between signs having the same pronunciation but different meanings. In the chart at right are 15 cuneiform words, their transliteration and their English translation.

STATUETTES show the appearance of the Sumerians. The four statuettes at left, made about 2500 B.C., were found at Tutub (modern Khafaje). The statuette at right, made about 1850 B.C., was found at Ur. It represents Princess Enannatumma, high priestess

mourned by the women of Jerusalem in the days of the prophet Ezekiel. It is not too much to say that, with the decipherment of the Sumerian tablets, we can now trace many of the roots of man's major religious creeds back to Sumer.

Cuneiform

But the Sumerians' chief contribution to civilization was their invention of writing. Their cuneiform script is the earliest known system of writing in man's history. The cuneiform system served as the main tool of written communication throughout western Asia for some 2,000 years—long after the Sumerians themselves had disappeared. Without it, mankind's cultural progress would certainly have been much delayed.

The Sumerian script began as a set of pictographic signs devised by temple administrators and priests to keep track of the temple's resources and activities. They inscribed the signs in clay with a reed stylus, and this accounts for the curious wedge-shaped characters. In the course of the centuries Sumerian scholars developed the signs into purely phonetic symbols representing words or syllables.

More than 90 per cent of the tablets that have been excavated in Sumer are economic, legal and administrative documents, not unlike the commercial and governmental records of our own day. But some 5,000 of the finds are literary works: myths and epic tales, hymns and lamentations, proverbs, fables, essays. They qualify as man's oldest known literature—nearly 1,000 years older than the *Iliad* and the Hebrew Bible. In addition the tablets include a number of Sumerian "textbooks," listing the names of trees, birds, insects, minerals, cities, countries and so forth. There are even commemorative narratives which constitute mankind's first writing of history.

From the Sumerians' invention of writing grew the first formal system of education—another milestone in human intellectual progress. They set up "professional" schools to train scribes, secretaries and administrators; in time these vocational schools became also centers of culture where scholars, scientists and poets devoted their lives to learning and teaching.

The head of the school was called "the school father"; the pupils, "school sons." Among the faculty members were "the man in charge of drawing," "the man in charge of Sumerian," "the man in charge of the whip." There was no sparing of the rod. The curriculum consisted in copying and memorizing the lists of

of the moon-god Nanna and sister of Lipit-Ishtar, king of Isin. Enannatumma presided at some of the most important reconstruction of Ur after it had been destroyed by the Elamites.

words and names on the textbook tablets, in studying and composing poetic narratives, hymns and essays and in mastering mathematical tables and problems, including tables of square and cube roots.

Teachers in ancient Sumer seem to have been treated not unlike their counterparts in the U. S. today: their salaries were low and they were looked upon with a mixture of respect and contempt. The Sumerians were an aggressive people, prizing wealth, renown and social prestige. As their tablets suggest, they were far more concerned with accounts than with academic learning.

Their restless ambition and aggressive spirit are reflected in the bitter rivalry among their cities and kings. The history of Sumer is a story of wars in which one city after another rose to ascendancy over the country. Although there are many gaps in our information, we can reconstruct the main outlines of that history from references in the tablets. The first recorded ruler of Sumer, as I have mentioned, was Etana, king of Kish. Probably not long afterward a king of Erech by the name of Meskiaggasher founded a dynasty which ruled the whole region from the Mediterranean to the Zagros Mountains northeast of Sumer. The city of Kish then rose to dominance again, only to be supplanted by the city of Ur, whose first king, Mesannepadda, is said to have ruled for 80 years and made Ur the capital of Sumer. After Mesannepadda's death, Sumer again came under the rule of the city of Erech, under a king named Gilgamesh who became the supreme hero of Sumerian history—a brave, adventurous figure whose deeds were celebrated throughout the ancient world of western Asia. The next great ruler who appears in the record was Lugalannemundu of the city of Adab; he is reported to have ruled 90 years and to have controlled an empire extending far beyond Sumer. But his empire also fell apart, and a king of Kish named Mesilim became the dominant figure in Sumer. Later rule over the country was won by the city of Lagash. The last ruler of the Lagash dynasty, a king named Urukagina, has the distinction of being the first recorded social reformer. He suppressed the city's harsh bureaucracy, reduced taxes, and brought relief to widows, orphans and the poor. One of King Urukagina's inscriptions contains the word "freedom"—the first appearance of this word in man's history. But within less than 10 years a king of the neighboring city of Umma overthrew Urukagina and put the city of Lagash to the torch.

The Fall of Sumer

The cities' incessant struggle for power exhausted Sumer. A Semitic people from the west, under the famous warrior Sargon the Great, marched into the country and established a new dynasty. Sargon founded a capital called Agade (from which came the name Akkadian) and made it the richest and most powerful city in the Middle Eastern world. He conquered almost all of western Asia and perhaps also parts of Egypt and Ethiopia. Sargon's sons held on to the empire, but his grandson, Naramsin, brought Sumer to disaster. For reasons unknown, he destroyed the holy city of Nippur, and soon afterward he was defeated by semibarbaric invaders from the mountains of Iran who overran Sumer and completely wiped out the city of Agade.

It took the Sumerians several generations to recover. But their civilization did come to life again, under a governor of Lagash named Gudea, whose face is the best known to us of all the Sumerians because a score of statues of him have been found in the ancient temples of Lagash. Gudea re-established contacts and trade with the rest of the known world and put Sumer on the path to prosperity. After Gudea, however, the rivalry among its cities broke out again and became Sumer's final undoing. The city of Ur, under a king named Ur-Nammu, defeated Lagash; Ur-Nammu founded a new rule called the Third Dynasty of Ur. It was to be Sumer's last dynasty.

Ur-Nammu was a strong and benevolent ruler. According to inscriptions that have recently come to light, he removed "chiselers" and grafters and established

AREA AROUND NIPPUR, one of the principal cities of Sumer (see map on pages 20 and 21), is covered with barren dunes today. Six thousand years ago much of the area was similarly barren. The Sumerians and their predecessors made it fertile by irrigation.

NIPPUR WAS EXCAVATED in 1951 and 1952 by a joint expedition of the University Museum of the University of Pennsylvania and the Oriental Institute of the University of Chicago. In this photograph the houses of Nippur's scribal quarter are uncovered.

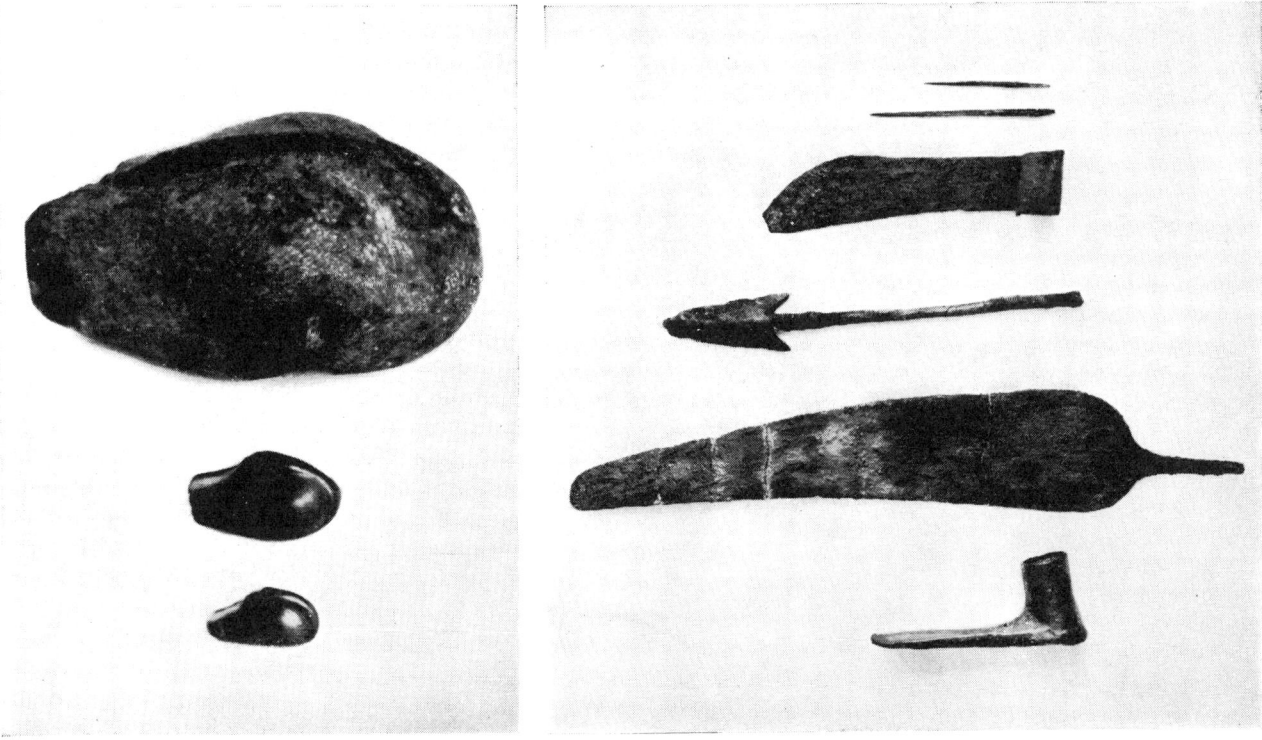

ARTIFACTS at left are Sumerian stone weights. The weight at top is one *mana* (505 grams); the weight at bottom, one *gin* (8.416 grams); the weight in middle, one *gin* 160 *shē* (15.896 grams).

At right is a group of copper and bronze tools and weapons. They are, from top to bottom, two bronze drills, a copper axhead, a copper spearhead, a copper saw blade and a bronze adzhead.

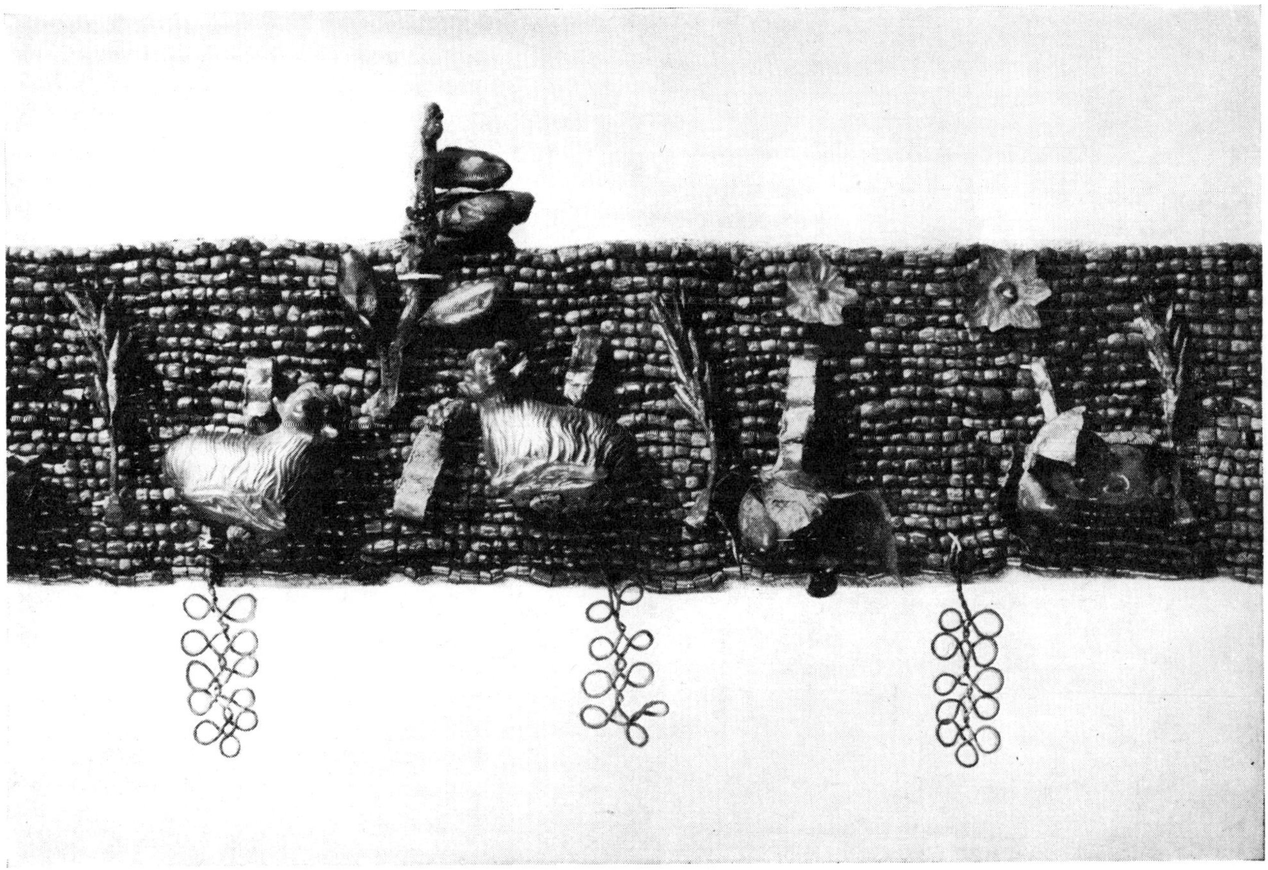

DIADEM of Queen Shub-Ad, who lived about 2500 B.C., was found in the royal cemetery of Ur. The horizontal band of the diadem is fashioned out of beads of lapis lazuli. Mounted on the band are tiny leaves, fruits, flowers and figures of rams, all made of gold.

a law code which insured honest weights and measures and took care that the poor should not "fall a prey to the wealthy." Ur-Nammu's code is especially significant for the fact that instead of the barbarous rule of "an eye for an eye and a tooth for a tooth" common among early societies it established a money fine as punishment for assaults.

In spite of Sumer's civilized kings and prosperity, time was running out for the Sumerians. Their internal rivalries and the growing pressure of surrounding peoples soon overwhelmed them. Semitic nomads from the Arabian desert to the west (the Amorites of the Bible) took over the Sumerian cities of Isin, Larsa and Babylon. Ur itself was conquered by the Elamites to the east, who carried off its last king, Ibbi-Sin. In the following two and a half centuries the Semitic rulers of Isin and Larsa, and then Larsa and Babylon, struggled for control of the country. Finally, in about the year 1720 B.C., Hammurabi defeated Rim-Sin, the last king of Larsa, and Babylon emerged as the dominant city of southern Mesopotamia. The Sumerians were submerged by the Semites and lost their identity as a people. In time their name was erased from the memory of man; the Sumerian language disappeared as a living, spoken tongue, though for centuries it continued to be the written language studied in schools.

The Sumerians firmly believed that when man died, his emasculated spirit descended to a dark, dreary nether world. The spirit and fame of this proud, vigorous people certainly suffered a remarkable eclipse after their empire fell. But what their minds created survives throughout the living corpus of present-day civilization: it appears in the form of a Biblical proverb, a statutory law, a heroic folktale, an Aesopic fable, a zodiacal sign, a Euclidean theorem, the weight of a coin, the degree of an angle. And in the cuneiform tablets which were the Sumerians' pre-eminent gift we have found the earliest intellectual record of man's strivings toward civilization.

Editor's Note

The author wishes to thank the following individuals for their generous cooperation and help in the presentation of this article: F. G. Rainey, A. V. Kidder, Robert Dyson, Edmund I. Gordon, Jane Kohn, and the Board of Managers of the University Museum of the University of Pennsylvania.

An Early City in Iran

by C. C. and Martha Lamberg-Karlovsky
June 1971

Tepe Yahyā, midway between Mesopotamia and India, was a busy center of trade 5,500 years ago. An outpost of Mesopotamian urban culture, it played a key role in the spread of civilization from west to east

The kingdom of Elam and its somewhat better-known neighbor, Sumer, were the two earliest urban states to arise in the Mesopotamian area during the fourth millennium B.C. Archaeological findings now show that the Elamite realm also included territory at least 500 miles to the east. For more than 10 centuries, starting about 3400 B.C., the hill country of southeastern Iran some 60 miles from the Arabian Sea was the site of a second center of Elamite urban culture.

Today all that is left of the city that stood halfway between the Euphrates and the Indus is a great mound of earth located some 4,500 feet above sea level in the Soghun Valley, 150 miles south of the city of Kerman in the province of the same name. Known locally as Tepe Yahyā, the mound is 60 feet high and 600 feet in diameter. Its record of occupation begins with a 6,500-year-old Neolithic village and ends with a citadel of the Sassanian dynasty that ruled Persia early in the Christian Era. Intermediate levels in the mound testify to the connections between this eastern Elamite city and the traditional centers of the kingdom in the west.

Such a long archaeological sequence has much value for the study of man's cultural development from farmer to city dweller, but three unexpected elements make Tepe Yahyā a site of even greater significance. First, writing tablets made of clay, recovered from one of the lower levels in the mound, have been shown by carbon-14 analysis of associated organic material to date back to 3560 B.C. (±110 years). The tablets are inscribed with writing of the kind known as proto-Elamite. Proto-Elamite inscriptions and early Sumerian ones are the earliest known Mesopotamian writings, which are the oldest known anywhere. The Tepe Yahyā tablets are unique in that they are the first of their kind that can be assigned an absolute date. It comes as a surprise to find these examples of writing—as early as the earliest known—in a place that is so far away from Mesopotamia.

The second surprise is evidence that Elamite trade with neighboring Sumer in an unusual commodity—steatite, the easily worked rock also known as soapstone—formed a major part of the commerce at Tepe Yahyā. Unlike Sumer, which was surrounded by the featureless floodplains of lower Mesopotamia, Elam was a hill kingdom rich in natural resources. Elamite trade supplied the Sumerians with silver, copper, tin and lead, with precious gems and horses, and with commoner materials such as timber, obsidian, alabaster, diorite and soapstone. To find that the soapstone trade reached as far east as Tepe Yahyā adds a new dimension to our knowledge of fourth-millennium commerce.

Third, the discovery of Tepe Yahyā has greatly enlarged the known extent of ancient Elam, which was hazily perceived at best. Susa, the most famous Elamite city, lies not far from such famous Sumerian centers as Ur and Eridu. As for other Elamite cities named in inscriptions (Awan, for example, or Madaktu), their location remains a mystery. To discover a prosperous Elamite city as far east of Mesopotamia as Tepe Yahyā is both a surprise and something of a revelation. It suggests how urban civilization, which arose in lower Mesopotamia, made its way east to the valley of the Indus (in what is now West Pakistan).

The British explorer-archaeologist Sir Aurel Stein was the first to recognize that southeastern Iran is a region with important prehistoric remains. Two sites that Stein probed briefly in the 1930's—Tal-i-Iblis near Kerman and Bampur in Persian Baluchistan—have recently been excavated, the first by Joseph R. Caldwell of the University of Georgia and the second by Beatrice de Cardi of the Council for British Archaeology. Although it is the largest mound in southeastern Iran, Tepe Yahyā remained unknown until the summer of 1967, when our reconnaissance group from the Peabody Museum at Harvard University discovered it during an archaeological survey of the region.

We have now completed three seasons of excavation at Tepe Yahyā in cooperation with the Iran Archaeological Service and have established a sequence of six principal occupation periods. The site was inhabited almost continuously from the middle of the fifth millennium B.C. until about A.D. 400. Following the end of the Elamite period at Tepe Yahyā, about 2200 B.C., there is a 1,000-year gap in the record that is still unexplained but finds parallels at major sites elsewhere in Iran. Tepe Yahyā remained uninhabited until 1000 B.C., when the site was resettled by people of an Iron Age culture.

Our main work at Tepe Yahyā began in the summer of 1968 with the digging of a series of excavations, each 30 feet square, from the top of the mound to the bottom [*illustration, pp. 32-33*]. Small test trenches were then made within the series of level squares. During our second and third season the excavations were extended by means of further horizontal exposures on the top of the mound and to the west of the main explorations. In addition we opened a stepped trench 12 feet wide on the opposite face of the mound as a check on the sequences we had already exposed.

The earliest remains of human occupation at Tepe Yahyā, which rest on virgin soil in a number of places, consist of five superimposed levels of mud-brick construction. We have assigned them to a single cultural interval—Period VI—that is shown by carbon-14 analysis to lie in the middle of the fifth millennium B.C. The structures of Period VI seem to be a series of square storage areas that measure about five feet on a side. Most of them have no doorways; they were probably entered through a hole in the roof. The walls are built either of sun-dried mud bricks that were formed by hand or of hand-daubed mud [*see top illustration on page 36*]. Fragments of reed matting and timber found on the floors of the rooms are traces of fallen roofs.

The tools of Period VI include implements made of bone and flint. Many of the flints are very small; they include little blades that were set in a bone handle to make a sickle. The most common kind of pottery is a coarse, hand-shaped ware; the clay was "tempered" by the addition of chaff. The pots are made in the form of bowls and large storage jars and are decorated with a red wash or painted with red meanders. Toward the end of Period VI a few pieces of finer pottery appear: a buff ware with a smooth, slip-finished surface and a red ware with decorations painted in black.

Human burials, all of infants, were found under the floor in a few of the structures. The limbs of the bodies had been tightly gathered to the trunk before burial, and accompanying the bodies are unbroken coarse-ware bowls. In one room a small human figurine was found face down on the floor, resting on a collection of flint and bone tools. The sculpture is 11 inches long and was carved out of dark green soapstone [*see illustration on page 34*]. The carving clearly delineates a female figure. Its elongated form and the presence of a hole at the top of the head, however, suggest a dual symbol that combines male and female characteristics.

The Neolithic culture of Period VI evidently included the practice of agriculture and animal husbandry. Identifiable animal bones include those of wild gazelles and of cattle, sheep and goats. Camel bones are also present, but it is not clear whether or not they indicate that the animal had been domesticated at this early date. The domesticated plants include a variety of cereal grains. In the Tepe Yahyā area today raising crops involves irrigation; whether or not this was the case in Neolithic times is also unclear. At any rate the Neolithic occupation of the mound continued until about 3800 B.C.

The transition from Period VI to the Early Bronze Age culture that followed occurred without any break in continuity. The structures of Period V contain coarse-ware pottery of the earlier type. The finer, painted pottery becomes commoner and includes some new varieties. One of these, with a surface finish of red slip, has a decorative geometric pattern of repeated chevrons painted in black. We have named this distinctive black-on-red pottery Yahyā ware, and we call the material culture of Period V the Yahyā culture.

The commonest examples of Yahyā ware are beakers. These frequently have a potter's mark on the base, and we have so far identified nine individual marks. Evidence that outside contact and trade formed part of the fabric of Early Bronze Age life at Tepe Yahyā comes from the discovery at Tal-i-Iblis, a site nearly 100 miles closer to Kerman, of almost identical painted pottery bearing similar potter's marks. There is other evidence of regional contacts. Yahyā ware shows a general similarity to the painted pottery at sites elsewhere in southeastern Iran, and a black-on-buff ware at Tepe Yahyā closely resembles pottery from sites well to the west, such as Bakun. Moreover, the Period V levels at Tepe Yahyā abound in imported materials. There are tools made of obsidian, beads made of ivory, carnelian and turquoise, and various objects made of alabaster, marble and mother-of-pearl. One particularly handsome figure is a stylized representation of a ram, seven inches long, carved out of alabaster [*see top illustration on page 39*]. No local sources are known for any of these materials.

Although the architecture of Period V demonstrates a continuity with the preceding Neolithic period, the individual structures are larger than before. Several of them measure eight by 11½ feet in area and are clearly residential in character. Some rooms include a hearth and chimney. In the early levels the walls are still built of hand-formed mud bricks. Bricks formed in molds appear in the middle of Period V, which carbon-14 analyses show to have been around 3660 B.C. (±140 years).

The bronze implements of Period V, like much of the earliest bronze in the world, were produced not by alloying but by utilizing copper ores that contained "impurities." This was the case in early Sumer, where the ore, imported from Oman on the Arabian peninsula, contained a high natural percentage of nickel. Early bronzesmiths elsewhere smelted copper ores that were naturally rich in arsenic. Chisels, awls, pins and spatulas at Tepe Yahyā are made of such an arsenical bronze.

Six artifacts from the site have been analyzed by R. F. Tylecote and H. McKerrell of the University of Newcastle upon Tyne. They found that the bronze had been produced by smelting, which shows that the metalworkers of Period V were able to obtain the high temperatures needed to smelt copper ores into molten metal. The final shapes were not made by casting, however, but by hot and cold forging, a more primitive technique. One of the articles, a chisel, proved to contain 3.7 percent arsenic, which leads us to believe that the metalworkers consciously selected for smelting ores with a high arsenic content. This finding is further testimony in support of trade at Tepe Yahyā; none of the copper deposits native to the region could have been used to make arsenical bronze.

With the beginning of Period IV, around 3500 B.C., the appearance of writing at Tepe Yahyā allows the city to be identified as a proto-Elamite settlement. Much of the pottery representative of the first two phases of this period, IV-C and IV B, is typical of the preceding Yahyā culture in both shape and decoration. Although there is plentiful evidence of external contact, the transition to Period IV at Tepe Yahyā, like the one that preceded it, occurred with-

Large earth mound, over a third of a mile in circumference, was raised to a out any break in continuity. There is no need at Tepe Yahyā to conjure up that hackneyed instrument of cultural change: a new people arriving with luggage labeled "Proto-Elamite."

Architecture, however, was considerably transformed. The site ceased to be a residential area and became an administrative one. A large structure we have unearthed at the IV-C level of the mound is carefully oriented so that its walls run north-south and east-west. The walls consist of three courses of mold-formed brick in a new size. The earlier mold-formed bricks had been six by six by 12 inches; the new ones were 9½ by 9½ by 4¾ inches—a third wider and less than half as thick. So far we have identified five of an undetermined number of rooms within the large structure, although we have fully cleared only part of one room. Both the structure and the partially excavated room continue toward the center of the mound; the size of each remains to be determined.

The part of the room that has been cleared measures about 10 by 20 feet. Its contents strongly suggest a commercial function. Among the objects in the room are bowls with beveled rims made of a coarse ware. The vessels have counterparts at numerous sites in Mesopotamia. They are believed to have served as standard measures. Three large storage jars, which proved to be empty, were also found in the room; near them were some 24 "sealings": jar stoppers made of clay and marked with a seal impression. The seals used to mark the sealings were cylindrical; the designs resemble those on cylinder seals found at Susa, the Elamite capital in the Mesopotamian area. The finding creates the possibility that goods from Susa were reaching Tepe Yahyā early in Period IV.

Lying on the floor of the room were 84 blank clay tablets and six others that bore inscriptions. The tablets are all the same shape; they are made of unbaked dark brown clay, are convex in profile and measure 1⅓ by two inches. The six inscribed tablets bear a total of 17 lines of proto-Elamite writing. The inscriptions were impressed in the soft clay with a stylus; they read from right to left along the main axis of the tablet and from top to bottom. When an inscription continues from one side of a tablet to the other, the writer rotated the tablet on its main axis so that the bottom line of the obverse inscription and the top line of the reverse inscription lie opposite each other.

The Tepe Yahyā inscriptions are being deciphered now. Preliminary examination indicates that they are records or receipts dealing with goods. The fact that inscribed and otherwise identical blank tablets were found in the same room is strong evidence that the writing was done on the spot. Therefore the goods they describe must have been either entering or leaving the administrative area.

Until the discovery at Tepe Yahyā the only other proto-Elamite tablets known were from Susa or from Sialk in northwestern Iran. Susa yielded nearly 1,500 such tablets, Sialk only 19. Proto-Elamite writing has been found recently at Shahdād, a site north of Kerman that is being excavated by the Iran Archaeological Service. The writing there is not on tablets but consists of brief inscriptions, with a maximum of seven signs, incised on pottery.

A second change in architectural style is evident in the single IV-B structure examined so far. It is a building, nine by 24 feet in area, that is oriented without reference to north-south and east-west. It is built of bricks of a still newer size and shape. They are oblong rather than square, and are either 14 or 17 inches long; the other two dimensions remained the same. The structure is subdivided into two main rooms and a few smaller rooms that contain large storage bins built of unbaked clay. Its walls are only

height of 60 feet over a 5,000-year period as new settlements were built on the rubble of earlier ones. Located in southeastern Iran and known locally as Tepe Yahyā, the site was first occupied by a Neolithic community in the middle of the fifth millennium B.C.

NEOLITHIC FIGURINE was found in one of the storerooms in the earliest structure at Tepe Yahyā, associated with tools made of flint and bone. The sculpture was apparently intended to be a dual representation: a female figure imposed on a stylized phallic shape.

one brick thick, and their inside surfaces are covered with plaster.

Storage vessels in one of the main rooms still held several pounds of grain. The grain was charred, which together with the fact that the matting on the floor and the bricks in the wall were burned indicates that the building was destroyed by fire. Amid the debris on the floors were cylinder seals and, for the first time at Tepe Yahyā, stamp seals as well.

Some bronze tools of the IV-B period have also been discovered. Needles and chisels, unearthed in association with soapstone artifacts, were probably used to work the soapstone. A bronze dagger some seven inches long was found by Tylecote and McKerrell to have been made by forging smelted metal, as were the bronze tools of Period V. Analysis showed that the dagger, unlike the earlier artifacts of arsenical bronze, was an alloy comprising 3 percent tin. Tin is not found in this part of Iran, which means that either the dagger itself, the tin contained in it or an ingot of tin-alloyed bronze must have been imported to Tepe Yahyā.

The proof that writing was known at Tepe Yahyā as early as it was known anywhere is a discovery of major importance to prehistory. Perhaps next in importance, however, is the abundant evidence suggesting a unique economic role for the city beginning late in the fourth millennium B.C. The IV-B phase at Tepe Yahyā is known from carbon-14 analyses to have extended from near the end of the fourth millennium through the first two centuries of the third millennium. During that time the city was a major supplier of soapstone artifacts.

Objects made of soapstone, ranging from simple beads to ornate bowls and all very much alike in appearance, are found in Bronze Age sites as far apart as Mohenjo-Daro, the famous center of Harappan culture on the Indus, and Mari on the upper Euphrates 1,500 miles away. Mesopotamia, however, was a region poor in natural resources, soapstone included. The Harappans of the Indus also seem to have lacked local supplies of several desired materials. How were the exotic substances to be obtained? Sumerian and Akkadian texts locate the sources of certain luxury imports in terms of place-names that are without meaning today: Dilmun, Maluhha and Magan.

Investigations by Danish workers on the island of Bahrein in the Persian Gulf have essentially confirmed the belief that the island is ancient Dilmun. There is also a degree of agreement that the area or place known as Maluhha lay somewhere in the valley of the Indus. Even before we began our work at Tepe Yahyā it had been suggested that the area known as Magan was somewhere in southeastern Iran. Our excavations have considerably strengthened this hypothesis. A fragmentary Sumerian text reads: "May the land Magan [bring] you mighty copper, the strength of... diorite, 'u-' stone, 'shumash' stone." Could either of the untranslated names of stones stand for soapstone? Were Tepe Yahyā and its hinterland a center of the trade? Let us examine the evidence from the site.

More soapstone has been found at Tepe Yahyā than at any other single site in the Middle East. The total is more than 1,000 fragments, unfinished pieces and intact objects; the majority of them belong to Period IV-B. Among the intact pieces are beads, buttons, cylinder seals, figurines and bowls. Unworked blocks of soapstone, vessels that are partially hollowed out and unfinished seals and beads are proof that Tepe Yahyā was a manufacturing site and not merely a transshipment point.

Some of the soapstone bowls are plain, but others are elaborately decorated with carvings. The decorations include geometric and curvilinear designs, animals and human figures. Among the decorations are examples of every major motif represented on the numerous soapstone bowls unearthed at Bronze Age sites in Mesopotamia and the Indus valley. Moreover, motifs found on pottery unearthed at sites such as Bampur, to the east of Tepe Yahyā, and Umm-an-Nai on the Persian Gulf are repeated on soapstone bowls from IV-B levels.

During our 1970 season we located what was probably one of the sources of Tepe Yahyā soapstone. An outcrop of the rock in the Ashin Mountains some 20 miles from the mound shows evidence of strip-mining in the past. This is unlikely to have been the only source. Soapstone deposits are often associated with deposits of asbestos and chromite. There is a chromite mine only 10 miles from Tepe Yahyā, and we have noted veins of asbestos in stones unearthed during our excavation of the mound. Reconnaissance in the mountains to the north might locate additional soapstone exposures.

Taking into consideration the large quantities of soapstone found at the site, the evidence that many of the soapstone articles were manufactured locally, the availability of raw material nearby and the presence in both Mesopotamia and Harappan territory of soapstone bowls that repeat motifs found at Tepe Yahyā, it is hard to avoid the conclusion that the city was a major producer of soapstone and a center of trade in the material. Before turning to the broader significance of such commercial activity in this geographically remote area, we shall briefly describe the remaining occupation periods at Tepe Yahyā.

At present there is little to report concerning the final phase of Period IV, which drew to a close about 2200 B.C. It is then that the break occurs in the continuity at Tepe Yahyā. The Iron Age reoccupation of the site, which lasted roughly from 1000 to 500 B.C., comprises Period III. It is evidenced by a series of living floors and by pottery that shows strong parallels to wares and shapes produced during the same period in northwestern Iran. We have not yet uncovered a major structure belonging to Period III; both the nature of the culture and Tepe Yahyā's relations with its Iron Age neighbors remain unclarified.

Period II at Tepe Yahyā, which consists of more than 200 years of Achaemenian occupation, was a time of large-scale construction. The building material remained mud brick, but we have yet to uncover a complete structure. The appearance of the two large rooms excavated thus far suggests, however, that the site had once more become at least partly residential.

A subsequent 600 years or so of Parthian and Sassanian occupation, representing Period I, is the final period of urban civilization at Tepe Yahyā. We have uncovered suggestions of large-scale architecture, including courtyards and part of a massive mud-brick platform made by laying four courses of brick one on the other. By Sassanian times (early in the third century) the accumulated debris of thousands of years had raised the mound to an imposing height; the structure that has been partly exposed probably was a citadel standing on the summit.

Most of the Sassanian pottery consists

TWO CYLINDER SEALS from the level at Tepe Yahyā overlying the first proto-Elamite settlement appear at left in these photographs next to the impressions they produce. The seal designs, which show pairs of human figures with supernatural attributes, are generally similar to the designs on seals of Mesopotamian origin but appear to be of local workmanship.

EARLIEST STRUCTURE at Tepe Yahyā is a storage area consisting of small units measuring five feet on a side. Few of the units have doorways; apparently they were entered through a hole in the roof. The walls were built either of sun-dried mud bricks, formed by hand rather than in molds, or simply of hand-daubed mud. White circle (*left*) shows where female figurine was found.

TWO ELAMITE BUILDINGS at Tepe Yahyā left the traces seen in this photograph. The walls of the earlier building (*left*) were built sometime around 3500 B.C. of mold-formed mud bricks 9½ inches on a side. The walls run from north to south and from east to west. The walls of the later structure (*right*) are not oriented in these directions. It was built sometime after 3000 B.C. of oblong mold-formed mud bricks of two lengths. Both structures seem to have been administrative rather than residential. The earlier one contained storage pots and measuring bowls. Near one angle of its walls a pile of 84 unused writing tablets is visible.

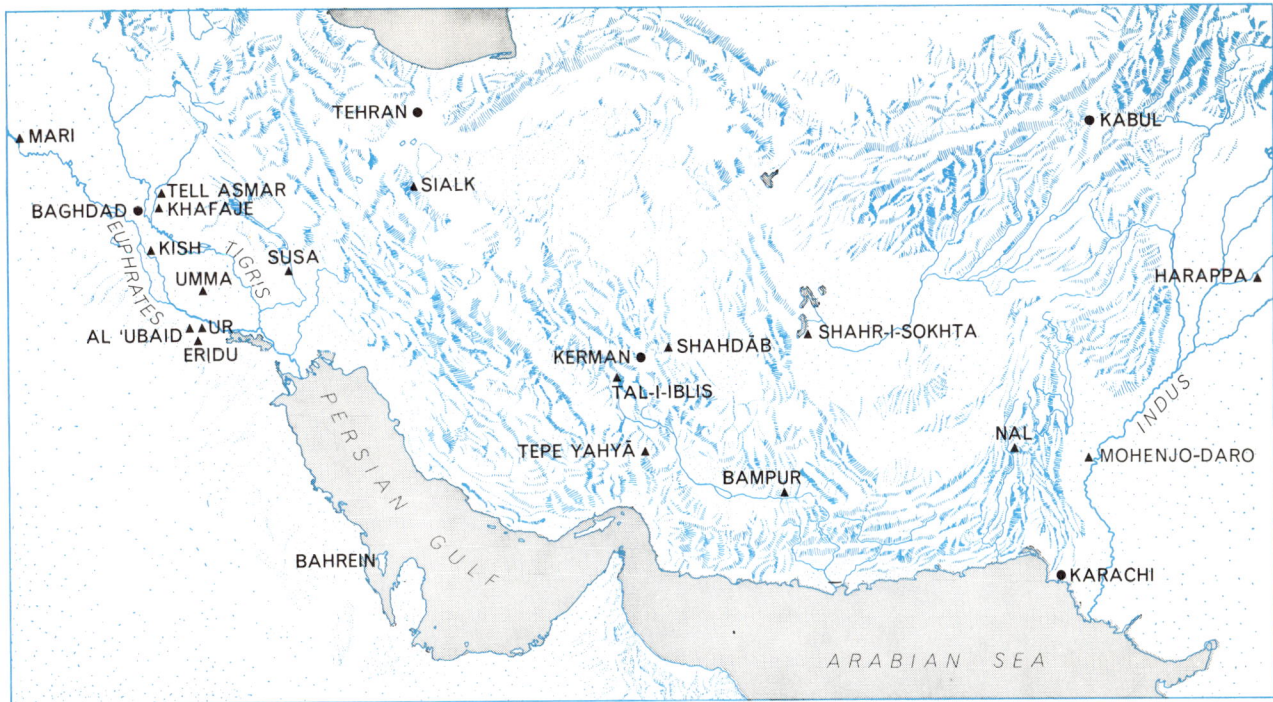

FIRST CITIES arose in the kingdom of Sumer in lower Mesopotamia (*left*). The earliest known forms of writing appeared in Sumer and in nearby Elam at cities such as Susa and Sialk. The discovery of proto-Elamite writing at Tepe Yahyā (*center*), which is 500 miles to the east, suggests that trade between the region and the early cities of Mesopotamia led to the rise of cities in this part of ancient Persia in the fourth millennium B.C. and to the later development of the urban Harappan civilization in the Indus region.

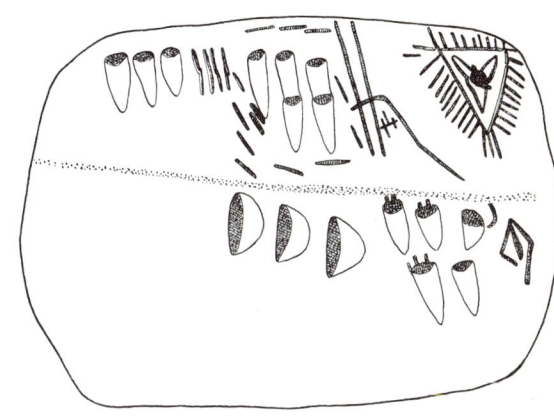

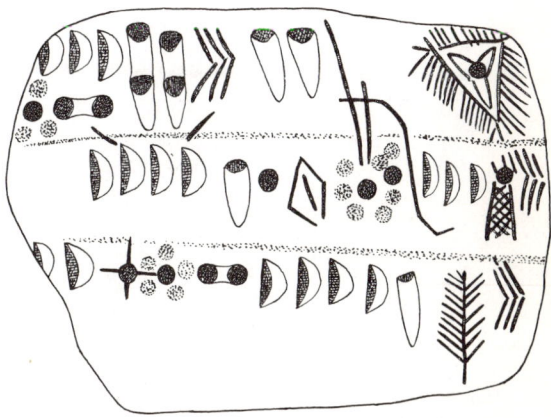

INSCRIBED TABLETS from Tepe Yahyā (*photographs*) are shown next to drawings that reproduce the written symbols. Only six inscribed tablets have been found so far. The inscriptions are in proto-Elamite, written from right to left across the length of the tablet by pressing the blunt or sharp end of a stylus into the soft clay. Similar written tablets have been unearthed at Susa and Sialk.

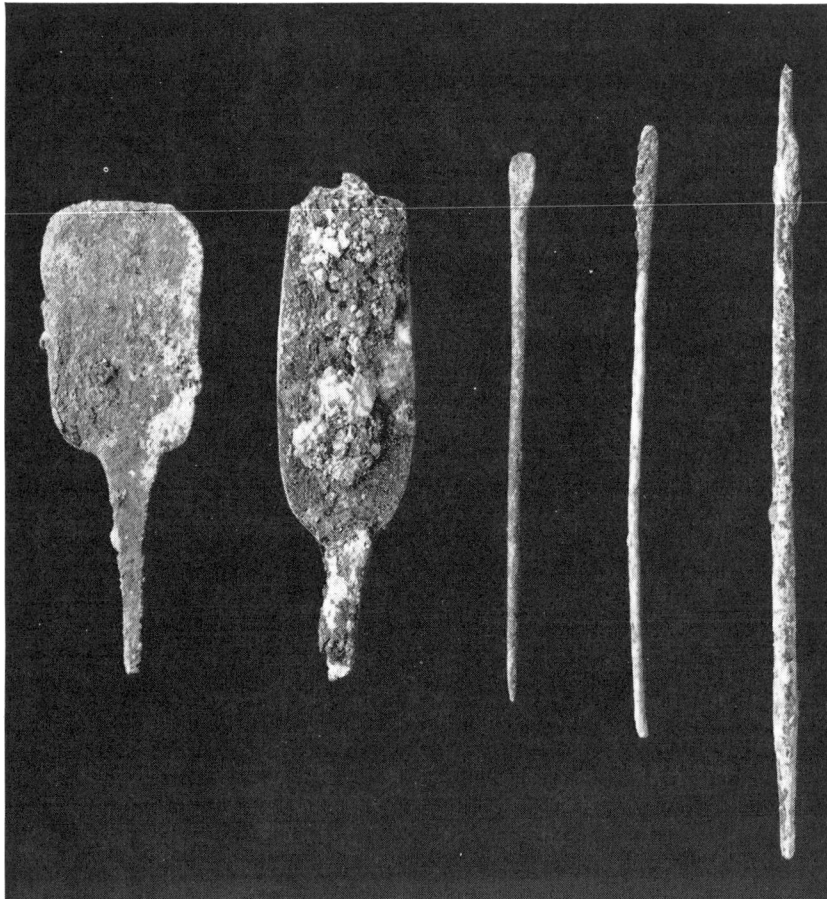

BRONZE OBJECTS contemporaneous with peak of work and trade in soapstone at Tepe Yahyā include two chisels (*left*) and three needle-like forms; the longest object measures 6½ inches. The bronze was not produced by alloying but by utilizing copper that naturally included significant amounts of arsenic. The enriched ores were obtained through trade.

SOAPSTONE BOWLS, many of them elaborately decorated, were among the numerous objects made at Tepe Yahyā and traded eastward and westward during the first half of the third millennium B.C. Fragments of bowls with decorations like the ones on these bowl fragments from Tepe Yahyā have been found from Mesopotamia to the Indus valley.

of coarse, thick-walled storage jars. An abundance of beads and several small glass and pottery bottles, perhaps containers for perfume, suggest a degree of prosperity during Period I. The presence of iron and bronze swords, axes and arrowheads adds a military flavor. A single work of art, a small clay figurine, represents a warrior with a distinctive headdress [*see bottom illustration on next page*]. Thereafter, from sometime in the fifth century on, Tepe Yahyā was occupied only by occasional squatters or transient nomads. The few scattered surface finds are of early Islamic age; none of the visitors lingered or built anything of substance.

What role did Elamite Tepe Yahyā play in the transmission of the urban tradition from west to east? The city's position suggests that Elamite culture, which is now revealed as being far more widespread than was realized previously, was instrumental in the contact between the first urban civilization in Mesopotamia and the civilization that subsequently arose in the Indus valley. It appears that the Elamites of eastern Persia may have accomplished much more than that. To assess this possibility it is necessary to examine the evidence for direct contact, as distinct from trade through middlemen, between Mesopotamia and the Indus valley.

A small number of artifacts that are possibly or certainly of Harappan origin have been found at sites in Mesopotamia. Because much of the archaeological work there was done as long as a century ago, it is not surprising that both the age and the original location of many of these artifacts can only be roughly estimated. Nonetheless, Mesopotamia has yielded six stamp seals, one cylinder seal and a single clay sealing, all of the Harappan type, that are evidence of some kind of contact between the two civilizations. Certain seals are engraved with Harappan writing. On others the writing is combined with animal figures that are indisputably Harappan in style: a "unicorn," an elephant, a rhinoceros. Evidence of contact, yes. But was the contact direct or indirect?

The single Indus sealing found in Mesopotamia was discovered by the French archaeologist G. Contenau at Umma in southern Iraq during the 1920's. It suggests the arrival there of freight from Harappan territory that had been identified with the sender's personal mark before shipment. The seven seals, however, are evidence of a more equivocal kind. Mesopotamian contact with the Indus evidently did not resemble the later trade between Mesopotamia and, say, the Hittite realm to the west. In that instance Assyrian trading colonies were housed within special quarters of such Hittite strongholds as Kültepe and Hattusha [see "An Assyrian Trading Outpost," by Tahsin Özgüç; Scientific American Feb. 1963]. There is simply no good evidence that Mesopotamians ever visited the Indus to set up residence and trade or that Harappans did the reverse.

What, then, were the seals of Harappan traders doing in Mesopotamia? What was the function of the three unearthed at Ur, the two at Kish and the two at Tell Asmar? So far there is no persuasive answer to these questions. It is tempting to look on these seals not as credentials but as souvenirs of indirect trade contact; all of them are handsome objects. At the same time another equally puzzling question presents itself. Some objects of Indus origin have been found in Mesopotamia. Why has nothing of any kind from Mesopotamia been found at any Indus site?

Evidence of direct trade contact between the two civilizations thus remains almost entirely absent. Other kinds of trade, however, are equally well known. One of the oldest and most widespread is simple exchange, which can interpose any number of witting or unwitting intermediaries between two principals. Exchange is notable for presenting the archaeologist with difficulties of interpretation; intangibles such as style and function are likely to travel along with the goods.

A system of exchange that involves a single intermediary seems to provide the theoretical model that best approximates the situation at Tepe Yahyā. Such a system is known as "central place" trade; we suggest that Tepe Yahyā was just such a central place in southeastern Persia during Elamite times.

A central place can lie outside the sphere of influence of either principal and at the same time produce goods or control natural resources desired by both. In addition to (or even instead of) exporting its own products, a central place can transship goods produced by either principal. Bahrein—ancient Dilmun—provides a good example of a central place whose prosperity was based on the transshipment of goods bound for Mesopotamia. Whether or not transshipment was important at Tepe Yahyā, the city's basic central-place role in Elamite times was clearly that of a producer manufacturing and exporting articles made of soapstone.

The names of the Mesopotamian sites that contain soapstone bowls identical

FIGURINE OF A RAM carved out of alabaster is one of the numerous articles made from imported materials that are found at Tepe Yahyā at the time of its first urban settlement about 3800 B.C. Evidences of trade between the city and outlying areas include, in addition to alabaster, mother-of-pearl from the Persian Gulf, marble, turquoise and carnelian.

FIGURINE OF A WARRIOR modeled in clay is from the final period of occupation at Tepe Yahyā, when a Sassanian military outpost stood on the top of the mound from sometime in the third century B.C. to about A.D. 400. Thereafter only nomads visited the dead city.

in shape and decorative motif with those we unearthed at Tepe Yahyā read like an archaeologist's checklist: Adab, Mari, Tell Asmar, Tell Aqrab, Khafaje, Nippur, Telloh, Kish, Al 'Ubaid and Ur. Bowls of Tepe Yahyā style have also been found at Mohenjo-Daro on the Indus and at Kulli-Damb in Pakistani Baluchistan. In addition to bevel-rim bowls of the Uruk type at Tepe Yahyā as evidence of contact with the west, the mound has yielded Nal ware, a kind of Indus painted pottery that predates the rise of Harappan civilization, as evidence of contact with the east.

Tepe Yahyā was not, however, the only central place in eastern Persia. It seems rather to have been one of several that comprised a local loose Elamite federation astride the middle ground between the two civilizations. Shahr-i-Sokhta, a site 250 miles northeast of Tepe Yahyā, appears to have been another central place, exporting local alabaster and transshipping lapis lazuli from Afghanistan. The links between Tepe Yahyā and other possible central places in the region such as Tal-i-Iblis, Shahdāb and Bampur—mainly demonstrated by similarities in pottery—have already been mentioned.

How did this remote Elamite domain, which in the case of Tepe Yahyā predates the appearance of Harappan civilization by at least three centuries, influence developments in the Indus valley? In spite of exciting new evidence that trade networks existed as long ago as the early Neolithic, a strong tendency exists to view trade exclusively as an ex post facto by-product of urbanism. Trade, however, has certainly also been one of the major stimuli leading to urban civilization. This, it seems to us, was exactly the situation in ancient Kerman and Persian Baluchistan.

We suggest that trade between resource-poor Mesopotamia and the population of this distant part of Persia provided the economic base necessary for the urban development of centers such as Tepe Yahyā during the fourth millennium B.C. It can further be suggested that, once an urban Elamite domain was established there, its trade with the region farther to the east provided much of the stimulus that culminated during the third millennium B.C. with the rise of Harappan civilization. Sir Mortimer Wheeler has declared that "the idea of civilization" crossed from Mesopotamia to the Indus. It seems to us that the Elamite central places midway between the two river basins deserve the credit for the crossing.

Teotihuacán

by Renê Millon
June 1967

The first and largest city of the pre-Columbian New World arose in the Valley of Mexico during the first millenium A.D. At its height the metropolis covered a larger area than imperial Rome

When the Spaniards conquered Mexico, they described Montezuma's capital Tenochtitlán in such vivid terms that for centuries it seemed that the Aztec stronghold must have been the greatest city of pre-Columbian America. Yet only 25 miles to the north of Tenochtitlán was the site of a city that had once been even more impressive. Known as Teotihuacán, it had risen, flourished and fallen hundreds of years before the conquistadors entered Mexico. At the height of its power, around A.D. 500, Teotihuacán was larger than imperial Rome. For more than half a millennium it was to Middle America what Rome, Benares or Mecca have been to the Old World: at once a religious and cultural capital and a major economic and political center.

Unlike many of the Maya settlements to the south, in both Mexico and Guatemala, Teotihuacán was never a "lost" city. The Aztecs were still worshiping at its sacred monuments at the time of the Spanish Conquest, and scholarly studies of its ruins have been made since the middle of the 19th century. Over the past five years, however, a concerted program of investigation has yielded much new information about this early American urban center.

In the Old World the first civilizations were associated with the first cities, but both in Middle America and in Peru the rise of civilization does not seem to have occurred in an urban setting. As far as we can tell today, the foundation for the earliest civilization in Middle America was laid in the first millennium B.C. by a people we know as the Olmecs. None of the major Olmec centers discovered so far is a city. Instead these centers—the most important of which are located in the forested lowlands along the Gulf of Mexico on the narrow Isthmus of Tehuantepec—were of a ceremonial character, with small permanent populations probably consisting of priests and their attendants.

The Olmecs and those who followed them left to many other peoples of Middle America, among them the builders of Teotihuacán, a heritage of religious beliefs, artistic symbolism and other cultural traditions. Only the Teotihuacanos, however, created an urban civilization of such vigor that it significantly influenced the subsequent development of most other Middle American civilizations—urban and nonurban—down to the time of the Aztecs. It is hard to say exactly why this happened, but at least some of the contributing factors are evident. The archaeological record suggests the following sequence of events.

A settlement of moderate size existed at Teotihuacán fairly early in the first century B.C. At about the same time a number of neighboring religious centers were flourishing. One was Cuicuilco, to the southwest of Teotihuacán in the Valley of Mexico; another was Cholula, to the east in the Valley of Puebla. The most important influences shaping the "Teotihuacán way" probably stemmed from centers such as these. Around the time of Christ, Teotihuacán began to grow rapidly, and between A.D. 100 and 200 its largest religious monument was raised on the site of an earlier shrine. Known today as the Pyramid of the Sun, it was as large at the base as the great pyramid of Cheops in Egypt [*see bottom illustration on page 48*].

The powerful attraction of a famous holy place is not enough, of course, to explain Teotihuacán's early growth or later importance. The city's strategic location was one of a number of material factors that contributed to its rise. Teotihuacán lies astride the narrow waist of a valley that is the best route between the Valley of Mexico and the Valley of Puebla. The Valley of Puebla, in turn, is the gateway to the lowlands along the Gulf of Mexico.

The lower part of Teotihuacán's valley is a rich alluvial plain, watered by permanent springs and thus independent of the uncertainties of highland rainfall. The inhabitants of the valley seem early to have dug channels to create an irrigation system and to provide their growing city with water. Even today a formerly swampy section at the edge of the ancient city is carved by channels into "chinampas": small artificial islands that are intensively farmed. Indeed, it is possible that this form of agriculture, which is much better known as it was practiced in Aztec times near Tenochtitlán, was invented centuries earlier by the people of Teotihuacán.

The valley had major deposits of obsidian, the volcanic glass used all over ancient Middle America to make cutting and scraping tools and projectile points. Obsidian mining in the valley was apparently most intensive during the city's early years. Later the Teotihuacanos appear to have gained control of deposits of obsidian north of the Valley of Mexico that were better suited than the local material to the mass production of blade implements. Trade in raw obsidian and obsidian implements became increasingly important to the economy of Teotihuacán, reaching a peak toward the middle of the first millennium A.D.

The recent investigation of Teotihuacán has been carried forward by specialists working on three independent but related projects. One project was a monumental program of excavation and reconstruction undertaken by Mexico's National Institute of Anthropology, headed by Eusebio Dávalos. From 1962 to 1964 archaeologists under the direction of Ignacio Bernal, director of the

National Museum of Anthropology, unearthed and rebuilt a number of the structures that lie along the city's principal avenue ("the Street of the Dead"); they have also restored Teotihuacán's second main pyramid ("the Pyramid of the Moon"), which lies at the avenue's northern end. Two of the city's four largest structures, the Pyramid of the Sun and the Citadel, within which stands the Temple of Quetzalcoatl, had been cleared and restored in the 1900's and the 1920's respectively. Among other notable achievements, the National Institute's work brought to light some of the city's finest mural paintings.

As the Mexican archaeologists were at work a group under the direction of William T. Sanders of Pennsylvania State University conducted an intensive study of the ecology and the rural-settlement patterns of the valley. Another group, from the University of Rochester, initiated a mapping project under my direction. This last effort, which is still under way, involves preparing a detailed topographic map on which all the city's several thousand structures will be located. The necessary information is being secured by the examination of surface remains, supplemented by small-scale excavations. One result of our work has been to demonstrate how radically different Teotihuacán was from all other settlements of its time in Middle America. It was here that the New World's urban revolution exploded into being.

It had long been clear that the center of Teotihuacán was planned, but it soon became apparent to us that the extent and magnitude of the planning went far beyond the center. Our mapping revealed that the city's streets and the large majority of its buildings had been laid out along the lines of a precise grid aligned with the city center. The grid was established in Teotihuacán's formative days, but it may have been more intensively exploited later, perhaps in relation to "urban renewal" projects undertaken when the city had become rich and powerful.

The prime direction of the grid is slightly east of north (15.5 degrees). The basic modular unit of the plan is close to 57 meters. A number of residential structures are squares of this size. The plan of many of the streets seems to repeat various multiples of the 57-meter unit. The city's major avenues, which run parallel to the north-south axis, are spaced at regular intervals. Even the river running through the center of the city was canalized to conform to the grid. Miles from the city center the remains of buildings are oriented to the grid, even when they were built on slopes that ran counter to it. A small design composed of concentric circles divided into quadrants may have served as a standard surveyor's mark; it is sometimes pecked into the floors of buildings and sometimes into bare bedrock. One such pair of marks two miles apart forms a line exactly perpendicular to the city's north-south axis. The achievement of this kind of order obviously calls for an initial vision that is both audacious and self-confident.

A city planner's description of Teotihuacán would begin not with the monumental Pyramid of the Sun but with the two complexes of structures that form the city center. These are the Citadel and the Great Compound, lying respectively to the east and west of the city's main north-south avenue, the Street of the Dead. The names given the various structures and features of Teotihuacán are not, incidentally, the names by which the Teotihuacanos knew them. Some come from Spanish translations of Aztec names; others were bestowed by earlier archaeologists or by our mappers and are often the place names used by the local people.

The Street of the Dead forms the main axis of the city. At its northern end it stops at the Pyramid of the Moon, and

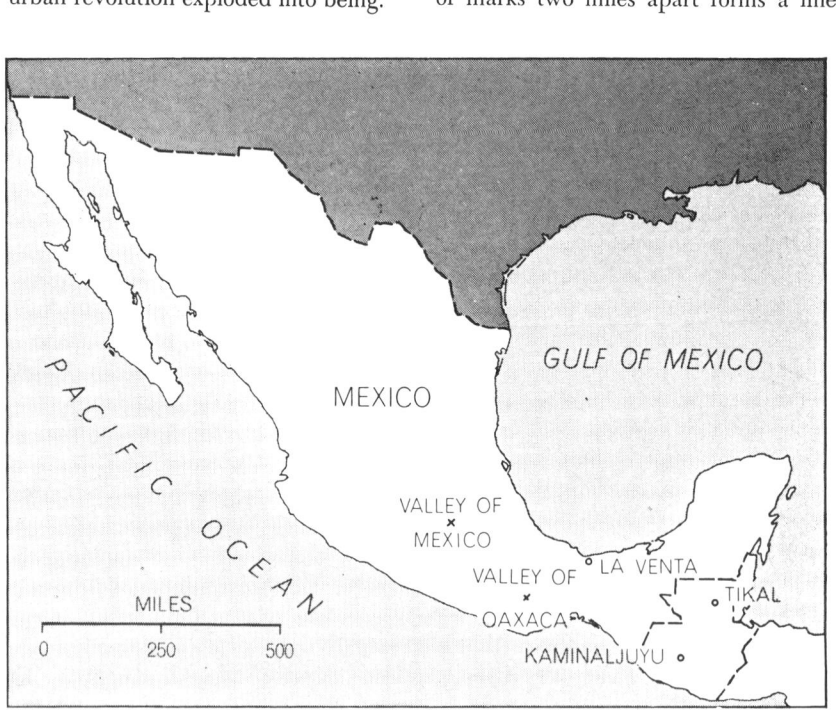

EARLY CIVILIZATION in Middle America appeared first in the lowlands along the Gulf of Mexico at such major centers of Olmec culture as La Venta. Soon thereafter a number of ceremonial centers appeared in the highlands, particularly in the valleys of Oaxaca, Puebla and Mexico. Kaminaljuyu and Tikal, Maya centers respectively in highlands and lowlands of what is now Guatemala, came under Teotihuacán's influence at the height of its power.

CEREMONIAL HEART of Teotihuacán is seen in an aerial photograph looking southeast toward Cerro Patlachique, one of a pair of mountains that flank the narrow valley dominated by the city. The large pyramid in

we have found that to the south it extends for two miles beyond the Citadel-Compound complex. The existence of a subordinate axis running east and west had not been suspected until our mappers discovered one broad avenue running more than two miles to the east of the Citadel and a matching avenue extending the same distance westward from the Compound.

To make it easier to locate buildings over so large an area we imposed our own 500-meter grid on the city, orienting it to the Street of the Dead and using the center of the city as the zero point of the system [see bottom illustration, p. 47]. The heavy line defining the limits of the city was determined by walking around the perimeter of the city and examining evidence on the surface to establish where its outermost remains end. The line traces a zone free of such remains that is at least 300 meters wide and that sharply separates the city from the countryside. The Street of the Dead, East Avenue and West Avenue divide Teotihuacán into quadrants centered on the Citadel-Compound complex. We do not know if these were formally recognized as administrative quarters of the city, as they were in Tenochtitlán. It is nonetheless possible that they may have been, since there are a number of other similarities between the two cities.

Indeed, during the past 25 years Mexican scholars have argued for a high degree of continuity in customs and beliefs from the Aztecs back to the Teotihuacanos, based partly on an assumed continuity in language. This hypothetical continuity, which extends through the intervening Toltec times, provides valuable clues in interpreting archaeological evidence. For example, the unity of religion and politics that archaeologists postulate at Teotihuacán is reinforced by what is known of Aztec society.

The public entrance of the Citadel is a monumental staircase on the Street of the Dead. Inside the Citadel a plaza opens onto the Temple of Quetzalcoatl, the principal sacred building in this area. The temple's façade represents the most successful integration of architecture and sculpture so far discovered at Teotihuacán [see bottom illustration on page 50].

The Great Compound, across the street from the Citadel, had gone unrecognized as a major structure until our survey. We found that it differs from all other known structures at Teotihuacán and that in area it is the city's largest. Its main components are two great raised platforms. These form a north and a south wing and are separated by broad entrances at the level of the street on the east and west. The two wings thus flank a plaza somewhat larger than the one within the Citadel. Few of the structures on the platforms seem to have been temples or other religious buildings. Most of them face away from the Street of the Dead, whereas almost all the other known structures along the avenue face toward it.

the foreground is the Pyramid of the Moon. The larger one beyond it is the Pyramid of the Sun. Many of the more than 100 smaller religious structures that line the city's central avenue, the Street of the Dead, are visible in the photograph. South of the Pyramid of the Sun and east of the central avenue is the large enclosure known as the Citadel. It and the Great Compound, a matching structure not visible in the photograph, formed the city's center. More than 4,000 additional buildings, most no longer visible, spread for miles beyond the center. At the peak of Teotihuacán's power, around A.D. 500, the population of the city was more than 50,000.

One therefore has the impression that the Compound was not devoted to religious affairs. In the Citadel there are clusters of rooms to the north and south of the Temple of Quetzalcoatl, but the overall effect conveyed by the temples and the other buildings that surround the Citadel's plaza is one of a political center in a sacred setting. Perhaps some of its rooms housed the high priests of Teotihuacán.

The plaza of the Compound is a strategically located open space that could have been the city's largest marketplace. The buildings that overlook this plaza could have been at least partly devoted to the administration of the economic affairs of the city. Whatever their functions were, the Citadel and the Compound are the heart of the city. Together they form a majestic spatial unit,

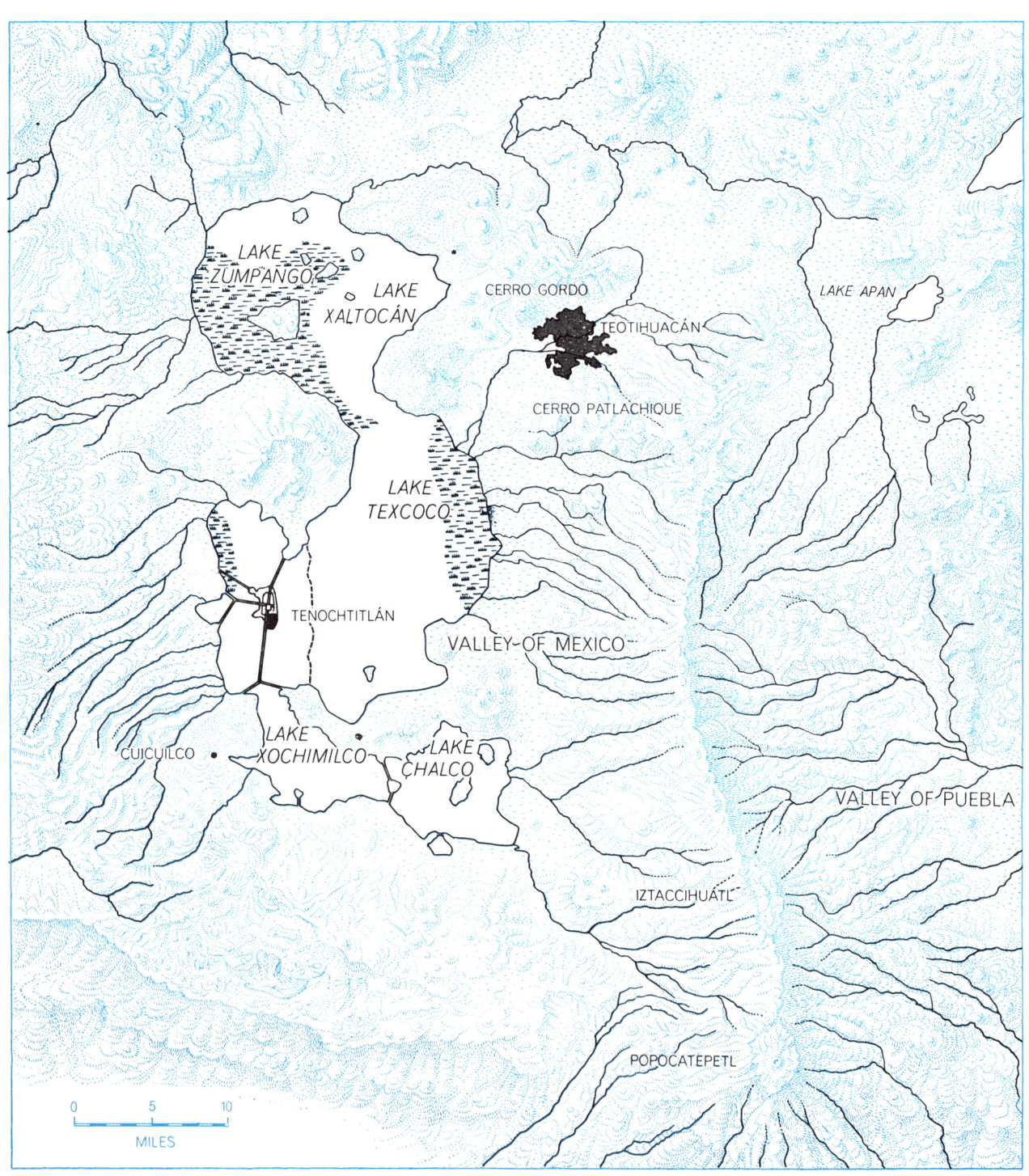

VALLEY OF MEXICO was dominated by shallow lakes in late pre-Hispanic times; in the rainy season they coalesced into a single body of water. Teotihuacán was strategically located; it commanded a narrow valley a few miles northeast of the lakes that provided the best route between the Valley of Mexico and the Valley of Puebla, which leads to the lowlands along the Gulf of Mexico (*see map at bottom of page 42*). It was an important center of trade and worship from 100 B.C. until about A.D. 750. Centuries after its fall the Aztec capital of Tenochtitlán grew up in the western shallows of Lake Texcoco, 25 miles from the earlier metropolis.

a central island surrounded by more open ground than is found in any other part of Teotihuacán.

The total area of the city was eight square miles. Not counting ritual structures, more than 4,000 buildings, most of them apartment houses, were built to shelter the population. At the height of Teotihuacán's power, in the middle of the first millennium A.D., the population certainly exceeded 50,000 and was probably closer to 100,000. This is not a particularly high figure compared with Old World religious-political centers; today the population of Mecca is some 130,000 and that of Benares more than 250,000 (to which is added an annual influx of a million pilgrims). One reason Teotihuacán did not have a larger population was that its gleaming lime-plastered residential structures were only

APARTMENT HOUSE typical of the city's many multiroomed dwellings was excavated in 1961 by Laurette Séjourné. The outer walls of the compound conform with the 57-meter module favored by the city's planners. Within its forbidding exterior (*see south façade at bottom of illustration*) individual apartments comprised several rooms grouped around unroofed patios (*smaller white areas*).

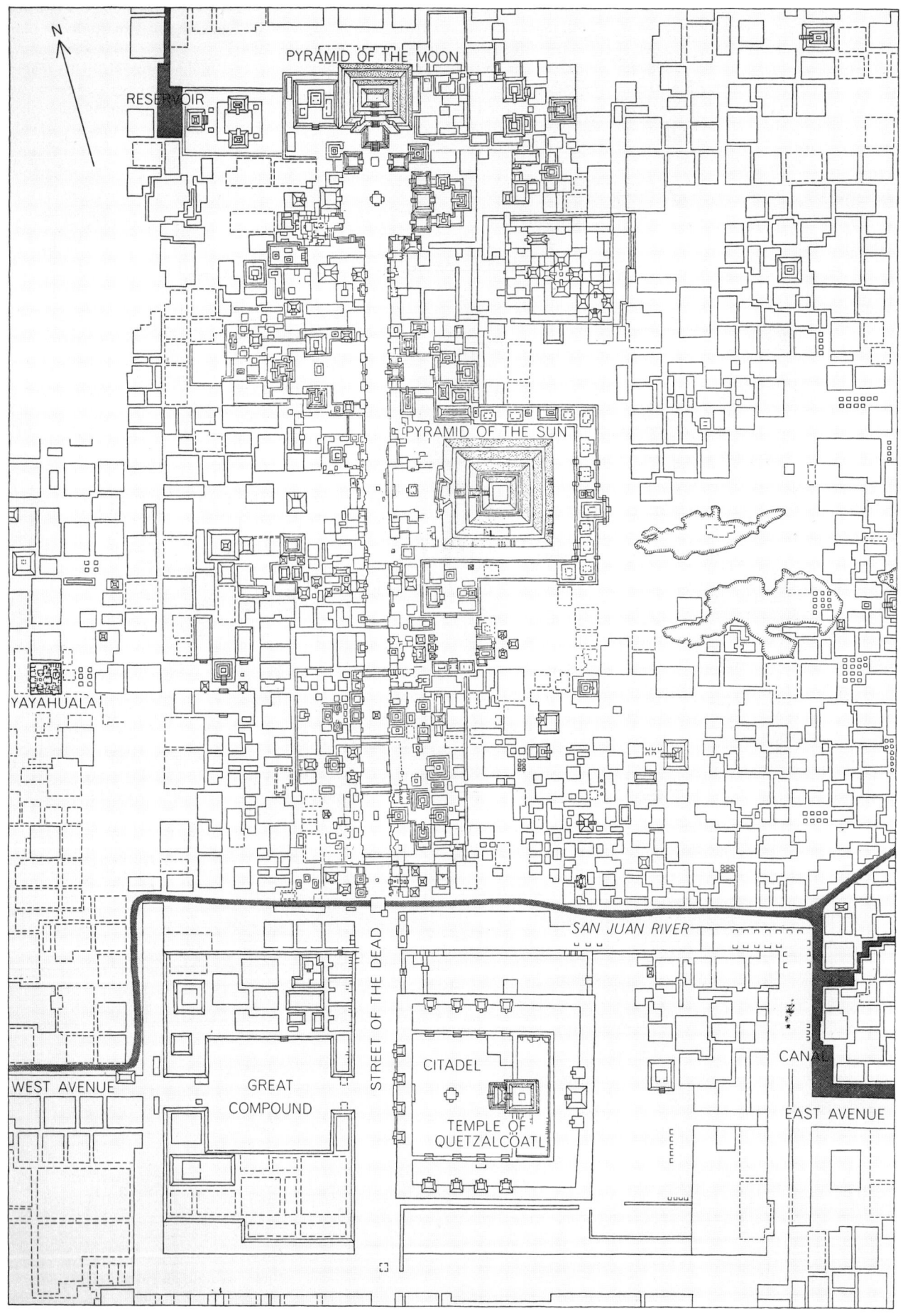

one story high. Although most of the inhabitants lived in apartments, the buildings were "ranch-style" rather than "high-rise."

The architects of Teotihuacán designed apartments to offer a maximum of privacy within the crowded city, using a concept similar to the Old World's classical atrium house [*see illustration on page 45*]. The rooms of each apartment surrounded a central patio; each building consisted of a series of rooms, patios, porticoes and passageways, all secluded from the street. This pattern was also characteristic of the city's palaces. The residential areas of Teotihuacán must have presented a somewhat forbidding aspect from the outside: high windowless walls facing on narrow streets. Within the buildings, however, the occupants were assured of privacy. Each patio had its own drainage system; each admitted light and air to the surrounding apartments; each made it possible for the inhabitants to be out of doors yet alone. It may be that this architectural style contributed to Teotihuacán's permanence as a focus of urban life for more than 500 years.

The basic building materials of Teotihuacán were of local origin. Outcrops of porous volcanic rock in the valley were quarried and the stone was crushed and mixed with lime and earth to provide a kind of moisture-resistant concrete that was used as the foundation for floors and walls. The same material was used for roofing; wooden posts spaced at intervals bore much of the weight of the roof. Walls were made of stone and mortar or of sunbaked adobe brick. Floors and wall surfaces were then usually finished with highly polished plaster.

What kinds of people lived in Teotihuacán? Religious potentates, priestly bureaucrats and military leaders presumably occupied the top strata of the city's society, but their number could not have been large. Many of the inhabitants tilled lands outside the city and many others must have been artisans: potters, workers in obsidian and stone and craftsmen dealing with more perishable materials such as cloth, leather, feathers and wood (traces of which are occasionally preserved). Well-defined concentrations of surface remains suggest that craft groups such as potters and workers in stone and obsidian tended to live together in their own neighborhoods. This lends weight to the hypothesis that each apartment building was solely occupied by a "corporate" group, its families related on the basis of occupation, kinship or both. An arrangement of this kind, linking the apartment dwellers to one another by webs of joint interest and activity, would have promoted social stability.

If groups with joint interests lived not only in the same apartment building but also in the same general neighborhood, the problem of governing the city would have been substantially simplified. Such organization of neighborhood groups could have provided an intermediate level between the individual and the state. Ties of cooperation, competition or even conflict between people in different neighborhoods could have created the kind of social network that is favorable to cohesion.

The marketplace would similarly have made an important contribution to the integration of Teotihuacán society. If the greater part of the exchange of goods and services in the city took place in one or more major markets (such as the one that may have occupied the plaza of the Great Compound), then not only the Teotihuacanos but also the outsiders who used the markets would have felt a vested interest in maintaining "the peace of the market." Moreover, the religion of Teotihuacán would have imbued the city's economic institutions with a sacred quality.

The various social groups in the city left some evidence of their identity. For example, we located a walled area, associated with the west side of the Pyramid of the Moon, where large quantities of waste obsidian suggest that obsidian workers may have formed part of a larger temple community. We also found what looks like a foreign neighborhood. Occupied by people who apparently came to Teotihuacán from the Valley of Oaxaca, the area lies in the western part of the city. It is currently under study by

CITY CENTER is composed of two sets of structures, the Great Compound and the Citadel (*bottom of illustration on opposite page*). They stand on either side of the Street of the Dead, the main north-south axis of the city. A pair of avenues approaching the center of the city from east and west form the secondary axis. The city's largest religious monuments were the Pyramid of the Sun, the Pyramid of the Moon and the Temple of Quetzalcoatl, which lies inside the Citadel. Yayahuala (*left of center*) was one of many residential compounds. Its architecture is shown in detail on page 45.

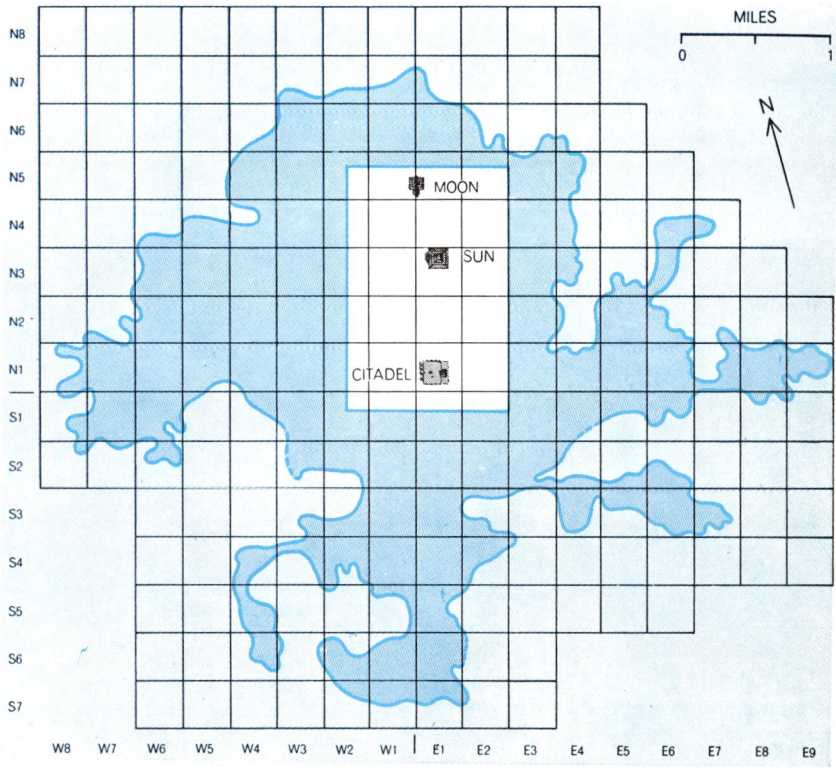

IRREGULAR BOUNDARY of Teotihuacán is shown as a solid line that approaches the edges of a grid, composed of 500-meter squares, surveyed by the author's team. The grid parallels the north-south direction of the Street of the Dead, the city's main avenue. One extension of the city in its early period, which is only partly known, has been omitted. A map of Teotihuacán's north-central zone (*light color*) is reproduced on page 46.

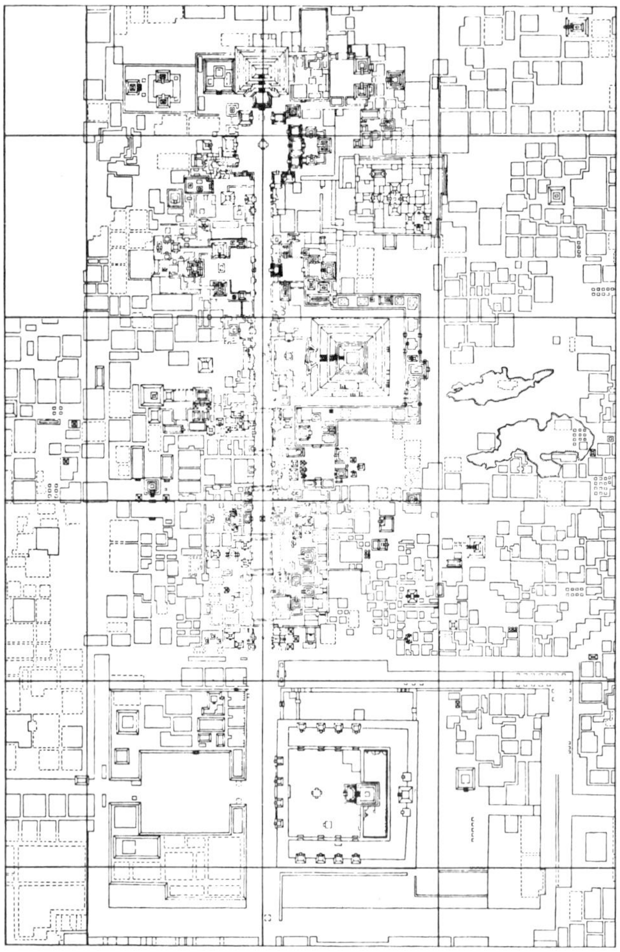

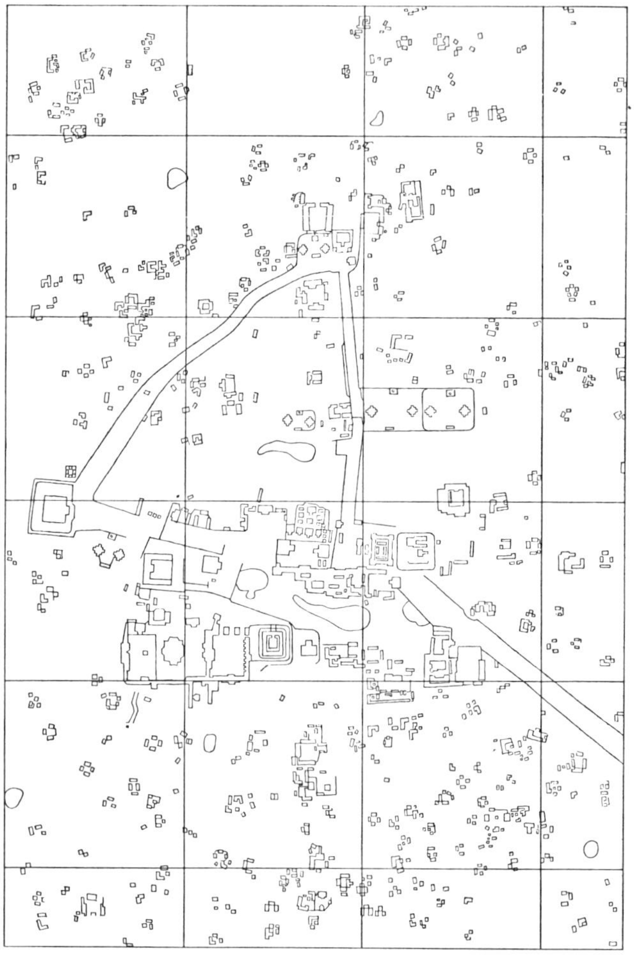

DENSITY OF SETTLEMENT at Teotihuacán is compared with that at Tikal, largest of the lowland Maya ceremonial centers in Middle America. The maps show the central area of each settlement at the same scale. The data for Teotihuacán (*left*) are from surveys by the author and the Mexican government. Those for Tikal (*right*) are from a survey by the University of Pennsylvania. Even though its center included many public structures, Teotihuacán's concentrated residential pattern shows its urban character.

PYRAMID OF THE SUN is as broad at the base as the great pyramid of Cheops in Egypt, although it is only half as high. It was built over the site of an earlier shrine during Teotihuacán's first major period of growth, in the early centuries of the Christian era.

John Paddock of the University of the Americas, a specialist in the prehistory of Oaxaca. Near the eastern edge of the city quantities of potsherds have been found that are characteristic of Maya areas and the Veracruz region along the Gulf of Mexico. These fragments suggest that the neighborhood was inhabited either by people from those areas or by local merchants who specialized in such wares.

We have found evidence that as the centuries passed two of the city's important crafts—the making of pottery and obsidian tools—became increasingly specialized. From the third century A.D. on some obsidian workshops contain a high proportion of tools made by striking blades from a "core" of obsidian; others have a high proportion of tools made by chipping a piece of obsidian until the desired shape was obtained. Similar evidence of specialization among potters is found in the southwestern part of the city. There during Teotihuacán's period of greatest expansion one group of potters concentrated on the mass production of the most common type of cooking ware.

The crafts of Teotihuacán must have helped to enrich the city. So also, no doubt, did the pilgrim traffic. In addition to the three major religious structures more than 100 other temples and shrines line the Street of the Dead. Those who visited the city's sacred buildings must have included not only peasants and townspeople from the entire Valley of Mexico but also pilgrims from as far away as Guatemala. When one adds to these worshipers the visiting merchants, traders and peddlers attracted by the markets of Teotihuacán, it seems likely that many people would have been occupied catering to the needs of those who were merely visiting the city.

Radical social transformations took place during the growth of the city. As Teotihuacán increased in size there was first a relative and then an absolute decline in the surrounding rural population. This is indicated by both our data from the city and Sanders' from the countryside. Apparently many rural populations left their villages and were concentrated in the city. The process seems to have accelerated around A.D. 500, when the population of the city approached its peak. Yet the marked increase in density within the city was accompanied by a reduction in the city's size. It was at this time, during the sixth century, that urban renewal programs may have been undertaken in areas

HUMAN FIGURE, wearing a feather headdress, face paint and sandals, decorates the side of a vase dating from the sixth century A.D. Similar figures often appear in the city's murals.

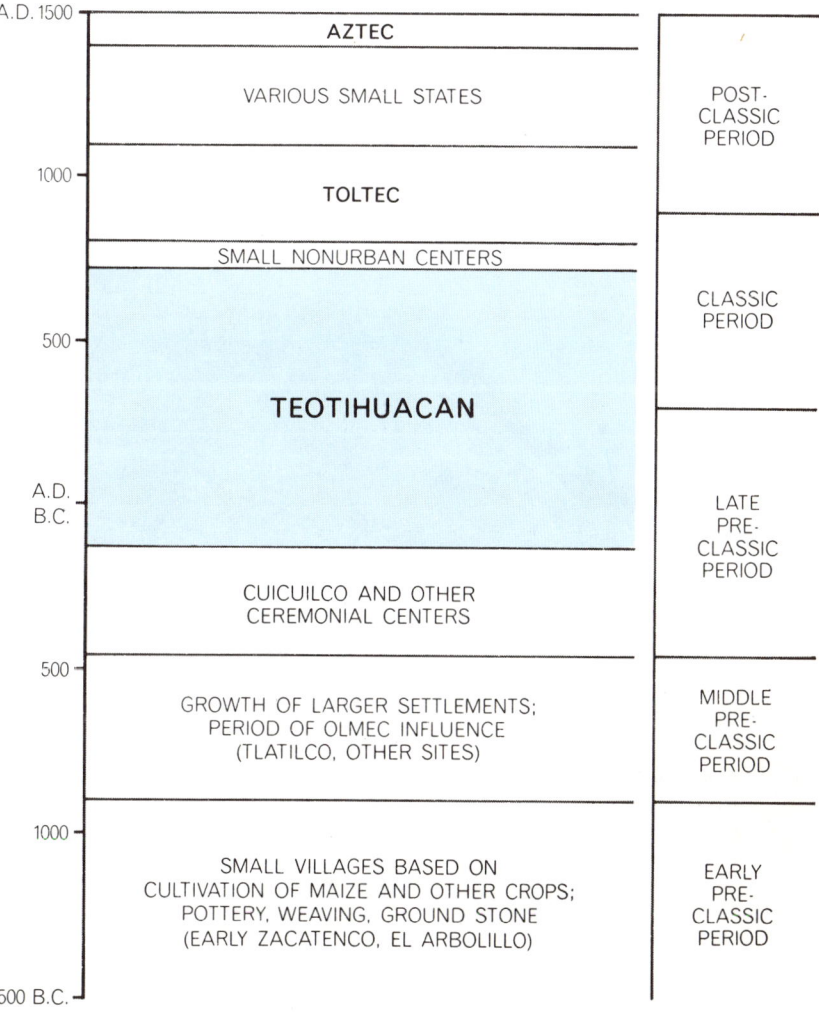

CITY'S BIRTH took place during the late pre-Classic Period in the Valley of Mexico, about a century before the beginning of the Christian era. Other highland ceremonial centers such as Cuicuilco in the Valley of Mexico and Cholula in the Valley of Puebla were influential at that time. Although Teotihuacán fell in about A.D. 750, near the end of the Classic Period, its religious monuments were deemed sacred by the Aztecs until Hispanic times.

PYRAMID OF THE MOON, excavated in the early 1960's by a Mexican government group under the direction of Ignacio Bernal, stands at the northern end of the Street of the Dead. The façade presented to the avenue (*above*) consists of several interlocking, truncated pyramids thrusting toward the sky. The structure, 150 feet high and 490 feet wide at the base, is smaller than the Pyramid of the Sun but is architecturally more sophisticated.

TEMPLE OF QUETZALCOATL is the major religious structure within the Citadel, the eastern half of Teotihuacán's city center. The building is believed to represent the most successful integration of sculpture and architecture to be achieved throughout the city's long history. A covering layer of later construction protected the ornate facade from damage.

where density was on the rise.

Such movements of rural and urban populations must have conflicted with local interests. That they were carried out successfully demonstrates the prestige and power of the hierarchy in Teotihuacán. Traditional loyalties to the religion of Teotihuacán were doubtless invoked. Nevertheless, one wonders if the power of the military would not have been increasingly involved. There is evidence both in Teotihuacán and beyond its borders that its soldiers became more and more important from the fifth century on. It may well be that at the peak of its power and influence Teotihuacán itself was becoming an increasingly oppressive place in which to live.

The best evidence of the power and influence that the leaders of Teotihuacán exercised elsewhere in Middle America comes from Maya areas. One ancient religious center in the Maya highlands—Kaminaljuyu, the site of modern Guatemala City—appears to have been occupied at one time by priests and soldiers from Teotihuacán. Highland Guatemala received a massive infusion of Teotihuacán cultural influences, with Teotihuacán temple architecture replacing older styles. This has been recognized for some time, but only recently has it become clear that Teotihuacán also influenced the Maya lowlands. The people of Tikal in Guatemala, largest of the lowland Maya centers, are now known to have been under strong influence from Teotihuacán. The people of Tikal adopted some of Teotihuacán's artistic traditions and erected a massive stone monument to Teotihuacán's rain god. William R. Coe of the University of Pennsylvania and his colleagues, who are working at Tikal, are in the midst of evaluating the nature and significance of this influence.

Tikal provides an instructive measure of the difference in the density of construction in Maya population centers and those in central Mexico. It was estimated recently that Tikal supported a population of about 10,000. As the illustration at the top of page 48 shows, the density of Teotihuacán's central area is strikingly different from that of Tikal's. Not only was Teotihuacán's population at least five times larger than Tikal's but also it was far less dispersed. In such a crowded urban center problems of integration, cohesion and social control must have been of a totally different order of magnitude than those of a less populous and less compact ceremonial center such as Tikal.

What were the circumstances of Teotihuacán's decline and fall? Almost certainly both environmental and social factors were involved. The climate of the region is semiarid today, and there is evidence that a long-term decline in annual rainfall brought the city to a similar condition in the latter half of the first millennium A.D. Even before then deforestation of the surrounding hills may have begun a process of erosion that caused a decrease in the soil moisture available for crops. Although persistent drought would have presented increasingly serious problems for those who fed the city, this might have been the lesser of its consequences. More ominous would have been the effect of increasing aridity on the cultivators of marginal lands and the semisedentary tribesmen in the highlands north of the Valley of Mexico. As worsening conditions forced these peoples to move, the Teotihuacanos might have found themselves not only short of food but also under military pressure along their northern frontier.

Whether or not climatic change was a factor, some signs of decline—such as the lowering of standards of construction and pottery-making—are evident during the last century of Teotihuacán's existence. Both a reduction in population and a tendency toward dispersion suggest that the fabric of society was suffering from strains and weaknesses. Once such a process of deterioration passed a critical point the city would have become vulnerable to attack.

No evidence has been found that Teotihuacán as a whole had formal defenses. Nonetheless, the valley's drainage pattern provides some natural barriers, large parts of the city were surrounded by walls or massive platforms and its buildings were formidable ready-made fortresses. Perhaps the metropolis was comparatively unprotected because it had for so long had an unchallenged supremacy.

In any case, archaeological evidence indicates that around A.D. 750 much of central Teotihuacán was looted and burned, possibly with the help of the city's own people. The repercussions of Teotihuacán's fall seem to have been felt throughout civilized Middle America. The subsequent fall of Monte Alban, the capital of the Oaxaca region, and of many Maya ceremonial centers in Guatemala and the surrounding area may reasonably be associated with dislocations set in motion by the fall of Teotihuacán. Indeed, the appropriate epitaph for the New World's first major metropolis may be that it was as influential in its collapse as in its long and brilliant flowering.

FEATHERED SERPENT, from one of the earlier murals found at Teotihuacán, has a free, flowing appearance. The animal below the serpent is a jaguar; the entire mural, which is not shown, was probably painted around A.D. 400. It may portray a cyclical myth of creation and destruction. The city's principal gods were often represented in the form of animals.

LATER SERPENT GOD, with a rattlesnake tail, is from a mural probably painted less than a century before the fall of Teotihuacán. The figure is rendered in a highly formal manner. A trend toward formalism is apparent in the paintings produced during the city's final years.

II

INVENTIONS AND THE URBAN TRADITION

II INVENTIONS AND THE URBAN TRADITION

INTRODUCTION

The articles in Section II deal with two consequences of early civilization: technological innovation and the evolution of urban settlements over centuries of civilized rule. Technological innovation progressed hand in hand with political and economic development. The innovations described by Robert Maddin and his colleagues and by Stuart Piggott are two technologies that we take for granted—iron and wheeled transport. Our present-day industrial civilization could never have developed its extraordinary technological complexity without these two critical innovations.

An abundance of cheap iron tools and weapons produced from readily available ores enabled early civilizations to clear land more easily and to wage war with sharp, deadly weapons. After 900 B.C., iron implements became more and more common as Old World technologies adjusted to the new metal. Bronzesmiths developed the basic techniques of ironworking by trial and error. During a long period of experimentation, smiths developed ironworking techniques, such as steeling, quenching, and tempering, that enabled them to develop properties in the metal appropriate to the functions of the objects they were making. The practical experience of thousands of smiths through centuries of experimentation resulted in sophisticated methods for making strong, durable iron tools. Their very durability gave iron implements an important advantage in the forest or on the battlefield, enabling the societies that used iron to expand the capabilities of their armies and to develop plow agriculture. Surprisingly, iron technology underwent little change throughout the Iron Age and Classical times up until Medieval times. The skilled craftspeople who experimented with the new metal provided the basic technology that enabled the Romans to conquer much of the Mediterranean and European world and more than a millennium later, allowed the Conquistadores to destroy the non–iron-using Aztec and Inca civilizations in the New World.

The early history of the wheel and wheeled transport has attracted surprisingly little attention, partly because the wooden parts of chariots, wagons, and similar vehicles are among the first items to perish in any potential archaeological site. But the wheel was a revolutionary invention—one that immediately enabled its inventors to carry much greater loads, provided they had abundant timber to make the carts and cattle to haul them. Early trade routes relied heavily on water-borne transport and on human backs for load carrying. Wheeled carts opened up new dimensions of land travel, leading to the development of overland routes that soon became heavily traveled highways and caravan routes. Lightweight chariots revolutionized warfare as soon as horses were trained to draw them.

Stuart Piggott argues that wheeled carts were used in Eastern Europe at least 5,500 years ago. The earliest wheeled vehicles were presumably developed somewhere between Lake Van in Asia Minor and Lake Urmia in Northern Iran, in relatively level terrain where timber was abundant. The inhabi-Piggott points to vehicle burials found by Soviet archaeologists in Georgia and Armenia that are at least 4,500 years old. These suggest that wheeled vehicles were first invented not in Mesopotamia but in the highland areas to the north. The Sumerians drew pictures of wheeled vehicles about 2800 B.C. Once castration was found to produce docile cattle or asses, the hauling of carts became possible. And once the Sumerians had domesticated the horse, it was an easy step to develop chariots and radically expand the sphere of military operations. Use of the wheel soon developed into a close marriage of human and vehicle—an interdependence that continues into our own times. No other major technological innovation has ever had such a dramatic effect on the course of history.

Both iron tools and wheeled transport had drastic effects on the history of preindustrial cities. Settlements such as Carthage and Winchester survived wars, sieges, famines, legal disputes, and the onslaughts of revolutionary technologies. The archaeology of cities is extraordinarily complex, for the excavator must unravel a long story of successive dwellings, new street plans, and the archaeological remains of sieges and earthquakes, fires and house remodelings. This type of archaeology is exemplified in Carthage, a great city of antiquity that survived centuries of warfare and religious controversy before being razed by Moslems in A.D. 698. An international effort has been under way for several years to rescue Roman Carthage from modern real estate development. The article by Humphrey and Pedley shows not only how complex urban archaeology can become, but also how durable cities can be. Carthage was completely destroyed by the Romans in 146 B.C.; but so strategic was the site that the conquerors resettled it only a quarter-century later. The new city soon became one of the most prosperous in the Roman Empire. Here and at other key locations, urban life became more than a transitory phenomenon—rather an ongoing process of rebuilding and expansion. Even after its second razing, Carthage has risen again to become one of the urban centers of the Mediterranean.

In the case of Winchester as well as that of Carthage, the Industrial Age has placed new pressures on an ancient preindustrial city that survived the transition into our automated, mechanized century. The ruins of Roman Carthage are threatened by modern urban expansion. Much of Medieval Winchester in England still stands, however. The magnificent cathedral and its quiet green overlook a bustling settlement of 33,000 people whose history can be traced back to Roman times 2,000 years ago. Dead cities such as Troy or Ur-of-the-Chaldees are easier to study, for their shattered remains can be reached without disturbing modern inhabitants. Roman, Saxon, and Medieval Winchester lie under the streets of the modern city. The town center is currently being redeveloped in response to the needs of a motorized and industrialized age. The deep foundations of new developments reach down into the complex earlier occupation levels of the city, whose history is recorded not only in local archives but in the ground as well. For more than a decade the Winchester Excavations Committee has worked on the foundations of the city, studying the origin and changing character of Winchester's urban community from the first permanent settlement to the emergence of the modern Victorian city. The committee studied the city in its entirety, comparing different stages of the settlement's evolution. Martin Biddle's article describes more than 2,000 years of urban life in a durable city that changed in response to shifting economic, political, and social conditions. Winchester experienced three principal periods of efflorescence and two of decline—the second beginning in the sixteenth century. This slump lasted until the railroad came to the city in the nineteenth century. In 1860, Victorian Winchester was larger than the city in Roman times, but only slightly bigger than the Medieval city. The more rapid growth of Winchester during the past century is a phenomenon of an industrial civilization whose survival depends on city life and the urban economy.

Carthage and Winchester grew somewhat haphazardly. The Romans gave Winchester a grid street plan—a layout that became largely obscured in later times. We can only guess at the psychological perspectives of those who planned Roman Carthage or Winchester. Did they care whether successive generations would adhere to their master plan and develop their city in systematic manner? Did they have faith that their city would survive for hundreds of years? Could they confidently leave their planned settlement for future generations to complete according to plan? What were their feelings about the future?

In an unmechanized, preindustrial society, the building of any major religious complex or urban center is an enormous undertaking that requires control of huge labor forces. Norman Hammond's article on the planning of the great Maya ceremonial center at Lubaantun shows how successive generations of builders erected a pattern of eleven major structures and at least twenty plazas in a minimum of five stages during a 150-year period. By the standards of Carthage or Teotihuacán, Lubaantun is relatively small. But what is impressive is the way that the builders followed an architectural master plan for generation after generation. Motivated by their unbounded faith in the religion that dictated the master plan, thousands of people contributed to the long-term completion of a vast ceremonial center. Even more remarkable, those who erected Lubaantun carried out their designs with the labor of a scattered rural population supported by subsistence agriculture. And when Maya civilization collapsed, the vast structures of Lubaantun reverted to the rain forest and were forgotten until recent times. Lubaantun lacks the continuity of urban civilization represented by Carthage and Winchester, but the sheer magnitude of the collective labor to build this and other Maya ceremonial centers and cities testifies to the faith of their inhabitants in the future of their city and their civilization.

How the Iron Age Began

by Robert Maddin, James D. Muhly and
Tamara S. Wheeler
October 1977

Until almost the end of the second millennium B. C. bronze was the utilitarian metal of the Mediterranean world. Within a few centuries it was replaced by a new kind of metal: "steeled" iron

It is an old adage that necessity is the mother of invention. The many unanticipated inventions of modern times would seem to be counterexamples, but over the span of human history the adage probably has a certain rough justice. A current investigation in the history of technology is providing a case in point: the appearance some 3,000 years ago of a kind of steel as a substitute for bronze, which until then had been the dominant metal of the civilized world.

For some two millenniums, up to about 1200 B.C., the civilizations of the Old World had satisfied their needs for a utilitarian metal—for tools, weapons, armor and many other durable articles—with various types and alloys of copper, including bronze. Toward the end of that era, known loosely as the Bronze Age, the civilizations of the eastern Mediterranean suffered a series of disturbances. Exactly what caused these disturbances is not known, but one fact about the ensuing centuries has become clear: the use of bronze rapidly diminished and the use of iron—specifically "steeled," or carburized, iron—increased even more rapidly.

Various items of evidence, necessarily fragmentary but diverse enough to inspire a degree of confidence, suggest the speed of the transition. Iron was known as a workable metal during most if not all of the Bronze Age. Nevertheless, Bronze Age sites in the eastern Mediterranean and Southwest Asia representative of a 2,000-year span of history have yielded a total of fewer than 500 iron artifacts, most of them ornamental. The bronze artifacts recovered from the same sites are numbered in the scores of thousands.

Contrast this picture with the number of knives and weapons made from both metals that have been found at sites in Greece representative of the period between 1050 and 900 B.C. A. Snodgrass of the University of Cambridge tabulated the relative abundance of bronze and iron as follows: bronze knives none, iron knives more than 15; bronze swords one, iron swords more than 20; bronze spearheads eight, iron spearheads more than 30.

This distribution is remarkable on two counts. First, bronze articles of this kind can be made by casting, a quick and easy production method, whereas similar iron articles must be individually shaped by forging, a comparatively arduous process. Second, bronze, like its principal constituent, copper, is remarkably durable and can be scrapped and recast repeatedly. Why had the people at these sites substituted a complex process for a simple one? And what had become of the bronze articles they had made in earlier years?

Future archaeological investigation may reveal why bronze went into a decline. Among the causes could have been a breakdown of the trade in tin, the principal alloying ingredient in the articles of the later Bronze Age. With respect to the rapid rise of iron as a substitute metal the picture is a good deal clearer. Both archaeological investigations and studies of ancient inscriptions have in recent years substantiated much that was conjectural and revealed much that was entirely unknown. To present this information in context let us briefly describe copper and iron metallurgy as it was known in the last millenniums before the Christian Era.

Copper is found both as a metal (in lumps of "native" copper) and as an ore that must be heated to yield the metal. For the purposes of this discussion native copper can be ignored. The oldest copper-smelting sites known are at locations in Iran and Israel and date from the fifth and fourth millenniums B.C. Copper ores are found in modest abundance on Cyprus, in various parts of Turkey, in Iran and in Israel. The commonest ore is chalcopyrite, a complex copper iron sulfide that must be roasted in the open air to remove the sulfur before it can be smelted. Certain copper ores contain arsenic; when they are smelted they yield an arsenical copper alloy that can be characterized as "natural bronze."

The early metalworkers of the eastern Mediterranean commonly smelted copper by filling a stone furnace with alternating layers of charcoal and ore combined with a flux. The flux served the purpose of removing from the copper ore the constituents the metalworker did not want in his finished product. These constituents are collectively known as gangue (a word originally derived from the Greek for a vein of ore). In the hot furnace the flux tended to combine with the gangue and remove it from the metal. In many ores of the eastern Mediterranean the gangue was silica: any one of a number of silicon oxides. The appropriate flux for these ores was the iron oxide hematite; the heat of the furnace combined the silicon and iron oxides to form an iron silicate.

When the metalworker had filled his furnace, he ignited the charcoal. In some furnaces the heat of the fire was increased by the natural draft provided by a flue; in others air was forced into the top, sides or bottom of the furnace through clay pipes. As the charge in the furnace got hotter the charcoal was oxidized to carbon monoxide; the hot gas flowed upward through the mixture of ore and flux, chemically reducing both. Reduction took place at about 1,100 degrees Celsius, and the molten copper trickled down to form a puddle at the bottom of the furnace, leaving the gangue behind as a slag. The early metalworkers could not have accurately predicted or measured the furnace temperature; presumably if no puddle of copper appeared, they let the furnace cool off and started over again with a different charge or more draft.

If the ore happened to contain more than a few percent of arsenic what the metalworker found was a puddle of natural bronze. The bronze had the advantage of being harder than copper. Even if the puddle was merely soft pure copper, however, the cast metal could be made harder by hammering. Working the copper in this way made it possible for metalworkers to fashion reasonably durable copper articles during a pre-

Bronze-Age period that varied in its duration in different parts of the eastern Mediterranean and Southwest Asia.

Arsenical copper ores eventually came to be widely smelted because of the greater hardness of natural bronze. It was later discovered that copper combined with tin instead of arsenic was also hard. It may be that the toxicity of arsenic led to the replacement of arsenical bronze by tin bronze. In the eastern Mediterranean and Southwest Asia tin bronze first appeared around the beginning of the third millennium B.C.; by the early years of the second millennium the production of tin bronze had surpassed that of arsenical.

Late in the second millennium B.C. upheavals in the eastern Mediterranean, some of them attributed in Egyptian texts of the time to the activities of interlopers known collectively as the "Peoples of the Sea," led to the collapse of local authority in a number of areas. In the centuries that followed, described by students of the ancient world as a dark age, iron soon replaced bronze as the metal most commonly used for tools, weapons and other articles. Since bronze had been satisfactory for the same purposes for several thousand years and iron did not appear to be as useful, it must be inferred that iron was not suddenly adopted as a result of technical innovation but rather that bronze suddenly became scarce. The further inference is that the scarcity resulted from an interruption in the supply of tin and even of copper to the bronze smelters of the eastern Mediterranean. Where the tin had been coming from is not known. The source may have been such relatively nearby mining areas as the Balkans or the Eastern Desert of Egypt; it may even have been such distant areas as Cornwall or eastern Iran.

The early metalworkers produced iron from ores, mostly hematite and magnetite, by a smelting process much like the one used to produce copper. There was, however, an important difference. Iron does not melt at temperatures below 1,537 degrees C., and the highest temperature that could be reached in a primitive smelter appears to have been about 1,200 degrees. Smelting iron ore at that temperature yields not a puddle of metal but a spongy mass mixed with iron oxide and iron silicate. These nonmetallic substances, which collectively represent slag, arise from the combination of ferrous oxide and silica gangue in the reduction process.

The commonest of the nonmetallic substances is fayalite, which remains viscous at temperatures down to 1,177 degrees C. The metalworker therefore withdrew a mass of spongy iron from the furnace, reheated it in a forge and quite literally squeezed the fayalite out of it by hammering.

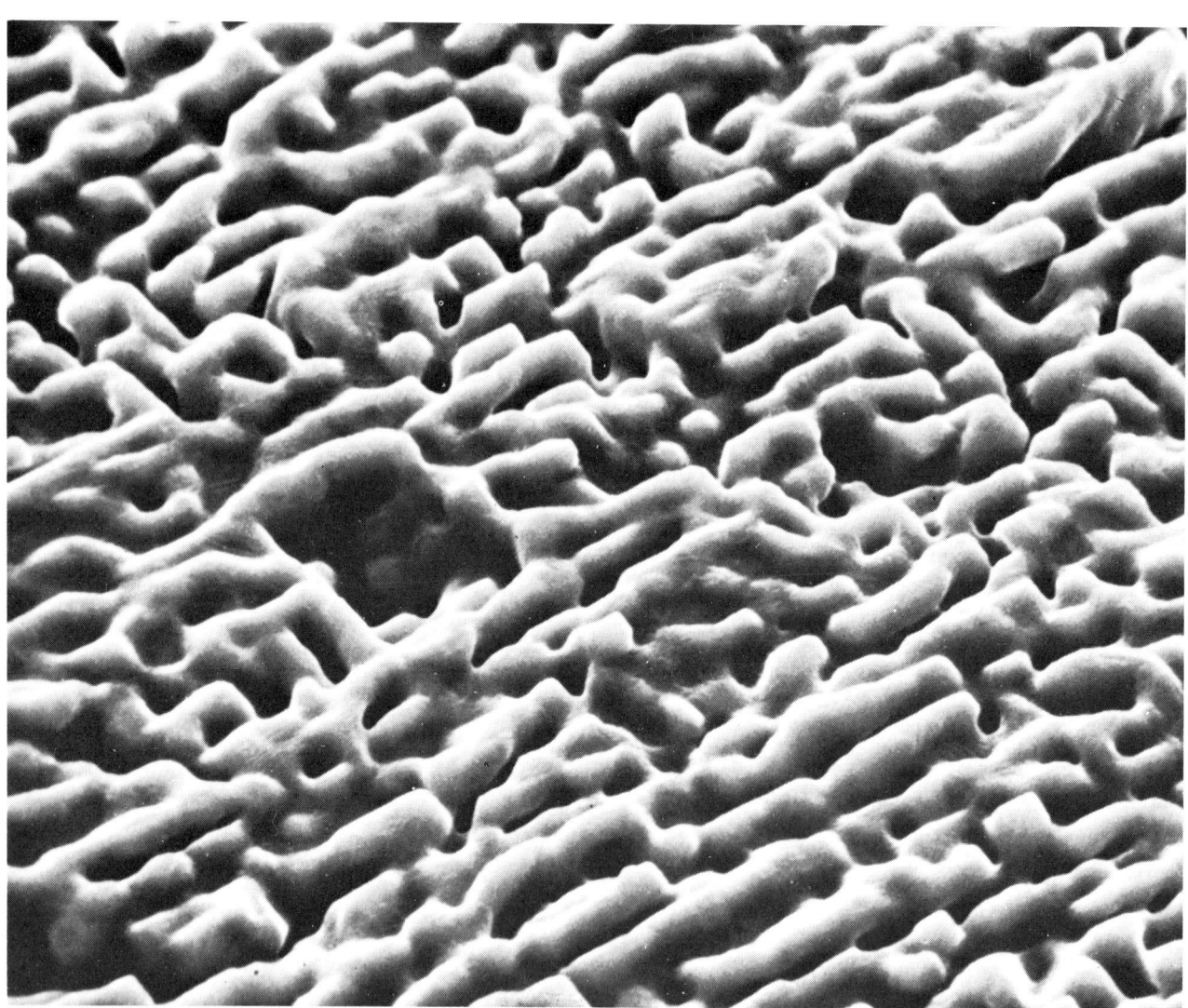

SPONGY STRUCTURE of bloomery iron is revealed in this scanning electron micrograph which shows a modern sample of iron that was smelted at a temperature below its melting point. To produce the sponge a very pure oxide of iron was reduced in an atmosphere of helium and carbon monoxide; the result is seen magnified 2,400 diameters. With a sample of ordinary iron ore the interstices of the sponge would be filled with slag, which could be expelled by hammering. The sample was prepared by Y. K. Rao of the University of Washington.

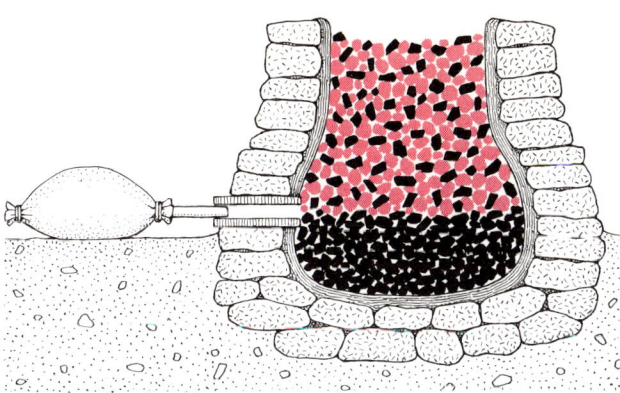 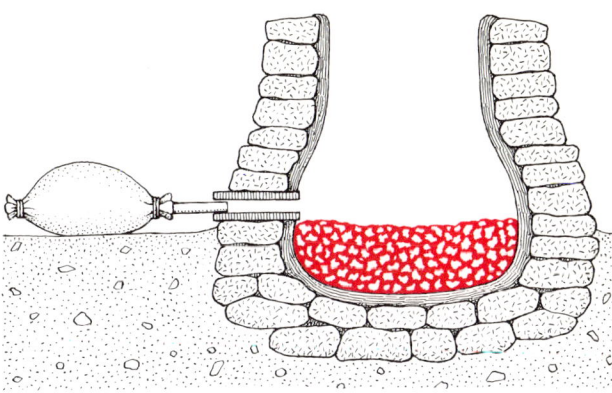

IRON SMELTER, seen here in a speculative reconstruction based on the remains of European Iron Age furnaces, was first filled with a mixed charge of ore, usually hematite or magnetite, and charcoal (*left*). The charge was ignited and the furnace temperature was raised to about 1,200 degrees Celsius by a draft. Because iron does not melt below 1,537 degrees C. the product of the smelting process (*right*) was the spongy mixture of nonmetallic wastes and iron (*color*) known as a bloom. The blacksmith reheated the bloom on a forge to above 1,170 degrees C., making the wastes viscous. The smith then removed the wastes from the iron by hammering. What remained was soft iron.

The hammering at the same time turned the porous iron "bloom" into a continuous network of iron grains interspersed with a few stringers of slag that had not been eliminated. The bloom was the blacksmith's raw material; the iron articles were made by heating and hammering the bloom further.

What the blacksmith had to work with was a poor substitute for bronze. Bloomery iron is a soft metal; its tensile strength is about 40,000 pounds per square inch, only slightly more than the strength of pure copper (about 32,000 p.s.i.). Work-hardening, that is, continued hammering, will bring the strength of iron up to almost 100,000 p.s.i. A bronze containing 11 percent tin, however, has a tensile strength after casting of some 60,000 p.s.i. and a strength after cold-working of as much as 120,000 p.s.i. Bronze was clearly a better material than bloomery iron for the manufacture of weapons and tools.

Bronze had other major advantages over iron. Since it melted at temperatures that the early metalworkers could attain, it was suited to casting. A bronze containing 11 percent tin begins to lose fluidity when it cools to 1,000 degrees C., and it is completely solid at 831 degrees. Since pure iron does not melt below 1,537 degrees, it could not be cast. When iron is alloyed with large amounts of carbon, say 4 percent, it can be made to melt at about 1,150 degrees. The resolidified metal, however, is very brittle. In any event iron was not cast before the middle of the first millennium B.C., when the process was pioneered by the Chinese in the Far East.

The casting methods used in the

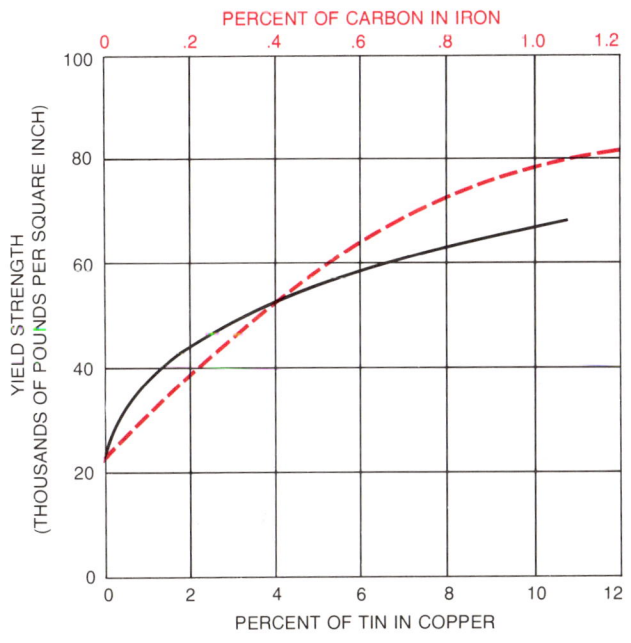 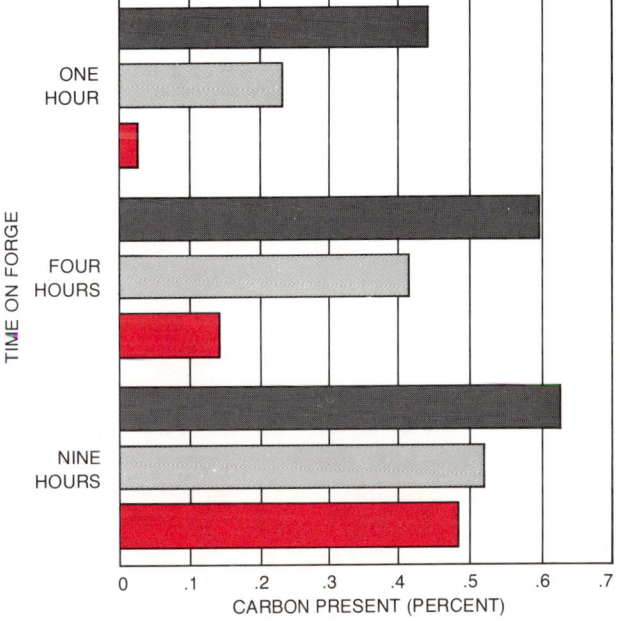

EFFECT OF STEELING, the carburization of bloomery iron by alloying the metal with carbon, is to strengthen the metal until its yield strength is substantially greater than the yield strength of bronze. The addition of 1 percent of tin to copper produces a bronze alloy (*black*) with a yield strength of 30,000 pounds per square inch and the addition of 5 percent tin produces a bronze alloy with a yield strength of 50,000 p.s.i. The addition of .4 percent carbon to iron produces a carburized alloy (*color*) with a yield strength of more than 50,000 p.s.i. An iron that contains 1 percent carbon, in turn, is more than 10,000 p.s.i. stronger than a bronze that contains as much as 8 percent tin.

CARBURIZATION OF IRON results from the diffusion of carbon into the iron from a charcoal fire. The diffusion rate depends on the heat of the fire and the length of time the iron is in the forge. At a temperature of 920 degrees C. the amount of carbon diffused to a depth of half a millimeter below the surface of the iron in an hour (*top bars*) is nearly .5 percent by weight (*black*) but only .02 percent of the carbon has penetrated to a depth of 1.5 mm. (*color*). As the middle and bottom bars show, prolonged exposure increases the percentage of carbon diffused to depths of one mm. (*gray*) and 1.5 mm. below the surface of the iron without greatly increasing percentage at .5 mm.

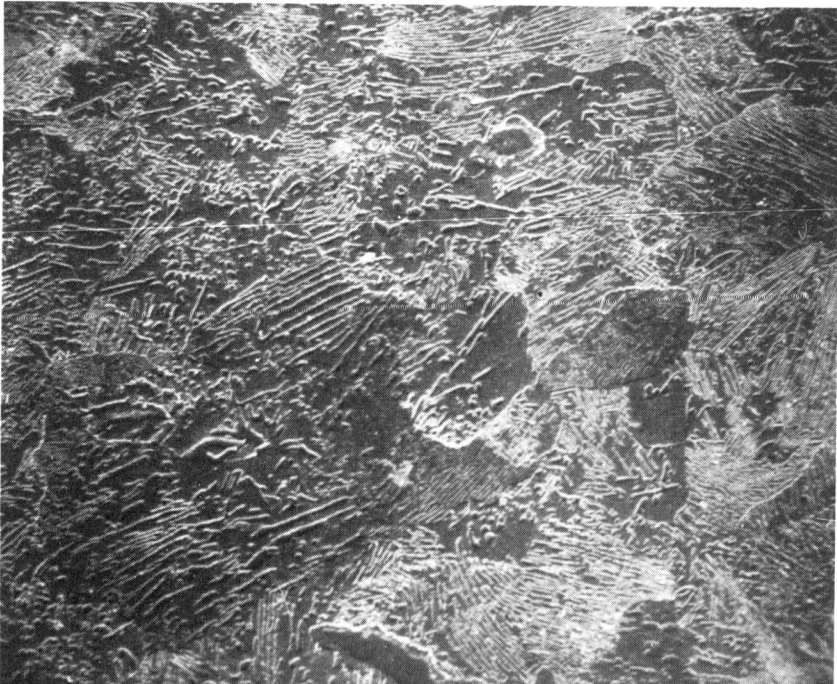

PEARLITE, a characteristic microstructure of carbon steels, has a layered pattern at high magnifications. This scanning electron micrograph enlarges the sample 1,250 diameters. It shows a gold-covered replica of the corroded surface of a steeled-iron blade found at a site in Israel: Tel Fara South. Although the iron is oxidized a relic pearlite microstructure is preserved. The blade was made available for study by the Institute of Archaeology of the University of London.

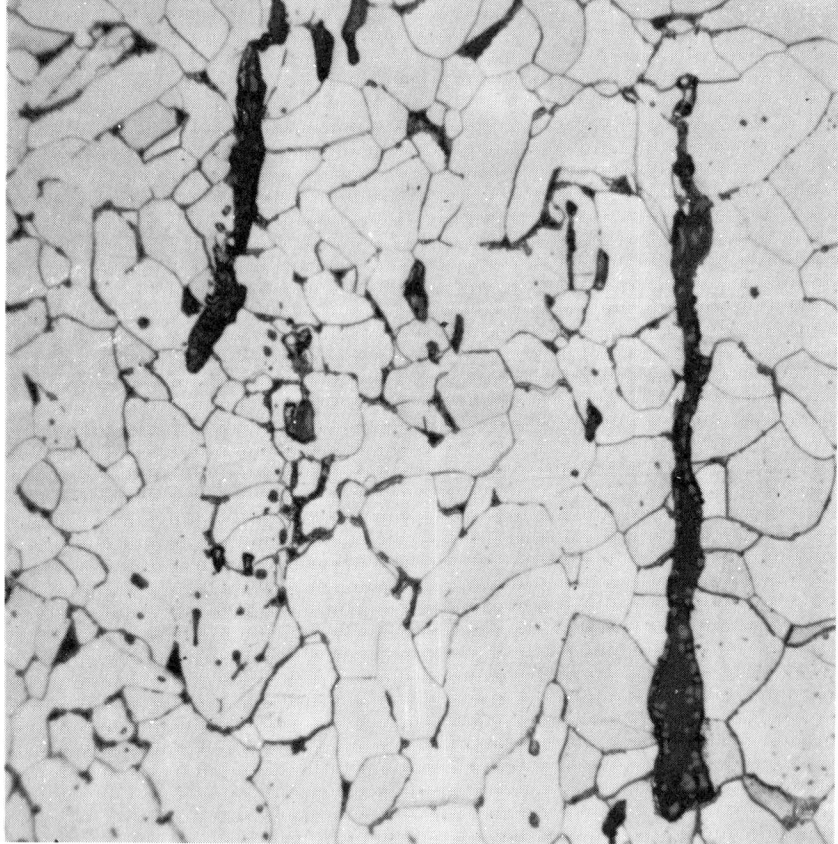

IRON SPIT from a site in Greece is seen in longitudinal section at a magnification of 200 diameters. The narrow dark areas are stringers: fragments of slag in the original iron bloom that were deformed but not expelled by the hammering preparatory to the forging of the spit. The iron artifact was made available for study by the staff of the Numismatic Museum in Athens.

Bronze Age, as indicated by actual molds that have survived or as inferred from written references, were remarkably diverse. There were one-piece, two-piece and multipiece molds made of earth, clay and stone. Some molds had cores, and the lost-wax process made it possible to cast the bronze in complex shapes and with elaborate surface decoration. Iron, except for the brittle high-carbon metal, was useless for any of these processes, which turned out not only utilitarian articles but also a great number of purely ornamental objects such as figurines and jewelry. Bronze had one further advantage. It corrodes slowly, and the characteristic green patina is considered decorative. Iron corrodes rapidly, and in the process often suffers considerable damage.

How, then, could iron become a satisfactory substitute for bronze as the second millennium B.C. drew to a close? The answer is that if bloomery iron is treated in a certain way, it can be transformed into an alloy that is for most purposes far superior to bronze. That treatment was steeling, and its initial discovery was probably accidental. What happened was as follows. When the blacksmith reheated the iron bloom in order to hammer out the slag, he did so with a charcoal fire in the forge. He needed to heat the bloom to 1,200 degrees C. to make the slag viscous, and he probably did not let the temperature go much below 800 degrees until the work was finished. The bloom was in direct contact with the white-hot charcoal and with the hot carbon monoxide evolved by its combustion. In that temperature range a small amount of carbon from both sources slowly diffused into the iron, in effect converting it into carbon steel down to a certain depth below the surface.

The time required for carbon to diffuse into iron follows simple physical laws. For example, if one plots carbon concentration and depth of penetration at a temperature of 950 degrees C., one finds that after nine hours the concentration at a depth of 1.5 millimeters below the surface is .5 percent. At higher temperatures the carbon atoms diffuse into the iron more rapidly; at 1,150 degrees C. after nine hours the concentration at the same depth can reach 2 percent.

In modern metallurgical terms carburized iron at a temperature higher than 910 degrees C. has the microstructure of the form of steel known as austenite. When the temperature falls below 727 degrees C., the austenite breaks down into two components. One is ferrite, or pure iron. The other is the iron carbide known as cementite. Called the eutectoid reaction, this two-phase breakdown gives rise to the microstructure of the form of steel known as pearlite: alternating layers of ferrite and

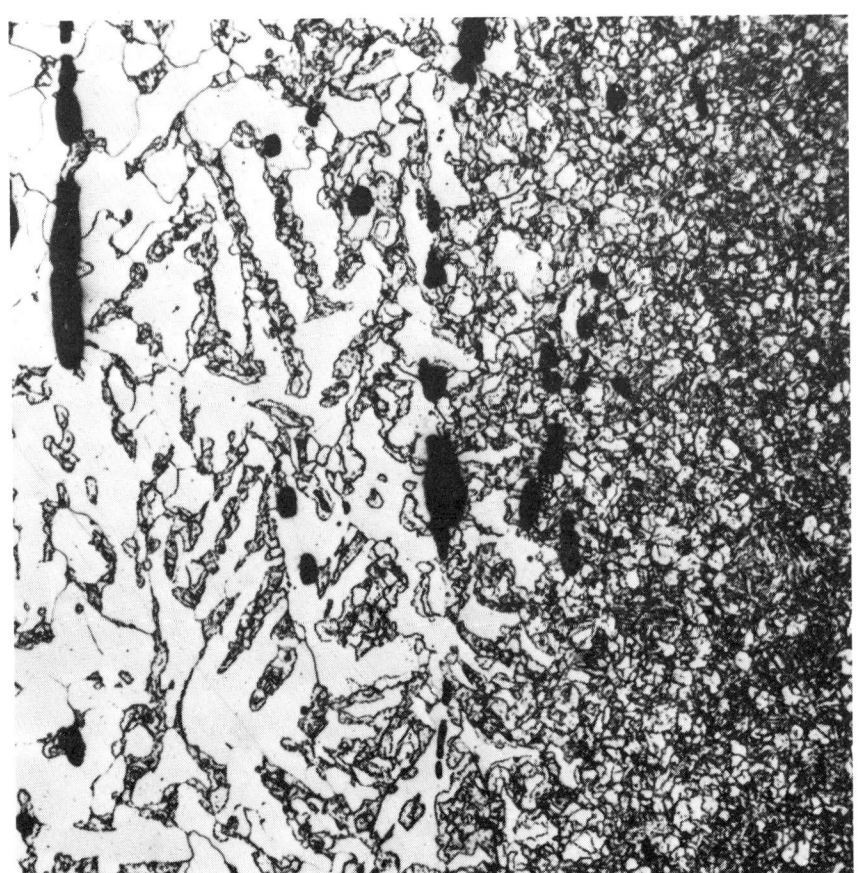

METALLURGICAL SKILL in the fourth century B.C. is indicated in this micrograph. Shown at a magnification of 300 diameters is a section of an adze blade unearthed at Al Mina, the ruins of a Greek trading colony on the coast of Turkey near Syria. The blacksmith who made the implement used a sheet of carburized iron for the working face of the adze but economized by using soft iron for the other face. The micrograph, showing the juncture between fine-grained steeled iron and coarse-grained uncarburized iron, is clear proof of the blacksmith's mastery.

On the basis of our research and that of others it seems evident that by the beginning of the 10th century B.C. blacksmiths were intentionally steeling iron. Very few iron artifacts of the 12th century B.C. or earlier have been metallurgically analyzed, so that the prevalence of steeling in that period remains uncertain. Nevertheless, a 12th-century knife from Idalion, a site on Cyprus, was certainly carburized to improve its hardness. A site on Mount Adir in northern Israel has yielded an iron pick in association with 12th-century pottery. One would hesitate to remove a sample from the pick for analysis, but it has been possible to test the tip of it for hardness. The readings averaged 38 on the Rockwell "C" scale of hardness. This is a reading characteristic of a modern hardened steel.

Unlike the Mount Adir pick, many of the ancient iron artifacts that have survived in eastern Mediterranean sites are badly corroded, a condition that complicates metallurgical study. Several techniques, however, make it possible to detect pearlite even in objects that are totally oxidized. In one such technique a polished surface is prepared for study under the microscope at magnifications greater than 1,000 diameters. Since the ferrite layers of the pearlite differ from the cementite layers in their chemical composition, it is sometimes possible to detect them even in iron oxide. An even more promising technique makes use of the scanning electron microscope. Here it is not the polished surface that is examined but a gold-plated thin-film replica of it. The ferrite layers are softer than the cementite ones, even in a corroded artifact, and they stand out clearly when the replica is tilted to accentuate the different levels of the two constituents. The presence of pearlite in an iron artifact is a clear indication that the artifact has been carburized.

After 900 B.C. the production of iron implements rapidly increased. Even though at this time tin again became available in the eastern Mediterranean, bronze did not replace iron. Sites dating from the 10th century B.C. to the sixth have yielded great hoards of iron implements. At Hasanlu in northwestern Iran a University of Pennsylvania expedition unearthed iron weapons numbering in the thousands. At Gordion, the capital of ancient Phrygia, another University of Pennsylvania expedition discovered one of the largest collections of iron artifacts ever found in the eastern Mediterranean. At Nimrud in Iraq, the excavations of Max Mallowan of the University of Oxford uncovered another major iron assemblage.

The evidence for the growing popularity of iron goes beyond archaeological finds. Neo-Assyrian and Neo-Babylonian writings reflect a world technologically quite different from that of the

cementite. Reflected in this microstructure is the proportion of carbon in the metal. If the iron is free of carbon, no pearlite will be present. If the alloy contains as much as .8 percent carbon, the microstructure that is formed will be 100 percent pearlite.

It is illuminating to compare the tensile strengths of carburized iron and bronze. A carbon content ranging from .2 to .3 percent gives the steeled iron a strength equal to that of unworked bronze: about 60,000 p.s.i. If the carbon content is raised to 1.2 percent, the steeled iron has a tensile strength of 140,000 p.s.i., which is somewhat greater than the strength of cold-worked bronze. If the blacksmith then cold-hammers the steeled iron, its tensile strength can be increased to 245,000 p.s.i., or more than twice the strength of cold-worked bronze.

The accidental discovery of steeling must have encouraged experimentation, because in due course the early blacksmiths could control the process well enough to develop properties in the metal appropriate to the function of the object they were making. It is possible that future metallurgical studies (and even some that are now in progress) will help to trace the progression from accidental steeling to purposeful steeling. For example, carbon can get into iron by pathways other than carburization. It can be trapped in the pores of the iron bloom; forging would then form the trapped carbon into stringers within the metal. In a polished metallographic section of such an accidentally steeled piece the stringers would appear as uneven streaks. Entirely accidental carburization through exposure to charcoal in the course of heating and forging, although more difficult to detect microscopically, should leave some trace. The carbon content would probably be low and the concentration would be uneven. It is incontrovertible proof of deliberate steeling, however, when one finds an iron object consisting of layers with dissimilar percentages of carbon. The blacksmith would have no reason to make such an object unless he understood the different properties of the different layers. The earliest-known object of this kind is an Egyptian iron knife that was probably made between 900 and 800 B.C.

period before 900 B.C. References are made to iron axes, iron hoes, iron picks, iron saws, iron arrowheads, iron scissors, iron fetters and even iron furniture and iron lamps. Iron also became the metal of choice for knives and daggers. A passage from the corpus of Babylonian "wisdom literature" strikes a sour note to this effect: "A woman is a pitfall, a hole, a ditch, a woman is a sharp iron dagger that cuts a man's throat."

We have not yet mentioned a second process that significantly enhances the quality of carburized iron. This is quenching: quickly cooling a hot piece of metal by plunging it into water. An article of steeled iron that is left to cool by itself in the open air develops a microstructure of coarse pearlite. If the blacksmith instead waves the finished article in the air, accelerating the process of cooling, the pearlite microstructure is much finer. Even faster cooling by quenching can suppress the development of pearlite altogether; the steeled material has a quite different microstructure and is known as martensite. Martensite is significantly harder than pearlite, although it is quite brittle.

When one displays the results of quenching graphically, it appears that different rates of cooling—from the temperature of the furnace or forge, about 1,200 degrees C., to the temperature of transformation, about 700 degrees—give rise to different microstructures. In an iron containing .8 percent carbon, if the cooling period is approximately 60 seconds, coarse pearlite will form. To produce fine pearlite the cooling period should be only two or three seconds. To produce martensite the temperature must be reduced from the forge level to below 220 degrees C. in less than a second; only quenching can cool the material so quickly. One may assume that for small objects such as arrowheads hardness would be important and brittleness could be tolerated. If such small objects were made from iron with a .8 percent carbon content quick quenching would make them martensite. The same could have been accomplished with the surface layers of larger iron objects where hardness was important and brittleness could be tolerated, even though the interior of the object, being slower to lose heat, would remain pearlite.

It is not possible to estimate when the quenching process was invented; like steeling, it could easily have been discovered accidentally. One item of literary evidence, however, clearly indicates that blacksmiths of the eastern Mediterranean were familiar with the process in the eighth or seventh century B.C. The passage is in the ninth book of the *Odyssey*. Trapped in the cave of Polyphemus, the one-eyed giant, Odysseus and his men manage to get the giant drunk. They decide to blind him by snatching a burning olive trunk out of a fire and thrusting it into his eye. Our translation follows Richmond Lattimore's:

"As when a man who works as a blacksmith plunges into cold water a great axe or adze which hisses aloud, 'doctoring' it, since this is the way that steel is made strong, even so Cyclops' eye sizzled about the beam of the olive."

The description could only have been written by someone who had watched a blacksmith quench hot iron and knew that the quenching was done to increase the hardness of the metal. It also suggests that quench-hardening was something of a novelty in the Greek world at that time. "'Doctoring' it" is a free rendering of the Greek word *pharmasso;* the

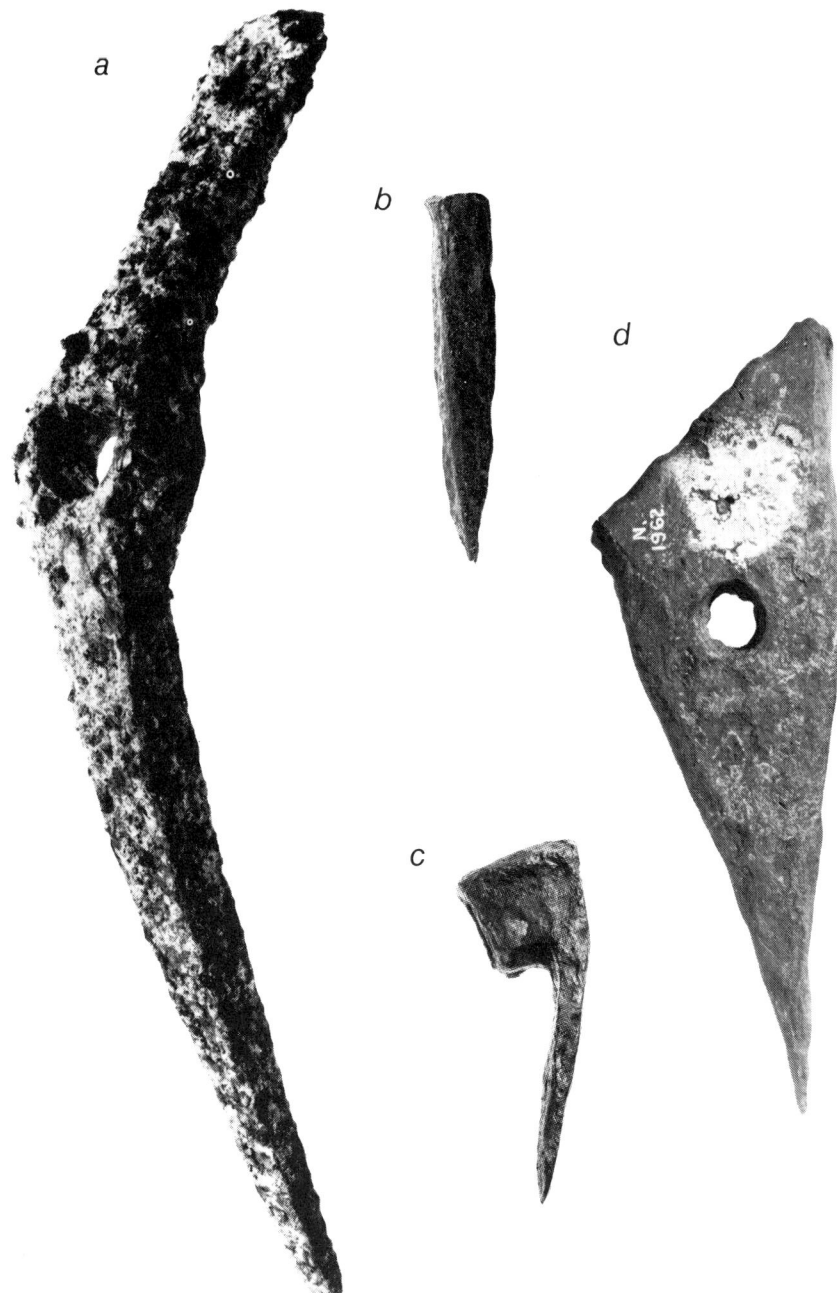

FOUR IRON IMPLEMENTS made in the Near East come from sites of late in the second millennium B.C. to late in the first millennium B.C. The largest (*a*) is a 39-centimeter pick from northern Isreal that was found in association with pottery of the 12th century B.C. Its tip, tested for hardness, yielded an average reading characteristic of a modern hardened steel. The chisel (*b*), from Al Mina, is almost 13 centimeters long; it was cleverly quenched to make its matrix hard without leaving its cutting edge brittle. The small adze (*c*), from Al Mina, is almost 12 centimeters long. It may have been made from the same bloom of iron as the chisel and perhaps by the same blacksmith. Its microstructure is shown in the illustration on page 61. The fourth tool (*d*), 25 centimeters long, comes from the ruins of Nimrud in northern Iraq. Under microscopic examination it shows the pearlite structure characteristic of carburized iron.

implication is that the iron was being treated in some magical way, as if by means of drug potions. Perhaps Homer was puzzled by the fact that whereas water softened or even dissolved many materials, it turned carburized iron into a metal harder than any that had been known before.

It is more difficult to obtain evidence of deliberate quenching than evidence of deliberate steeling. For one thing, water quenching could have been done simply to cool a forged object quickly, perhaps to be able to use it immediately or perhaps to avoid having too many hot objects around the smithy. For another, with an object of any size it is the outer layer that consists of martensite, and it is this layer that is most likely to have been removed by corrosion over the centuries. Nevertheless, some meager evidence of deliberate quenching exists. For example, so far 11 iron artifacts from Nimrud have been analyzed metallurgically. Although all are heavily corroded, five of them show possible indications of quenching. The rest show signs of some carburization but evidently were not quenched.

A third technique of ironworking arises directly from quenching. This is the process of tempering, a practice that reduces the brittleness induced by quenching. The early blacksmiths must have realized soon that quenching made their products brittle. The quenching would have left cracks along the edges of many articles, and users would have complained of breakage. Tempering, that is, reheating up to but not above the temperature of transformation (727 degrees C.), affects the iron carbide that quenching forces into the microstructure of iron so as to give rise to martensite. The carbide precipitates and then coalesces by diffusion. Both the exact temperature attained and the time that the article is held at that temperature determine the amount of iron carbide that coalesces and hence the final hardness and ductility of the metal. As ductility increases, hardness decreases.

For the blacksmiths of antiquity tempering was probably never done intentionally. There is no change in the color of the hot iron at the critical range of temperatures and thus no obvious way of gauging the correct heat in the forge. A method was developed early in the fourth century B.C., however, that surmounted the difficulty of achieving true tempering and at the same time produced carburized-iron tools that were both hard and durable. Our evidence for this statement is a stonecutter's chisel unearthed at the Greek trading colony of Al Mina, a site in coastal Turkey near the Syrian border. The chisel has a matrix composed largely of martensite but containing nodules of pearlite that increase in density toward the tip of the

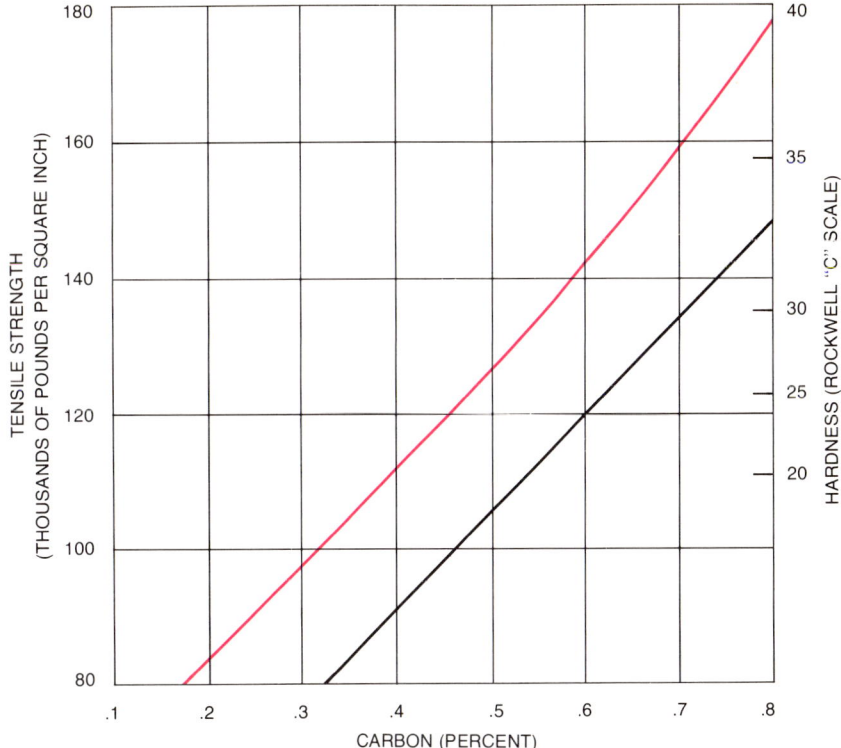

STRENGTH AND HARDNESS of carburized iron both increase as the percentage of carbon in the alloy rises. Degrees of hardness here are measured on the Rockwell "C" scale. If the speed of cooling is not rapid, the steel microstructure that develops is coarse pearlite (*black*). Regardless of its carbon content, coarse pearlite steel is less durable than fine pearlite steel (*color*).

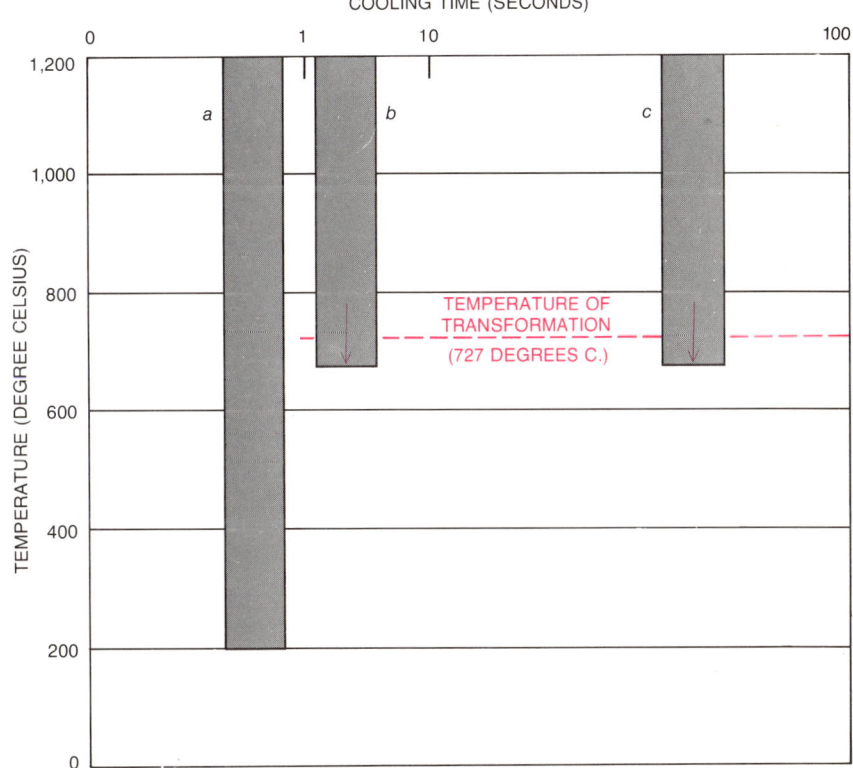

EFFECT OF QUENCHING on the microstructure of carburized iron is shown on this graph in terms of the length of time required to lower the temperature of the iron from its forging heat (about 1,200 degrees C.). If cooling requires less than one second (*a*), the microstructure that forms is martensite, tough but somewhat brittle. If up to three seconds is required, the resulting microstructure is fine pearlite (*b*). Cooling as quick as this calls for quenching. Prolonged cooling, in excess of 10 seconds, forms a third kind of microstructure: coarse pearlite (*c*).

tool, rather than toward the interior as one would expect. Laboratory experiments suggest that this reverse distribution was achieved by covering the tip of the tool with some kind of insulating material, such as clay, heating the piece and then quenching it. Clay would crack off as soon as the tool hit the water, but it would nonetheless slow the cooling rate enough to reduce the amount of martensite formed at the cutting end of the tool. It was evidently by some cheap and simple means such as this one that the blacksmith of Al Mina created a chisel with a strong body and a durable edge.

Another example of innovative smithing was found at Al Mina. Analysis of the elements present in an adze uncovered with the chisel suggests that both tools were made from the same bloom of iron and thus perhaps even made by the same smith. The adze was formed by hot-hammering two sheets of iron together. One sheet was carburized and the other was not. The combined sheets were forged into shape, and the finished adze was air-cooled rather than quenched. The blacksmith, if he was the same man who made the chisel, evidently appreciated the fact that a woodworking adze need not have as hard an edge as a stoneworking chisel. He adjusted the manufacturing process accordingly, probably at a net saving in time and effort. The moment when smiths were first able to control the ironworking process so that the properties of the products were suited to their end uses is clearly a significant one in the history of technology. Such a moment may well be what we see in the finds at Al Mina.

To sum up, by the beginning of the seventh century B.C. at the latest the blacksmiths of the eastern Mediterranean had mastered two of the processes that make iron a useful material for tools and weapons: carburizing and quenching. And by the beginning of the fourth century B.C. at the latest a method had been found to overcome the disadvantages of brittle steel while preserving the advantage of its hardness. The smiths' quest had involved hundreds of years of experimentation and uncountable hours at the furnace and the forge. All the craftsmen of antiquity—potters, masons, stonecutters, weavers, carpenters and smiths of bronze, copper and precious metals—shared the blacksmith's empirical approach to their work, but none of them faced as large a challenge as he did. To be made strong and durable iron needs sophisticated treatments. The blacksmith could not have understood, at least at first, why these treatments improved the iron, but his tenacity, pragmatic knowledge and skill in the centuries following the end of the second millennium B.C. enabled the peoples of the eastern Mediterranean to take the momentous step from the Bronze Age to the Iron Age.

The Beginnings of Wheeled Transport

by Stuart Piggott
July 1968

Mankind has traveled on wheels for at least 5,000 years. The recent discovery of ancient wagons at sites in the U.S.S.R. casts doubt on the accepted hypothesis that vehicles were invented in Mesopotamia

Professor Marshall McLuhan, in one of his oracular pronouncements, defined the relationship of the automobile to modern man as that of the mechanical bride. Recent archaeological studies help to trace the earliest stages in man's romance with the wheel that ultimately led to this strange, if not unholy, consummation. Like all first courtships, it was inexpert and tentative in its beginnings, but more than 5,000 years ago the bride of wheeled transport had been won in Eurasia. For whatever reason, the early Americans failed to duplicate this invention.

It is not excessively determinist to suggest that certain prerequisites are needed for the development of wheeled vehicles. The vehicles will be invented only in societies that have a need to move heavy or bulky loads considerable distances over land that is fairly flat and fairly firm. A suitable raw material, such as timber, must be on hand for building the vehicle. And a prime mover stronger than a man must be available to make the wheels turn. In the Old World the power problem had been solved at least 7,000 or 8,000 years ago by the domestication of cattle. Once it was realized that castration produced a docile, heavy draft animal, oxen were available for traction; their strength and patience more than compensated for their slowness. Timber was available in quantity in the parts of the Near East that were neither desert nor steppe. These are the regions that saw the emergence of the earliest agricultural communities, beginning about 9000 B.C. The same communities were among the first to possess polished stone axes and adzes and, soon thereafter, copper and bronze tools suitable for elaborate carpentry.

The archaeological evidence shows that the first stages of wheeled transport depended on heavy vehicles with disk (as opposed to spoked) wheels. The wheels were either cut from a single massive plank or were made from three (and occasionally more) planks doweled and mortised together. Light vehicles with spoked wheels, harnessed to swift draft animals, were a later development that combined an advanced technology in bronze tools—and thus in the wheelwright's craft—with the domestication of the small wild horse of the steppe. Such vehicles first appear in the Near East in response to military needs during the first half of the second millennium B.C. Here, however, we are concerned mainly with developments earlier than the second millennium, when vehicles were usually drawn by oxen.

From the standpoint of the archaeologist wood is a miserable material; it is resistant to decay only in exceptional conditions of waterlogging or desiccation. Under normal circumstances to detect and recover traces of wood encountered in an excavation calls for a high degree of technical skill. It may therefore surprise the reader to learn that in Europe and Asia nearly 50 wheeled vehicles—or their wheels—have been recovered from sites that predate the second millennium B.C. This type of direct evidence concerning early vehicles is supported by discoveries of other kinds, such as models of vehicles or their wheels made from pottery, which of course is much less susceptible to disintegration than wood.

The earliest examples of wheeled vehicles have all been found within a region no more than 1,200 miles across centered between Lake Van in eastern Asia Minor and Lake Urmia in northern Iran. Presumably the first wheeled vehicle originated somewhere within this region. The oldest evidence dates back to the final centuries of the fourth millennium B.C., indicating that wheeled transport came into existence somewhat more than 5,000 years ago.

The region within which wheeled vehicles made their first appearance embraces desert and open steppe as well as forested slopes along the mountain belt that includes the ranges of the Taurus, the Caucasus and the Zagros. Deciduous timber does not grow below the 1,000-foot contour of these mountains and often not below 3,000 feet. A mosaic of communities, with economies based on mixed agriculture and copper or bronze metallurgy, flourished in the region from about 3000 B.C. onward. In Mesopotamia to the south the population was already literate and urban societies were beginning to form. To the north the zone of farming communities probably merged gradually into the area occupied by the pastoralists of the steppe beyond the Caucasus. All three societies were ones in which wheeled transport would constitute a valuable technological addition to the existing economy.

Our earliest evidence for vehicles with wheels, as opposed to simple sledges that could be dragged overland, is provided by symbols in the pictographic script of Uruk, a Sumerian city in southern Mesopotamia. The Uruk pictographs represent man's earliest known writing; they are believed to date from somewhat before 3000 B.C. Some Uruk signs depict a schematized profile view of a sledge; others show the sledge pictograph with two little disks added below it—an abbreviated symbol for a four-wheeled vehicle. Beginning about 2700 B.C. in Mesopotamia the evidence is no longer symbolic but concrete. By that time the Sumerians and their neighbors buried vehicles along with their dead; sometimes the vehicles even contained the dead. The vehicle remains often survive as nothing more than stains in the soil such as have been de-

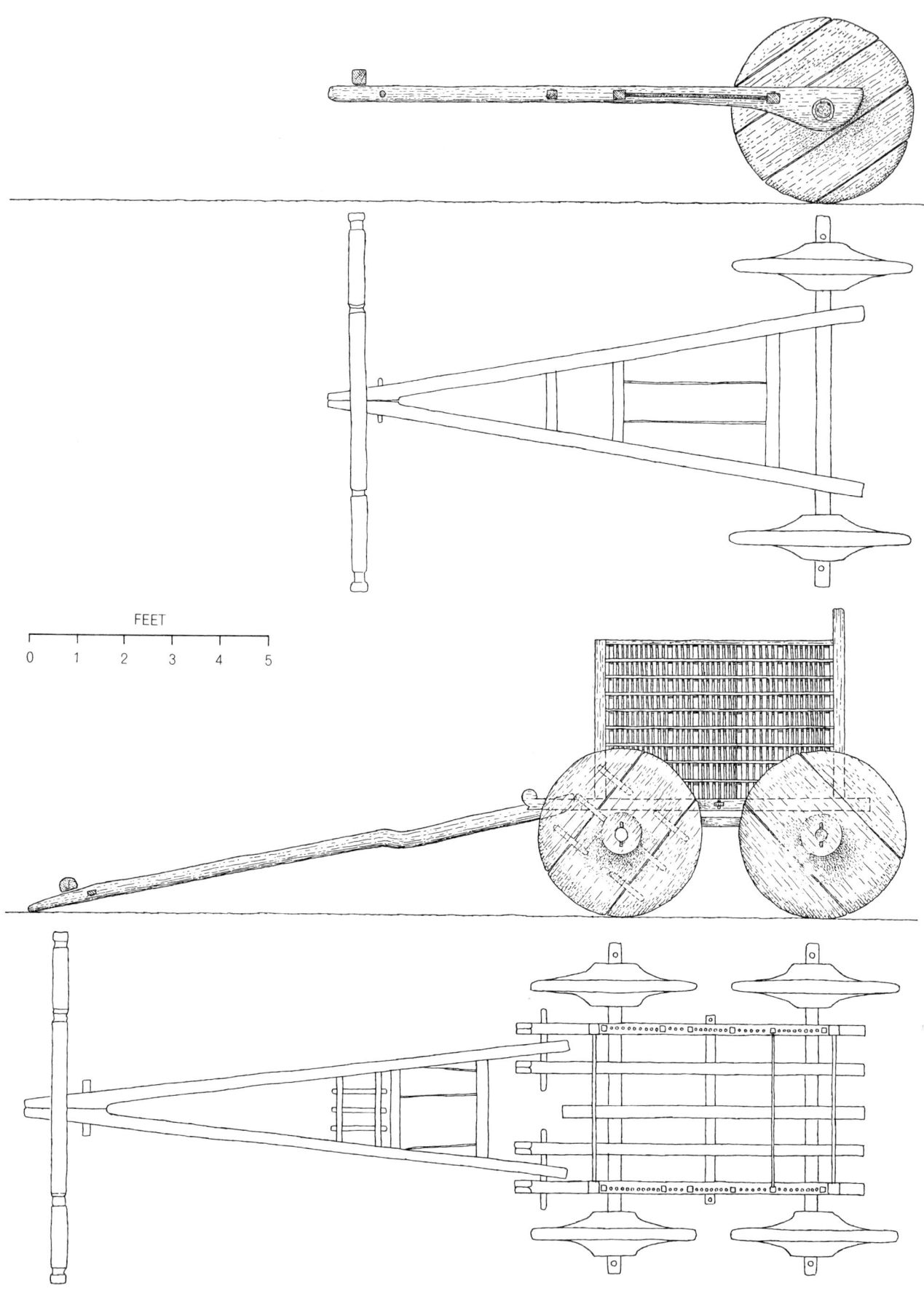

CART AND WAGON from the latter half of the second millennium B.C. were found by Soviet archaeologists in tombs at Lake Sevan in the Armenian S.S.R. They closely resemble the wheeled vehicles of much earlier times. The simple design of the A-frame cart (*top*) suggests that these vehicles came into being through the addition of an axle and wheels to a two-pole "slide car" that was formerly dragged along the ground by draft animals. The wagons at Lake Sevan (*bottom*) were complex and utilized mortise-and-tenon joining. Their draft poles, however, were apparently nothing more than cart A-frames, pegged to the wagon's chassis.

tected in the Royal Tombs at Kish and Ur and at Susa in Elam. They are of two kinds: vehicles with two wheels (carts) and vehicles with four wheels (wagons).

Carts and wagons alike were drawn by oxen or by Asiatic asses (*Equus onager*), cousins of the horse that the early Mesopotamians had managed to domesticate. The vehicles' wheels were light disks made by joining three planks. The representations in Mesopotamian art and the model vehicles that have survived from this period and the periods that follow it show that disk-wheeled vehicles were known both in Mesopotamia and among the nonliterate peoples along the Mesopotamian frontier, from Asia Minor on the west to Turkmenia on the east. The vehicles were present along most of the periphery before 2000 B.C.; soon thereafter they were common throughout it.

It had been assumed until recently that the adoption of wheeled transport among peoples to the north and west of the central zone outlined above, as well as the eventual adoption of vehicles by the peoples who inhabited Europe, were events that took place measurably later than adoption of vehicles within the central zone. Indeed, the spread of wheeled transport is often cited as a classic example of diffusion from a primary center. Since World War II, however, the picture has changed as archaeologists in southern Russia and in the Soviet republics of Georgia and Armenia have unearthed large quantities of new prehistoric material.

Among the discoveries are more than 25 burials in which vehicles were included; these apparently date from at least 2500 B.C. up to about 1200 B.C. Indirect evidence from several Soviet sites for even earlier knowledge of wheeled

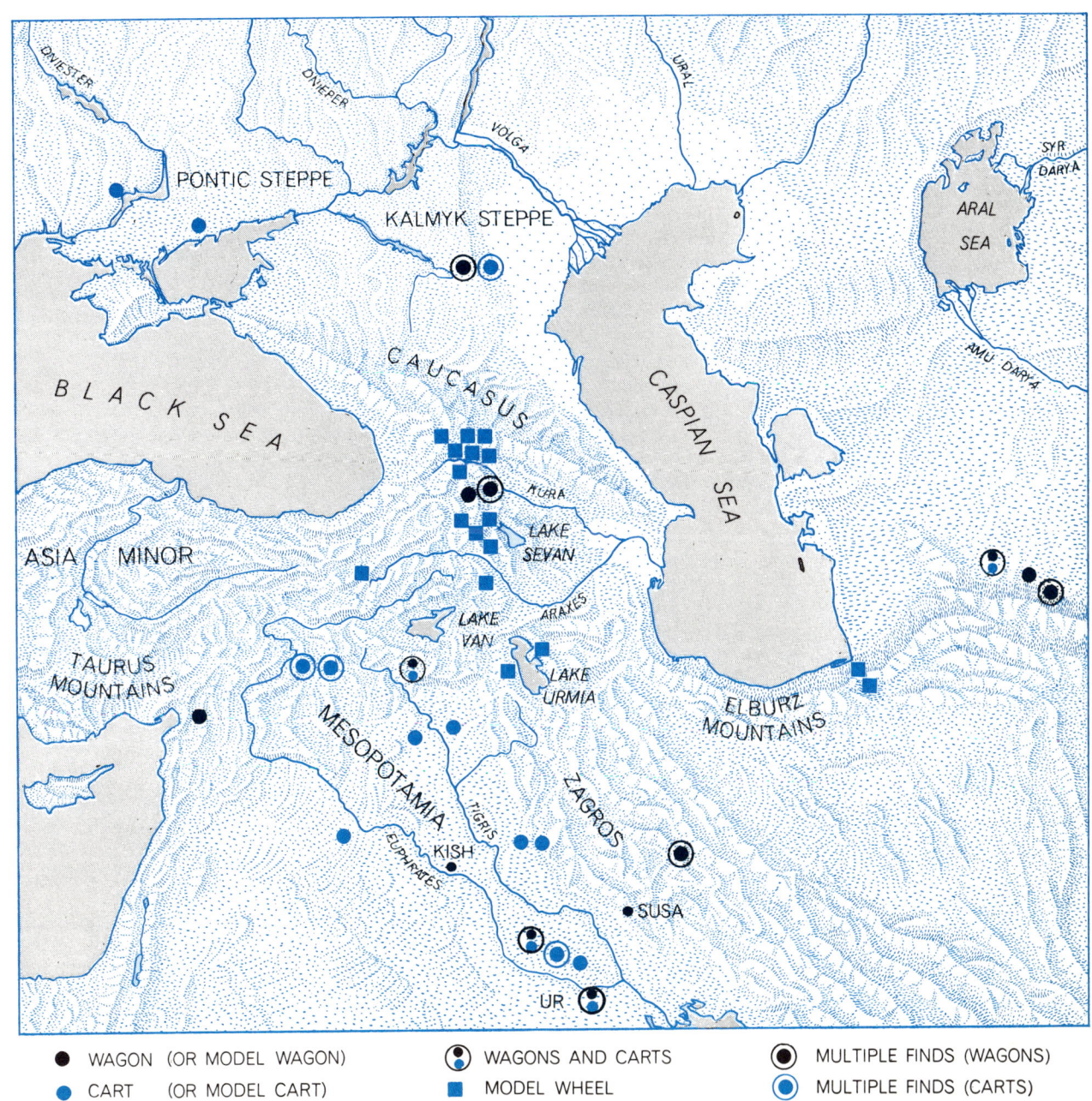

VEHICLES built before 2000 B.C. in a zone between the Black Sea and central Asia are found in two main concentrations. One is Transcaucasia and the open steppe to the north. The other is Mesopotamia, including the headwaters of the Tigris and Euphrates. It was formerly believed that the first wheeled vehicles were made in Mesopotamia. The discovery that such vehicles were made in Soviet Georgia and Armenia before the second millennium B.C. diminishes the probability of a Mesopotamian origin of wheeled transport.

vehicles—in the form of model wheels made from pottery—pushes the starting date back perhaps as far as 3000 B.C. Nothing has been found at the new Soviet sites that is demonstrably as old as the pictographs from Uruk. Nonetheless, the Soviet evidence considerably weakens the case for absolute priority in the invention of wheeled transport previously conceded to Mesopotamia. The challenge is a serious one because the Mesopotamian claim rests on the pictograph of a modified sledge and on nothing else.

Because the recent evidence from the U.S.S.R. is little known outside that country it is worth describing in some detail. By way of preface I should explain that a number of excavations in Transcaucasia—the region between the Black Sea and the Caspian Sea lying south of the greater Caucasus—have made it evident that this region was once occupied by a single homogeneous culture. Marked by a complex of sedentary mixed farming, village settlements and some copper-working, the culture extended from the river valleys of the Kura and the Araxes in Georgia and Armenia, southward to Lake Urmia and westward well beyond Lake Van [see illustration on preceding page]. The period during which the Kura-Araxes culture flourished is known on the basis of carbon-14 determinations. It began about 3000 B.C., continued until sometime after 2500 B.C. and may even have lasted down to the end of the third millennium B.C. Pottery models of disk wheels with well-marked hubs are found at a number of Kura-Araxes sites. They are identical with the wheels of model vehicles unearthed in the Near East; evidently the existence of wheeled transport was at least known in Transcaucasia at the same time that actual vehicles were being entombed at Kish and Ur.

As a matter of fact the Kura-Araxes culture possesses vehicle burials of its own. One tomb at Zelenyy, in the Tsalka region of the Georgian S.S.R., was found to have contained a wagon. It had evidently been interred in working order, since the floor of the tomb bore long grooves made by the vehicle's wheels. The burial at Zelenyy, a pit grave covered by a round kurgan, or barrow mound, belongs to a style of burial that moved into the Caucasus from the southern Russian steppe. On the steppe the burials have given their name to the Pit Grave culture, which flourished during much of the third millennium B.C. Similar burials—including in two instances the remains of wagons—have been unearthed at Trialeti, another site in the Tsalka district.

The waterlogged soil of one of these tombs, excavated in 1958, contained a wagon with massive three-piece wheels. The wagon had an A-shaped draft pole, of which the stumps were preserved. It had apparently been equipped with an arched canopy to shelter its occupants. As we shall see, several more or less complete examples of similar "covered wagons" have been found elsewhere. The Trialeti burial probably took place sometime before 2000 B.C., although the date is not known precisely.

Some 350 miles north of the Tsalka district, beyond the passes of the greater Caucasus range and well into the southern Russian steppe, Soviet archaeologists have unearthed several other buried carts and wagons. The sites are located in the Elista region of the Kalmyk Steppe, no more than a month's ox-trek distant from Transcaucasia. The first Elista burials were found in 1947; others were located in 1962 and 1963. They belong to the final phase of the Pit Grave culture or to a culture that overlapped and succeeded it, and appear to be dated between 2400 and 2300 B.C.

The carts buried in the Elista graves are represented by pairs of wheels and by one pottery model of a cart with an arched canopy. The most interesting of the Elista burials, however, are those containing four-wheeled wagons. Like the model cart, the Elista wagons had arched canopies; in some cases remains of the wickerwork of which the canopies were made have survived. The Soviet excavators maintain that one of the Elista wagons had a pivoted front axle, a device that would have permitted steering the wagon. This is remarkable. If accepted, the Elista innovation antedates by many centuries the first previously known appearance of a most important advance in vehicle design. Heretofore no ancient vehicle was known to have a pivoted front axle until the time of the Celtic ritual wagons at Djebjerg in Denmark, in the first century B.C. Indeed, the very existence of the feature before medieval times has sometimes been called into question, and we are certain of pivoted axles only from the Middle Ages onward.

The resemblance between the Elista vehicle burials and vehicle burials in the Georgian S.S.R. is not the only evidence that implies contact between the steppe and Transcaucasia. Near the Black Sea and the Dnieper River in southern Russia, an area that also lies within the ancient boundaries of the Pit Grave culture, two more vehicle burials

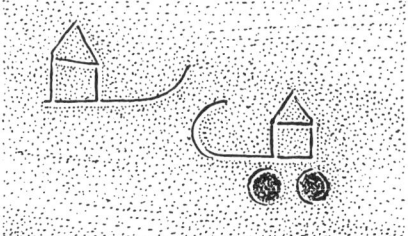

OLDEST PORTRAYAL of a vehicle with wheels is a Sumerian pictograph used shortly before 3000 B.C. It is derived from the sign for a sledge (*left*). The addition of two circles (*right*) turns it into the sign for a wagon.

CHINESE PICTOGRAPHS for a chariot or cart, apparently with spoked wheels, are first seen in inscriptions of the Shang dynasty, somewhat later than 1500 B.C. Two inverted "y" strokes (*top right*) represent the horses.

have been found. The graves were dug late in the third millennium B.C.; in both instances the vehicles are carts with one-piece disk wheels.

In 1956 the initiation of a hydroelectric project at Lake Sevan in the Armenian S.S.R. lowered the lake's level by many feet. Near Lchashen, as the level fell, a number of formerly submerged tombs were revealed; in them were found nearly a dozen carts and wagons. The vehicles are comparatively recent, having been buried over a period of some centuries, beginning about 1400 B.C. They are so well preserved, however, and have so many features in common with carts and wagons of much greater age that they merit special attention. Each burial was made in a huge boulder-lined pit, originally with a sloping ramp at one end. The vehicles were apparently maneuvered down the ramps and the pits were then covered with stone cairns. Soon afterward the level of Lake Sevan rose and immersion preserved the wood of the vehicles. In addition to vehicles with three-part disk wheels some of the tombs contained light carts—virtually chariots—that had spoked wheels.

From the viewpoint of technological development two-wheeled vehicles are more primitive than four-wheeled ones. In spite of their relatively late date the

Lchashen carts reflect this. They are of the simplest kind and embody a design that is still found today among nonindustrialized peoples in parts of Europe and Asia from the Iberian peninsula and the Mediterranean coast to Asia Minor, the Crimea, the Kalmyk Steppe and the Caucasus. (The same simple carts are found even farther east, of course, but their distribution in the Orient need not concern us here.) The basic design is an A-frame. The design presumably evolved from a simple travois, or slide car, made by lashing the butts of two poles together and letting the tips of the poles trail along the ground behind the draft animals. The addition of an axle and a pair of wheels near the wide end of the A-frame turns such a travois into a cart.

Wagons, on the other hand, are comparatively complex structures. With their intricate frames and often elaborate ornamentation, the Lchashen wagons were plainly vehicles of prestige just as much as today's Cadillac. The tombs at Lchashen contained six wagons in all. Four of them had arched canopies and one had upright wickerwork sides and a decorated panel at the back. Their complicated carpentry testifies to the need for adequate coachbuilders' tools. One covered wagon was an assembly of 70 component parts; the parts were either pegged together or joined by a mortise-and-tenon system that required cutting no fewer than 12,000 mortises. (The frame of the canopy alone required 600.) In spite of the excellence of their workmanship, the Lchashen wagons must have been slow and clumsy: the estimated unloaded weight of the wagon with the wickerwork sides is two-thirds of a ton.

Although the covered wagons of Lchashen are nearly 1,000 years younger than the steppe vehicles of the Elista region, they have counterparts among them. Moreover, the same form of wagon was common in the Near East during the third millennium B.C., as is indicated by pottery models unearthed in northern Iraq and Syria. The draft poles of the Lchasen wagons provide a lesson in vehicle evolution. They are plainly derived from cart A-frames; each wagon looks as if a cart A-frame had been pegged to the front of its chassis [see illustration on page 66]. This suggests continued use the familiar A-frame cart was the earliest form of vehicle known and that, when four-wheeled wagons came to be built, the designers continued to use the familiar A-frame shape instead of devising a single central pole for the draft animals.

What do the various Soviet discoveries signify as far as the beginning of wheeled transport is concerned? One way of interpreting this evidence is to suggest that during the third millennium B.C. the wagon found its way to Transcaucasia from the Russian steppe to the north, along with a funeral rite that required the burial of the vehicles in pit graves. At the time of the wagons' emergence, however, wheeled transport must already have existed in Transcaucasia, perhaps in the form of A-frame carts (the evidence for this being the pottery models of wheels found in Kura-Araxes sites of earlier date). Another interpretation might suggest instead that the covered wagons came to Transcaucasia from the south and that their presence in the Pit Grave sites represents an exotic intrusion into the steppe that has its ultimate origins in the early civilizations of the Near East.

The problems presented by such alternative explanations will be discussed later. Meanwhile one should remember that the Caucasus do not in fact form an insuperable barrier to movement across them in either direction. There are good passes through the greater Caucasus, particularly the one through which the Georgian Military Highway runs from Tiflis to Ordzhonikidze. Whichever way the current of diffusion may have run between urban and barbarian zones during the third millennium B.C., carts and wagons with one-piece and three-piece wheels certainly were in use throughout the region well before 2000 B.C.

MESOPOTAMIAN CHARIOT, pulled by Asiatic asses, was modeled in copper by an artisan at Tell Agrab around 2800 B.C. Although such vehicles were used for sport and war rather than for cartage, their three-piece disk wheels are identical with earlier cart wheels.

Let us now turn to the spread of wheeled transport into prehistoric Europe and see how, if you will, the West was won by the covered wagons of antiquity. Recently a number of large one-piece disk wheels have been discovered in the Netherlands. Carbon-14 determinations indicate that they were made a century or so before 2000 B.C. Two similar disk wheels, slightly earlier in date, have been found in Denmark. The wheels that most closely resemble the Dutch and Danish discoveries are ones found in the cart burials of the Pontic Steppe in southern Russia. This area is some 2,500 miles removed from the North Sea, even as the crow flies, and is considerably farther in terms of feasible overland routes of travel. What connections can be found between two such widely separated areas?

In all the land between the steppe and the North Sea the only direct evidence of the ancient use of wheeled vehicles consists of model wheels made of pottery and of a single model wagon. The pottery objects all appear to have been made before the end of the third millennium B.C., although precise dating is difficult. The model wagon, equipped with disk wheels, was found in a cemetery of the copper-using Baden culture, located at Budakalasz, on the outskirts of Budapest. It has a stunted one-piece draft pole. Above the chassis the wagon's sides rake outward; their concave upper edges suggest a body made of matting, supported by four corner poles [see lower illustration on page 72].

The Baden culture appears to have flourished in the period between 2700 and 2300 B.C. Chronologically this is not far removed from the era that saw wagons being buried at Ur, and it is contemporary with the vehicles found to the north and south of the Caucasus. The pottery models of single wheels are distributed at random. The one found deepest in central Europe was unearthed near Brno in Czechoslovakia; in general they are all contemporary with the later centuries of the Baden culture.

These few bits of clay constitute our only direct evidence of linkages between Europe and the steppe, but they are not the only evidence. In the Baden culture and in other roughly contemporaneous societies that flourished in what are now

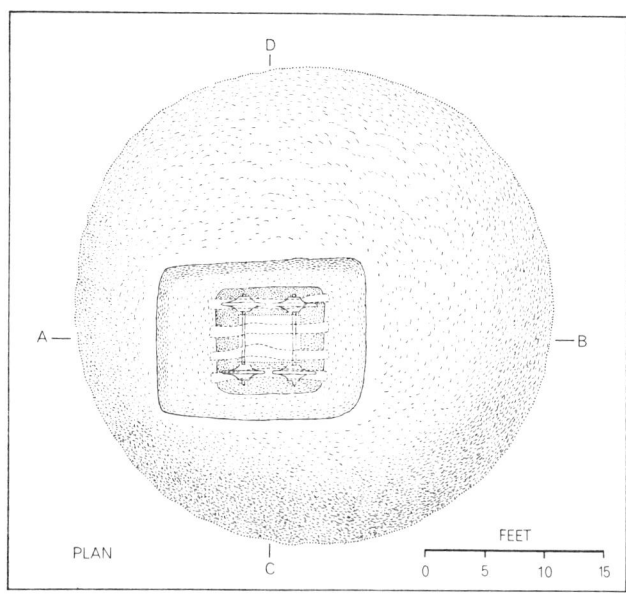
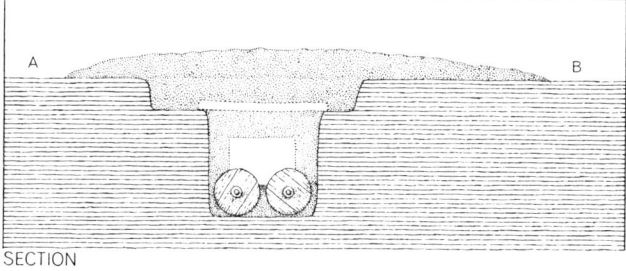
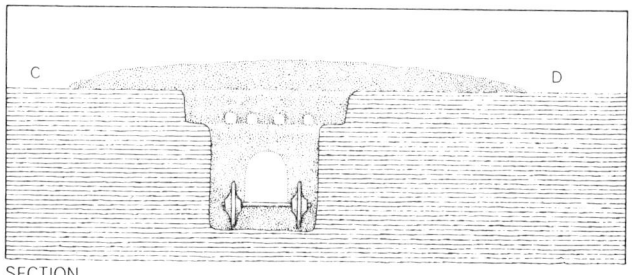

WAGON IN A TOMB was unearthed by Soviet archaeologists at Trialeti, in the Tsalka district of the Georgian S.S.R., in 1958. The wagon's wooden wheels and parts of its draft pole and chassis were preserved in the burial pit's waterlogged soil (see illustration below). Traces were found of an arched canopy that sheltered the occupants. The wagon probably was buried before 2000 B.C.

TRIALETI BURIAL PIT resembles a bog as the diggers probe for remnants of an entombed wagon. The vehicle's distinctive three-piece wheels have been almost wholly exposed. Trialeti is one of two Caucasus sites containing vehicles that predate 2000 B.C.

Poland and East Germany it was not uncommon to give ceremonial burial to animals as well as to men and women. Frequently the buried animals were pairs of cattle; more than 15 such burials belonging to the third millennium B.C. have been unearthed. One of them was found in the same Hungarian cemetery that yielded the model wagon. There a pair of oxen occupied one end of a long grave and human remains occupied the other end. In other cases paired oxen have been found lying at one end of a grave that was dug longer than necessary to accommodate the animals alone.

One inference to be drawn from the burials is that we are seeing pairs of draft animals; the discovery in Poland of two models of yoked pairs of oxen, of about the same age as the animal burials, lends weight to the inference. It is uncertain, however, whether we are seeing burials that originally included wheeled vehicles. The vehicles might have decayed without leaving a trace, or the traces could have gone unrecognized by the excavators. There also could have been no buried vehicles at all; the oxen may have been plow teams or animals that pulled a sledge. Nonetheless, if we take into account the burials of vehicles that have survived elsewhere, it seems most probable that burial of pairs of oxen is

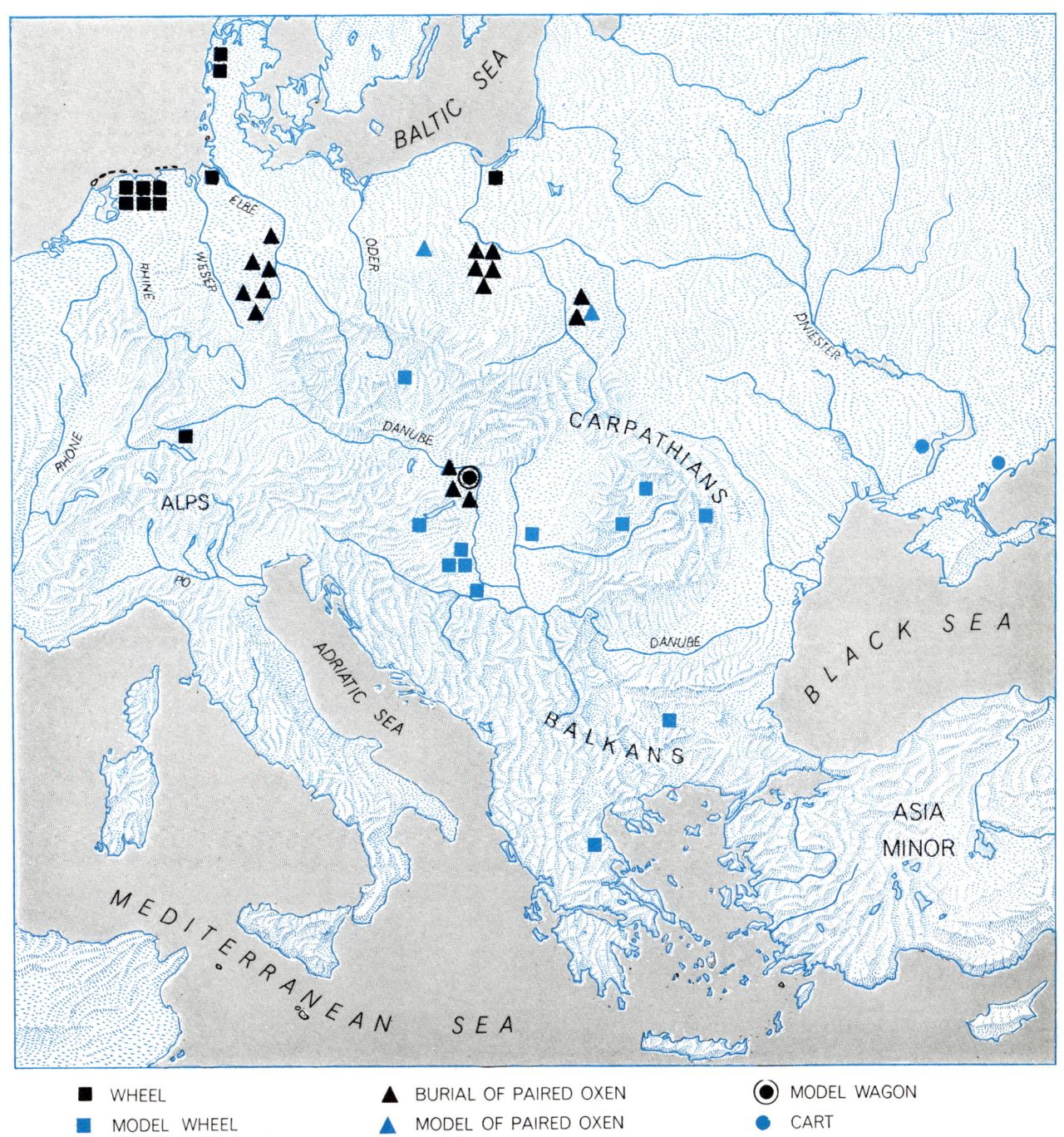

■ WHEEL
■ MODEL WHEEL
▲ BURIAL OF PAIRED OXEN
▲ MODEL OF PAIRED OXEN
◉ MODEL WAGON
● CART

PRESENCE OF WAGONS in Europe before 2000 B.C. is shown by the discovery of one-piece disk wheels in the Netherlands and in Denmark that yield carbon-14 dates earlier than the second millennium B.C. Direct evidence, in the form of pottery models of wheels and a single pottery model of a wagon, suggests that some vehicles entered central Europe via the Ukraine, the Romanian plain and Hungary. Indirect evidence, in the form of buried pairs of oxen and models of yoked oxen, suggests that another influx of wagons moved northwest from the Ukraine, skirting the Carpathian Mountains and arriving in the forested plain of northern Europe.

another variant of a general funeral rite in which at times a vehicle and its animals were buried together (as at Uruk), and at other times the animals were buried alone as a token representation. Accepting such an interpretation tentatively, we find that the indirect evidence of the animal burials fits in well with the direct evidence provided by the model wagon and model wheels. Both lines of evidence give added substance to a picture of Europe in which wheeled transport was used from the middle Danube to the Low Countries and Jutland at least by 2500 B.C. and probably earlier.

Thus, as in the Soviet excavations, we see that new or reassessed archaeological evidence, given the secure dating provided by carbon-14 analysis, is serving to narrow the ancient Near East's supposed margin of priority in the innovation of wheeled transport. What remains to be seen is whether valid inferences can be drawn with respect to two interlinked questions. The first question is whether or not the available evidence is sufficient to test the traditional diffusionist hypothesis about wheeled vehicles. This is the contention that the first such transport originated in a restricted region of western Asia where other technological innovations were under way among the precociously developing societies that immediately preceded the literate civilization of Sumer and Elam. The other question is more restricted in scope but is nevertheless important: Assuming that the area can be found in which wheeled vehicles were first used, by what routes and in what context of prehistory was the technology transferred from the point of innovation to Europe?

The answers to both questions depend heavily on the acceptability of the estimated ages of many archaeological finds and even of the actual dates of past events. In the context where the evidence is most needed, alas, it is not precise. For example, the date assigned to the earliest Uruk pictographs is derived from reasoned guesses and historical computation backward from the 24th century B.C., the point at which history of a sort begins in Mesopotamia, along with a glance at one or two relevant carbon-14 dates. Yet physicists have recently questioned whether "carbon-14 years" are exactly equivalent to calendar years during the period in question. The carbon-14 readings apparently give "true" dates that are several centuries earlier than the ones now in use, and correlation of the historical time scale with the carbon-14 time scale is fraught with difficulties. Even if carbon-14 dates themselves are no more than expressions of statistical probabilities, comparison of one with another should still provide a good relative scale. In this way, for example, one could validly equate part of the Kura-Araxes culture with part of the Baden culture. The scarcity of carbon-14 determinations for the Soviet vehicles is particularly regrettable when one considers the wealth of wood available for analysis. In spite of these handicaps, however, it is hard to escape the conclusion that the closely spaced dates of early wheeled vehicles unearthed from the Caucasus to the Netherlands must reflect a basic reality that indicates a rapid transmission of ideas over great distances.

Where was the first wheeled vehicle made? Let us return briefly to some of the factors considered at the outset. Timber would be needed both for the

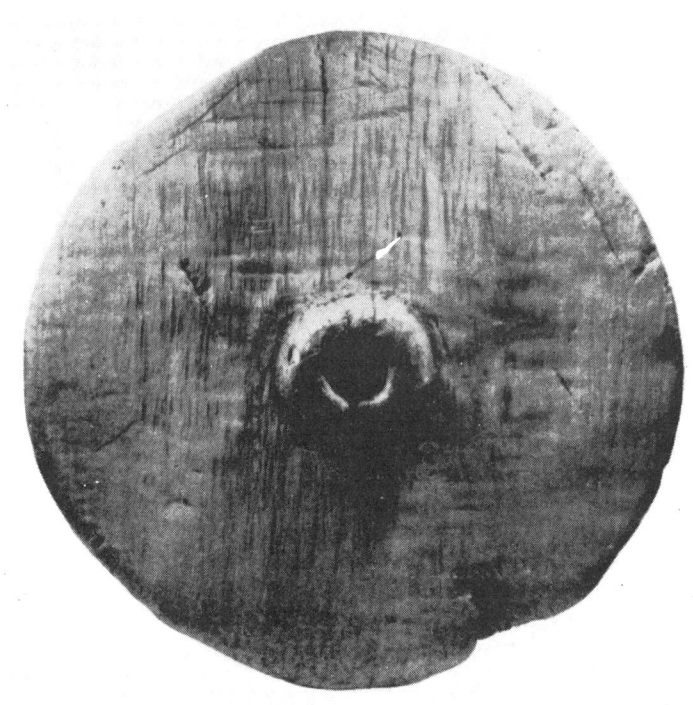

HEAVY WHEEL, fashioned from a single massive plank of wood, was found by Dutch archaeologists in Overijssel in 1960. Carbon-14 analysis dates it earlier than 2000 B.C.

MODEL OF A WAGON was found in a Hungarian cemetery that contains remains of the Baden culture. The Baden culture flourished in the middle of the third millennium B.C.

wheels and for the chassis; thus one is inclined to look toward regions adjacent to natural woodlands. In the case of Mesopotamia, timber would have had to come from the Zagros Mountains or from the Kurdish highlands. In support of Mesopotamia as the scene of the invention we should bear in mind that the Sumerians themselves seem to have come down from hill country, perhaps as early as the sixth millennium B.C.

Alternatively, the first wheeled vehicles could have been made within easy reach of the timber of the Caucasus. From there the invention could have been transmitted on the one hand to Mesopotamia (in the context of long-standing Sumerian ancestral relationships with the mountain peoples) and on the other into the treeless steppe to the north. Without drawing on resources beyond its bounds, however, the steppe itself certainly could not have been the birthplace.

In the light of our limited present knowledge it seems prudent to assume that the invention of wheeled vehicles took place in a wide area rather than a narrow one. The area should include Transcaucasia. Furthermore, the inventors should have not only access to raw materials but also suitable draft animals and adequate metal tools. Finally, the possibility of multiple invention is not beyond imagining. A vehicle of Sumerian design, with small one-piece wheels, could have provided a starting point. Later such developments as the covered wagon, with its heavy three-piece wheels, may well have taken place elsewhere and then been introduced into Mesopotamia. Mesopotamian wagon wheels are of noticeably lighter construction than those of the steppe; they can hardly have been the prototypes of the massive, doweled and mortised wheels of Transcaucasia. They could, however, represent a timber-saving version of a Transcaucasian original.

As for tracing the routes by which a knowledge of vehicles, or for that matter the vehicles themselves, moved westward into Europe, we must depend largely on inference. The evidence for cultural connections between the southern Russian steppe and the areas to the north and west is general rather than specific. Moreover, a new technological addition to a culture, such as the use of wheeled transport, does not necessarily carry any other traits of the parent culture with it. In spite of these caveats it has long been recognized that the cultures of the Hungarian plain in the late third millennium B.C. possess features that are difficult to explain on a basis of evolution from indigenous antecedents alone. A likely source for at least some of the obviously intrusive elements, such as new types of copper implements that resemble Caucasus copperwork, is southern Russia. The route of the intrusion could have been by way of the Ukraine and the plains of Romania, and thence into Hungary either over the mountains or by way of the Danube's Iron Gate. Along this route too could have come knowledge of the first wheeled vehicles.

The evidence of buried oxen in Poland and buried wheels in the Netherlands and Denmark may be related to an entirely separate intrusion. The pattern of cultures in the northern European plain around the middle of the third millennium B.C. includes a culture complex characterized by cord-ornamented pottery, stone battle axes and the custom of burying the dead in single graves covered by earth barrows. It has long been held that the complex is an intrusive one and is ultimately to be derived from sources in southern Russia related to the Pit Grave culture, although this interpretation has recently been disputed, and a case has been made instead for indigenous evolution.

The championing of local origins arises perhaps in part as a healthy reaction to earlier, overworked models of European prehistory that too strongly emphasized "invasions" and "folk movements." Nevertheless, even if some features of early northern European cultures can better be explained in terms of local growth, there still remains ample evidence of contact between southern Russia and northern Europe during the period. Dutch archaeologists have sought the origin of their disk-wheeled vehicles in Russia with good reason. A practicable route for the contact would also involve the Ukraine steppe, but from there it would cross the forest steppe and run beside the Dniester River, skirting the northern slopes of the Carpathian Mountains until it reached northern Europe's forested plain.

As in all questions of prehistory, we can at most advance working hypotheses that seem, in accordance with Occam's law, to account most economically for the archaeological facts. Indeed, what we call the facts are themselves only inferences derived from the surviving material culture of extinct communities. The investigation is nonetheless worthwhile, since it was during prehistoric times that the foundations of all our technology were laid down. No innovation was more fraught with ambiguous consequences than the invention and development of wheeled transport.

CHARIOTEER OF THE BLUES, whip held high in his right hand and reins gathered in his left hand, is portrayed in mosaic. He is one of four charioteers shown in the starting gates of a circus; the mosaic decorated the threshold of a dining room unearthed recently at a house site in Roman Carthage, where an international rescue-archaeology campaign began under UNESCO auspices in the mid-1970's.

Roman Carthage

by John H. Humphrey and John Griffiths Pedley
January 1978

An international campaign of rescue archaeology at the ruined city is uncovering significant information about its successive roles as a Roman colony, Vandal prize and outpost of the Byzantine Empire

In the last quarter of the first millennium B.C. Carthage, the greatest Phoenician colony in Africa, and Rome, then a young expansionist republic in central Italy, fought bitterly for control of the western Mediterranean. Between 264 and 146 B.C. the two powers were at war with each other on three occasions. Although some 50 years of uneasy peace separated the end of the second Punic War from the start of the third, the Roman senate could not forget the rivalry. The senators heard Cato the Elder demand on every possible occasion that Carthage be destroyed.

Cato did not live to see his demand met; he died at age 85 in 149 B.C. just as Rome mounted its final campaign against the Carthaginians. After a grim three-year siege Scipio Aemilianus, the adopted grandson of the victorious Roman commander in the second Punic War, captured Carthage in 146 B.C. His first orders after the city's surviving defenders were dispersed would have won Cato's approval. Scipio's troops leveled every building in the city; the site was then placed under a curse and ceremonially sown with salt.

The seeming finality of Scipio's gesture was short-lived. Less than 25 years later the Romans reversed their policy. Reborn as a Roman colony, Carthage was soon once again a great city, destined to survive for another 800 years. The remarkable history of these Punic and post-Punic centuries is being read in the city's ruins today as the result of an unprecedented international project in rescue archaeology. Launched by the director general of the United Nations Educational, Scientific and Cultural Organization in 1972, the project involves workers not only from the host nation, Tunisia, but also from nine other nations of Europe and America.

That there is more than enough work for all these participants will be made clear by a brief outline of the history of Roman Carthage. The capital of Roman Africa by the end of the first century B.C., the new city of Carthage eventually became the third-richest metropolis in the Roman Empire, rivaling Rome itself in magnificence. The Emperor Augustus renamed the city Colonia Julia Carthago, and with the advent of Christianity it became a center of religious ferment. By A.D. 439, the year Carthage surrendered to the advancing Vandals, the city had at least 22 great churches, its own bishop, more than 500 other clerics and a population estimated at 250,000 or more.

Imperial troops eventually expelled the Vandals, but they were troops of the Eastern Roman Empire; the liberated city was renamed Colonia Justiniana Carthago in honor of the ruler at Byzantium, Justinian the Great. Carthage remained a Byzantine city from A.D. 533 to 697. It might have stood to this day if its people had not risen in 697 against a small Arab garrison left there by the Moslem governor of Egypt, Hassan ibn en Noman. As the French classical scholar E. C. F. Babelon relates the story, Hassan, whose forces were busy adding Algeria and Morocco to the expanding realm of Islam, was infuriated by what he considered a treacherous attack. He repeated the Roman razing of nearly 1,000 years earlier in A.D. 698, and the city of Carthage was once again left in ruins.

Today, some 1,300 years later still, the twice-obliterated city has become a modern building site, its empty acres disappearing under the suburban sprawl of adjacent Tunis. In 1881 Tunis was occupied by the French, and in the years after World War II what had been a trickle of urban development became a flood. By the early 1970's deserted Carthage was the most desirable real estate in all Tunisia. The new palace of the president had been built over the northern ruins of Carthage, and large villas appeared on the heights overlooking the coast where the ancient Byrsa, or citadel, of the Punic city had stood. The adjacent heights, known in Roman times as the Hill of Juno and where the ruins of a Roman theater are still visible, were also invaded. Still other villas were built along the coast northward from Tunis up to and beyond the former Roman city wall, creating the present-day suburbs of Salammbo, Dermech and Sayda.

When the program of rescue archaeology was begun in the mid-1970's, the few undeveloped sections of the ruined city were apportioned among the various participating archaeologists. The Tunisian National Institute of Archaeology and Art, under the direction of Azedine Beschaouch, and Abdelinajid Eunatti, the conservator for the site of Carthage, have continued earlier work at Roman villas near the Roman theater. The principal undertaking of the host country, however, has been a massive cataloguing program, covering not only current discoveries but also the scattered findings of the past 150 years. A British group, directed by Henry Hurst, was assigned the island in the middle of one of the city's two artificial harbors: a circular harbor traditionally considered to have been military. The British were also given a second site on the north side of that harbor and a third area a short distance inland on the line of the Roman city wall.

From the circular harbor northward to city limits only one small unoccupied area remained on the shore of the Gulf of Tunis (except for the ruins of the Antonine baths, a part of Roman Carthage that was turned into an archaeological park some years ago); it was assigned to German excavators under the leadership of F. Rakob. Several other groups concentrated on parts of the city lying farther inland: the French, under S. Lancel, chose to continue earlier work by a succession of French investigators at the Punic citadel; one Canadian group, under P. Sénay, undertook to extend earlier French work at a circular monument on the Hill of Juno and another, under C. Wells and E. Wightman, traced the city wall nearby. Still farther inland an Italian group under A. Carandini set out to survey the street grid and city wall at the northwest corner of the city; archaeologists from the Institute of the History of Material Culture in Warsaw surveyed the southwest sector, particularly in the vicinity of the Roman circus, measuring variations in the electrical resistivity of the soil. The Danish group, under S. Dietz, chose a coastal site north of the Antonine baths, outside the city limits, where earlier Danish excavations had taken place. A Bulgarian group worked on another site outside the city limits: Damous el Karita, a famous early Christian church.

Two American groups were engaged in the rescue project. One group, a joint enterprise of Harvard University and the University of Chicago, was assigned an area on the western edge of the second harbor at Carthage, a rectangular harbor traditionally considered to have been mercantile, located just south of the circular one. The area extends westward into the adjacent Punic tophet, or burial ground, and the sanctuary of the Carthaginian goddess Tanit. Our own group, from the University of Michigan, was assigned a rectangular field 100 by 400 meters. Modern urban development had been forestalled in this area parallel to the rail line from Tunis to La Marsa, which lies west of the circular harbor. We were in a very real sense continuing a Michigan tradition: the first American archaeologist to work in Carthage, in 1925, was a classics scholar from the university, Francis W. Kelsey; his name was given to the university museum we represent as field director and principal investigator respectively. The work of both American groups is sponsored by the American Schools of Oriental Research and is funded largely through the Foreign Currency Program administered by the Smithsonian Institution.

The father, or perhaps more appropriately the grandfather, of modern Carthaginian studies was a 19th-century scholar, C. T. Falbe, who served as the Danish consul at Tunis and published the first detailed map of the ruined city in 1833. A number of other antiquarians, including the Anglican chaplain at Tunis, Nathan Davis, worked at the site in the years that followed, and soon after the French occupation French scholars drew up a comprehensive but wildly overambitious plan for excavating all the city's most important features.

The efforts of these and later investigators, however, served mainly to fill the museums of Europe with works of art such as mosaics and statuary whose exact location and archaeological context were generally undocumented. Indeed, until the current campaign began Carthage's checkered history of excavation and documentation gave it the reputation of being perhaps the hardest Classical Mediterranean site to study. Even the most resolute student of antiquity, attempting to interpret the work that had been done there, was frustrated by an absence of stratigraphic records, of pottery analyses, of numismatic studies and even of such a basic tool as an accurate large-scale map of the city.

That is now changing. Each of the groups working at Carthage has its own particular interests and specialties that for the first time are contributing to an overall view of the city's long history. For example, our group decided to concentrate on the later history of the city: from about A.D. 400, some 40 years before the Vandal takeover, to A.D. 698 and later, a period that includes the subsequent Byzantine revival of the city as Colonia Justiniana and its eventual seizure by the Moslems.

The long field that was assigned to us was ideal for the purpose. A preliminary survey of the site by the Tunisian National Institute of Archaeology and Art in 1971 showed that the field included the ruins of a late Christian church and baptistry and those of a number of wealthy private houses of the late Roman (that is, Colonia Julia) period and of the subsequent Vandal and Byzantine periods. In a broadening of the traditional focus of Classical archaeology, long known for its emphasis on such artifacts of history as inscriptions, coins and the products of artists and artisans, we number among our group specialists interested in evidence relating to the economy of the city and the people's way of life. For example, the Carthaginians' diet is reflected in the remains of plants and animals, and their exploitation of the physical environment is indicated by their choices of building stone and of clay for pottery.

A chronological framework is a prerequisite for the study of any Classical site: it enables the investigators to relate

MARBLE PAVEMENT covered the floor of the dining room after extensive rebuilding of the house that followed the Byzantine defeat of the Vandals in A.D. 533. The pavement, of a kind known as *opus sectile*, was repaired twice by the occupants of the house over the next century.

the various excavated levels and the objects found in each level to known periods of history. The greater the chronological precision is, the more detail that can be applied in the interpretation of different kinds of data. At Carthage, as at most Classical sites, the two kinds of artifacts that provide the basis for a firm chronological framework are coins and pottery. As an example, because of the relatively narrow intervals of time that are involved, coins usually provide a means of dating strata that is much more precise than carbon-14 determinations can be. Coins, however, are not necessarily found in abundance, whereas broken pottery is likely to be a major component of the rubbish at any Classical site.

In our oblong plot this once again proved to be the case. The coins we excavated in 1975 and 1976 were quickly identified for us by a University of Michigan colleague, T. V. Buttrey, and provided us with an overall chronological framework. It was, however, the potsherds found in stratigraphic association with the coins and the additional thousands of sherds from various intermediate strata at the site that enabled us to construct a series of quite precise chronological subdivisions based on pottery type and sequence.

The work was not without its difficulties. Until the rescue operation began at Carthage not even one publication had appeared describing the relative stratigraphy of the pottery unearthed in any part of the city. For example, what is known as African red-slip ware, a fine pottery produced in and around Carthage and elsewhere in northern Tunisia, was the main tableware in use not only in Carthage but also throughout the Roman Empire for half a millennium beginning in about A.D. 100. The history of this famous ware was painstakingly reconstructed by John W. Hayes of the Royal Ontario Museum in his book *Late Roman Pottery*. His definitive work, however, was based exclusively on the results of excavations elsewhere than in Tunisia, and the pottery classification depended largely on stylistic rather than chronological considerations. As for coins, until the rescue work began no catalogue of the coins excavated from the soil of Carthage had ever been published.

It is fortunate that Hayes and his colleague J. A. Riley of the University of Manchester have had charge of pottery analysis at our site. Because the fine red-slip tableware is easily recognized it has provided a general framework to which the other fine and coarse wares have been related. The two pottery specialists might readily have found themselves swamped with potsherds if they had not followed a program of selective preservation and disposal. The earth from each locus (that is, a distinguishable unit of soil) at the site was sifted after removal, and all the potsherds were segregated in buckets for washing (and for treatment with acid if they were heavily encrusted with earth). The sherds from each bucket were then sorted according to preestablished categories. Some were classified in terms of function. For example, pieces of lamps, jugs, basins, bowls, amphoras and cooking ware were separated. Other categories were based on the style of pottery, for example buff-finish wares, painted wares and red-slip wares.

The next step was to divide the sherds from each category into four groups: rim fragments, base fragments, fragments of the handle and fragments of the body of the vessel. The first quantitative measurements were made at this stage; the fragments in each of the four groups were counted and weighed and the data were recorded. If in the processing up to this point there was no evidence that the site had been contaminated, Hayes and Riley thought it was safe to combine all the buckets of pottery that had come from any single locus.

The next decision to be made was whether or not the locus was important. If the locus formed part of a "sealed" stratum (that is, an undisturbed level completely buried under an overlying stratum), or if the locus seemed important for some other reason, such as the presence of an unusual ware, Hayes and Riley kept and marked all the pottery recovered from it and assigned catalogue numbers to selected pieces, which were also measured and either photographed or drawn. If the locus was neither sealed nor otherwise important, they would discard most of the body sherds.

Because the body sherds usually far outnumbered rims, bases and handles, the actual quantity of pottery that was finally stored for later study was only a fraction of the quantity excavated. For example, on the basis of associated coins we were able to distinguish 81 varieties of pottery in strata belonging to the third quarter of the sixth century, an interval early in the Byzantine period at Carthage. Of a total of 7,343 sherds excavated only 881 were fragments of rims, bases and handles, and so more than 6,000 sherds could be discarded. Incidentally, the latest coin associated with this group of sherds was minted sometime between A.D. 548 and 565.

In 1976 Hayes and Riley published data relating to 17 separate groups or deposits of pottery from Carthage; the pottery ranged in date from early in the first century to the second half of the sixth. Last year they went on to publish

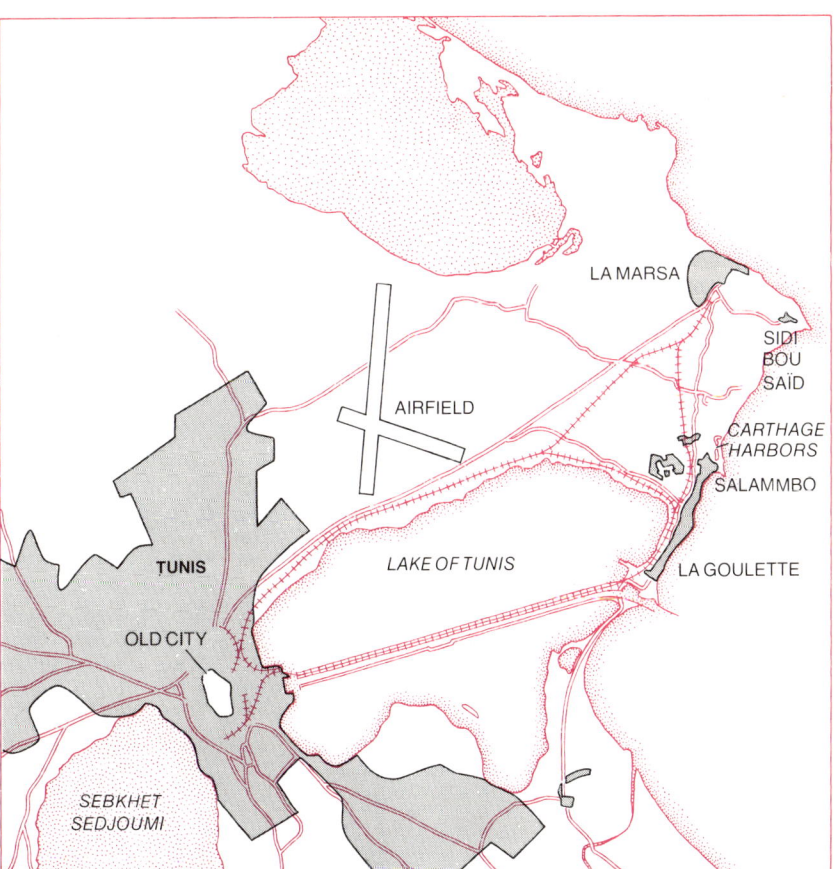

RUINS OF CARTHAGE lie to the north of modern Tunis, the capital city of Tunisia. In recent decades the northward spread of the suburbs of Tunis has almost engulfed the old city.

several additional pottery groups, most of them dating to the seventh century.

Among their findings is a decline in importation of fine wares from Italy early in the history of Colonia Julia. During the first century imported Arretine fine ware made up 27 percent of such wares at our site and imported amphoras made up another 2.5 percent. The proportion of imported wares fell to a fraction of that percentage early in the second century.

The sifting process yielded much more than potsherds alone. It enabled us to recover a far larger number of coins than might have come to light through more traditional methods of excavation. For example, we recovered more than 600 coins in our 1975 season and more than 1,200 in 1976. Unfortunately their quality did not match their quantity. The coins from the later centuries at Carthage, particularly those from the Vandal period, are very small and poorly minted and also are severely corroded by burial in the acid soil. Still another advantage of sifting, as will be seen below, was the recovery of an abundance of animal bones and plant materials.

Once a secure chronological framework is established it becomes possible to interpret the successive phases of occupation at a site as they relate to the surviving annals of Classical history. For example, we are now able to present at least in broad outline the history of the area we have excavated so far. Our work began in 1975 with the clearing of an area some 15 by 25 meters in the northwest part of our 100-by-400-meter field. The excavation exposed much of the floor plan of a Roman house fronting on one of the regular north-south streets of Colonia Julia. The Roman rebuilders of Carthage had constructed a terrace in this part of the city by piling a massive layer of fill over the underlying rubble of Punic Carthage. We have yet to excavate the Punic levels. Here, as evidently elsewhere in the city, the building of terraces over the Punic ruins took place before the laying out of the main street grid and its lesser subdivisions: the *insulae*, or city blocks. The main street our house fronts on is designated Kardo IX East on the street plan of Roman Carthage.

The date of the terrace construction falls early in the first century A.D. Thus it appears that this area, west of the circular harbor, was not among the first parts of the city to be rebuilt when Julius Caesar and his successor Augustus established Colonia Julia. In any event the city planners evidently subdivided the new city blocks into 16 equal lots, each lot about 17.5 meters square. The earliest of the Roman houses on our site, built no later than the middle of the first century, occupied one such lot or at most two.

We have not excavated all the earlier Roman levels at the house site. What we have exposed proves that a large cistern was built under the courtyard of the house early in the second century. In about the middle of that century pits were evidently dug at the edge of the street immediately outside the house; they were soon refilled and covered by a plastered sidewalk. If this outside activity marks some break in the continuity of occupation, it may have been associated with a great fire that swept Carthage in the reign of the emperor Antoninus Pius (A.D. 138–61) and destroyed much of this section of the city.

Our work has concentrated on the house remains that are attributable to the late Roman, Vandal and Byzantine periods at Carthage. With regard to the late Roman period it is apparent that the house was completely reconstructed just before A.D. 400. It may also have been enlarged at that time, although it still appears to have occupied only half of the width of the block. The main room of the house, roughly seven by nine meters, was a dining room; the dining-room wall on the east, or street, side of the house is five meters west of the outside wall. To the north the dining room opened onto a colonnaded courtyard, and the room itself was paved with a figured mosaic. The occupants of the house after the Vandal interlude at Carthage replaced the original Roman mosaic, but some of the mosaic's border, with an acanthus-scroll design, has survived.

It happens that in the centuries after 100 B.C. Roman Carthage was the home of one of the most important schools of mosaic construction in the empire. The Tunisian reconnaissance of our field uncovered one example that was quite well preserved, and in 1975 we were able to show that the mosaic had stood at the threshold between the dining room and the courtyard of our house. The mosaic depicts four Greek charioteers standing in their chariots at the starting gates of a circus [*see illustration on page 74*]. A small pool occupied the southeast corner of the courtyard colonnade; both the courtyard and the colonnade were paved with mosaics, but only fragments of these paved areas have escaped destruction.

Where these and other mosaic fragments survive they tell us something

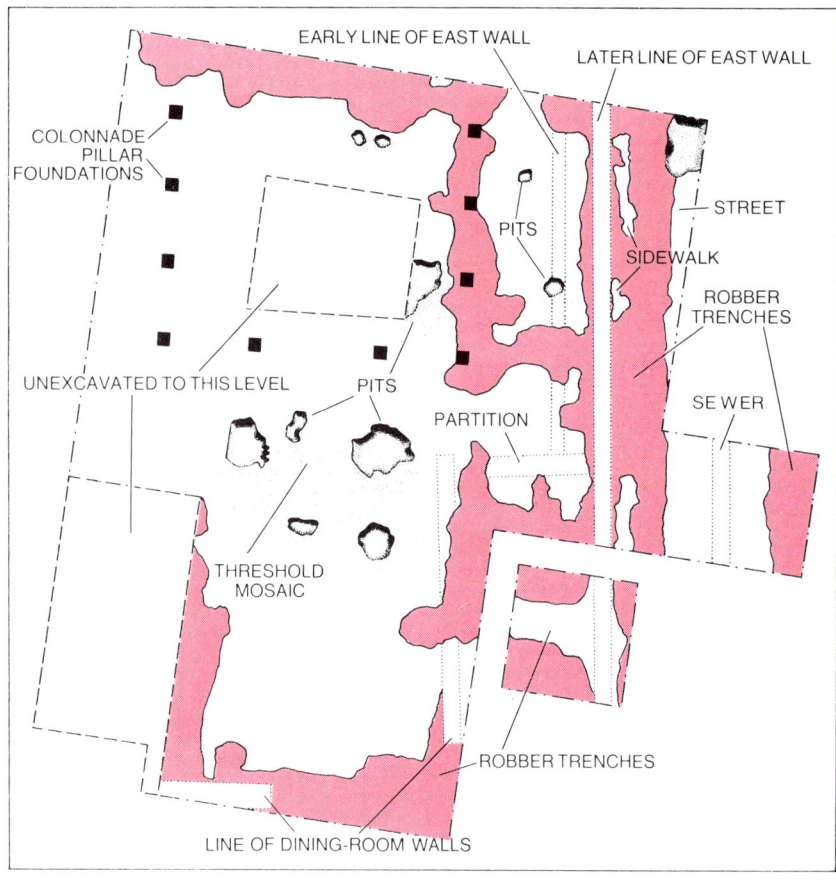

ROMAN RESIDENCE, later rebuilt according to the same ground plan, is being excavated by the University of Michigan group at Carthage. Located on one of the many terraces built by the Romans to cover the ruins of Punic Carthage, the first house was built on this site no later than the middle of the first century A.D. Just before A.D. 400 it was reconstructed as is shown here; the mosaic representing the Greek charioteers was at the threshold leading from dining room to courtyard. The extensive trenches (*color*) were dug by later masonry robbers.

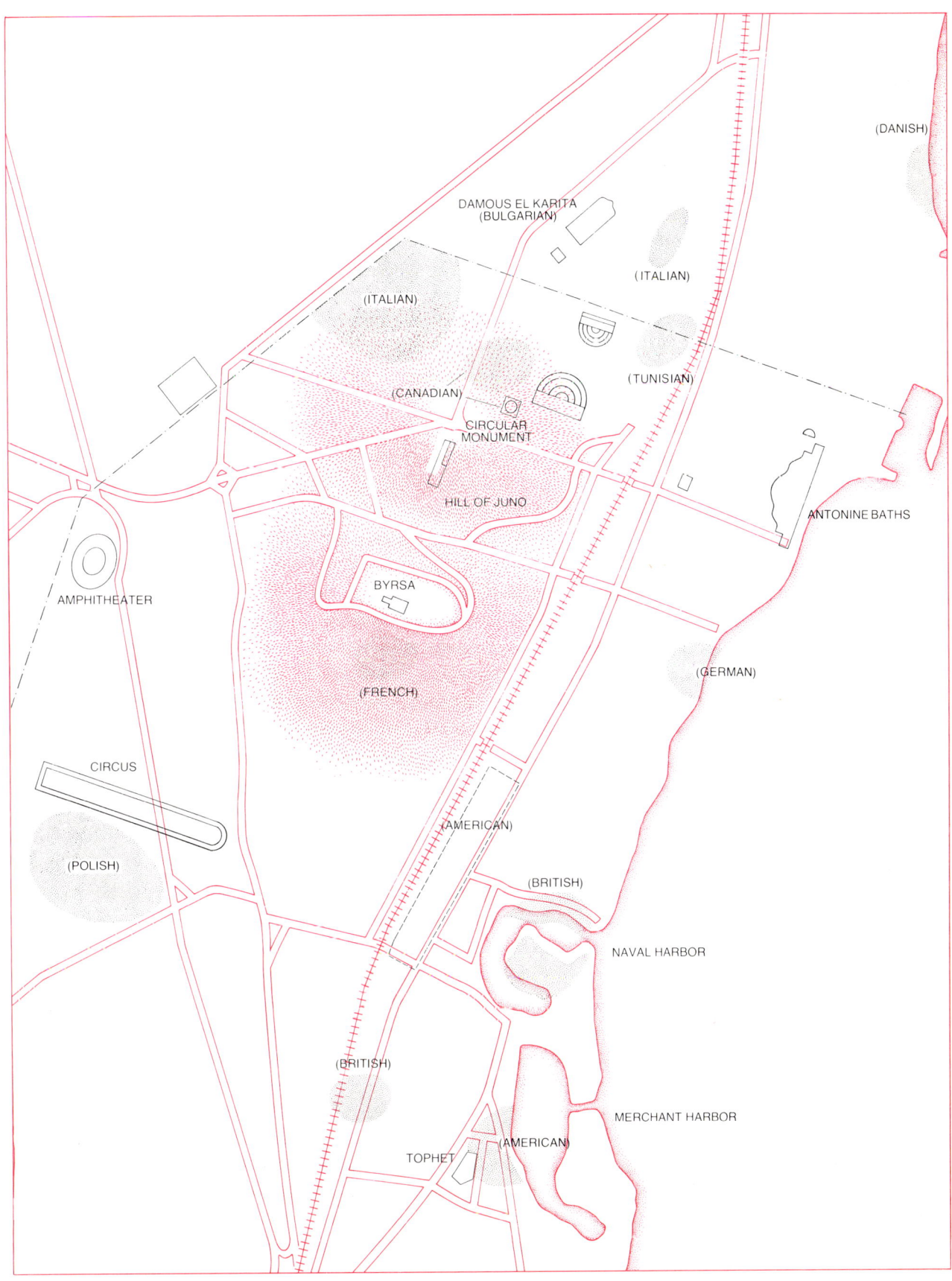

RESCUE CAMPAIGN is under way at 13 locations in Carthage. These are, from north to south, a site north of the Antonine Baths (Danish), a Christian church (Bulgarian), a street and city-wall survey (Italian), a circular monument and wall survey (Canadian), Roman villas (Tunisian), the Punic citadel (French), a site south of the baths (German), the University of Michigan area, a survey near the circus (Polish), two military-harbor sites and a city-wall site (British) and a joint Harvard University–University of Chicago concession.

about the occupants of the house during the Vandals' rule. Katherine Dunbabin of McMaster University has analyzed all our mosaics. She finds that as the Roman mosaics wore through or otherwise became outdated the householders continued to put down new mosaics as replacements and even extended the paved areas. For example, remodeling during the Vandal period extended the house eastward until it included the area of the street that had formerly been a plastered sidewalk. The remodeling enlarged the rooms along the east side of the house, and at the same time the floors of the enlarged rooms were covered with new mosaics. Except for these repairs and alterations the century or so of Vandal rule at Carthage appears to have had little effect on what we now call the House of the Greek Charioteers.

Soon after the Byzantine general Belisarius expelled the Vandals from Carthage our house was extensively rebuilt. The work followed the existing floor plan and wall lines, but the dining-room floor was repaved with pieces of marble arranged in an elaborate pattern. This kind of pavement is known as *opus sectile* (the Latin phrase for cut work), and the example in our house is the first Byzantine *opus sectile* floor found in a private house in Carthage that can be confidently dated. The marble pieces have been studied by our geologist, Reuben G. Bullard. He reports that many of them were not freshly cut for the purpose but were salvaged from similar pavements elsewhere and reused here.

The Byzantine work on the house included the redesign of the area between the dining room and the street as an open court paved with flagstones. The remaining rooms fronting on the street received new mosaics, but afterward the house remained unaltered until the third quarter of the sixth century. At that time the courtyard in front of the dining room, which then had a plastered floor, was also covered with flagstones. The house appears to have been occupied until the Arab conquest of A.D. 698, but no new mosaics were laid. The occupants did make an attempt to preserve the *opus sectile* pavement in the dining room. Two distinct phases of repair can be detected. The first repair conformed as closely as possible to the original design; the second abandoned conformity and the repair disrupted the pattern.

When the railroad from Tunis was built adjacent to our site in 1909, the laborers who raised the right-of-way embankment scraped away the top levels of our house for fill. As a result little of the later Byzantine and post-Byzantine record of occupation remains. Fortunately traces of this period of Carthaginian history exist elsewhere on our plot, just to the south of the church and baptistry ruins located earlier by the Tunisian National Institute. We spent our entire 1976 season working in this part of the plot, and we uncovered evidence of five successive phases of occupation that extend from about A.D. 650 to about the 11th century.

During the earliest of the five phases the area had been part of an active ecclesiastical complex that included the church adjacent to our house. Our chronology indicates that the church and its associated structures had reached their final phase sometime before A.D. 647–59. The succeeding phase, which is dated slightly later than A.D. 659–68, marks

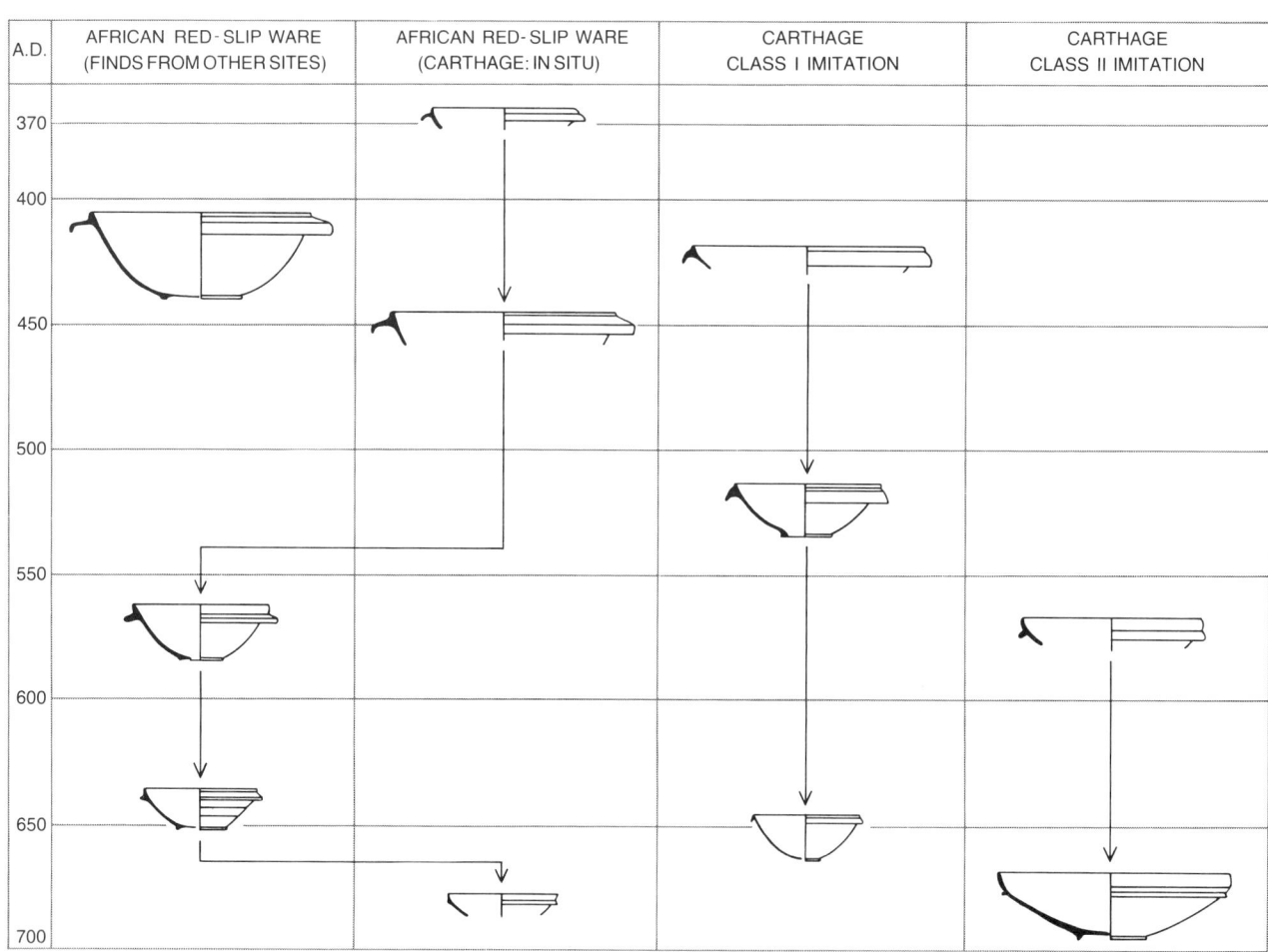

CHANGING POTTERY STYLE over some 300 years is exemplified by a kind of flanged bowl that first became popular in late Roman times. A fine red-slip ware, it was copied throughout the empire; examples made in Africa (*first and second columns*) are found at Carthage and elsewhere. The bowls were imitated by potters in and near Carthage (*third and fourth columns*), who omitted the slip.

the apparent collapse of the church complex. This collapse is indicated by the beginning of a process particularly familiar to Classical archaeologists: foundation robbing, that is, the theft of building stone from an abandoned site for use elsewhere.

The third phase, dated slightly later than A.D. 668–73, shows evidence of at least three distinct efforts to renew the flooring of the abandoned site; all were of poor quality. It is significant that the second and third phases at the site, which collectively imply less than prosperous and stable conditions in Carthage, both precede by many years the Moslem destruction of the city in A.D. 698. It would seem that the running conflict between Islam and the Byzantine Empire, starting in the Near East half a century earlier, had by this time also unsettled the North African provinces.

The fourth phase at our former church site, dated later than A.D. 687–95 and perhaps as late as the 10th century, is notable for a second major incursion by foundation robbers. The fifth and final phase may with some confidence be placed in the Islamic period: the 10th or even the 11th century. One of the floors of this phase overlaid and sealed an Islamic coin, and it seems safe to presume that the floor is later in date than the coin.

Classical archaeology normally pays little attention to a site in its declining phase, after the monumental buildings have fallen into disuse. Later occupations are likely to be marked by construction less substantial than masonry, for example partitions of mud brick or wattle and daub. Recent archaeological work in England has revealed something of what happened there after the Roman occupation of Britain had ended, but similar studies in other parts of the Roman Empire are rare. Therefore our findings in this corner of post-Punic Carthage throw a valuable light on the last days of the city.

In summary, even after the roofs had collapsed and the walls had been robbed of their stones, the shell of the church complex sheltered a series of domestic habitations where we can still recognize individual housing units. The conditions were mean, the partitions were superficial and the floors were paved not with mosaic or fine mortar but with trampled mud brick. Yet the quantity of coins and potsherds found even in the uppermost levels indicates that the last days of Colonia Justiniana were characterized by intense activity. The advance of Islam had in effect left Carthage besieged. The Christians from the surrounding countryside who flocked to the city evidently welcomed refuge however rudimentary it was.

The animal remains (which we have recovered by dry sifting) and the plant remains (recovered from the sifted soil by flotation) provide an additional dimension to our picture of life in post-Punic Carthage. Bones and shells have not normally been regarded with any great enthusiasm by the Classical archaeologist, and we have been fortunate in having David Reese, a graduate student at the University of Cambridge, analyze our finds of these materials. He has discovered that pigs and sheep or goats were the city's most abundant meat animals. Cattle bones are less common; evidently these larger animals were more often harnessed to the plow and the cart than slaughtered for meat. At Carthage this preference remains the same from the early Roman period to the late Byzantine, and the evidence contrasts sharply with Latin literary sources that would have us believe beef was the most popular meat. That the camel was present here long before the Arab influx is evident from the discovery of camel bones in a pit filled with trash soon after A.D. 100.

Fishbones representative of various species indicate that seafood formed an important part of the Carthaginian diet. Curiously the tuna, the fish that bulks largest in the Tunisian diet today, is not in evidence. A wide variety of mollusk shells, both marine and terrestrial, are present. There is no evidence, however, that the land snails were eaten, and signs of water wear suggest that the marine snails and bivalves were not eaten either but were accidentally gathered along with beach sand that was used to make mortar.

Richard I. Ford and Naomi Miller of the University of Michigan have analyzed the botanical materials from the site. They include a variety of seeds and numerous fragments of burned wood. Olive pits are the most abundant of the seeds. Olives were eaten on the spot not only by the various inhabitants of our plot but also by the workers who prepared mortar for the stonemasons: pits appear frequently in the mortar of all the construction phases. Other seeds Ford and Miller have identified include wheat grains, grape seeds and a single peach stone. Meanwhile a representative collection of wood from various species of trees that grow in Tunisia today has been established, and Classical works are being searched for information about the main sources of timber in antiquity and the kinds of wood preferred for different purposes. The next step will be to see how the burned wood we have salvaged from our excavations

QUARRIES FOR CARTHAGE included one quarry on the city outskirts and three near enough to the coast to allow water shipment. Other main quarry sites were located between 12 kilometers (gypsum at Jebel Ayari) and 160 kilometers away (Numidian marble at Simitthu).

fits into such a conceptual framework.

A similar effort has been launched with regard to the varieties of building stone used at Carthage. Both the immediate hinterland of the city and more distant areas of Tunisia and even Algeria are well known for abandoned quarries of both Punic and Roman times. What has been less apparent, however, is how the various quarry products were utilized.

Bullard, our geologist, has studied the question. He finds that the Romans followed Punic practices with respect to a porous coarse sandstone taken from Ghar el Kebir, a quarry some 60 kilometers northeast of Carthage. This stone, which could be brought to the city by water, was used as a general construction material. A local lithified sand and a quartz sandstone from the Hamilcar quarries just north of the city were used by the Romans as a filler rather than for surface masonry. Durable and easily worked limestone was available from quarries at Jebel Djelloud and Jebel er Rorouf, from which the stone could also be brought by water, and at Jebel Ayari, an overland haul of some 12 kilometers. The Romans used this excellent stone for posts, lintels and paving blocks and on occasion for wall courses.

For elaborate facings the Romans quarried a near-marble, gray with pink and white veins, at an outcropping of Jurassic sediments some 60 kilometers southwest of Carthage near Thuburbo Maius. For massive columns they selected a white-and-brown-veined limestone from an adjacent deposit. Gypsum-rich clays from a deposit at Jebel Azeis, north of Thuburbo Maius, and quantities of gypsum available even closer to Carthage account for the frequent use of molded gypsum blocks in city construction. The marble quarry at Simitthu, 160 kilometers west of Carthage, was the Romans' source of *marmor Numidicum*, a mottled pink-and-yellow facing stone that was not only used in the city but also exported in large quantities to cities all over the empire.

As our work continues we expect to link still other Tunisian quarry sites to the building stones of post-Punic Carthage in the same way that our other interdisciplinary workers are adding to a growing sum of knowledge. An immediate example is the work conducted throughout our 100-by-400-meter field last year. Surveys using an electrical-resistivity meter in the southern half of the field have yielded important information on the presence and absence of cisterns, information that will allow value judgments with respect to such broader topics as architectural development, town planning and population density. Together with our colleagues in this international rescue effort we are with each season expanding the traditional bounds of Classical archaeology.

The Archaeology of Winchester

by Martin Biddle
May 1974

This English cathedral city was faced with the loss of its past as a result of urban redevelopment. Excavation has now revealed the pattern of its growth since its birth some 2,000 years ago

How is a city born and how does it grow? If it is long dead, like Troy or royal Ur, archaeology can readily provide some of the answers. If the city is still very much alive, like Rome or London, the evidence is harder to obtain. Nonetheless, over the past 12 years an intensive archaeological campaign has uncovered the early periods and amplified the recorded history of one such city. The site was a major defended settlement during the latter part of the British Iron Age, was the island's fifth-largest town in Roman times, was a prosperous bishopric from the seventh century, was a royal seat until well after the Norman Conquest and is today one of England's leading cathedral cities, with a population of 33,000. The city is Winchester, and what more than a decade of urban archaeology has revealed about it is a fair indication of how much can be achieved elsewhere in the world when the work is begun before the past is irretrievably destroyed.

The River Itchen, the trout stream made famous by Izaak Walton in *The Compleat Angler*, rises in central Hampshire and flows south through a range of chalk downs on its way to Southampton Water, behind the Isle of Wight. Since remote antiquity the river valley and the grassy downs have provided natural lines of communication, the one north-south and the other east-west. At the point where the two routes cross and the alluvial valley floor is narrowest a spur of the chalk downs slopes more gently than elsewhere toward the riverbank.

A mile or so southeast of this spur the valley of the Itchen is commanded on its opposite eastern side by an Iron Age hill fort: St. Catharine's Hill [*see illustration on page 85*]. Built during the third or second century B.C. and enclosing an area of more than 20 acres, the defenses give evidence of having been reconstructed several times before being burned in the first century B.C. By then a settlement had appeared on the western side of the valley, on the same chalk spur where Winchester would later lie. In about the middle of the first century B.C. the new settlement was formally defined by the construction of a rampart and ditch that enclosed an area of just over 40 acres, or nearly twice the area of the eastern hill fort. This enclosure was the dominant feature of the valley in the later Iron Age. It lay astride the east-west route and commanded the river crossing.

Although little is known of the interior of the western settlement, its central area seems to have been densely occupied. The economy of the inhabitants was based on agriculture, but there is also evidence for long-distance trade connections. Fragments of southern Italian wine amphoras of the first century B.C. have been found, and the enclosure and its immediate vicinity have produced nine large bronze Ptolemaic coins of the third century B.C. from Egypt. These, of course, may have been imported for the value of their metal long after the time when they were first minted.

The size of the western enclosure is impressive, but there is not yet enough evidence to suggest that it contained an urban or even a proto-urban community. Moreover, the settlement appears to have been a false start; there is a break of as much as 100 years in its habitation. When the area was reoccupied soon after the Roman conquest of Britain in A.D. 43, the settlement was on the valley floor near the river, outside and downhill from the Iron Age enclosure.

Much of what we know about the growth of the settlement in Roman times is the result of emergency excavations first undertaken in 1961, when preparations were being made for the building of a new hotel in the center of the city. The rescue excavation soon revealed two facts. The first was the immense and virtually untapped wealth of Winchester's archaeological record. The second was the rate at which that record would be destroyed by the modern developments then planned for the decade ahead.

The city today is an important administrative, judicial, military, ecclesiastical and business center. The pressures generated by these urban functions find expression in plans for new roads and buildings, all potentially destructive of the buried remains of the city's past. A special body, the Winchester Excavations Committee, was set up in 1962 to deal with the problem of investigating and recording the archaeological evidence before its destruction. During the next 10 years the committee administered the largest program of urban excavation yet undertaken in Britain (or elsewhere in Europe for that matter). For seven years the work has been a joint Anglo-American venture, done in collaboration with the University of North Carolina and Duke University and supported by government and foundation funds from both sides of the Atlantic.

The project had from the start the principal objective of studying the origin and changing character of the urban community throughout its entire existence, from the first permanent settlement down to the emergence of the modern city in the reign of Victoria. The city itself was to be the subject, rather than any one period or aspect of its past. We hoped to try to grasp the totality of the urban phenomenon and the interaction of the city and its setting, both at distinct moments in time and between one period of its development and another.

The project involved not only rescue

excavations on threatened sites but also excavations on unthreatened ones, some of them large enterprises that yielded information essential to any balanced concept of the city's evolution. The project also required the integrated utilization of all the available evidence, whether it was from archaeology, from the natural sciences or from written records (in which the city is immensely rich from the 12th century on).

In 1968 the Winchester Research Unit was set up to prepare this large body of material for publication. A series of perhaps 12 volumes of *Winchester Studies* is planned. They will come from the Clarendon Press at Oxford and the University of North Carolina Press. The first volume will appear late this year or early in 1975.

The new Romano-British settlement on the Itchen was peopled not by Romans from Italy but by Romanized Celts. Their settlement may have grown up in a rather formless way at the junction of the new Roman roads that met close to the old river crossing. These roads, built shortly after the Roman conquest, were perhaps protected by a detachment of troops housed in a fort at or near their junction. If the fort ever existed, and the evidence is still unclear, its life was no more than 20 years. The development of the civil settlement was in contrast rapid: by the end of the first century it had become a walled city with a chessboard street plan and public buildings. The earth-and-timber ramparts of the city defenses enclosed an area of more than 143 acres. Their line was followed by all subsequent walls of the city down to the end of the Middle Ages.

The size of the enclosed area made Winchester the fifth-largest city in Roman Britain. Two long-distance Roman roads formed the axes of the rectilinear street system that divided the city into *insulae*, or blocks. A central block was occupied by the forum and basilica, constructed by about A.D. 100 to house the judicial, administrative and principal commercial functions of the city. The city was now known as Venta Belgarum. As "Venta" may imply, it was the market center of its region, and as "Belgarum" indicates, that region was populated by the Celtic tribesmen known as the Belgae, from among whose principal landowners the city's chief citizens were drawn.

Little is known of the detailed development of Roman Winchester. At first its houses, even if they were provided with such amenities as glazed windows, painted walls, tiled roofs and mosaic floors, were built of timber. Increasing prosperity in the later second century led to their being rebuilt in stone. About A.D. 200 the defenses, which must long have been out of repair, were totally remodeled. Within a generation the earth-and-timber perimeter was strengthened by the addition of a stone wall that was to stand for 1,500 years. The influence of the stone ramparts is still reflected in the traffic problems of the modern city.

The Romano-Britons left behind one common kind of archaeological evidence: the remains of their dead. In the Roman fashion the cemeteries lay along the roads outside the city gates. Here in the mid-fourth century, among the burials of the native population, is found the first clear evidence of the arrival of aliens at Winchester. Some graves, distinguished by the leather belts with bronze fittings they contained, are apparently those of soldiers. Their equipment is of a kind well known along Rome's frontiers on the Rhine and the Danube.

During the second half of the fourth century, following the barbarian ravaging of Britain in A.D. 367, the defenses of the island provinces were reorganized. An important element in the revised strategy was a system of "defense in depth," which was to be provided by walled towns. The towns' fortifications were strengthened by the addition of projecting towers, evidently to mount catapults that could rake attackers with arcs of intersecting fire. Winchester was included in the defense system. The maintenance and use of such artillery probably required the services of specialized troops; the alien element now recognized in burials of this period at Winchester and at other towns may well indicate the presence of such specialists. They were foreigners (perhaps Germans), either regular soldiers or mercenaries.

The movement of troops and even of entire peoples in the interests of frontier defense was a normal part of Roman policy. That policy was evidently continued even after the departure of the Roman administration of Britain at the beginning of the fifth century. In A.D. 410 the Emperor Honorius told the citics of Roman Britain to look after their own defense; this they did by continuing to hire mercenaries. The foreign levies now came not from the distant frontiers of the empire but from the barbarian shores around the North Sea, the traditional homeland of the Anglo-Saxon peoples.

The presence of Anglo-Saxons among the Romanized Celts of Winchester shortly after A.D. 400 is indicated by the

WINCHESTER LIES beside the River Itchen near the center of Hampshire, some 12 miles to the north of Southampton and 60 miles southwest of London, the city that eclipsed it.

presence of pottery identical with the pottery used in their home settlements along the lower reaches of the German rivers Weser and Elbe. Together with the evidence from the cemeteries, the pottery shows that the population of late Roman Winchester was already mixed and that before the end of Roman Britain the first forerunners of the English were already established in and around the city that was eventually to emerge as the capital of an English kingdom: Wessex.

It appears that urban life in Roman Winchester came slowly to an end during the fifth century. At every site of excavation the evidence of decay, the abandonment of buildings and the loss of streets is the same. No objects and only a little pottery of the period from A.D. 450 to 650 have been found. The ruined Roman city nonetheless remained an important focal point as Anglo-Saxon settlement of the region progressed, and this is indicated by two lines of evidence.

First, comparatively few Anglo-Saxon cemeteries of the pagan period from the fifth to the seventh century have been found in the county of Hampshire. The most striking cluster of these cemeteries lies in the immediate area of Winchester, outside the city walls to the east and west. Moreover, an early cemetery that was in use by A.D. 500 lies two miles upstream from the city. Unless the former Roman center was still a focus of some kind, why should these cemeteries, each of which presumably holds the burials of a farm or a small village, be concentrated in its vicinity?

Second, in about A.D. 648 Cenwalh, king of Wessex, founded a church dedicated to St. Peter and St. Paul inside the still standing Roman walls of Winchester. About a decade later this church became the see of the bishop of Wessex. Cenwalh had built the Winchester church not as a bishop's see but simply as a minster, that is, a church served by a group of priests and clerks not necessarily living under monastic rule. One may ask what function and what community this church in the center of a ruined city was intended to serve.

The Anglo-Saxon cemeteries suggest that from the late fifth century into the seventh Winchester was still an important place. (The Saxons transformed the name Venta into Wintancæster.) King Cenwalh's church may indicate the nature of that focus. Excavation of the seventh-century church has shown that it lies adjacent to the Roman forum. In the late Saxon period the Anglo-Saxon royal palace was immediately west of the church and was intimately associated

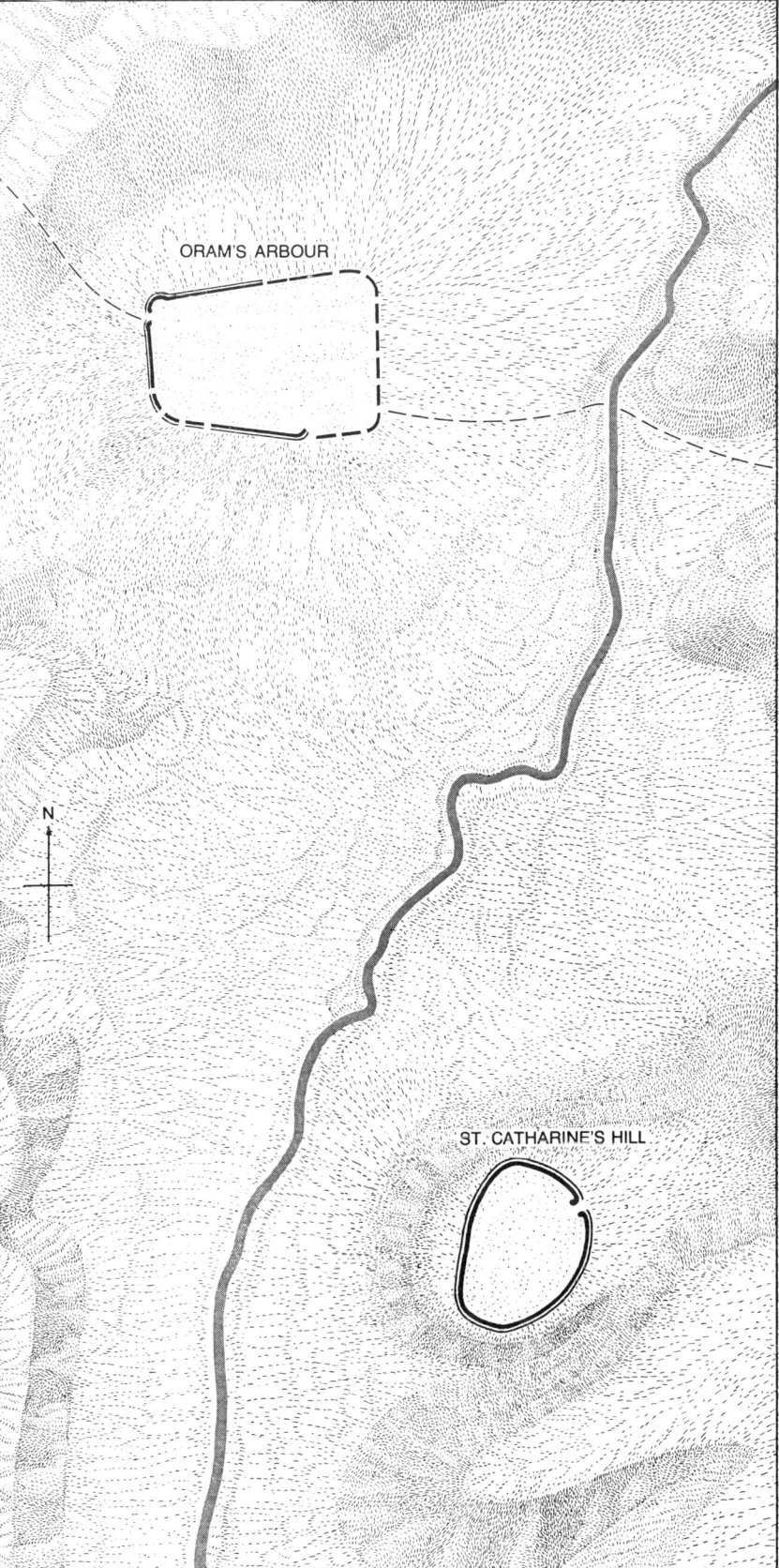

EARLIEST SETTLEMENTS in the Winchester area were two Iron Age defended enclosures. The earlier of the two (*bottom*), the hill fort now known as St. Catharine's Hill, was built in the third or second century B.C. By the time it was abandoned a second defense, twice the size of the first, had been constructed to the north on the opposite side of the river. Commanding the east-west route across the chalk downs, the new enclosure, now known as Oram's Arbour, has yielded pottery made in Italy and large bronze coins minted in Egypt. Both the route location and parts of earthworks shown at Oram's Arbour are hypothetical.

86 II | INVENTIONS AND THE URBAN TRADITION

with it. The royal palace also lay close to the forum, in particular to the south end of the basilica, the principal public building of Roman Venta. The origins of the royal palace are unknown, and the site has not been excavated. The relationship of these structures may nonetheless support the following interpretation.

We know that the Germanic mercenaries serving in post-Roman Britain revolted against their native masters, thereby destroying the fabric of the life they had been engaged to protect. Power passed to the victorious rebels, who did not entirely forget, even when they were augmented by successive waves of settlers from barbarian Europe, that they were in some sense heirs of Rome. Continental analogies, for example the towns of Trier and Cologne, show that the buildings that had been the seat of Ro-

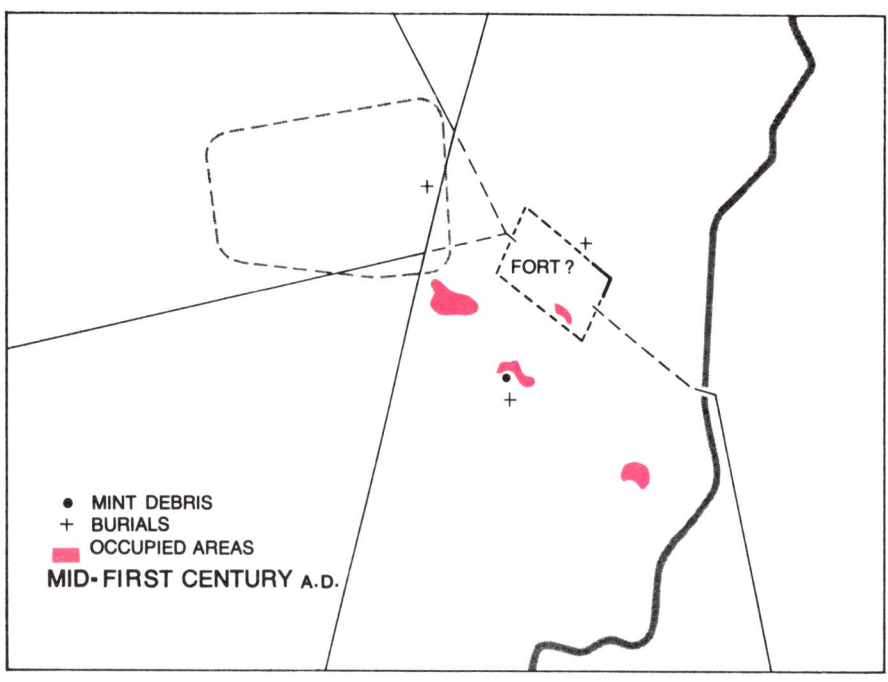
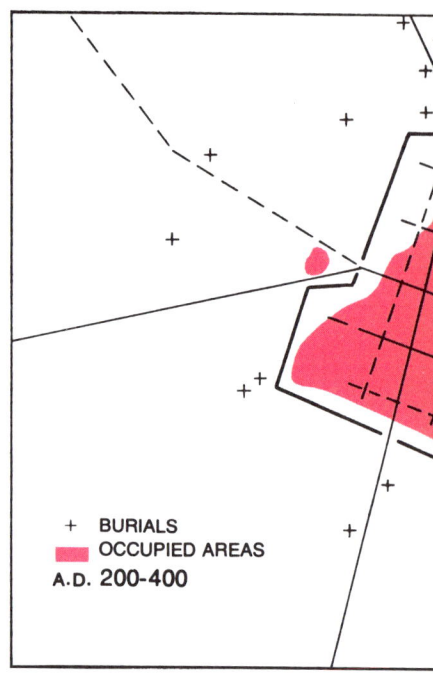

THREE MAJOR CYCLES of urban efflorescence at Winchester are illustrated on these two pages. The city's first roots were planted (*above*), perhaps in the form of a military post, to the east of the abandoned Iron Age enclosure (*light gray*) at the juncture of five Roman roads; this took place in the middle of the first century B.C. Broken lines indicate conjectural restoration.

VENTA BELGARUM, as the growing settlement was known in Roman times, was a fortified town with its streets comprising a rectangular

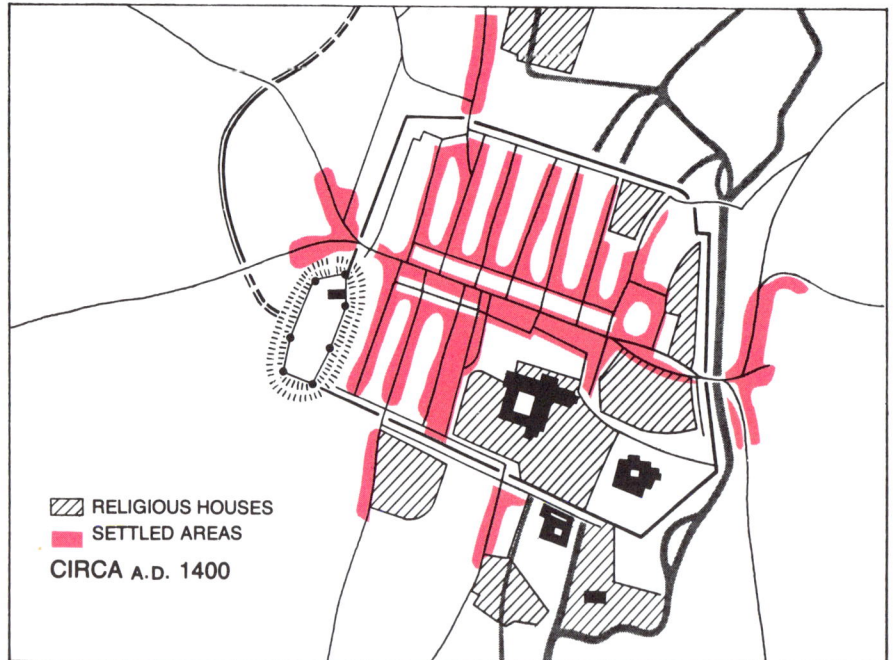
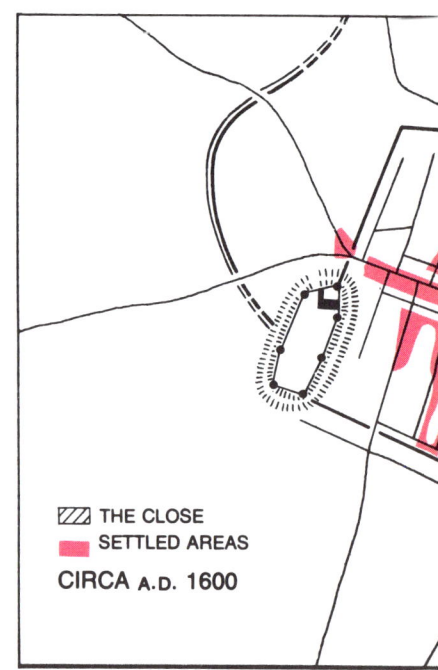

MEDIEVAL REVIVAL, first under English and then under Norman rule, raised Winchester above its former eminence as a Roman town. As seen here, some two centuries after the Conquest it had already begun to diminish in importance in spite of the great new Norman cathedral that had obliterated Old Minster. Growth of city in this period is illustrated on next two pages.

SECOND SLUMP saw the city drop to 37th place among English towns by the 1520's. Winchester fell even lower after England's monasteries

man authority sometimes survived as the residences of the new rulers. The same may have happened at Winchester. Germanic peoples of Saxon origin were established in the Roman city before its collapse. To them authority over the city and its lands may have passed by conquest or by survival, and their leaders, later to be kings, may have taken up residence in or next to the basilica that was the symbol of that authority.

On that hypothesis the Anglo-Saxon cemeteries outside the walls would reflect the presence of this ruling element within the old walled city, and the founding of the church by a king of Wessex in the middle of the seventh century would represent the establishment of a chapel to serve the royal household. The lack of archaeological material from this period is negative evidence of a certain

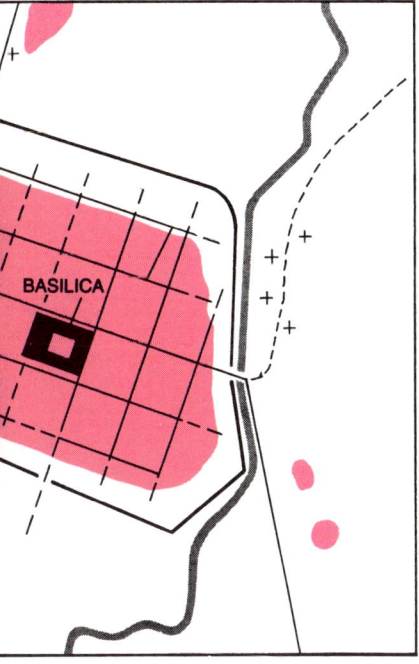

grid surrounding a central basilica and forum. In the third and fourth centuries A.D. it was the fifth-largest of the settlements in Roman Britain.

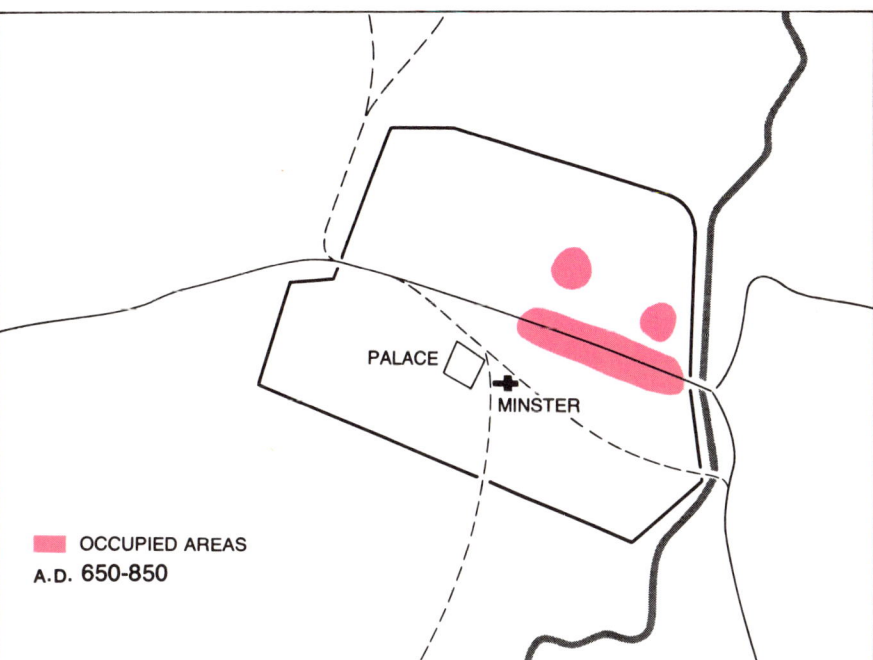

FIRST DECLINE came in the centuries after the end of Roman rule. By the sixth century only the wall and a single road bisecting the enclosed area remained of Venta Belgarum. For the next three centuries the town, called Wintancæster by the Saxons, may have sheltered a "king's hall" near the ruined basilica; the bishop's minster nearby could also have served as a royal chapel.

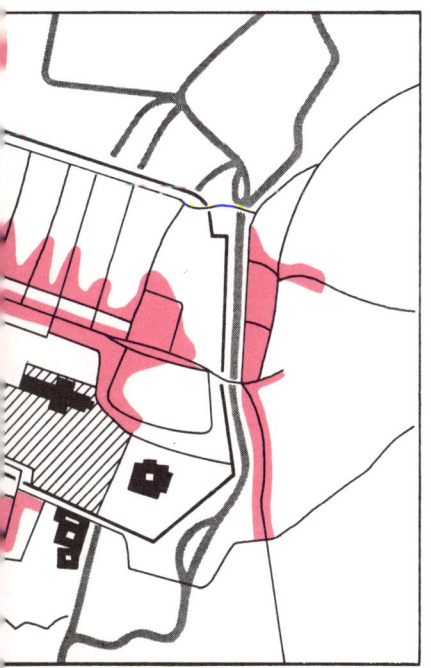

were dissolved during the 1530's. Depressed for 300 years thereafter, the cathedral city largely marked time until early in the 19th century.

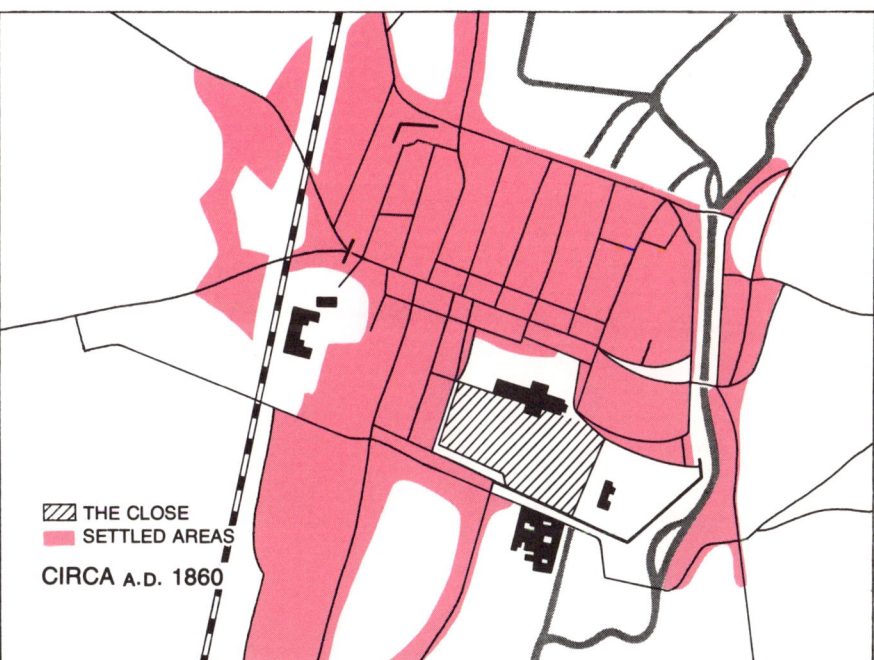

VICTORIAN REVIVAL of Winchester included construction of a railway just west of the city, which now stretched beyond the bounds of its Roman walls although only slightly exceeding its maximum extent in medieval times. The southeast quadrant of the old walled area remained dominated by the cathedral and its "close." Just south stands Winchester College, a public school.

88　II | INVENTIONS AND THE URBAN TRADITION

value: it shows that the greater part of the walled area was uninhabited. On the other hand, it has nothing to say about the Anglo-Saxon royal palace that has been buried under the cathedral graveyard for eight centuries and remains unexcavated.

With the founding of the church, which later became known as Old Minster, the city of Winchester entered a new phase. A few contemporary written records, an increasing amount of archaeological evidence and comparisons with other English and continental centers make it possible to present a less hypothetical picture of the character of the city in the two centuries following A.D. 648.

Within the walled area of Winchester four components become evident. One is the bishop's church and its community.

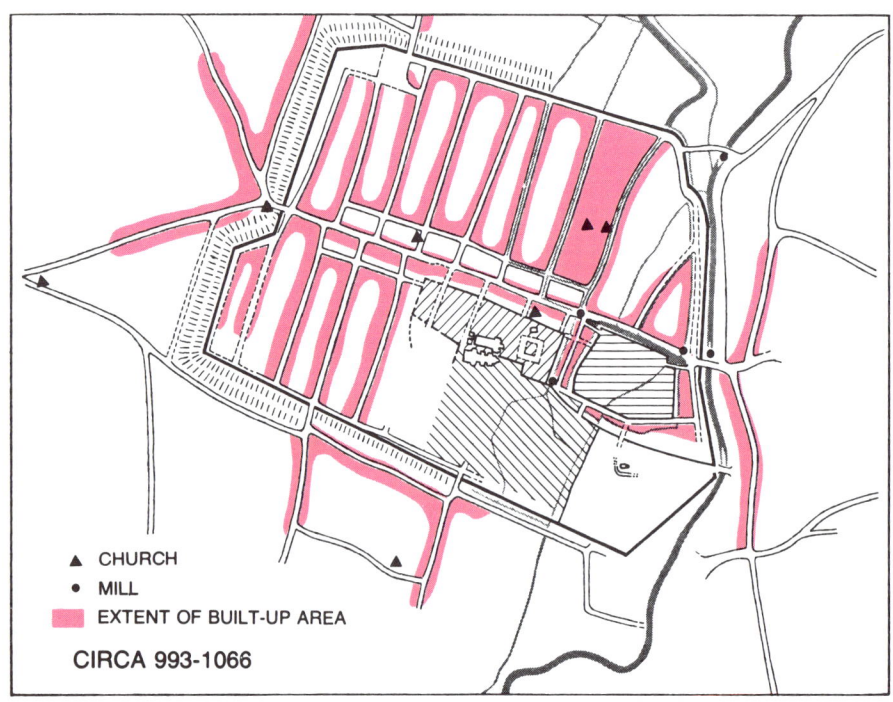

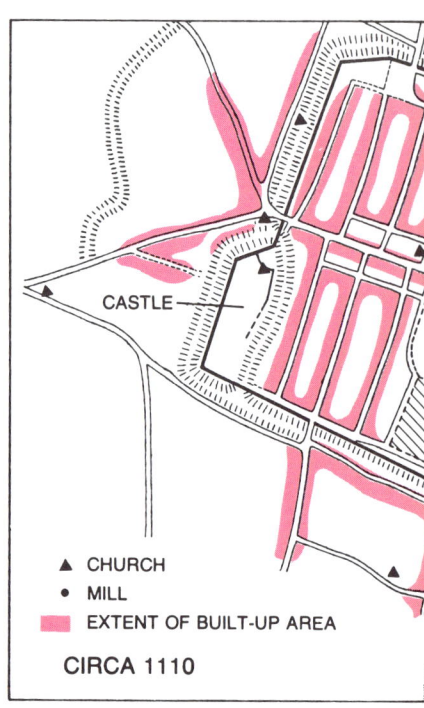

ANGLO-SAXON WINCHESTER just before the Conquest was a town with regularly aligned streets, elaborate defenses and many churches in addition to the Old and New Minsters and Nunnaminster. The illustration directly below shows the city's southeast quadrant in detail.

POST-CONQUEST DECADES were notable for Norman expansion. A new castle (*lower left*) enhanced the

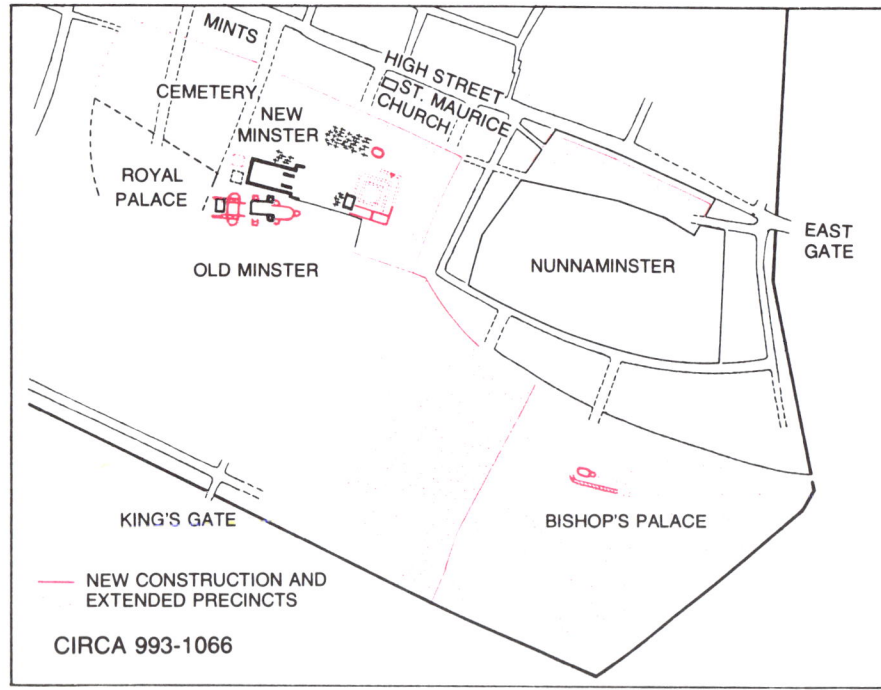

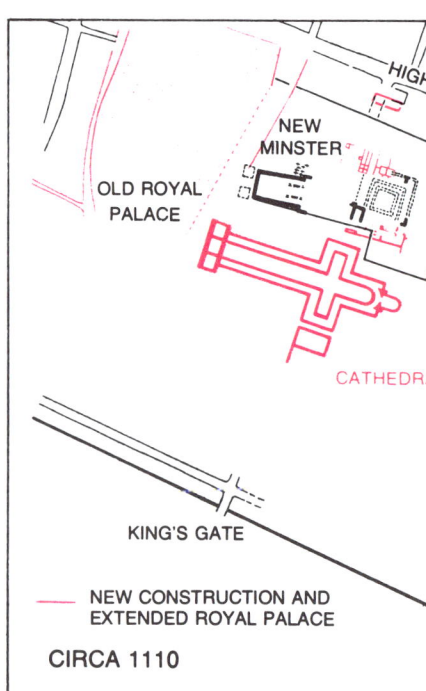

SOUTHEAST QUADRANT of Winchester at the close of the Anglo-Saxon era was the site of the royal palace, the bishop's palace and, in addition to lesser churches, the cathedral church or Old Minster, New Minster and Nunnaminster (nuns' church). Mints may have been located here.

NORMAN CHANGES doubled the size of the royal palace, rebuilt and extended the bishop's palace and also

Another is the royal residence; there is more circumstantial evidence for its existence during this period, when the church was the burial place of the Wessex kings. A third component is the presence of an unknown number of private residences; there is evidence of two such residential complexes. Of one, only the name survives as a description of an area within the city's East Gate: Coitburi. Names of this type, the second element signifying a defensible enclosure, are known from early London. The other private residence has actually been excavated in part; its earliest feature is a small private cemetery of the seventh century, probably adjacent to the earliest buildings, which remain unexcavated. The area of the cemetery was eventually built up; the first structures here were of timber, and in about A.D. 800 a stone

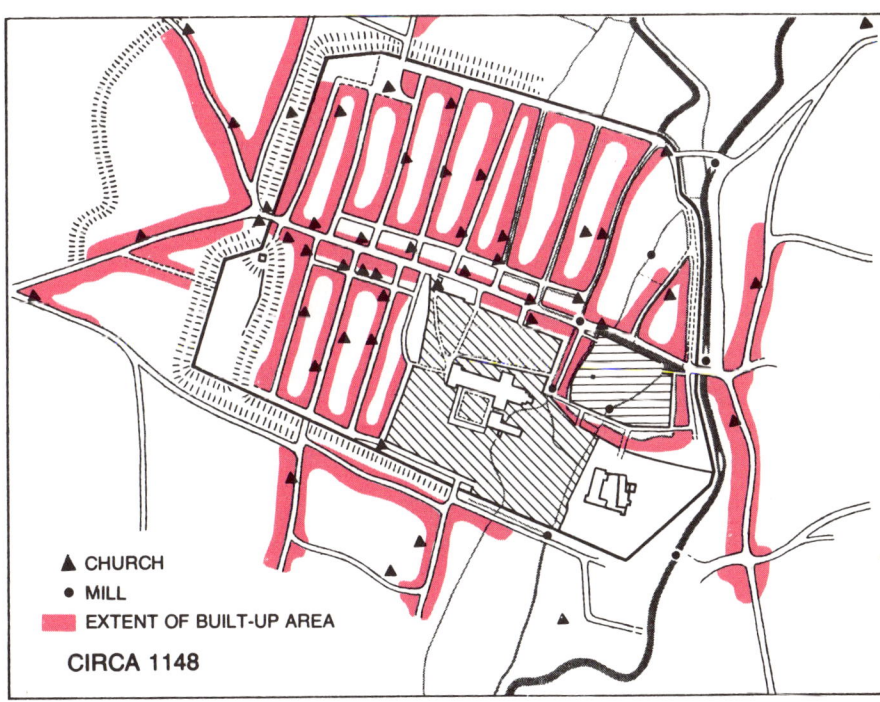

defenses and a great new cathedral rose. As a Norman seat the city stood second among English towns.

NORMAN APOGEE at Winchester came in the 12th century, when the city's churches numbered more than 50. Winchester's decline began that same century with a loss of close contact with the court. The trend was accelerated by removal of the royal treasury to London during the 1180's.

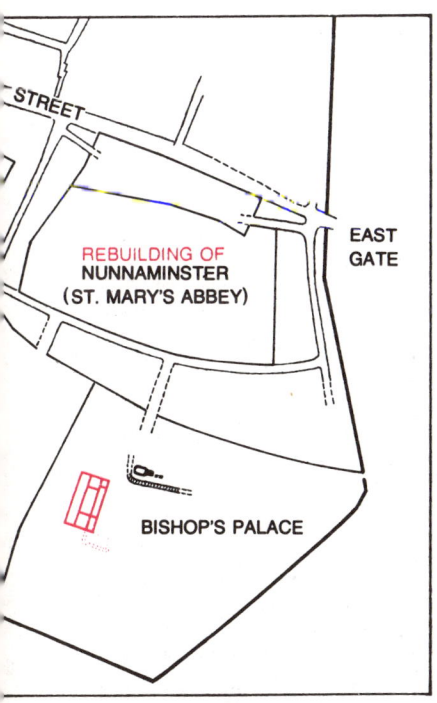

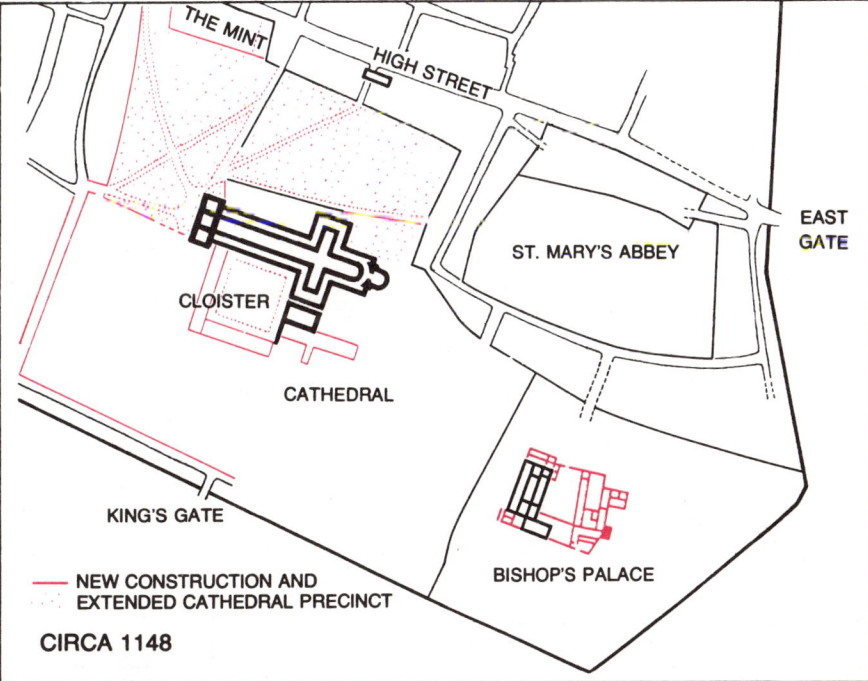

raised a great new cathedral. At the time of completion the cathedral was the longest church in all England.

CATHEDRAL PRECINCT had extended over the sites of the royal palace and New Minster by 1148. Nunnaminster, now called St. Mary's Abbey, was rebuilt once again. The bishop's palace, one of the greatest houses of its age, had by now almost reached its ultimate dimensions.

house was built [*see illustration on opposite page*]. Its remains contain evidence for the working and assaying of gold. The wealth of the burials in the private cemetery (one contained a necklace with gold and garnet pendants and 27 silver rings), the construction of a stone building and the working of precious metal all suggest occupants of high social status.

The fourth component is more problematical. It seems likely that the royal, ecclesiastical and private residences must have been supported by some service population, perhaps in the form of a developing street market along the eastern part of High Street, in the area known by about A.D. 900 as *ceapstræt*, or market street. As extensive excavations have shown, much of the walled area of the city was certainly uninhabited at this time, but contemporary records and the archaeological evidence both indicate that some of the walled acres were used for the grazing of livestock and the raising of crops.

The existence of these four components does not make Winchester an urban community at this time; there is no evidence of industry, of a dense population, of trade or of a full social hierarchy. Indeed, only the higher levels of society seem to be present. Comparisons with Anglo-Saxon Hamwih (modern Southampton), some 12 miles downstream, are instructive. At Winchester we have a royal residence and royal burials, a bishop and his church, the homes (two at least) of subjects of substance and just possibly a mint. Southampton had a mint but no other obvious marks of social greatness. At this time, however, Southampton had a substantial population, much industrial activity and the elements of a regular street plan. Moreover, there is evidence of long-range trade. In contrast, none of these is found in Winchester.

Here are two different kinds of settlement: the old royal and ceremonial center, limited in its extent and functions, and the complementary port and industrial settlement emerging as a true town at the head of a superb natural harbor. Now, Anglo-Saxon kings had many residences, and the primitive apparatus of government moved with the king as he journeyed among his estates. Winchester therefore was not at this time a capital any more than it was an urban community. It was, however, one of the more important royal residences, perhaps because of its church and the city's close association with the royal house.

Beginning toward the close of the eighth century England was subjected to a series of Viking attacks that steadily increased in severity. By the middle of the ninth century these had evolved into a phase of extensive Scandinavian settlement. Alone among the English kingdoms Wessex survived. After the Battle of Edington in 878 and the Treaty of Wedmore in the same year King Alfred, who ruled Wessex from 871 to 899, set about bolstering the defenses of his kingdom. Alfred's strategy was based on a series of "burhs," or fortified places, so located that no part of Wessex was more than 20 miles from one of them. The burhs were of several kinds: simple forts, refurbished Roman fortresses, newly created towns and former Roman towns that had been refortified and replanned. Winchester was in the last category.

The Roman defenses of the city were brought back into commission and the city gates repaired or rebuilt. Within the walls a new street system was laid out along the axis of the main east-west street; this street had survived in modified form from the Roman period. The other new streets, however, had no connection with the Roman pattern, which had long since vanished. The elements of the new pattern—the east-west High Street, the back streets parallel to it and the intersecting north-south streets—

ROW OF SMALL DWELLINGS, built in the 13th century, lies exposed by excavation. Only the earth floors and the clay sills of walls have survived. Medieval records place cloth-finishing works in this area; the cottages may have housed workers in the industry.

have remained in use with minor changes down to the present. A fourth element, a street running around the entire city inside the wall and providing direct access to the city's perimeter defenses in time of war, is partly lost today. As its original function became unnecessary it was built on in many places.

The ninth-century street plan shows that the entire walled area of the Roman city—143 acres—was brought back into use by the end of the century. Similar street systems can be seen in many of the other burhs set up by Alfred, and there can be no doubt that they represent a deliberate intent to establish urban communities; this English episode of organized town foundation is without parallel in early medieval Europe. The blocks formed by the new streets seem to have represented land apportioned for permanent settlement. In such places military effectiveness was to be secured by economic success.

Not all Alfred's burhs were successful, but Winchester never looked back. By the 960's the privacy of its monasteries had to be protected against a rising tide of urban life. Before the end of the century several city streets were named after the trades practiced in them. There was a Tanner Street, a Fleshmonger Street, a Shieldmaker Street and later a Shoemaker Street (to give their names in modern English), and suburbs were growing outside each of the city's five gates.

The southeastern quarter of Winchester gave the city its unique character. Here, 100 years before the Norman Conquest, was the most remarkable group of royal and ecclesiastical buildings in Anglo-Saxon England. Edward the Elder (899–924) founded New Minster and Nunnaminster, that is, a "nuns' minster." In the reign of King Edgar (959–975), Old Minster, New Minster and Nunnaminster were reformed and reconstructed. The bishop's palace was established in the same quarter of the city at about the same time, and between 971 and 994 Old Minster was entirely rebuilt. By this time written evidence at last confirms the existence of the royal palace immediately east of the cathedral.

It was in these buildings toward the end of the Anglo-Saxon period that the apparatus of a centralized English state began to emerge. By the reign of Cnut, or Canute (king of both England and Denmark from 1016 to 1035), Winchester had become the permanent repository of the king's treasure. The time of Edward the Confessor (1042–1066) may have seen the emergence of an embryo financial and secretarial administration. The cathedral continued its ancient association with the ruling house: Cnut was buried in it in 1035 and Edward was crowned there at Easter, 1043, thus formalizing his accession the preceding year. Even before the Norman Conquest the custom seems to have been established of the king of England's wearing his crown in Winchester Cathedral at Easter, the most important feast of the Christian year.

ANGLO-SAXON HOUSE, some 23 feet square, may have been built around A.D. 800. The four corners and the doorway incorporate masonry, much of it taken from Roman buildings, but the walls are mainly courses of flint rubble. The two graves (*right*) continue under wall; antedating the house construction, they form part of a cemetery of seventh century.

No other place in England and few places in all Europe played such a central role in the life of a state during the 11th century. Yet Winchester was not the largest city in the realm. It was perhaps fourth in size and economic power, being surpassed by London, York and Lincoln in that order. Yet it was emerging as a kind of national capital, a distinction that was destined to pass to Westminster and London in the century that followed.

Victorious at Hastings on October 14, 1066, William the Conqueror seized Winchester without opposition in November, opening the way for the surrender of London and his coronation in Westminster Abbey on Christmas Day. The effects of the Conquest on Winchester were as complex as they were considerable. In the larger buildings, in the composition of the upper levels of urban society and in social fashion there were profound changes. In administration, in the bulk of the population and in the basic fabric of the houses and the streetscape there was essential continuity. If for many in Winchester the immediate dislocation caused by the Conquest and the appropriation of land for new buildings was serious, the massive Norman financial investment in major public works during the remainder of the century and the presence of royal officials, barons and magnates of the newly rich Anglo-Norman aristocracy ensured for the city a rapid recovery and a clear improvement in its wealth and status.

By about 1100 the ancient role of Winchester as a royal center had been given new emphasis. In February, 1067, a Norman castle had been begun at the point where the Roman defenses at the southwest corner of the city formed a salient. In about 1070 the Anglo-Saxon royal palace was extended northward to High Street and doubled in area, the additional space being required for the construction of the Conqueror's hall and palace. East of the palace the total rebuilding of Old Minster was begun in 1079. The eastern part of the new cathedral was dedicated 14 years later, in 1093, and the entire project was completed in 30 or 40 years.

The Norman cathedral demonstrated most clearly, as perhaps its builders had intended, not only the eminent role of the city but also the finality of the Norman acquisition of the Anglo-Saxon

SITE OF OLD MINSTER, the principal cathedral church of the Anglo-Saxon kingdom of Wessex, is seen under excavation (*left*) in this aerial photograph. The excavation lies to the north of the cathedral built by the Normans following their conquest of England.

MORE THAN 1,100 REINTERRED SKELETONS were found near the west end of the cathedral. In digging foundations for the Norman cathedral the builders disturbed many burials. In filling the trench dug to gather stone from Old Minster for use in the new building they disposed of the disturbed remains. Skulls were placed toward west according to tradition, but other bones were jumbled.

state. The new cathedral was more than 500 feet long, making it larger than any other church in England or Normandy, longer than old St. Peter's or any of the churches on the pilgrims' route to Santiago de Compostela in Spain. Only the contemporary abbey church built by St. Hugh at Cluny in Burgundy was longer.

With the building of the castle, the rebuilding of the palace and the cathedral, the repair and reconstruction of New Minster and Nunnaminster (renamed St. Mary's Abbey), Winchester in about 1100 was a principal residence of the Norman kings, the seat of the royal administration and a center of great ecclesiastical importance. Englishmen had yielded place to Normans in the houses along the most important streets of the city. The English had also adopted Norman fashions to such an extent that 70 percent of the citizens' names recorded in about 1110 were foreign, whereas only 15 percent had been before the Conquest. The English were nonetheless still prominent in affairs. Winchester's mint was now second in importance only to London's, and the moneyers, whose ranks included the leading burgesses and property owners in the city, were almost all English.

Winchester probably reached its zenith in the early years of the 12th century. After 1104 Henry I abandoned the custom of the annual Easter crown-wearing at the cathedral, a practice that had been regularly observed by his predecessors. Royal interest shifted from the palace in the center of the city, in intimate contact with the cathedral, to the new castle on the hill beside the wall. By the 1130's the palace was no longer a royal residence; it may by then have passed to the bishop, whose role in city affairs was now increasing. At that time the rebuilding of the episcopal palace at Wolvesey in the southeastern corner of the city was undertaken. Successive kings also extended the period over which the bishops of Winchester might enjoy the profits of St. Giles Fair, held on the hill east of the city. The three days originally granted by William Rufus in 1098 were increased to 16 days under Henry II. Although the fair was probably of pre-Conquest origin, its heyday came in the 13th century, when it was one of the most important fairs in England and was attended by traders from many parts of Europe.

In the civil war of 1141 Winchester was seriously damaged. The old royal palace was burned down, and St. Mary's and Hyde Abbey and many parish churches and private houses suffered severely when the city was sacked by the London contingent supporting the king. By that time London had been the largest and wealthiest city in England for some 200 years. Westminster had emerged as a royal residence in the 11th century and increased greatly in importance with the rebuilding of the Abbey by Edward the Confessor and his burial there in 1066. By the middle of the 12th century an increasing number of administrative functions were located at Westminster. Finally in the 1180's even the tradition of Winchester as the site of the royal treasury gave way, and the king's treasure was transferred to London.

The close link between Winchester and the crown was now severed. The castle remained an important royal residence, often embellished and often visited, but it was of no more importance than many another great house. The economy of the city held up during the rest of the 12th century, but there are signs of trouble in the 13th century, as first the western suburb and then the western neighborhood within the walls began to decline. Large areas of the city passed into religious hands. By the 14th century considerable tracts within the walls were no longer built up. A petition of 1440 cited the destruction of 11 streets, 17 parish churches and 987 houses as a result of pestilence and the withdrawal of trade. Where Winchester had occupied second place among English cities at the end of the 11th century, by 1200 it was sixth or lower. By 1334 it was 14th, by 1377 it was 29th and by 1527 it was 37th. Many of the city parishes were amalgamated in the early 16th century, but it was the suppression of the monasteries in 1536–1539 that wrought the greatest changes, removing three monastic communities, four friaries and several lesser institutions.

The built-up area of the city was by now confined to the central and eastern parts of High Street, to the adjacent areas of the side streets, to the main north-south street and to the eastern and southern suburbs. So it was to remain for three centuries. By the early 19th century a revival had begun, encouraged by the growing role of Winchester as a garrison town and by the advent of the railway in 1839.

Ancient Winchester now lies under the streets and buildings of an active and dynamic modern urban center. Reconstruction, redevelopment and the redesign of approach roads and internal streets are destroying the evidence of the city's past at a quantifiable rate. The pattern of the city's Roman-built defenses was effectively breached for the first time only in 1939. By 1950, 2 percent of the defenses had been destroyed and by 1965, 8 percent. By 1980 completion of the city's traffic plan will have raised this figure to 35 percent. A third of the 2,000-year-old defensive system will have been removed in 40 years. There are many similar examples.

In such a situation the raw material for the study of urban evolution has to be rescued now or not at all. Winchester is exceptionally rich in written records, but they barely touch the first 1,000 years of the community's existence, its Iron Age and Roman cycles and its Anglo-Saxon rebirth. Historical data only become full during the time of Winchester's long medieval decline. This is a pattern that is repeated all over Europe. The basic evidence for the study of urban origins and growth, for the waxing and waning of our towns and cities, has not been recognized until the last moment before its destruction. In London not more than 15 years remain in which to undertake an inquiry that will never again be possible. The example of Winchester may show what can be won. It also shows how much may be lost.

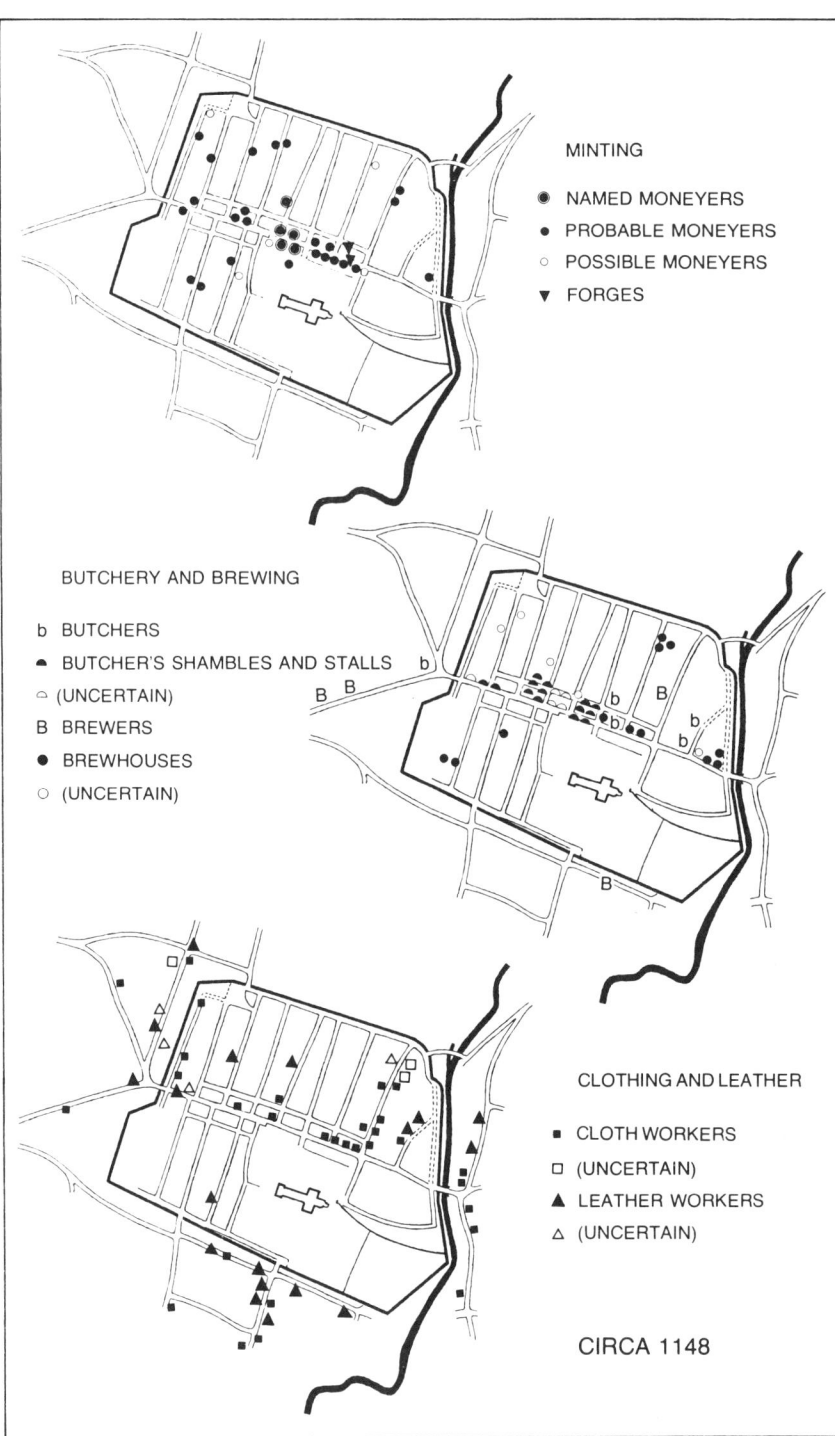

URBAN TRADES AND INDUSTRIES in mid-12th-century Winchester included victualing and manufacture in addition to the minting of coins. Five properties, four of them on High Street, were occupied by moneyers whose names appear in an 1148 survey. Another 27 properties are identifiable as probably or possibly moneyers', and two moneyers' forges are known.

The Planning of a Maya Ceremonial Center

by Norman Hammond
May 1972

The center at Lubaantún in British Honduras called for a huge investment in labor and materials. When a choice had to be made between cutting costs and adhering to the plan, the plan won out

Among the pre-Columbian civilizations of the New World the Aztec and Inca empires that the conquistadors overthrew are commonly believed to have been the most advanced, but this distinction may well belong to the Maya, whose culture reached its apogee in the first millennium of the Christian Era during what is known as the Classic period. The brilliance of Maya aesthetics is apparent in Classic stucco work, vase-painting and fresco; the intellectual achievements of the Classic period include not only a written language but also calendric and astronomical studies of a high order. Classic Maya civilization was centered in the lowland jungle province of Petén in Guatemala and in adjacent Belize (British Honduras), extending northward and westward into Mexico and southward and eastward into Honduras and El Salvador.

The civilization of the Classic period flourished within a surprisingly loose framework compared, for example, with the partly contemporaneous pre-Columbian culture centered on Teotihuacán a few hundred miles away in the Valley of Mexico. In the first half of the first millennium the rulers of Teotihuacán built one of the largest and most precisely planned urban complexes known in ancient times [see the article "Teotihuacán," by René Millon, beginning on page 221]. Where the Maya held sway in the tropical lowlands, however, there were no such cities. The numerous population was scattered among widely dispersed farmers' hamlets. Living in relative isolation and sheltered in dwellings built of perishable materials, the great majority of the Maya supported themselves by raising crops (principally maize and beans) in forest clearings they prepared for planting by the slash-and-burn method. At intervals were a few clusters of more permanent structures built of stone, but these were not cities in any conventional sense; the most spectacular of their masonry edifices are lofty pyramids like those the first Spaniards saw used as temples in Aztec Mexico. As a result it has become customary to call these clusters of stone buildings "ceremonial centers."

From an economic viewpoint the construction of a Maya ceremonial center constituted an enormous investment in energy and materials. More than a century of archaeological investigation has shown that within a range of regional variation the centers are all much alike architecturally. Where uneven terrain had to be leveled, this was achieved by building foundation platforms of rough stone rubble retained by masonry walls. Rising from these foundations are stone structures arrayed around a number of open plazas.

Each structure consists of a freestanding masonry wall that encloses a more or less rectangular area, filled with rubble up to the height of the retaining wall; in general the greater the area enclosed, the higher the wall. On top of these structures stood superstructures of various kinds. It is customary to call the superstructures on high pyramidal substructures "temples" and those on lower and more extensive substructures "palaces." Most of the superstructures on lower and smaller substructures, having been made of perishable materials, have entirely disappeared; many are known to have been residences, whereas others are buildings of unknown purpose.

Amid the cluster of interconnected plazas with structures grouped around them, each Maya center is likely to have one or more "ball courts." Unlike the term palace, the term ball court is not guesswork. It is known from sculptured monuments that these distinctive structures were used for playing a game that might be described as a cross between volleyball and soccer. Each ball court consists of a pair of steep rubble mounds faced with masonry; these mounds form the sides of a long, narrow field of play where the Maya engaged in the ritual contest they called *pok-ta-pok*.

In most Maya centers built during the Classic period the plaza in front of the major temple pyramid contained sculptured stone monuments that archaeologists call by the Greek name "stelae." These bear the images of rulers, some of them shown with their captives, and long hieroglyphic inscriptions that seem to contain historical information. The portions of the inscriptions that record dates in Maya calendric notation can be read. The dates inscribed on stelae and on sculptured altars at the Classic sites of Piedras Negras and Yaxchilán, two ceremonial centers on the Usumacinta River in the Petén region, and Quiriguá, a third center to the southeast, seem to record events in the lives of several rulers. The first of these dated monuments was erected during the third century of the Christian Era and the last at the end of the ninth century.

The emphasis in recent years on settlement-pattern research in the Maya area has resulted in the common presumption that the location and layout of ceremonial centers and the distribution of settlements around them are due solely to environmental dictates, without the deliberate planning apparent in such places as Teotihuacán. On the other hand, the social investment in labor and materials required for the construction of such a center suggests that a certain amount of consideration must have gone into the work: the marshaling of labor, the specification of dimensions, the collecting of vast amounts of rubble fill and masonry facing blocks, and the feeding of all these things into the construction program. The successful integration of such elements and the abilities of a range of specialized artisans argues strongly in favor of a preordained plan, and one that specified the layout and subsequent function of the site.

My opportunity to seek evidence for Maya planning came recently. The occasion was the surveying and excavation of Lubaantún, a small Maya ceremonial center in the Rio Grande basin of southern Belize. Field studies were pursued there, primarily under the sponsorship of the University of Cambridge and the Peabody Museum of Archaeology and Ethnology of Harvard University, in 1970. Three main programs were undertaken. The first was the detailed mapping of the center and of a sample of the surrounding settlement area; this work was done by Michael Walton, a professional architect, and Basilio Ah, a local Mopan Maya Indian with previous mapping experience. The second program called for excavation at the center to determine both the sequence of construction and the dates of occupation. The third was an ecological survey of the Rio Grande region, including a study of the local geology by John Hazelden of the University of Cambridge, to determine what kinds of natural resources—building stone, materials for tools, forest products for construction, plants for medicine and ritual, wild game and other foodstuffs—were or had once been locally available.

Lubaantún lies in the foothill zone of the Maya Mountains [*see illustration on opposite page*]; it occupies a long sloping ridge that runs from north to south. To the east and west the ridge falls away steeply and is bounded by creeks. The slope of the ridge is gradual, eventually descending sharply to the level of the Rio Columbia, a branch of the Rio Grande that passes a few hundred meters south of the site. Stream erosion has carved the surrounding land into a maze of low, round-topped hillocks; as a result the ridge is the only fairly level tract of any size in the area.

The region around Lubaantún is well endowed with natural resources. The Rio Columbia contains an abundance of freshwater mollusks. It also provides a waterway, navigable by canoe, that runs via the Rio Grande all the way to the Caribbean; the seacoast is some 25 kilometers east of Lubaantún as the crow flies. Hazelden's survey showed that thinly bedded sandstone, limestone and siltstone are available along the riverbanks and in the nearby foothills, and that all the stone needed for the center could have been quarried within a radius of three kilometers. Potter's clay is also found along the river, and such forest products as copal gum, valued by the Maya as incense, can be gathered on the wooded coastal plain. Moreover, the foothill zone where Lubaantún is situated has some of the most fertile soil in all southern Belize. There is game in the hills and on the coastal plain, waterfowl in swampy areas, and mollusks, crustaceans and fish along the coast. The canoe route to the coast covers 90 kilometers, or almost four times the straight-line distance, and might be thought to have been traveled infrequently by the people of Lubaantún. When Elizabeth S. Wing of the Florida State Museum analyzed the animal remains we recovered at the ceremonial center, however, she found that nearly 40 percent of them were of marine origin.

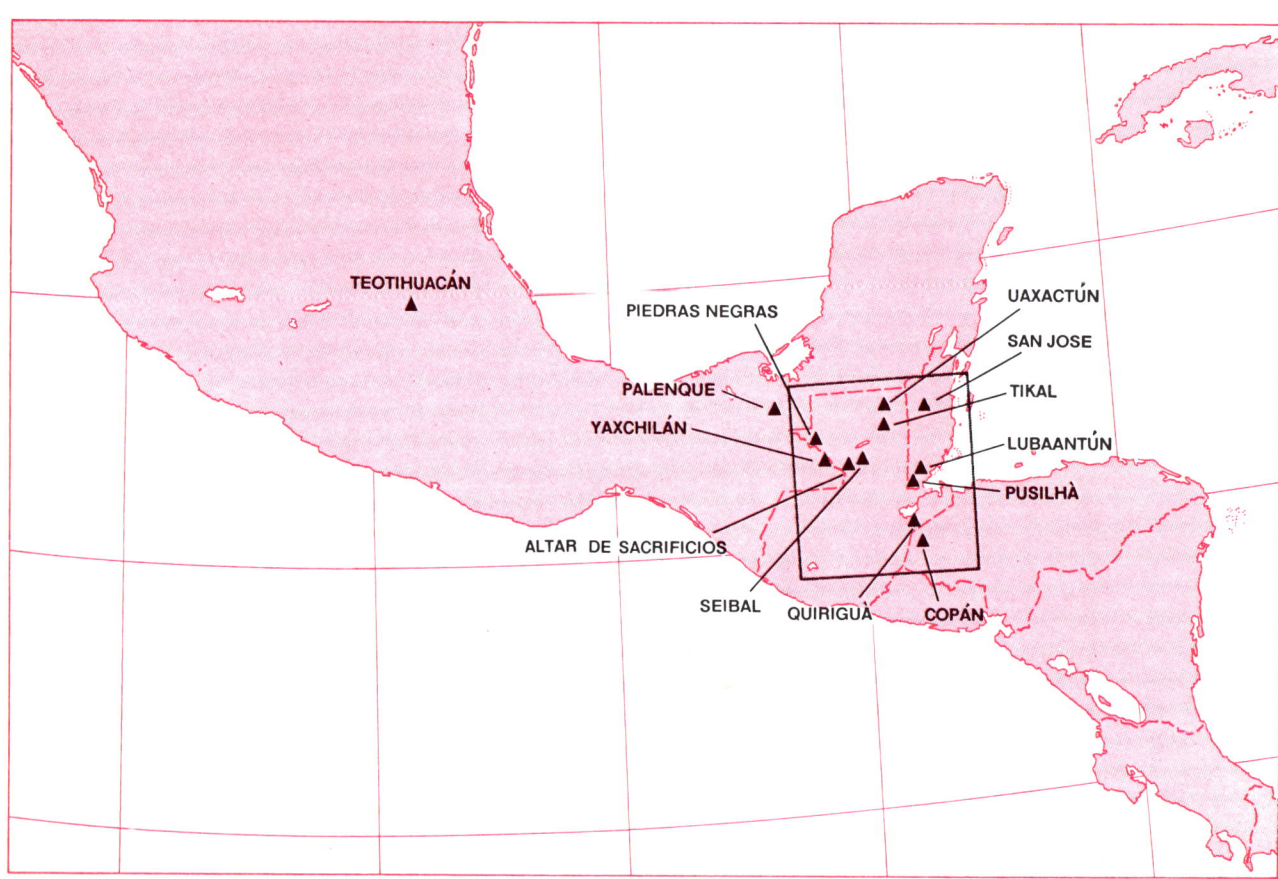

PETÉN LOWLANDS of northern Guatemala border on Mexico to the north and west and on Honduras and British Honduras to the south and east. Twelve lowland Maya centers of the Classic period are shown; the region is shown in more detail on the opposite page.

Our excavations showed that when the Lubaantún center was founded early in the eighth century, it consisted of a single large platform covering an area of some 2,500 square meters on the part of the ridge that was later occupied by an open plaza we have designated Plaza IV [see "b" in illustration on pages 100 and 101]. On the north side of this first platform stood a series of narrow rubble-filled substructures faced with stone. We were surprised to find that the original construction had begun so late; by early in the eighth century the Late Classic florescence of Maya civilization was already at its height. As will be seen, the lateness of the date has important historical implications.

In any event the first platform at the center was almost completely buried under later construction. In the second phase of the work two more large platforms were built north and south of the first, and large plaza areas were laid out beyond the north platform [see "c" in illustration on pages 100 and 101], quadrupling the area of Lubaantún. At one side of the north platform, facing what was later to be Plaza IV, the builders raised their first temple pyramid. We have designated it Structure 12. Its present size is the result of later construction that has entirely engulfed the original pyramid. Construction of a ball court on the southern extension completed the second-phase work at Lubaantún.

The first undeniable evidence that planning outweighed expediency in the building of the center appeared during the third phase of construction. Early work during the third phase had extended the north platform southward until it covered most of the 2,500-square-meter platform built in the first phase. It was then decided to enlarge the first pyramid and add two new ones. The size of these, as planned, meant that space in the center of the site was going to be very short indeed; for the first time a crucial decision was forced on the rulers of Lubaantún. Was the site to be extended still farther north and south along the ridge, where the shallow curve of the crest meant that a large surface area could be gained with the construction of a relatively shallow platform? Or was centralization more important than economy and should the center be expanded laterally even though the acquisition of a small area meant the construction of high platforms and the investment of a prodigious amount of labor and material resources? The latter decision was taken, and the growth of Lubaantún changed

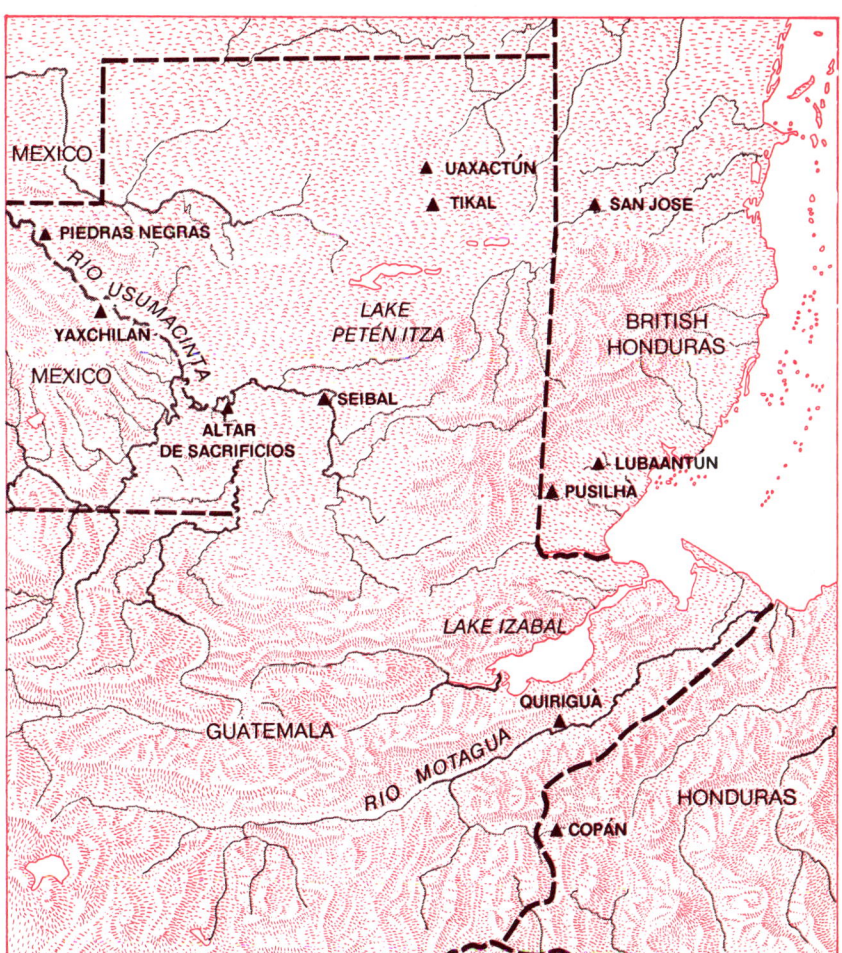

LUBAANTÚN IS SITUATED in the foothills of the Maya Mountains, an isolated highland area in southern British Honduras. It is among the last of the centers built by the Maya.

from modification of the local topography to the creation of an artificial topography [see "d" in illustration on pages 100 and 101]. The retaining walls that gained the builders six meters' horizontal space to the east and west are multiterraced and more than 11 meters high. The amount of rubble that fills the space between ridge slope and wall must exceed 3,000 cubic meters. It is hard to imagine clearer proof that the planned layout of Lubaantún was sufficiently important to force the builders to overcome the limitations of local topography.

In the fourth phase of construction at the center still more artificial topography was created. Just beyond the newly extended main platform was a gully cut by a small stream on the west side of the ridge. This watercourse was now covered by rubble-filled platforms, forming a series of broad plazas that led down the steep slope almost to the bank of the creek at the bottom [see "e" in illustration on pages 100 and 101]. Whether the most southerly part of this extension was built during the fourth phase or the fifth remains uncertain. In any event the major enterprise during the fifth and final phase of construction at Lubaantún was the refurbishing of the central part of the site. Broad staircases were built at the north and south ends of Plaza V, and a second ball court was constructed on a new platform east of the plaza. At the same time a new staircase was added to Structure 12, the largest of the temple pyramids at the site.

The building of Lubaantún, which had been in progress for between 100 and 150 years, was now essentially complete. Begun early in the eighth century, the work ended not long before the ceremonial center was abandoned sometime between A.D. 850 and 900. The plan of Lubaantún that we have now is a palimpsest, so to speak, of all five periods, but it is essentially the plan of the site as it was functioning at the time of its abandonment. It is only at this period that we can fully comprehend the zonal structure and traffic pattern within the ceremonial center.

As a result of the mapping project we

know not only the total number of edifices that were built at Lubaantún but also exactly where they stood in relation to one another and the exact dimensions of each. The structures range in height from as little as 20 centimeters to more than 12 meters and in basal area from 40 square meters to more than 500 square meters. As at other Maya ceremonial centers, each structure served as a foundation for some kind of superstructure. Elsewhere a number of these superstructures, in particular the temples and palaces, were built of stone and still survive. At Lubaantún, however, all the superstructures apparently were built of wood and no longer exist. They presumably had walls of poles and roofs of palm thatch, like the Maya houses in the vicinity today. Fragments of the clay that was daubed on the pole walls of one temple have been preserved by fire; the impressions show that the poles were a little over three inches in diameter.

When we compared the dimensions of the various foundation structures, we found that they fell into four distinct clusters. The pyramids are at the top of the scale; the smallest of the three has a basal area of more than 500 square meters and is more than five meters high. Our system of classification placed structures this large or larger in the "religious" category. At the bottom of the scale are numerous small, low structures, all less than 1.2 meters high and 100 square me-

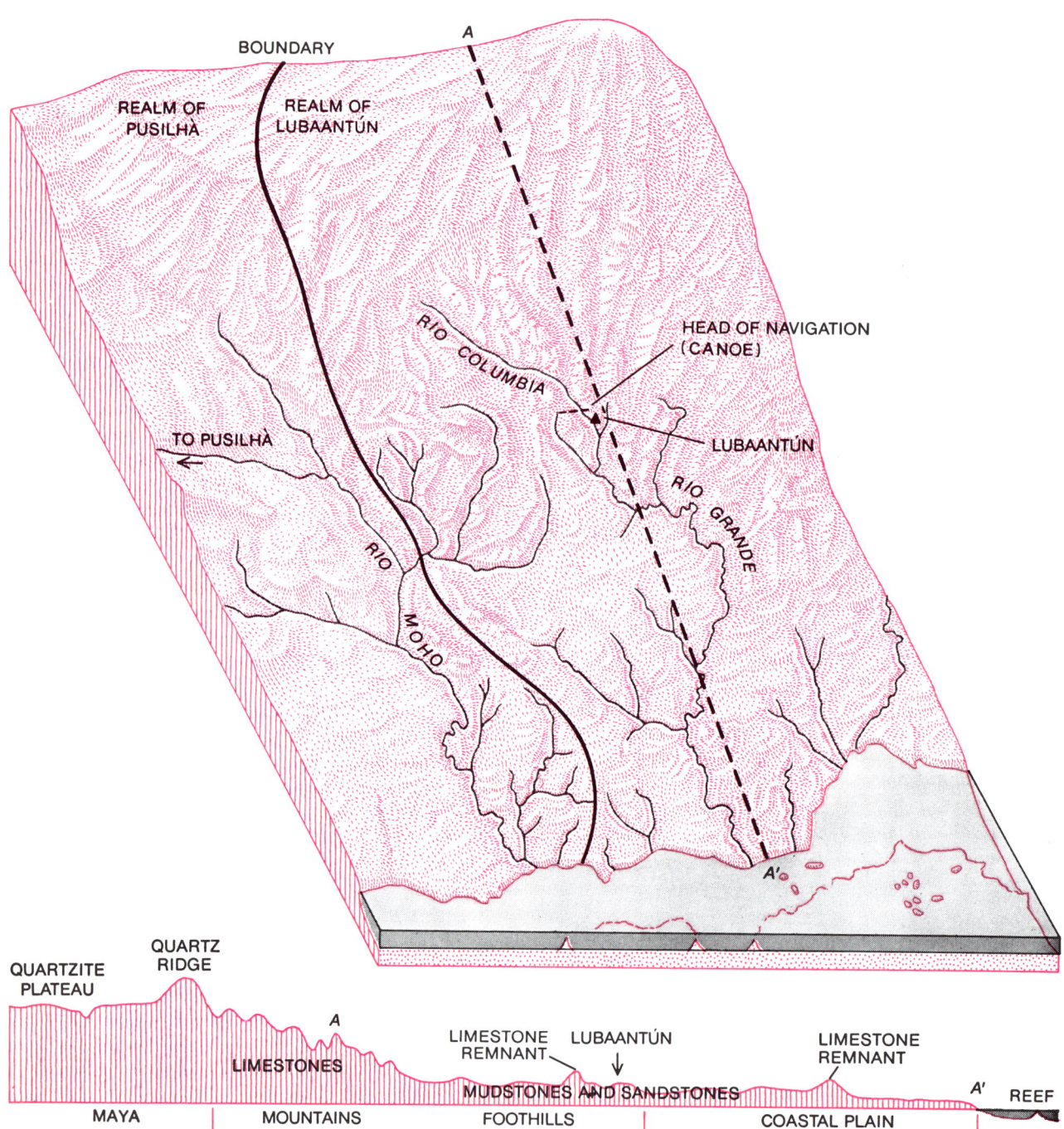

REALM OF LUBAANTÚN extended northwest some 25 kilometers from the foothills of the Maya Mountains to the highland plateau and southeast another 25 kilometers to the low-lying Caribbean coast and the sheltered waters of the barrier reef offshore (see cross section at bottom). The region controlled by the ceremonial center consisted of some 1,600 square kilometers, and the population may have numbered 50,000. The soil in the foothills was fertile, and the realm was rich in raw materials and wild foods.

ters in area. We assume that they were house foundations and have classified them as "residences." Between these extremes are two groups of structures with dimensions that overlap with respect to area but not with respect to height. The structures of the smaller group range from more than 1.2 meters in height to less than two meters; none is less than 150 or more than 280 square meters in basal area. On the basis of size and location we have dubbed this group of structures "elite residences." The structures of the larger group, ranging in height from two to 3.6 meters with a basal area as large as 330 square meters, include the two Lubaantún ball courts and a number of other structures that are neither obviously residential nor obviously ritual. We have placed all of them in a nonspecific category: "ceremonial structures."

When we marked the structures on the site map according to this four-category classification, an interesting correlation emerged. The structures surrounding any particular plaza usually belonged in the same category. Plaza IV, with its three pyramids, is a prime example; it is the only one of the 20 plazas at Lubaantún that belongs in the "religious" category. Furthermore, the five plazas immediately contiguous to Plaza IV all belong to the "ceremonial" category, and six of the seven most remote plazas at the site fall in the "residential" category. The master plan for Lubaantún seems to have called for a religious core surrounded by an inner zone of ceremonial plazas and an outer zone of residences. Such a layout follows a simple concentric-zone model, modified at Lubaantún only by the requirements of topography.

Common sense suggests that the traffic plan for such a concentric-zone model would call for residential areas with low accessibility and public areas with high accessibility. Religious areas would be either accessible or secluded depending on the nature of the cult. For example, if access to a central religious area was restricted, this fact would suggest worship of an exclusive and elitist nature.

In order to test this hypothesis we conducted a topological analysis of the potential traffic flow at Lubaantún without regard for the presumed functions of the plazas as deduced from the categories of structures surrounding them. Our first step was to reduce the pattern of the major plazas and their interconnections to a planar graph [see graph in bottom illustration at right]. The graph en-

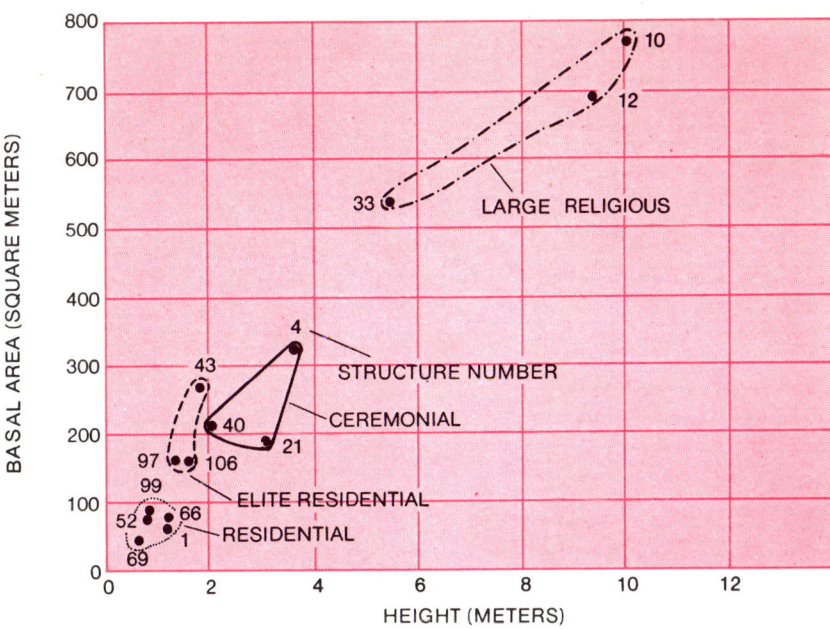

MEASUREMENT OF THE STRUCTURES at Lubaantún showed a proportional relation between height and basal area. When both measurements are plotted on a graph, the structures typically fall within one of four clusters. The pyramids of Plaza IV cover the most area and are the highest of all the structures at the site. Adjacent to the more remote plazas were the lowest and smallest structures; these had presumably been house foundations. Of the structures in two intermediate clusters, the higher were probably foundations for buildings that served "ceremonial" purposes; the lower may have been occupied by the elite.

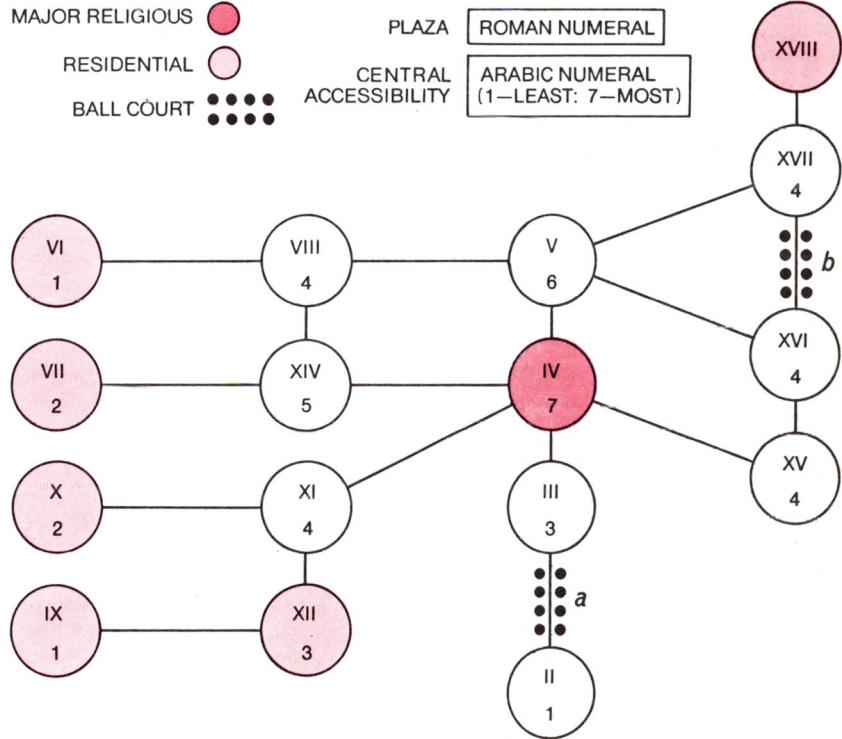

PLANAR GRAPH OF THE PRINCIPAL PLAZAS at Lubaantún and their interconnections allowed a topological analysis of the accessibility and centrality of each. An index of central accessibility showed that Plaza IV, the religious center of the site, was the most centrally accessible, with a maximum index value of 7. Of the eight least accessible plazas, all with an index value no greater than 3, six were bordered by small, low structures that were probably occupied by houses. A major difference is evident between the first ball court at the site, which was quite private (a), and the second, which was more public (b).

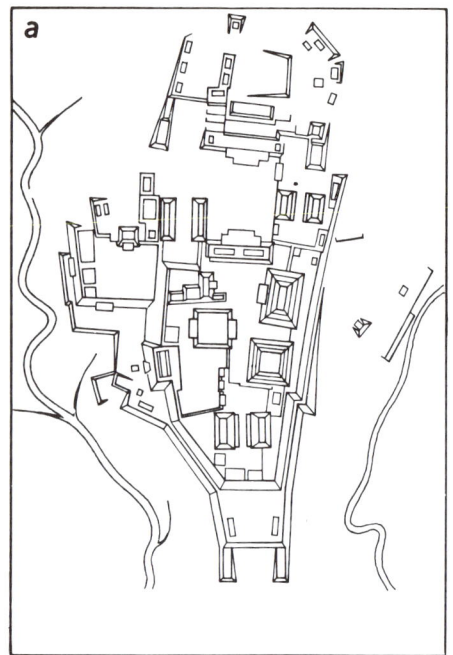 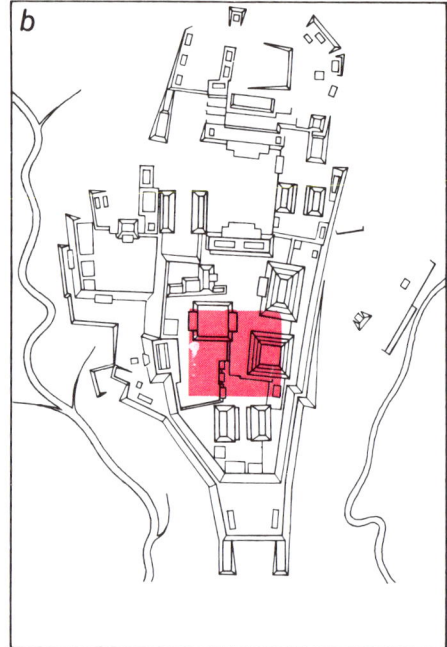 

LUBAANTÚN GREW in the five phases outlined in this sequence of illustrations. The center after its completion is shown schematically at far left (*a*). In the first construction phase (*b*) a rectangular platform covering 2,500 square meters was built astride the north-south ridge that forms the long axis of the site. During the second phase (*c*) another platform was added to the south of the first, and plaza areas and a third platform were added to the north. The first pyramid at the site was built on one side of the north platform and the first ball court was built on the south platform. During the third phase (*d*) a southerly addition to the north plat-

abled us to calculate for each plaza an index of centrality and an index of accessibility. Combined, these indexes provided a rating of central-accessibility that ranged from a minimum value of 1 to a maximum value of 7.

We then compared the topological analysis with our estimates of the functions served by the various plazas. Our hypothesis of low accessibility in residential areas was confirmed. The most secluded of all the plazas, with the minimum rating of 1, were the plazas numbered VI, IX and XVIII, which we had classified as residential, and Plaza II, which we had classified as ceremonial. The next most secluded, with ratings of 2 or 3, were the residential plazas numbered VII, X and XII and a second ceremonial plaza, Plaza III. The most centrally accessible plaza at the site, with the maximum rating of 7, proved to be Plaza IV, the religious center of the site.

The fact that two ceremonial plazas, Plaza III and Plaza II, were among those with minimal accessibility ratings meant that the site layout called for a striking decline in accessibility southward along the central axis of Lubaantún. The accessibility rating of Plaza III is four points lower than the rating of its neighboring plaza to the north, and the rating of Plaza II is the minimum possible. Since these two plazas form the end zones of the first ball court built at Lubaantún and because the ball court can only be reached by way of Plaza IV, the site's religious center, the question arises: Were playing and watching the ball game restricted activities?

It is known from early Spanish accounts that the Maya ball game had ritual overtones; sculptures at Chichén Itzá indicate that some matches even ended with the sacrifice of the losing players. Taking this evidence and the restricted access at Lubaantún into consideration, it seems probable that if any part of the religious practice during the early days at the ceremonial center was confined to the elite, that part was the ball game.

The Spanish accounts, however, indicate that for all its ritual overtones the ball game was open to public view. This suggests that the fact the second ball court at Lubaantún, the one constructed late in the history of the center, is located in a much more public part of the center is significant. The second court lies just off Plaza V, a highly accessible area: plazas XVII and XVIII, which are its end zones, also rate high in accessibility. Perhaps a change in Maya attitudes regarding the esoteric nature of the game occurred in the interval between the building of the first court and the building of the second. If that is what happened, the trend toward a more public ritual that seems evident in the middle of the ninth century at Lubaantún persisted throughout the post-Classic period and on down to the time of the Conquest.

In summary, the traffic-flow analysis confirmed our commonsense hypothesis that the center's residential areas were secluded and its public areas more accessible. Concerning the question of whether the religious observances were public or restricted, common sense had identified Plaza IV, with its three pyramids, as the religious center of Lubaantún. By showing that Plaza IV was also the most accessible plaza at the site, traffic analysis suggests unrestricted public access to religious activities.

Plaza V, just to the north, ranks next in accessibility. This open area, with its broad stairways, is perhaps the most spacious of all the plazas at Lubaantún, and its high accessibility strengthens our suspicion that, with or without the contiguous Plaza VIII, this was the marketplace for the center. Finally, the fact that for a century or more the only ball court at Lubaantún was an area with sharply restricted access suggests that, at least until very late in Classic times, the ball game was confined to an elite group within a well-stratified society.

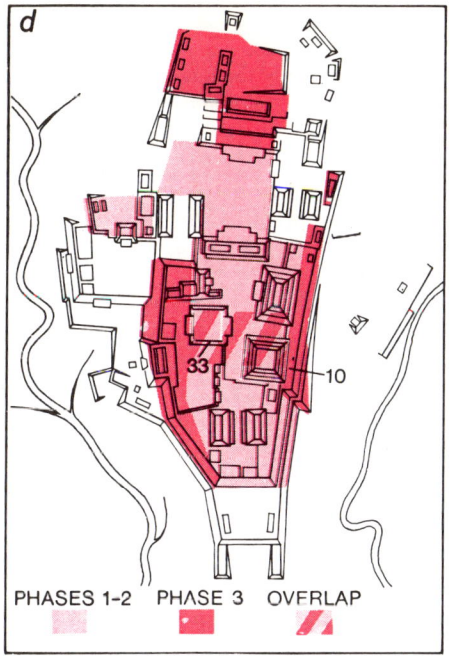
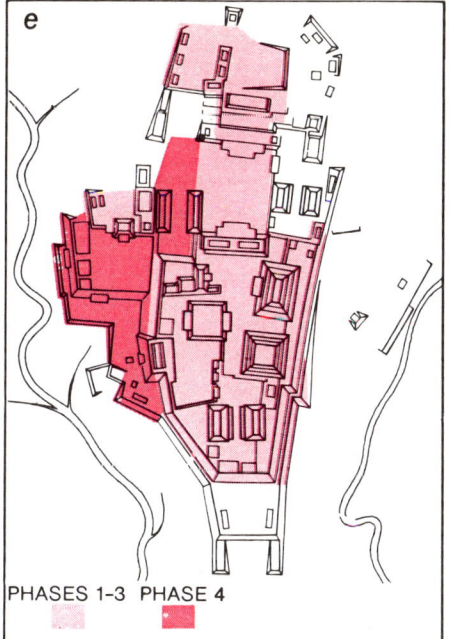
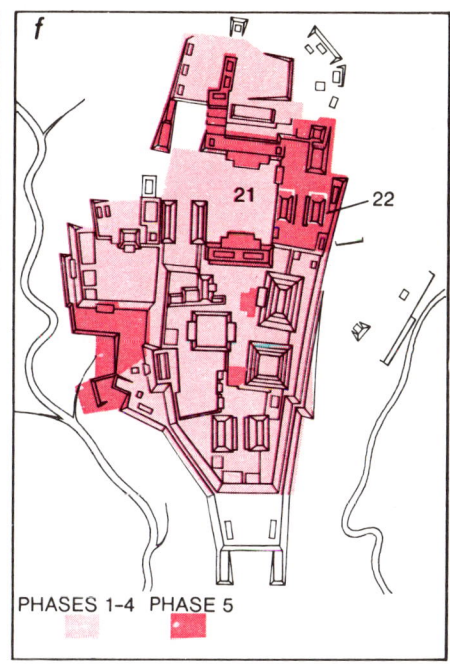

form covered up most of the first-phase platform at the site, and adequate foundations for two more pyramids were provided by new platforms built over the steep east and west slopes of the ridge. Construction in the fourth phase (*e*) included a series of platforms on the west slope that descended almost to the creek at the bottom of the ridge. In the final phase the main construction (*f*) consisted of a second ball court east of Plaza V and new staircases for Plaza V and for Structure 12, the first of the pyramids at the center. Growth of the center to the east and west regardless of the immense cost indicates the builders' adherence to a fixed plan.

Perhaps it is not too much to propose here a wider archaeological application of assessments of this kind. Analysis of the centrality and accessibility of the different areas that make up "palace" complexes in, for example, Mesopotamia or Crete or Mycenaean Greece might suggest functions quite different from those enshrined in long accepted but essentially poetic phrases such as "the queen's antechamber" or "lustral area."

Why was Lubaantún built where it was? The answer to the question is suggested by the results both of our mapping and ecological surveys and of our excavations. These show that the influence of the ceremonial center was felt not only adjacent to but well away from the site itself. Most of the low, round-topped hills on all sides of Lubaantún are surmounted by small masonry and rubble platforms; the dressed-stone retaining walls are one or two meters high and the rubble serves to level off the summit. These structures, on a smaller scale, are exactly like the great platforms at Lubaantún. Furthermore, they support house foundations in numbers sufficient to indicate that 1,200 to 1,300 people resided within a one-kilometer radius of the ceremonial center. This is scarcely a large population, but it is as densely concentrated as the local topography permits.

These hill platforms and house foundations represent a social investment in labor and materials that, although it is dispersed, is comparable to the more concentrated investment that produced the complex structures of the ceremonial center. The scale of the work also implies an adequate supply of food for the inhabitants of the district, which suggests in turn that location of the center in the belt of fertile soil along the foothills of the Maya Mountains was scarcely accidental.

Why was the center built, however, at precisely this place? The soil zone extends a considerable distance to both the northeast and the southwest, which suggests that factors in addition to the prospect of good crops must have entered into the decision to build the center here. One of the factors must have been the propinquity of the site to the Rio Columbia. Not only was the stream a source of water and the mollusks from it a reliable source of protein (their shells appeared by the thousands in our excavations) but also the head of navigation by canoe lies near Lubaantún. Goods coming upstream from the Caribbean would have been transferred from canoe to porter in this area. Moreover, this spot is also where the main overland trail along the base of the foothills crosses the river. Lubaantún was thus in a position to control canoe traffic to and from the coast and overland traffic along the foothills. In effect, the center dominated the entire Rio Grande basin, a "realm" extending for some 50 kilometers from the high plateau of the Maya Mountains southeastward to the Caribbean shore. The entire realm is some 1,600 square kilometers in extent; its population may have numbered as many as 50,000.

Our excavations made it clear that Lubaantún was the center of a flourishing regional marketing system. From the Maya Mountains came the metamorphic rock used to make not only axe heads of stone but also the *manos*, or stone rollers, and *metates*, or shallow stone troughs, that are used together to grind maize. From the Caribbean coast, which was as far away in the opposite direction, came marine shells used for ornaments and the seafood that forms such a high percentage of the animal remains at the site. In addition, trade extended far beyond the frontiers of the realm. Two sources in the highlands of Guatemala, identified by Fred H. Stross of the University of California at Berkeley, provided obsidian, which can be flaked into fine blades with a razor-sharp edge. Also from the highlands came tripod *metates* made of lava. From the south came plumes from the cock quetzal to adorn the rulers of Lubaantún and from an unidentified highland source came jade for their jewels.

In exchange for these imports the inhabitants of Lubaantún evidently traded the beans of the cacao tree, which are used to make chocolate and were the universal currency of Middle America in pre-Columbian times. As I have noted, the soil around Lubaantún is fertile. A

CEREMONIAL CENTER at Lubaantún consisted of 11 major structures and many minor ones grouped around 20 plazas. A number of these are identified in the map on the opposite page by Arabic and Roman numerals respectively. Construction of the center began in the eighth century after Christ, late in the Classic Maya period, and continued for 150 years.

study of all the soils in the region in terms of their utility to the Maya of the Classic period was conducted recently by Charles Wright of the United Nations Food and Agriculture Organization. He found that Lubaantún stands in the center of the largest zone of top-quality soil for cacao-tree culture in all of southern Belize. As Spanish records attest, cacao beans were traded between this lowland area and the highlands of Guatemala in post-Conquest times. That the tree and its fruit were known in Lubaantún is apparent from a figurine of the Classic period excavated there; it depicts a musician wearing a cacao-pod pendant [see illustration at left]. It seems clear that the prosperity of the realm was in large measure due to its possession of one of the sources of this scarce product, which was in constant demand. The trade with the Guatemalan highlands, where a completely different range of resources was available, was in many ways a form of economic symbiosis, existing for the mutual benefit of both partners and fostering diplomatic as well as commercial contacts that it was mutually useful to maintain.

MUSICIAN WEARING A PENDANT in the form of a pod from the cacao tree is the subject of a figurine of the Classic period found at Lubaantún. Evidence that cacao was known to the people of Lubaantún, taken together with evidence that local soils are particularly suited to raising cacao trees, suggests that cacao beans were exchanged for foreign imports.

The question of why Lubaantún was built when it was remains unanswered. The entire Rio Grande basin appears to have been unoccupied territory until the eighth century, when the center was founded. So far not a single object made before Late Classic times, not even a potsherd, has been discovered at any site in the region. To the southwest of the Rio Grande basin another Maya site, a ceremonial center named Pusilhà, has been discovered in the basin of the Moho River. Some 20 stelae have been found there; the dates they bear range from A.D. 573 to 731. Pusilhà was therefore functioning as a ceremonial center during all of the seventh century. Moreover, the most recent of the Pusilhà stelae dates and the presence there of Lubaantún-style figurines show that the center was still occupied well after the foundation of Lubaantún.

Pusilhà was flourishing before Lubaantún was even built. This fact has given rise to a number of cause-and-effect hypotheses. According to one of them, the Maya who built Lubaantún were former residents of the Pusilhà realm who migrated northward as a re-

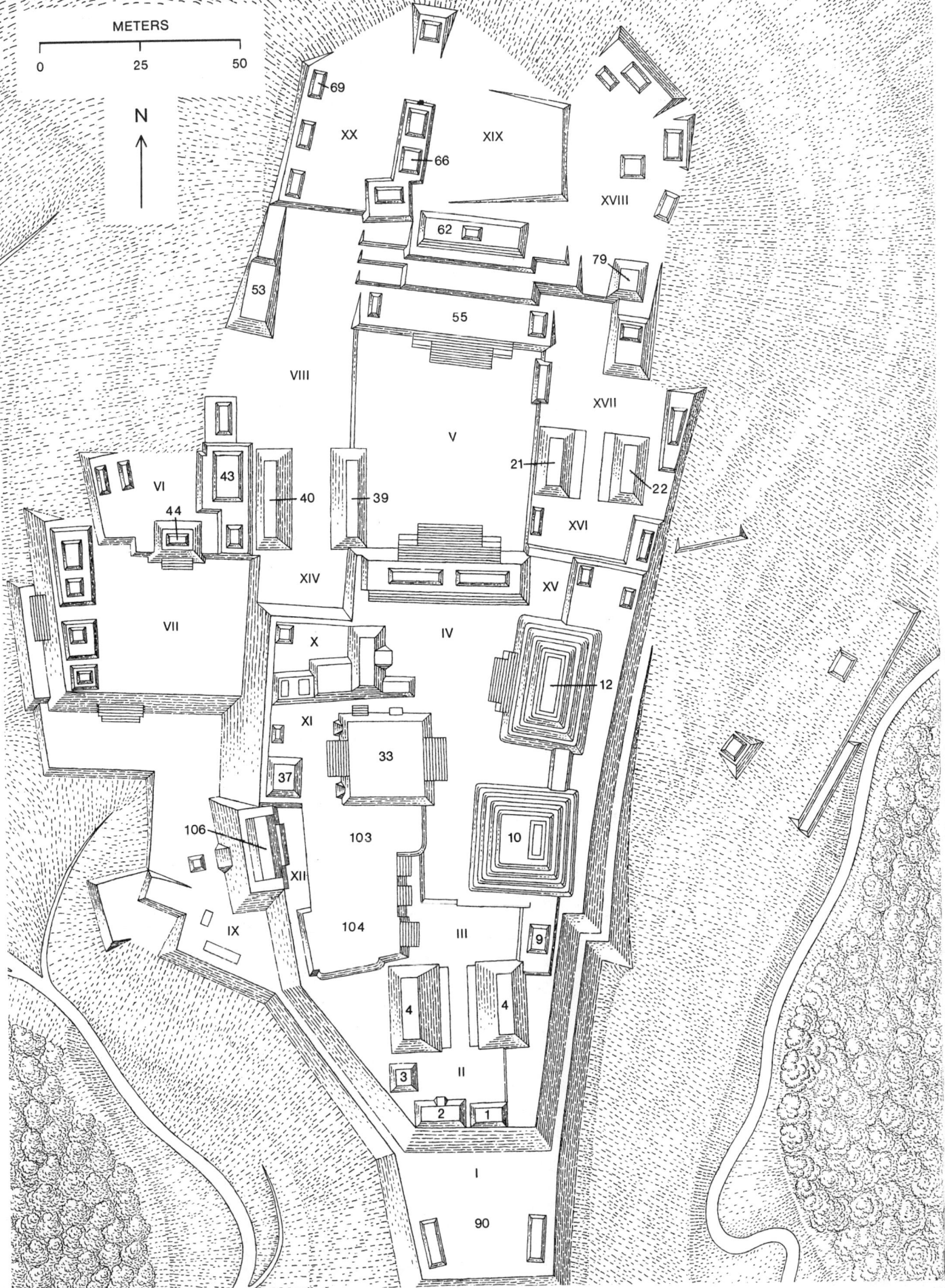

sult of population pressure or political expansion within or beyond that realm. Another hypothesis, first advanced in 1938 by Sylvanus Griswold Morley, suggested that political control had been transferred from Pusilhà to Lubaantún in the eighth century, the time when the Maya at Pusilhà ceased to raise stelae. According to the Morley hypothesis, the halt in stela-raising was evidence that the use of Pusilhà as a ceremonial center had also ceased.

The Morley hypothesis, applied more generally, has been the controlling model for much of the speculation about the collapse of Classic Maya civilization. In this view the end of the "stela cult" at each ceremonial center marked the end of the religious, political, administrative and commercial control exerted by the realm's rulers. Our studies at Lubaantún cast doubt on that line of speculation. Although this Late Classic ceremonial center exerted control over a wide realm for some 150 years, not one stela, sculptured or plain, appears to have been raised there. It thus seems clear that the presence of the stela cult was not crucial to the exercise of effective religious, political and commercial control. If a center such as Lubaantún could flourish without instituting such a cult, then other ceremonial centers could have continued to exercise authority after stelae were no longer raised. Excavation at Maya sites of the Classic period to obtain articles for carbon-14 or thermoluminescence analysis might well shed more light on the decline of Maya civilization than do hypotheses that depend on the terminal dates preserved on stelae.

The stelae cult might better be viewed as a product of ideological fashion than as an integral part of the social and economic infrastructure that supported the culture of the Maya for more than 2,000 years. Maya ceremonial centers, if Lubaantún is a fair example, drew their power not so much from the gods as from the integration of a broad range of economic resources. The economic effort may often have included, as it did at Lubaantún, the exploitation of a commodity in great demand. Seen in this light the Maya ceremonial center seems to have been more the focus of a regional marketing system and, as a result, a seat of administrative and political power than the headquarters of a primarily religious institution. In almost every aspect except population density the Maya centers equate in form and function with the preindustrial cities of the Old World.

III
CONSEQUENCES

III CONSEQUENCES

INTRODUCTION

The early cities of the Near East, Asia, and the New World all had certain organizational features in common. Each one was ruled by an elite of priests and kings. Religious and secular power often coincided in one person, a divine ruler. The elite lived in the center of the city, in the prestigious quarter where the temples and other public buildings were concentrated. The elite's sacred, and well-protected, precincts were surrounded by the workshops and dwellings of artisans and merchants. Often potters would concentrate in one quarter, metal workers in another, and so on. On the outskirts of the city lived small farmers. These early cities were centers of trade, technological innovation, and changes in social evolution as urban societies responded to increasingly advanced technology and better communications.

The early city-states of Sumer were little more than small urban centers with very restricted hinterlands. But as trade extended over larger regions and technological innovations continued apace, the size of major city-empires increased, and the extent and grandeur of their urban centers grew steadily. After the advent of ironworking, the spread of urbanization accelerated, partly because some rulers—notably the Persians and later the Romans—deliberately founded cities on existing, strategic village sites. Gideon Sjoberg, who describes the origins and evolution of cities, points out that empires were effective disseminators of city life because their rulers used cities to consolidate ceremonial, military, and political gains in the outposts of their territory. But these same cities rose and fell with the fortunes of empires. The continuity of urban life was assured by the survival of some key cities ruled by literate elites. These rulers managed to maintain their cities into more prosperous times when new political forces such as the Byzantine and Arab empires, established contact with the survivors of Roman imperialism.

The Industrial Revolution brought far-reaching changes in city life and urban civilization. Sjoberg points out that nearly 80 percent of the British now live in cities—a striking contrast to the situation in the seventeenth century. This dramatic shift toward city dwelling results from both the expansion of European power into other continents and the development of a technology based on inanimate energy sources. Sjoberg argues that the advent of experimental scientific methods in the seventeenth century linked the learning of the elite with the trial-and-error knowledge of the artisans. The resulting scientific revolution led to the Industrial Revolution and the industrial city.

When people lived as hunters and gatherers, the biosphere supported a population of no more than 10 million—less than the population of London or Tokyo today. Then some 10,000 years ago, humans began to cultivate the soil and domesticate animals, shaping the biosphere for their own purposes.

As agricultural techniques became more efficient, the world's population began to increase slowly. Population growth in turn compelled people to produce even more food, to alter the biosphere to meet their food needs. With the advent of urban civilization, human stress on the biosphere increased even more. It took 2 million years or more for the world's human population to exceed a billion souls. We added our fourth billion in only 15 years, between 1950 and 1965. The consequences of this dramatic expansion have long been predicted and observed. Much human ingenuity is going into ways of checking this explosive growth and of feeding more mouths through new agricultural methods. Lester Brown's article chronicles our progress in feeding ourselves and argues for a global effort to monitor, investigate, and regulate human relationships with the environment. Brown points out that we have developed remarkable new breeds of crops and domesticated animals to produce higher yields of food with much less land, water, labor, and fertilizer. We rely heavily on mechanization, irrigation, fertilization, and chemical control of weeds and insects. But there are dangers, too: overgrazing and soil erosion have stripped millions of square miles of agricultural land all over the world. In response to these and other consequences of our burgeoning population, we have developed the technology to divert streams and rivers, conserve the soil, and alter global climatic patterns in a conscious way. The primary question for the future, as Brown points out, is whether we can cooperate sufficiently to use our technology for the benefit of humanity.

Energy crises are nothing new in the human experience. John Nef chronicles a remarkable shift in human energy use during the sixteenth century, when Britain ran out of wood and turned to coal as a new fuel source. Britain was the first large area to experience a catastrophic shortage of wood fuel. Between A.D. 1500 and 1700, the British population nearly doubled to 6 million. The demand for firewood and house lumber jumped during that period, and there were widespread complaints of deforestation. By 1700 London housed more than 530,000 people, and one in four people was living in a town. Large settlements placed heavy demands on nearby woodland. By the end of the seventeenth century, coal had become not only Britain's major fuel, but a major export commodity as well. As early as the sixteenth century, coal was shipped south to London from Newcastle and other ports, supporting millions of domestic hearths and ultimately providing the energy basis for the Industrial Revolution. After extensive experimentation, coal-burning furnaces were eventually adopted for metal smelting. Ultimately fossil fuel became a highly efficient energy source for the textile and manufacturing industries that were the vanguard of the Industrial Revolution. During the nineteenth century, coal production rose to such an extent that people in the 1920s began to realize that coal was a finite, exhaustible resource. But just at that time, oil came into widespread use.

The world's urban civilizations have been not only profligate consumers of energy and natural resources, but catalysts for major population displacements as well. In part, these result from trading and exploitation of natural resources, but they also stem from the accentuation of an innate human tendency to migrate. The first urban civilizations developed in the Near East, in Mesopotamia and the Nile Valley. Their flourishing markets attracted traders and craftspeople from neighboring lands. Soon large cities such as Teotihuacán were supporting actual enclaves of foreign merchants who lived and worked far from their original homelands. The growth of cities accelerated a process of human migrations that had begun millions of years before. Humans have always had a tendency to migrate, for the human sociocultural mode of adaptation enables us to adapt culturally to new environments without relying on slow organic evolution. How else could the world have been peopled so rapidly? By 400,000 years ago, *Homo erectus* had settled in China and Europe as well as Africa. *Homo sapiens* had crossed into the Americas and into Australia by 30,000 years ago. The sparse human populations of hunter-gatherers adapted to every extreme of environment from Arctic cold to humid tropical rain forest. With the advent of food production, new economies and technologies led to increased migration as great technological inequalities developed between neighboring human territories. The new cities of 3000 B.C. acted as magnets, attracting traders and peasants. But the rulers of the cities needed labor forces under their direct control, so they acquired them by force—organized raiding and warfare brought back slaves and led to colonization of other lands by the conquering people. Kingsley Davis argues that all the basic types of human migration, including barbarian invasion, were prevalent in Classical times. But our own era has brought about migrations on a truly global scale, as the technological imbalances among different parts of the world have increased. Since the sixteenth and seventeenth centuries, the world as a whole has been part of the same migratory network. Davis traces the awesome consequences of the great migrations involved in European exploitation and colonization of remoter parts of the world. As he points out, migration has helped to fill the world with people. Now that the world is full, the migration patterns will change, simply because the technological imbalances between different parts of the world will deepen rather than equalize. Just what direction these changes will take, no one can predict.

Today we are living with the cumulative effects of 5,000 years of uninterrupted cultural evolution since the world's first civilization emerged in Mesopotamia. But the pace of cultural evolution has accelerated dramatically since the Industrial Revolution, and even more rapidly within the twentieth century. The world's population is now so large, and growing so rapidly, that it is questionable whether future generations will be able to collect, grow, or breed sufficient food. Despite the development of new, higher-yield crops and advanced agricultural technologies, conscious limitation of the world's population may be the only solution.

Perhaps because of population pressure the social rules of the city and civilization—evolving since Sumerian times—have begun to change again, this time with dizzying speed. These changes prompt us to ask what the future holds for civilization. Will different nations and civilizations be able to cooperate in global solutions to our collective problems? The articles in this Reader encourage us to believe that humankind will continue to rise to the challenges imposed by the breathtaking pace of our cultural evolution.

The Origin and Evolution of Cities

10

by Gideon Sjoberg
September 1965

The first cities arose some 5,500 years ago; large-scale urbanization began only about 100 years ago. The intervening steps in the evolution of cities were nonetheless a prerequisite for modern urban societies

Men began to live in cities some 5,500 years ago. As the preceding article relates, however, the proportion of the human population concentrated in cities did not begin to increase significantly until about 100 years ago. These facts raise two questions that this article proposes to answer. First, what factors brought about the origin of cities? Second, through what evolutionary stages did cities pass before the modern epoch of urbanization? The answers to these questions are intimately related to three major levels of human organization, each of which is characterized by its own technological, economic, social and political patterns. The least complex of the three—the "folk society"—is preurban and even preliterate; it consists typically of small numbers of people, gathered in self-sufficient homogeneous groups, with their energies wholly (or almost wholly) absorbed by the quest for food. Under such conditions there is little or no surplus of food; consequently the folk society permits little or no specialization of labor or distinction of class.

Although some folk societies still exist today, similar human groups began the slow process of evolving into more complex societies millenniums ago, through settlement in villages and through advances in technology and organizational structure. This gave rise to the second level of organization: civilized preindustrial, or "feudal," society. Here there is a surplus of food because of the selective cultivation of grains—high in yield, rich in biological energy and suited to long-term storage—and often also because of the practice of animal husbandry. The food surplus permits both the specialization of labor and the kind of class structure that can, for instance, provide the leadership and command the manpower to develop and maintain extensive irrigation systems (which in turn make possible further increases in the food supply). Most preindustrial societies possess metallurgy, the plow and the wheel—devices, or the means of creating devices, that multiply both the production and the distribution of agricultural surpluses.

Two other elements of prime importance characterize the civilized preindustrial stage of organization. One is writing: not only the simple keeping of accounts but also the recording of historical events, law, literature and religious beliefs. Literacy, however, is usually confined to a leisured elite. The other element is that this stage of organization has only a few sources of energy other than the muscles of men and livestock; the later preindustrial societies harnessed the force of the wind to sail the seas and grind grain and also made use of water power.

It was in the context of this second type of society that the world's first cities developed. Although preindustrial cities still survive, the modern industrial city is associated with a third level of complexity in human organization, a level characterized by mass literacy, a fluid class system and, most important, the tremendous technological breakthrough to new sources of inanimate energy that produced and still sustains the industrial revolution. Viewed against the background of this three-tiered structure, the first emergence of cities at the level of civilized preindustrial society can be more easily understood.

Two factors in addition to technological advance beyond the folk-society level were needed for cities to emerge. One was a special type of social organization by means of which the agricultural surplus produced by technological advance could be collected, stored and distributed. The same apparatus could also organize the labor force needed for large-scale construction, such as public buildings, city walls and irrigation systems. A social organization of this kind requires a variety of full-time specialists directed by a ruling elite. The latter, although few in number, must command sufficient political power—reinforced by an ideology, usually religious in character—to ensure that the peasantry periodically relinquishes a substantial part of the agricultural yield in order to support the city dwellers. The second factor required was a favorable environment, providing not only fertile soil for the peasants but also a water supply adequate for both agriculture and urban consumption. Such conditions exist in geologically mature mid-latitude river valleys, and it was in such broad alluvial regions that the world's earliest cities arose.

What is a city? It is a community of substantial size and population den-

FAINT OUTLINES of a forgotten Persian city appear in the aerial photograph shown on page 117. The site is on the south bank of the Gurgan River, east of the Caspian Sea near the present border between Iran and the U.S.S.R. A natural frontier between Persia and the steppe country to the north, the Gurgan region served as a barrier to penetration by nomads at least since the Iron Age. The citadel on the opposite bank of the river (*top right*) defended the city from steppe raiders. The photograph is one of many made in Iran by Erich F. Schmidt for the Oriental Institute of the University of Chicago.

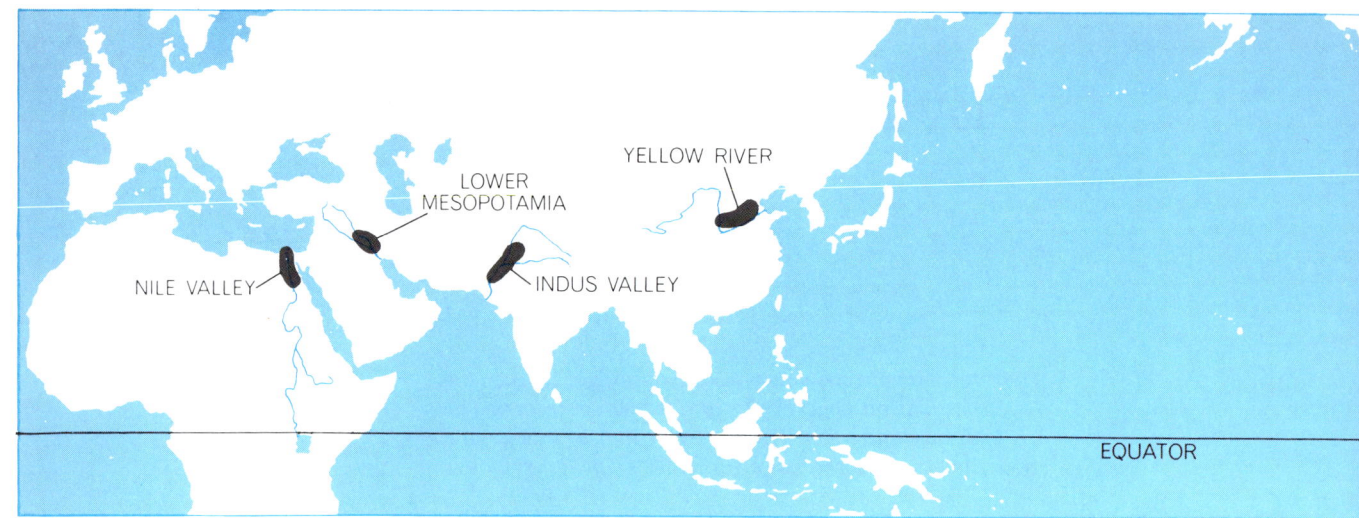

WORLD'S EARLIEST CITIES first evolved from villages in lower Mesopotamia and in the Nile valley (*left*). Soon thereafter cities also arose in similar alluvial regions to the east, first in the Indus valley and then along the Yellow River; Mesopotamian influences

sity that shelters a variety of nonagricultural specialists, including a literate elite. I emphasize the role of literacy as an ingredient of urban life for good reasons. Even though writing systems took centuries to evolve, their presence or absence serves as a convenient means for distinguishing between genuinely urban communities and others that in spite of their large size and dense population must be considered quasi-urban or nonurban. This is because once a community achieves or otherwise acquires the technological advance we call writing, a major transformation in the social order occurs; with a written tradition rather than an oral one it is possible to create more complex administrative and legal systems and more rigorous systems of thought. Writing is indispensable to the development of mathematics, astronomy and the other sciences; its existence thus implies the emergence of a number of significant specializations within the social order.

As far as is known, the world's first cities took shape around 3500 B.C. in the Fertile Crescent, the eastern segment of which includes Mesopotamia: the valleys of the Tigris and the Euphrates. Not only were the soil and water supply there suitable; the region was a crossroads that facilitated repeated contacts among peoples of divergent cultures for thousands of years. The resulting mixture of alien and indigenous crafts and skills must have made its own contribution to the evolution of the first true cities out of the village settlements in lower Mesopotamia. These were primarily in Sumer but also to some extent in Akkad, a little to the north. Some—such as Eridu, Erech, Lagash and Kish—are more familiar to archaeologists than to others; Ur, a later city, is more widely known.

These early cities were much alike; for one thing, they had a similar technological base. Wheat and barley were the cereal crops, bronze was the metal, oxen pulled plows and there were wheeled vehicles. Moreover, the city's leader was both king and high priest; the peasants' tribute to the city god was stored in the temple granaries. Luxury goods recovered from royal tombs and temples attest the existence of skilled artisans, and the importation of precious metals and gems from well beyond the borders of Mesopotamia bespeaks a class of merchant-traders. Population sizes can only be guessed in the face of such unknowns as the average number of residents per household and the extent of each city's zone of influence. The excavator of Ur, Sir Leonard Woolley, estimates that soon after 2000 B.C. the city proper housed 34,000 people; in my opinion, however, it seems unlikely that, at least in the earlier periods, even the larger of these cities contained more than 5,000 to 10,000 people, including part-time farmers on the cities' outskirts.

The valley of the Nile, not too far from Mesopotamia, was also a region of early urbanization. To judge from Egyptian writings of a later time, there may have been urban communities in the Nile delta by 3100 B.C. Whether the Egyptian concept of city living had "diffused" from Mesopotamia or was independently invented (and perhaps even earlier than in Mesopotamia) is a matter of scholarly debate; in any case the initial stages of Egyptian urban life may yet be discovered deep in the silt of the delta, where scientific excavation is only now being undertaken.

Urban communities—diffused or independently invented—spread widely during the third and second milleniums B.C. By about 2500 B.C. the cities of Mohenjo-Daro and Harappa were flourishing in the valley of the Indus River in what is now Pakistan. Within another 1,000 years at the most the mid-

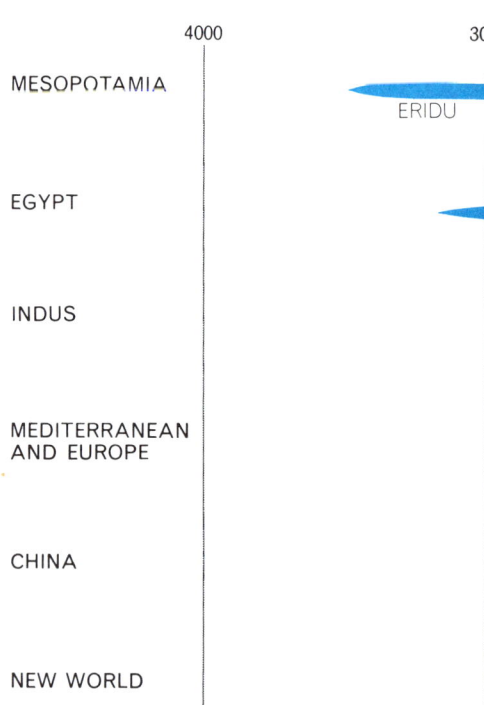

SEQUENCE of urban evolution begins with the first cities of Mesopotamia, makes its

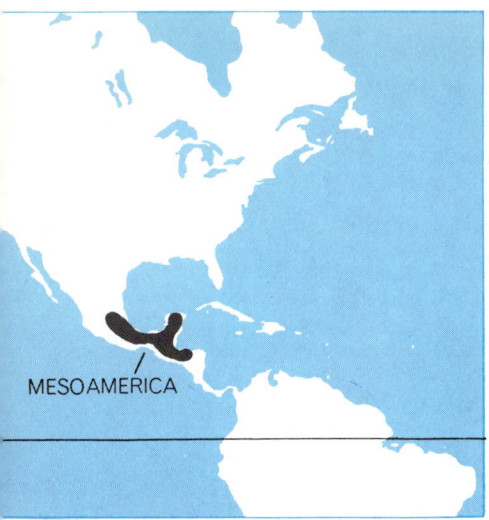

may have reached both areas. The cities of Mesoamerica (*right*) evolved independently.

dle reaches of the Yellow River in China supported urban settlements. A capital city of the Shang Dynasty (about 1500 B.C.) was uncovered near Anyang before World War II; current archaeological investigations by the Chinese may well prove that city life was actually established in ancient China several centuries earlier.

The probability that the first cities of Egypt were later than those of Sumer and the certainty that those of the Indus and Yellow rivers are later lends weight to the argument that the concept of urban living diffused to these areas from Mesopotamia. Be this as it may, none will deny that in each case the indigenous population contributed uniquely to the development of the cities in its own area.

In contrast to the situation in the Old World, it appears certain that diffusion played an insignificant role or none at all in the creation of the pre-Columbian cities of the New World. The peoples of Mesoamerica—notably the Maya, the Zapotecs, the Mixtecs and the Aztecs—evidently developed urban communities on a major scale, the exact extent of which is only now being revealed by current investigations. Until quite recently, for example, many New World archaeologists doubted that the Maya had ever possessed cities; it was the fashion to characterize their impressive ruins as ceremonial centers visited periodically by the members of a scattered rural population. It is now clear, however, that many such centers were genuine cities. At the Maya site of Tikal in Guatemala some 3,000 structures have been located in an area of 6.2 square miles; only 10 percent of them are major ceremonial buildings. Extrapolating on the basis of test excavations of more than 100 of these lesser structures, about two-thirds of them appear to have been dwellings. If only half the present-day average household figure for the region (5.6 members) is applied to Tikal, its population would have been more than 5,000. At another major Maya site—Dzibilchaltun in Yucatán—a survey of less than half of the total area has revealed more than 8,500 structures. Teotihuacán, the largest urban site in the region of modern Mexico City, may have had a population of 100,000 during the first millennium A.D. [*see illustration on next two pages*].

Although only a few examples of writing have been identified at Teotihuacán, it is reasonable to assume that writing was known; there were literate peoples elsewhere in Mesoamerica at the time. By the same token, the achievements of the Maya in such realms as mathematics and astronomy would have forced the conclusion that they were an urban people even in the absence of supporting archaeological evidence. Their invention of the concept of zero (evidently earlier than the Hindus' parallel feat) and their remarkably precise calculation of the length of the solar year would surely have been impossible if their literate elite had been scattered about the countryside in villages rather than concentrated in urban centers where a cross-fertilization of ideas could take place.

Mesoamerica was by no means the only area of large, dense communities in the New World; they also existed in the Andean region. A culture such as

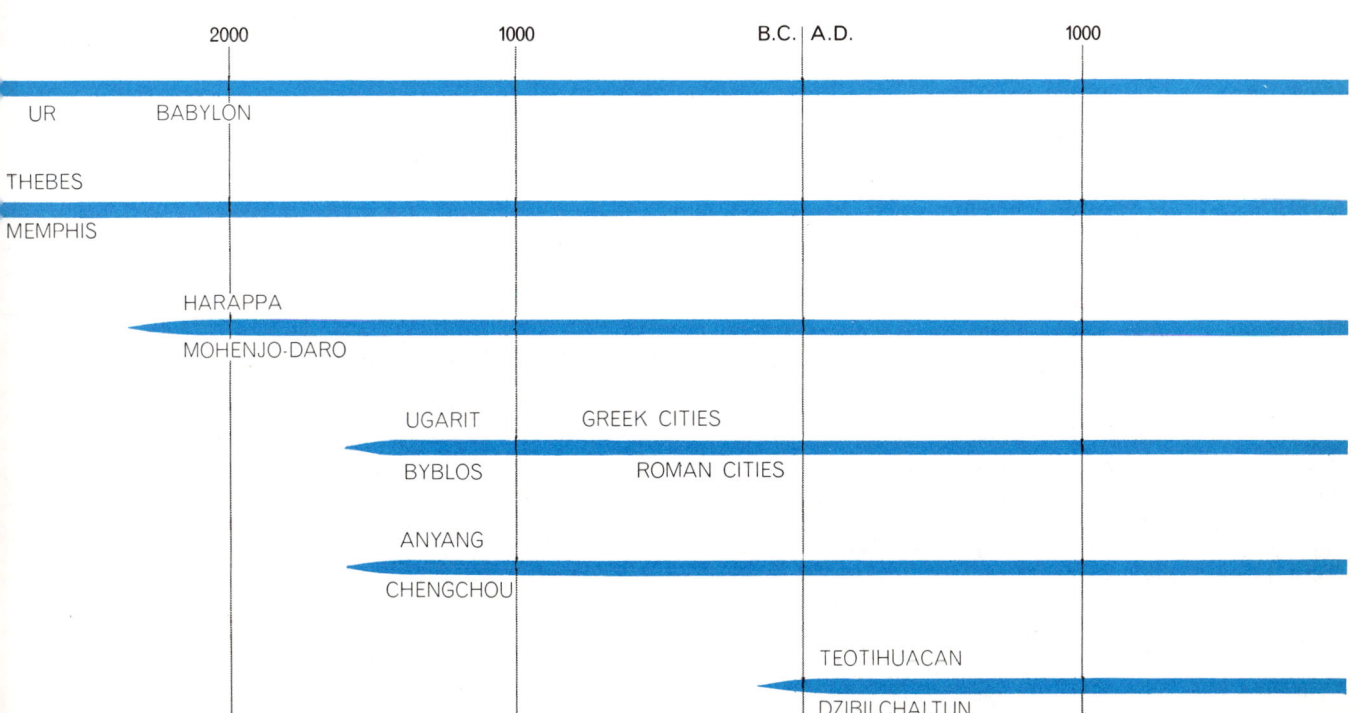

next appearance in the Nile valley, then extends to the Indus, to the eastern Mediterranean region and at last to China. In each area, the independently urbanized New World included, cities rose and fell but urban life, once established, never wholly disappeared.

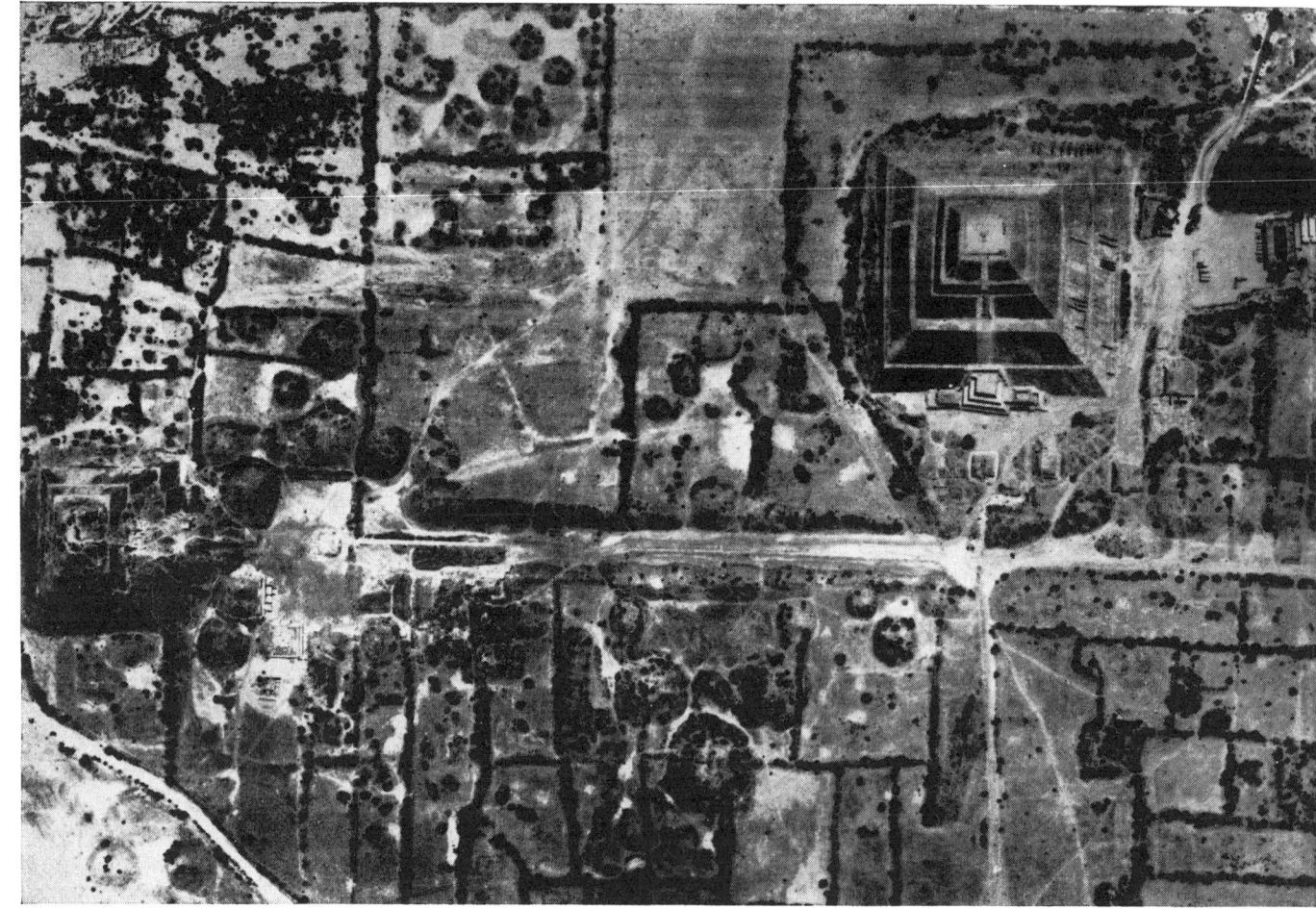

TEOTIHUACÁN is an extensive urban site near modern Mexico City that flourished during the first millennium A.D. Only the center of the city is seen in the photograph, but the precise grid layout of the city is partly revealed. The full extent of the grid, based on 60-meter-square city blocks, is not yet known, but it continues for miles beyond the city center. Aerial and ground surveys of the region by René Millon of the University of Rochester show that the north-south axis of the city was formed by a broad avenue (the

the Inca, however, cannot be classified as truly urban. In spite of—perhaps because of—their possession of a mnemonic means of keeping inventories (an assemblage of knotted cords called a quipu) the Incas lacked any conventionalized set of graphic symbols for representing speech or any concepts other than numbers and certain broad classes of items. As a result they were denied such key structural elements of an urban community as a literate elite and a written heritage of law, religion and history. Although the Incas could claim major military, architectural and engineering triumphs and apparently were on the verge of achieving a civilized order, they were still quasi-urban at the time of the European conquest, much like the Dahomey, Ashanti and Yoruba peoples of Africa.

The New World teaches us two lessons. In Mesoamerica cities were created without animal husbandry, the wheel and an extensive alluvial setting. One reason for this is maize, a superior grain crop that produced a substantial food surplus with relatively little effort and thus compensated for the limited tools and nonriverine environment. In the Andean region imposing feats of engineering and an extensive division of labor were not enough, in the absence of writing, to give rise to a truly urban society.

In spite of considerable cultural diversity among the inhabitants of the Near East, the Orient and the New World, the early cities in all these regions had a number of organizational forms in common. The dominant pattern was theocracy—the king and the high priest were one. The elite had their chief residences in the city; moreover, they and their retainers and servants congregated mainly in the city's center. This center was the prestige area, where the most imposing religious and government buildings were located. Such a concentration had dual value: in an era when communications and transport were rudimentary, propinquity enhanced interaction among the elite; at the same time it gave the ruling class maximum protection from external attack.

At a greater distance from this urban nucleus were the shops and dwellings of artisans—masons, carpenters, smiths, jewelers, potters—many of whom served the elite. The division of labor into crafts, apparent in the earliest cities, became more complex with the passage of time. Artisan groups, some of which even in early times may have belonged to specific ethnic minorities, tended to establish themselves in special quarters or streets. Such has been characteristic of preindustrial cities in all cultural settings, from the earliest times to the present day. The poorest urbanites lived on the outskirts of the city, as did part-time or full-time farmers; their scattered dwellings finally blended into open countryside.

From its inception the city, as a residence of specialists, has been a continuing source of innovation. Indeed, the very emergence of cities greatly accelerated social and cultural change; to

Street of the Dead) that starts at the Pyramid of the Moon (*far left*), runs past the larger Pyramid of the Sun (*left of center*) and continues more than three miles beyond the Ciudadela (*far right*). The east-west axis of Teotihuacán was formed by similar avenues that can be traced outward for two miles on either side of the central Ciudadela area. Although primarily a market and religious center for the surrounding countryside, Teotihuacán probably contained a resident population of 100,000 or more within its 16 square miles.

borrow a term from the late British archaeologist V. Gordon Childe, we can properly regard the "urban revolution" as being equal in significance to the agricultural revolution that preceded it and the industrial revolution that followed it. The city acted as a promoter of change in several ways. Many of the early cities arose on major transportation routes; new ideas and inventions flowed into them quite naturally. The mere fact that a large number of specialists were concentrated in a small area encouraged innovation, not only in technology but also in religious, philosophical and scientific thought. At the same time cities could be strong bulwarks of tradition. Some—for example Jerusalem and Benares—have become sacred in the eyes of the populace; in spite of repeated destruction Jerusalem has retained this status for more than two millenniums [see "Ancient Jerusalem," by Kathleen M. Kenyon; SCIENTIFIC AMERICAN, July 1965].

The course of urban evolution can be correctly interpreted only in relation to the parallel evolution of technology and social organization (especially political organization); these are not just prerequisites to urban life but the basis for its development. As centers of innovation cities provided a fertile setting for continued technological advances; these gains made possible the further expansion of cities. Advanced technology in turn depended on the increasingly complex division of labor, particularly in the political sphere. As an example, the early urban communities of Sumer were mere city-states with restricted hinterlands, but eventually trade and commerce extended over a much broader area, enabling these cities to draw on the human and material resources of a far wider and more diverse region and even bringing about the birth of new cities. The early empires of the Iron Age—for instance the Achaemenid Empire of Persia, established early in the sixth century B.C., and the Han Empire of China, established in the third century B.C.—far surpassed in scope any of the Bronze Age. And as empires became larger the size and grandeur of their cities increased. In fact, as Childe has observed, urbanization spread more rapidly during the first five centuries of the Iron Age than it had in all 15 centuries of the Bronze Age.

In the sixth and fifth centuries B.C. the Persians expanded their empire into western Turkestan and created a number of cities, often by building on existing villages. In this expansion Toprak-kala, Merv and Marakanda (part of which was later the site of Samarkand) moved toward urban status. So too in India, at the close of the fourth century B.C., the Mauryas in the north spread their empire to the previously nonurban south and into Ceylon, giving impetus to the birth of cities such as Ajanta and Kanchi. Under the Ch'in and Han dynasties, between the third century B.C. and the third century A.D., city life took hold in most of what was then China and beyond, particularly to the south and west. The "Great Silk Road" extending from China to Turkestan became studded with such oasis cities as Suchow, Khotan and Kashgar; Nanking and Canton seem to have attained urban status at this time, as did the settlement that was eventually to become Peking.

At the other end of the Eurasian land mass the Phoenicians began toward the end of the second millennium B.C. to spread westward and to revive or establish urban life along the northern coast of Africa and in Spain. These coastal traders had by then developed a considerable knowledge of shipbuilding; this, combined with their far-reaching commercial ties and power of arms, made the Phoenicians lords of the Mediterranean for a time. Some centuries later the Greeks followed a rather similar course. Their city-states—actually in a sense small empires—created or rebuilt numerous urban outposts along the Mediterranean shore from Asia Minor to Spain and France, and eastward to the most distant coast of the Black Sea. The empire that did the most to diffuse city life into the previously nonurban regions of the West—France, Britain, the Low Countries, Germany west of the Rhine, central and even eastern Europe—was of course Rome.

Empires are effective disseminators of urban forms because they have to build cities with which to maintain military supremacy in conquered regions. The city strongholds, in turn, require an administrative apparatus in order to tap the resources of the conquered area and encourage the commerce needed both to support the military garrison and to enhance the wealth of the homeland. Even when a new city began as a purely commercial outpost, as was the case under the Phoenicians, some military and administrative support was necessary if it was to survive and function effectively in alien territory.

There is a significant relation between the rise and fall of empires and the rise and fall of cities; in a real sense history is the study of urban graveyards. The capitals of many former empires are today little more than ghostly outlines that only hint at a glorious past. Such was the fate of Babylon and Nineveh, Susa in Persia, Seleucia in Mesopotamia and Vijayanagar in India. Yet there are exceptions. Some cities have managed to survive over long periods of time by attaching themselves first to one empire and then to another. Athens, for example, did not decline after the collapse of Greek power; it was able to attach itself to the Roman Empire, which subsidized Athens as a center of learning. Once Rome fell, however, both the population and the prestige of Athens dwindled steadily; it was little more than a town until the rise of modern Greece in the 19th century. On the other hand, nearby Byzantium, a city-state of minor importance under Roman rule, not only became the capital of the Eastern Roman Empire and its successor, the Ottoman Empire, but as Istanbul remains a major city to this day.

In the light of the recurrent rise and decline of cities in so many areas of the world, one may ask just how urban life has been able to persist and why the skills of technology and social organization required for city-building were not

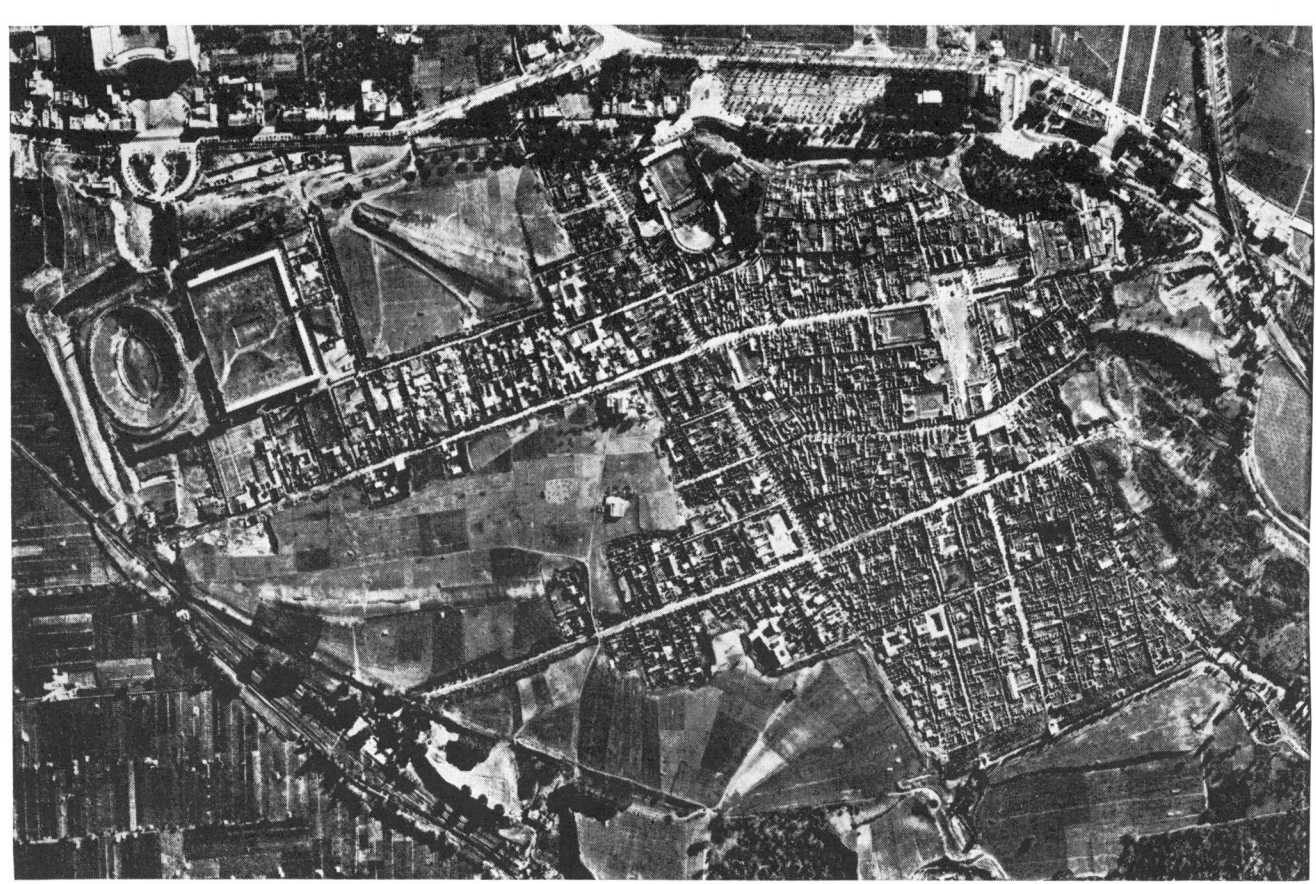

A ROMAN RESORT in Italy, Pompeii was buried by 18 feet of ash from Vesuvius in A.D. 79 after a lifetime of at least 400 years. Its rectangular ground plan was presumably designed by the Etruscans, who were among the city's first residents in pre-Roman days. Population estimates for the resort city are uncertain; its amphitheater (far left), however, could seat 20,000 people. Forgotten soon after its burial, Pompeii was rediscovered in 1748; systematic excavation of the site began in the middle of the 19th century.

lost. The answer is that the knowledge was maintained within the framework of empires—by means of written records and oral transmission by various specialists. Moreover, all empires have added to their store of skills relating to urban development as a result of diffusion—including the migration of specialists—from other civilized areas. At the same time various civilized or uncivilized subjects within empires have either been purposely educated by their conquerors or have otherwise gained access to the body of urban lore. The result on occasion is that the subjects challenge the power of the dominant ruling group.

The rise and fall of the Roman Empire provides a highly instructive case study that illuminates several relations between the life-span of cities and the formation and decline of empires. The Romans themselves took many elements of their civilization from the Etruscans, the Greeks and other civilized peoples who came under their sway. After Rome's northward expansion in western Europe and the proliferation of Roman cities in regions inhabited by so-called "barbarians"—in this instance preliterate, or "noncivilized," peoples—the Roman leaders were simply unable to staff all the bureaucratic posts with their own citizens. Some of the preliterates had to be trained to occupy such posts both in their own homelands and in the cities on the frontier. This process made it possible for the Romans to exploit the wealth of conquered regions and may have pacified the subjugated groups for a time, but in the long run it engendered serious conflicts. Eventually the Ostrogoths, Vandals, Burgundians and others —having been partially urbanized, having developed a literate elite of their own and having acquired many Roman technological and administrative skills—turned against the imperial power structure and engineered the collapse of Rome and its empire. Nor is this a unique case in history; analogies can be perceived in the modern independence movements of such European colonies as those in Africa.

With the breakup of the Roman Empire, not only did the city of Rome (which at its largest may have had more than 300,000 inhabitants) decline markedly but many borderland cities disappeared or shrank to small towns or villages. The decline was dramatic, but it is too often assumed that after the fall of Rome cities totally disappeared from western Europe. The historian E. Ewig has recently shown that many cities continued to function, particularly in Italy and southern France. Here, as in all civilized societies, the surviving cities were the chief residences and centers of activity for the political and religious elite who commanded the positions of power and privilege that persisted during the so-called Dark Ages.

In spite of Rome's decline many of the techniques and concepts associated with literate traditions in such fields as medicine and astronomy were kept alive; this was done both in the smaller surviving urban communities of Europe and in the eastern regions that had been ruled by the Romans—notably in the cities of the succeeding Eastern Roman Empire. Some of the technology and learning associated with Rome also became the basis for city life in the Arab empires that arose later in the Near East, North Africa, Spain and even central Asia. Indeed, the Byzantine and Arab empires—which had such major intellectual centers as Constantinople, Antioch, Damascus, Cairo and Baghdad —advanced beyond the knowledge inherited from antiquity. The Arabs, for example, took from the Hindus the concept of zero and the decimal system of numerals; by utilizing these concepts in both theory and practice they achieved significant advances over the knowledge that had evolved in the West. Eventually much of the new learning was passed on to Europe, where it helped to build the foundations for the industrial revolution.

In time Europe reestablished extensive commercial contact with the Byzantine and Arab empires; the interchange that followed played a significant role in the resurgence of urban life in southern Europe. The revitalization of trade was closely associated with the formation of several prosperous Italian city-states in the 10th and 11th centuries A.D. Venice and other cities eventually were transformed into small-scale empires whose colonies were scattered over the Mediterranean region—a hinterland from which the home cities were able to extract not only many of their necessities but also luxury items. By A.D. 1000 Venice had forged com-

A ROMAN OUTPOST in Syria, Dura Europos was founded on the Euphrates about 300 B.C. by the Seleucid successor to Alexander the Great. At first a center of Hellenism in the East, it was later a Roman stronghold until Valerian lost it in A.D. 257. Yale University archaeologists have studied the site since 1922; finger-like ramps are their excavation dumps.

A RENAISSANCE CITY, Lucca in northern Italy is no longer contained within the bastioned circuit of its walls, which were begun in 1504 and completed in 1645. Lucca's seesaw history is like that of many other southern European cities. A Roman town during the Punic wars, it was the site of Caesar's triumvirate meeting with Pompey and Crassus in 60 B.C. and was pillaged by Odoacer at the fall of the Roman Empire in A.D. 476. A fortress city once again by the seventh century A.D., Lucca had become a prosperous manufacturing center, specializing in the weaving of silk textiles, by the 12th century. It continues to produce silk and other textiles today.

mercial links with Constantinople and other cities of the Eastern Roman Empire, partly as a result of the activities of the Greek colony in Venice. The Venetians were able to draw both on the knowledge of these resident Greeks and on the practical experience of sea captains and other specialists among them. Such examples make it clear that the Italian city-states were not merely local creations but rather products of a multiplicity of cultural forces.

Beginning at the turn of the 11th century A.D. many European cities managed to win a kind of independence from the rulers of the various principalities and petty kingdoms that surrounded them. Particularly in northern Italy urban communities came to enjoy considerable political autonomy. This provided an even more favorable atmosphere for commerce and encouraged the growth of such urban institutions as craft guilds. The European pattern is quite different from that in most of Asia (for instance in India and China), where the city was never able to attain a measure of autonomy within the broader political structure. At the same time the extent of self-rule enjoyed by the medieval European cities can be exaggerated and often is; by the close of the Middle Ages urban self-rule was already beginning to be lost. It is therefore evident that the political autonomy of medieval cities was only indirectly related to the eventual evolution of the industrial city.

It was the industrial revolution that brought about truly far-reaching changes in city life. In some nations today, as Kingsley Davis notes in his first introduction, the vast majority of the inhabitants are city dwellers. Nearly 80 percent of the people in the United Kingdom live in cities, as do nearly 70 percent of the people of the U.S. Contrast this with the preindustrial civilized world, in which only a small, socially dominant minority lived in cities. The industrial revolution has also led to fundamental changes in the city's social geography and social organization; the industrial city is marked by a greater fluidity in the class system, the appearance of mass education and mass communications and the shift of some of the elite from the center of the city to its suburban outskirts.

Although there are still insufficient data on the rise of the industrial city—an event that took place sometime between 1750 and 1850—and although scholars disagree over certain steps in the process, the major forces at work in the two or three centuries before the industrial city emerged can be perceived clearly enough. Viewed in the light of Europe's preindustrial urban era, two factors are evident: the expansion of European power into other continents and the development of a technology based on inanimate rather than animate sources of energy. The extension of European trade and exploration (which was to culminate in European colonialism) not only induced the growth of cities in Asia, in parts of nonurban Africa and in the Americas but also helped to raise the standard of living of Europeans themselves and made possible the support of more specialists. Notable among the last was a new occupational group—the scientists. The expansion abroad had helped to shatter the former world view of European scholars; they were now forced to cope with divergent ideas and customs. The discoveries reported by the far-ranging European explorers thus gave added impetus to the advance of science.

The knowledge gained through the application of the scientific method is the one factor above all others that made the modern city possible. This active experimental approach has enabled man to control the forces of nature to an extent undreamed of in the preindustrial era. It is true that in the course of several millenniums the literate elite of the preindustrial cities added significantly to man's store of knowledge in such fields as medicine, astronomy and mathematics, but these scholars generally scorned mundane activities and avoided contact with those whose work was on the practical level. This meant that the scholars' theories were rarely tested and applied in the everyday realm. Moreover, in accordance with prevailing religious thought, man was not to tamper with the natural order or to seek to control it, in either its physical or its social aspect. For example, medical scholars in Greek and Roman cities did not dissect human cadavers; not until the 16th century in Europe did a physician—Andreas Vesalius of Brussels—actually use findings obtained from dissection to revise ancient medical theories.

In the field of engineering, as late as the 17th century most advances were made by artisans who worked more or less on a trial-and-error basis. With the development of the experimental method, however, the learning of the elite became linked with the practical knowledge of the artisan, the barber-surgeon and the like; the result was a dramatic upsurge of knowledge and a fundamental revision of method that has been termed the scientific revolution. Such was the basis of the industrial revolution and the industrial city.

That the first industrial cities appeared in England is hardly fortuitous; England's social structure lacked the rigidity that characterized most of Europe and the rest of the civilized world. The Puritan tradition in England —an ethical system that supports utilitarianism and empiricism—did much to alter earlier views concerning man's place in nature. In England scholars could communicate with artisans more readily than elsewhere in Europe.

The advent of industrialism brought vast improvements in agricultural implements, farming techniques and food preservation, as well as in transportation and communication. Improved water supplies and more effective methods of sewage disposal allowed more people to congregate in cities. Perhaps the key invention was the steam engine, which provided a new and much more bountiful source of energy. Before that time, except for power from wind and water, man had no energy resources other than human and animal muscle. Now the factory system, with its mass production of goods and mechanization of activity, began to take hold. With it emerged a new kind of occupational structure: a structure that depends on highly specialized knowledge and that functions effectively only when the activities of the component occupations are synchronized. This process of industrialization has not only continued unabated to the present day but has actually accelerated with the rise of self-controlling machines.

The evolution of the industrial city was not an unmixed blessing. Historians have argued through many volumes the question of whether the new working class, including many migrants from the countryside, lost or gained economically and socially as the factory system destroyed older social patterns. Today, as industrialization moves inexorably across the globe, it continues to create social problems. Many surviving traditional cities evince in various ways the conflict between their preindustrial past and their industrial future. Nonetheless, the trend is clear: barring nuclear war, the industrial city will become the dominant urban form throughout the world, replacing forever the preindustrial city that was man's first urban creation.

Human Food Production As A Process in the Biosphere

by Lester R. Brown

September 1970

Human population growth is mainly the result of increases in food production. This relation raises the question: How many people can the biosphere support without impairment of its overall operation?

Throughout most of man's existence his numbers have been limited by the supply of food. For the first two million years or so he lived as a predator, a herbivore and a scavenger. Under such circumstances the biosphere could not support a human population of more than 10 million, a population smaller than that of London or Afghanistan today. Then, with his domestication of plants and animals some 10,000 years ago, man began to shape the biosphere to his own ends.

As primitive techniques of crop production and animal husbandry became more efficient the earth's food-producing capacity expanded, permitting increases in man's numbers. Population growth in turn exerted pressure on food supply, compelling man to further alter the biosphere in order to meet his food needs. Population growth and advances in food production have thus tended to be mutually reinforcing.

It took two million years for the human population to reach the one-billion mark, but the fourth billion now being added will require only 15 years: from 1960 to 1975. The enormous increase in the demand for food that is generated by this expansion in man's numbers, together with rising incomes, is beginning to have disturbing consequences. New signs of stress on the biosphere are reported almost daily. The continuing expansion of land under the plow and the evolution of a chemically oriented modern agriculture are producing ominous alterations in the biosphere not just on a local scale but, for the first time in history, on a global scale as well. The natural cycles of energy and the chemical elements are clearly being affected by man's efforts to expand his food supply.

Given the steadily advancing demand for food, further intervention in the biosphere for the expansion of the food supply is inevitable. Such intervention, however, can no longer be undertaken by an individual or a nation without consideration of the impact on the biosphere as a whole. The decision by a government to dam a river, by a farmer to use DDT on his crops or by a married couple to have another child, thereby increasing the demand for food, has repercussions for all mankind.

The revolutionary change in man's role from hunter and gatherer to tiller and herdsman took place in circumstances that are not well known, but some of the earliest evidence of agriculture is found in the hills and grassy plains of the Fertile Crescent in western Asia. The cultivation of food plants and the domestication of animals were aided there by the presence of wild wheat, barley, sheep, goats, pigs, cattle and horses. From the beginnings of agriculture man naturally favored above all other species those plants and animals that had been most useful to him in the wild. As a result of this favoritism he has altered the composition of the earth's plant and animal populations. Today his crops, replacing the original cover of grass or forest, occupy some three billion acres. This amounts to about 10 percent of the earth's total land surface and a considerably larger fraction of the land capable of supporting vegetation, that is, the area excluding deserts, polar regions and higher elevations. Two-thirds of the cultivated cropland is planted to cereals. The area planted to wheat alone is 600 million acres—nearly a million square miles, or an area equivalent to the U.S. east of the Mississippi. As for the influence of animal husbandry on the earth's animal populations, Hereford and Black Angus cattle roam the Great Plains, once the home of an estimated 30 to 40 million buffalo; in Australia the kangaroo has given way to European cattle; in Asia the domesticated water buffalo has multiplied in the major river valleys.

Clearly the food-producing enterprise has altered not only the relative abundance of plant and animal species but also their global distribution. The linkage of the Old and the New World in the 15th century set in motion an exchange of crops among various parts of the world that continues today. This exchange greatly increased the earth's capacity to sustain human populations, partly because some of the crops transported elsewhere turned out to be better suited there than to their area of origin. Perhaps the classic example is the introduction of the potato from South America into northern Europe, where it greatly augmented the food supply, permitting marked increases in population. This was most clearly apparent in Ireland, where the population increased rapidly for several decades on the strength of the food supply represented by the potato. Only when the potato-blight organism (*Phytophthora infestans*) devastated the potato crop was population growth checked in Ireland.

The soybean, now the leading source of vegetable oil and principal farm export of the U.S., was introduced from China several decades ago. Grain sorghum, the second-ranking feed grain in the U.S. (after corn), came from Africa as a food store in the early slave ships. In the U.S.S.R. today the principal source of vegetable oil is the sunflower, a plant that originated on the southern Great Plains of the U.S. Corn, unknown in the Old World before Columbus, is now grown on every continent. On the other hand, North America is indebted to the Old World for all its livestock and poultry species with the exception of the turkey.

To man's accomplishments in exploiting the plants and animals that natural evolution has provided, and in improving them through selective breeding over the millenniums, he has added in this century the creation of remarkably productive new breeds, thanks to the discoveries of genetics. Genetics has made possible the development of cereals and other plant species that are more tolerant to cold, more resistant to drought, less susceptible to disease, more responsive to fertilizer, higher in yield and richer in protein. The story of hybrid corn is only one of many spectacular examples. The breeding of short-season corn varieties has extended the northern limit of this crop some 500 miles.

Plant breeders recently achieved a historic breakthrough in the development of new high-yielding varieties of wheat and rice for tropical and subtropical regions. These wheats and rices, bred by Rockefeller Foundation and Ford Foundation scientists in Mexico and the Philippines, are distinguished by several characteristics. Most important, they are short-statured and stiff-strawed, and are highly responsive to chemical fertilizer. They also mature earlier. The first of the high-yielding rices, IR-8, matures in 120 days as against 150 to 180 days for other varieties.

Another significant advance incorporated into the new strains is the reduced sensitivity of their seed to photoperiod (length of day). This is partly the result of their cosmopolitan ancestry: they were developed from seed collections all over the world. The biological clocks of traditional varieties of cereals were keyed to specific seasonal cycles, and these cereals could be planted only at a certain time of the year, in the case of rice say at the onset of the monsoon season. The new wheats, which are quite flexible in terms of both seasonal and latitudinal variations in length of day, are now being grown in developing countries as far north as Turkey and as far south as Paraguay.

The combination of earlier maturity and reduced sensitivity to day length creates new opportunities for multiple cropping in tropical and subtropical regions where water supplies are adequate, enabling farmers to harvest two, three and occasionally even four crops per year. Workers at the International Rice Research Institute in the Philippines regularly harvest three crops of rice per year. Each acre they plant yields six tons annually, roughly three times the average yield of corn, the highest-yielding cereal in the U.S. Thousands of farmers in northern India are now alternating a crop of early-maturing winter wheat with a summer crop of rice, greatly increasing the productivity of their land. These new opportunities for farming land more intensively lessen the pressure for bringing marginal land under cultivation, thus helping to conserve precious topsoil. At the same time they increase the use of agricultural chemicals, creating environmental stresses more akin to those in the advanced countries.

The new dwarf wheats and rices are far more efficient than the traditional varieties in their use of land, water, fertilizer and labor. The new opportunities for multiple cropping permit conversion of far more of the available solar energy

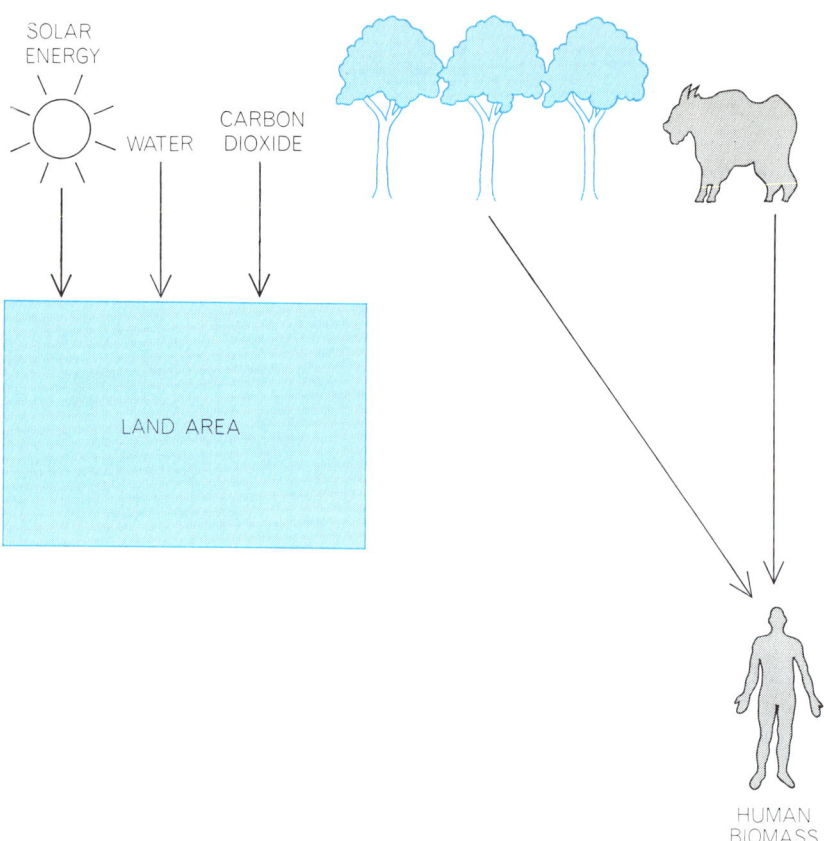

IMPACT OF THE AGRICULTURAL REVOLUTION on the human population is outlined in these two diagrams. The diagram at left shows the state of affairs before the invention of agriculture: the plants and animals supported by photosynthesis on the total land area could support a human population of only about 10 million. The diagram at right shows

into food. The new strains are not the solution to the food problem, but they are removing the threat of massive famine in the short run. They are buying time for the stabilization of population, which is ultimately the only solution to the food crisis. This "green revolution" may affect the well-being of more people in a shorter period of time than any technological advance in history.

The progress of man's expansion of food production is reflected in the way crop yields have traditionally been calculated. Today the output of cereals is expressed in yield per acre, but in early civilizations it was calculated as a ratio of the grain produced to that required for seed. On this basis the current ratio is perhaps highest in the U.S. corn belt, where farmers realize a four-hundred-fold return on the hybrid corn seed they plant. The ratio for rice is also quite high, but the ratio for wheat, the third of the principal cereals, is much lower, possibly 30 to one on a global basis.

The results of man's efforts to increase the productivity of domestic animals are equally impressive. When the ancestors of our present chickens were domesticated, they laid a clutch of about 15

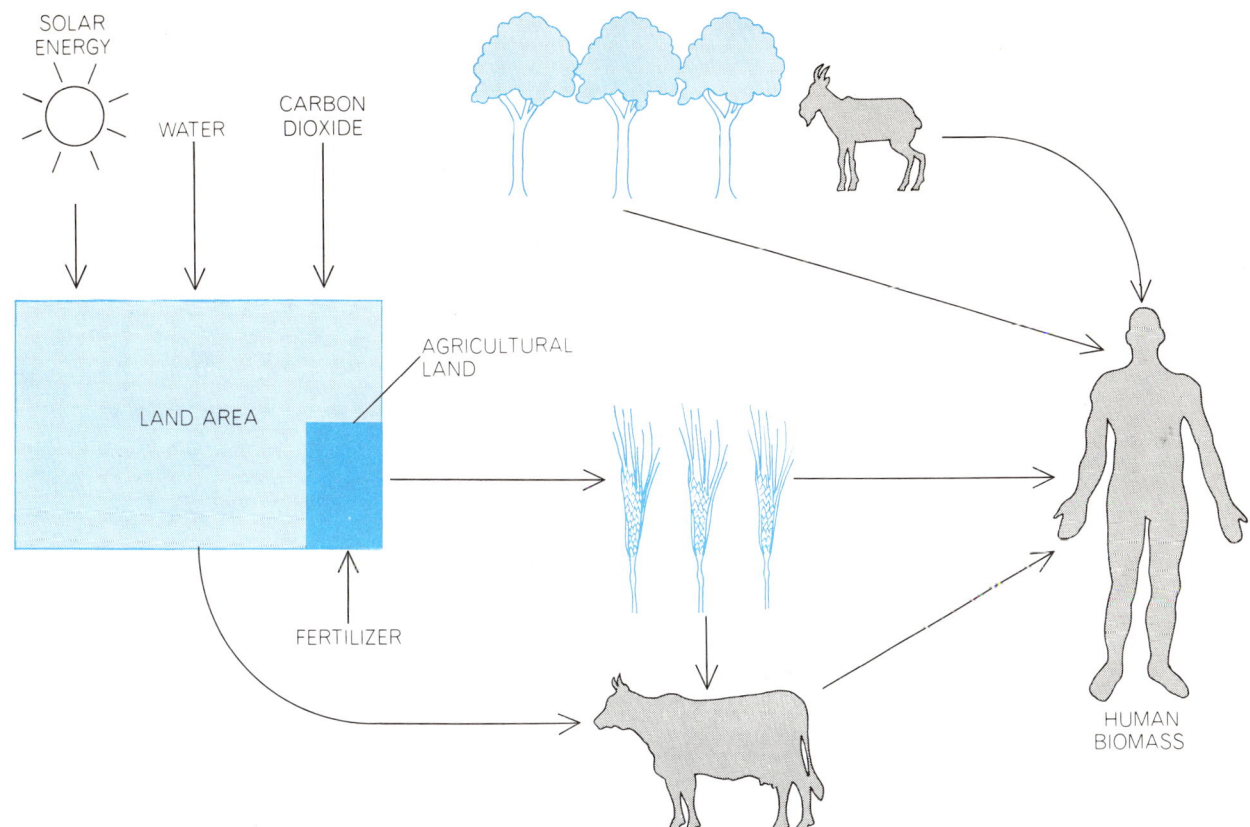

the state of affairs after the invention of agriculture. The 10 percent of the land now under the plow, watered and fertilized by man, is the primary support for a human population of 3.5 billion. Some of the agricultural produce is consumed directly by man; some is consumed indirectly by first being fed to domestic animals. Some of the food for domestic animals, however, comes from land not under the plow (curved arrow at bottom left). Man also obtains some food from sources other than agriculture, such as fishing.

eggs once a year. Hens in the U.S. today average 220 eggs per year, and the figure is rising steadily as a result of continuing advances in breeding and feeding. When cattle were originally domesticated, they probably did not produce more than 600 pounds of milk per year, barely enough for a calf. (It is roughly the average amount produced by cows in India today.) The 13 million dairy cows in the U.S. today average 9,000 pounds of milk yearly, outproducing their ancestors 15 to one.

Most such advances in the productivity of plant and animal species are recent. Throughout most of history man's efforts to meet his food needs have been directed primarily toward bringing more land under cultivation, spreading agriculture from valley to valley and continent to continent. He has also, however, invented techniques to raise the productivity of land already under cultivation, particularly in this century, when the decreasing availability of new lands for expansion has compelled him to turn to a more intensive agriculture. These techniques involve altering the biosphere's cycles of energy, water, nitrogen and minerals.

Modern agriculture depends heavily on four technologies: mechanization, irrigation, fertilization and the chemical control of weeds and insects. Each of these technologies has made an important contribution to the earth's increased capacity for sustaining human populations, and each has perturbed the cycles of the biosphere.

At least as early as 3000 B.C. the farmers of the Middle East learned to harness draft animals to help them till the soil. Harnessing animals much stronger than himself enabled man to greatly augment his own limited muscle power. It also enabled him to convert roughage (indigestible by humans) into a usable form of energy and thus to free some of his energy for pursuits other than the quest for food. The invention of the internal-combustion engine and the tractor 5,000 years later provided a much greater breakthrough. It now became possible to substitute petroleum (the product of the photosynthesis of aeons ago) for oats, corn and hay grown as feed for draft animals. The replacement of horses by the tractor not only provided the farmer with several times as much power but also released 70 million acres in the U.S. that had been devoted to raising feed for horses.

In the highly mechanized agriculture of today the expenditure of fossil fuel energy per acre is often substantially greater than the energy yield embodied in the food produced. This deficit in the output is of no immediate consequence, because the system is drawing on energy in the bank. When fossil fuels become scarcer, man will have to turn to some other source of motive energy for agriculture: perhaps nuclear energy or some means, other than photosynthesis, of harnessing solar energy. For the present and for the purposes of agriculture the energy budget of the biosphere is still favorable: the supply of solar energy—both the energy stored in fossil fuels and that taken up daily and converted into food energy by crops—enables an advanced nation to be fed with only 5 percent of the population directly employed in agriculture.

The combination of draft animals and mechanical power has given man an enormous capacity for altering the earth's surface by bringing additional land under the plow (not all of it suited for cultivation). In addition, in the poor-

EXPERIMENTAL FARM in Brazil, one of thousands around the world where improvements in agricultural technology are pioneered, is seen as an image on an infrared-sensitive film in the aerial photograph on the opposite page. The reflectance of vegetation at near-infrared wavelengths of .7 to .9 micron registers on the film in false shades of red that are proportional to the intensity of the energy. The most reflective, and reddest, areas (*bottom*) are land still uncleared of forest cover. Most of the tilled fields, although irregular in shape, are contour-plowed. Regular patterns (*left and bottom right*) are citrus-orchard rows. The photograph was taken by a National Aeronautics and Space Administration mission in cooperation with the Brazilian government in a joint study of the assessment of agricultural resources by remote sensing. The farm is some 80 miles northwest of São Paulo.

er countries his expanding need for fuel has forced him to cut forests far in excess of their ability to renew themselves. The areas largely stripped of forest include mainland China and the subcontinent of India and Pakistan, where much of the population must now use cow dung for fuel. Although statistics are not available, the proportion of mankind using cow dung as fuel to prepare meals may far exceed the proportion using natural gas. Livestock populations providing draft power, food and fuel tend to increase along with human populations, and in many poor countries the needs of livestock for forage far exceed its self-renewal, gradually denuding the countryside of grass cover.

As population pressure builds, not only is more land brought under the plow but also the land remaining is less suited to cultivation. Once valleys are filled, farmers begin to move up hillsides, creating serious soil-erosion problems. As the natural cover that retards runoff is reduced and soil structure deteriorates, floods and droughts become more severe.

Over most of the earth the thin layer of topsoil producing most of man's food is measured in inches. Denuding the land of its year-round natural cover of grass or forest exposes the thin mantle of life-sustaining soil to rapid erosion by wind and water. Much of the soil ultimately washes into the sea, and some of it is lifted into the atmosphere. Man's actions are causing the topsoil to be removed faster than it is formed. This unstable relationship between man and the land from which he derives his subsistence obviously cannot continue indefinitely.

Robert R. Brooks of Williams College, an economist who spent several years in India, gives a wry description of the process occurring in the state of Rajasthan, where tens of thousands of acres of rural land are being abandoned yearly because of the loss of topsoil: "Overgrazing by goats destroys the desert plants which might otherwise hold the soil in place. Goatherds equipped with sickles attached to 20-foot poles strip the leaves of trees to float downward into the waiting mouths of famished goats and sheep. The trees die and the soil blows away 200 miles to New Delhi, where it comes to rest in the lungs of its inhabitants and on the shiny cars of foreign diplomats."

Soil erosion not only results in a loss of soil but also impairs irrigation systems. This is illustrated in the Mangla irrigation reservoir, recently built in the foothills of the Himalayas in West Pakistan as part of the Indus River irrigation system. On the basis of feasibility studies indicating that the reservoir could be expected to have a lifetime of at least 100 years, $600 million was invested in the construction of the reservoir. Denuding and erosion of the soil in the watershed, however, accompanying a rapid growth of population in the area, has already washed so much soil into the reservoir that it is now expected to be completely filled with silt within 50 years.

A historic example of the effects of man's abuse of the soil is all too plainly visible in North Africa, which once was the fertile granary of the Roman Empire and now is largely a desert or near-desert whose people are fed with the aid of food imports from the U.S. In the U.S. itself the "dust bowl" experience of the 1930's remains a vivid lesson on the folly of overplowing. More recently the U.S.S.R. repeated this error, bringing 100 million acres of virgin soil under the plow only to discover that the region's rainfall was too scanty to sustain continuous cultivation. Once moisture reserves in the soil were depleted the soil began to blow.

Soil erosion is one of the most pressing and most difficult problems threatening the future of the biosphere. Each year it is forcing the abandonment of millions of acres of cropland in Asia, the Middle East, North Africa and Central America. Nature's geological cycle continuously produces topsoil, but its pace is far too slow to be useful to man. Someone once defined soil as rock on its way to the sea. Soil is produced by the weathering of rock and the process takes several centuries to form an inch of topsoil. Man is managing to destroy the topsoil

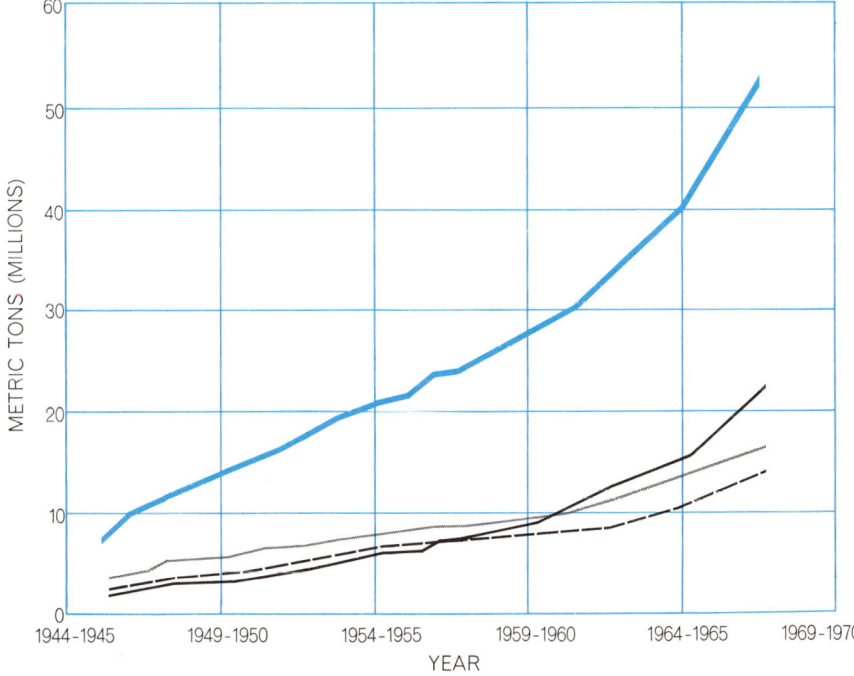

FERTILIZER CONSUMPTION has increased more than fivefold since the end of World War II. The top line in the graph (*color*) shows the tonnage of all kinds of fertilizers combined. The lines below show the tonnages of the three major types: nitrogen (*black*), now the leader, phosphate (*gray*) and potash (*broken line*). Figures, from the most recent report by the UN Food and Agriculture Organization, omit fertilizer consumption in China.

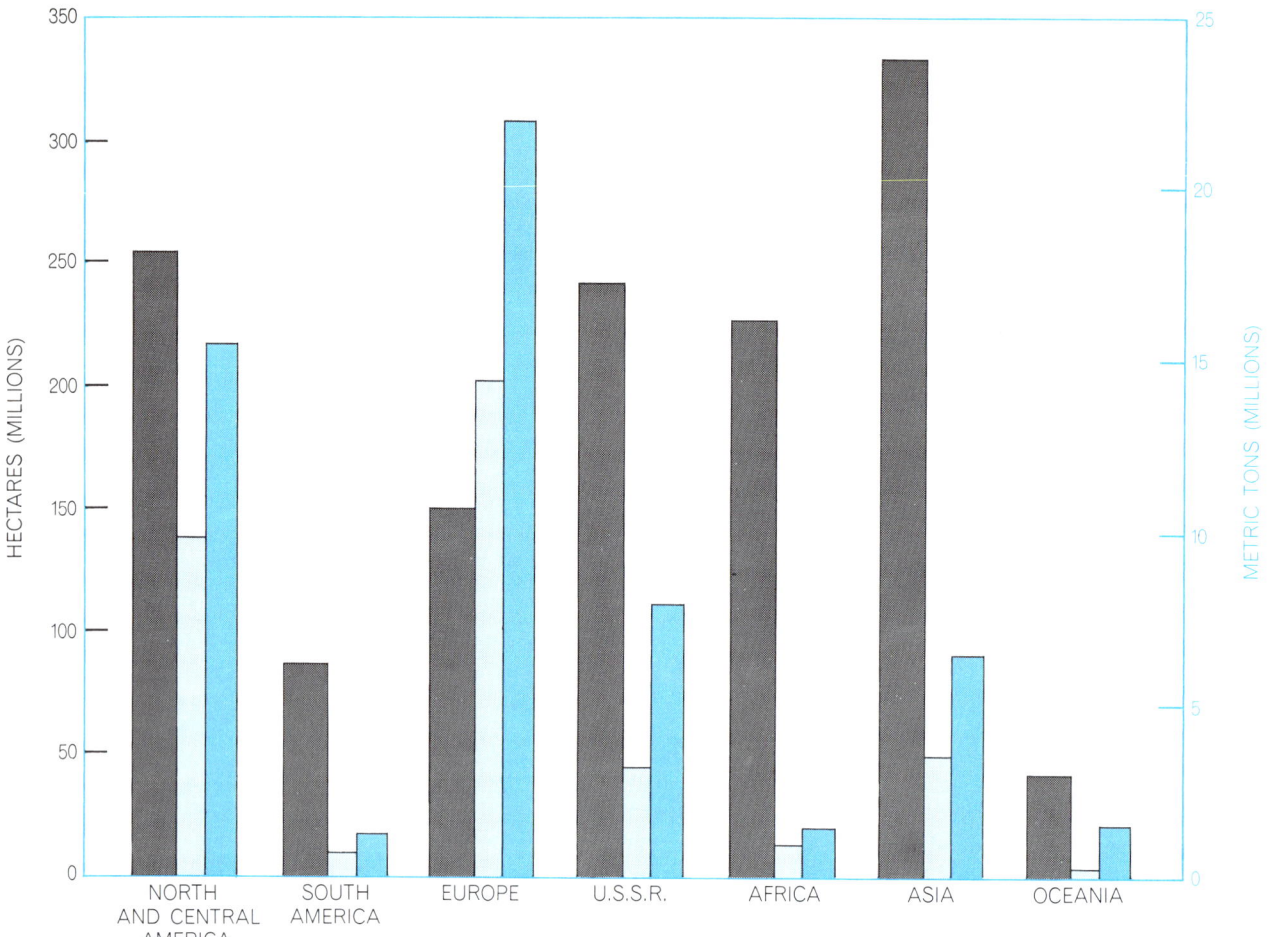

TONS OF FERTILIZER used in seven world areas are compared with the amount of agricultural land in each area. Two tonnages are shown in each instance: the amount used in 1962–1963 (*light color*) and the amount used in 1967–1968 (*solid color*). The greatest use of fertilizer occurs in Europe, the least fertilized area is Africa and the greatest percentage increase in the period was in Australia and New Zealand. Figures, from the Food and Agriculture Organization, omit China, North Korea and North Vietnam.

in some areas of the world in a fraction of this time. The only possible remedy is to find ways to conserve the topsoil more effectively.

The dust-bowl era in the U.S. ended with the widespread adoption of conservation practices by farmers. Twenty million acres were fallowed to accumulate moisture and thousands of miles of windbreaks were planted across the Great Plains. Fallow land was alternated with strips of wheat ("strip-cropping") to reduce the blowing of soil while the land was idle. The densely populated countries of Asia, however, are in no position to adopt such tactics. Their food needs are so pressing that they cannot afford to take large areas out of cultivation; moreover, they do not yet have the financial resources or the technical skills for the immense projects in reforestation, controlled grazing of cattle, terracing, contour farming and systematic management of watersheds that would be required to preserve their soil.

The significance of wind erosion goes far beyond the mere loss of topsoil. As other authors in this issue have observed, a continuing increase in particulate matter in the atmosphere could affect the earth's climate by reducing the amount of incoming solar energy. This particulate matter comes not only from the technological activities of the richer countries but also from wind erosion in the poorer countries. The poorer countries do not have the resources for undertaking the necessary effort to arrest and reverse this trend. Should it be established that an increasing amount of particulate matter in the atmosphere is changing the climate, the richer countries would have still another reason to provide massive capital and technical assistance to the poor countries, joining with them to confront this common threat to mankind.

Irrigation, which agricultural man began to practice at least as early as 6,000 years ago, even earlier than he harnessed animal power, has played its great role in increasing food production by bringing into profitable cultivation vast areas that would otherwise be unusable or only marginally productive. Most of the world's irrigated land is in Asia, where it is devoted primarily to the production of rice. In Africa the Volta River of Ghana and the Nile are dammed for irrigation and power purposes. The Colorado River system of the U.S. is used extensively for irrigation in the Southwest, as are scores of rivers elsewhere. Still to be exploited for irrigation are the Mekong of southeastern Asia and the Amazon.

During the past few years there has been an important new irrigation development in Asia: the widespread installation of small-scale irrigation systems on individual farms. In Pakistan and India, where in many places the water table is close to the surface, hundreds of thousands of tube wells with pumps have been installed in recent years. Interestingly, this development came about partly as an answer to a problem that had been presented by irrigation itself.

Like many of man's other interventions in the biosphere, his reshaping of the hydrologic cycle has had unwanted side effects. One of them is the raising of the water table by the diversion of river water onto the land. Over a period of time the percolation of irrigation water downward and the accumulation of this water underground may gradually raise the water table until it is within a few feet or even a few inches of the surface. This not only inhibits the growth of plant roots by waterlogging but also results in the surface soil's becoming salty as water evaporates through it, leaving a concentrated deposit of salts in the upper few inches. Such a situation developed in West Pakistan after its fertile plain had been irrigated with water from the Indus for a century. During a visit by President Ayub to Washington in 1961 he appealed to President Kennedy for help: West Pakistan was losing 60,000 acres of fertile cropland per year because of waterlogging and salinity as its population was expanding 2.5 percent yearly.

This same sequence, the diversion of river water into land for irrigation, followed eventually by waterlogging and salinity and the abandonment of land, had been repeated many times throughout history. The result was invariably the decline, and sometimes the disappearance, of the civilizations thus intervening in the hydrologic cycle. The remains of civilizations buried in the deserts of the Middle East attest to early experiences similar to those of contemporary Pakistan. These civilizations, however, had no one to turn to for foreign aid. An interdisciplinary U.S. team led by Roger Revelle, then Science Adviser to the Secretary of the Interior, studied the problem and proposed among other things a system of tube wells that would lower the water table by tapping the ground water for intensive irrigation. Discharging this water on the surface, the wells would also wash the soil's salt downward. The stratagem worked, and the salty, waterlogged land of Pakistan is steadily being reclaimed.

Other side effects of river irrigation are not so easily remedied. Such irrigation has brought about a great increase in the incidence of schistosomiasis, a disease that is particularly prevalent in the river valleys of Africa and Asia. The disease is produced by the parasitic larva of a blood fluke, which is harbored by aquatic snails and burrows into the flesh of people standing in water or in water-soaked fields. The Chinese call schistosomiasis "snail fever"; it might also be called the poor man's emphysema, because, like emphysema, this extremely debilitating disease is environmentally induced through conditions created by man. The snails and the fluke thrive in perennial irrigation systems, where they are in close proximity to large human populations. The incidence of the disease is rising rapidly as the world's large rivers are harnessed for irrigation, and today schistosomiasis is estimated to afflict 250 million people. It now surpasses malaria, the incidence of which is declining, as the world's most prevalent infectious disease.

As a necessity for food production water is of course becoming an increasingly crucial commodity. The projected increases in population and in food requirements will call for more and more water, forcing man to consider still more massive and complex interventions in the biosphere. The desalting of seawater for irrigation purposes is only one major departure from traditional practices. Another is a Russian plan to reverse the flow of four rivers currently flowing northward and emptying into the Arctic Ocean. These rivers would be diverted southward into the semiarid lands of southern Russia, greatly enlarging the irrigated area of the U.S.S.R. Some climatologists are concerned, however, that the shutting off of the flow of relatively warm water from these four rivers would have far-reaching implications for not only the climate of the Arctic but also the climatic system of the entire earth.

The growing competition for scarce water supplies among states and among various uses in the western U.S. is also forcing consideration of heroic plans. For example, a detailed engineering proposal exists for the diversion of the Yukon River in Alaska southward across Canada into the western U.S. to meet the growing need for water for both agricultural and industrial purposes. The effort would cost an estimated $100 billion.

Representing an even greater intervention in the biosphere is the prospect that man may one day consciously alter the earth's climatic patterns, shifting some of the rain now falling on the oceans to the land. Among the steps needed for the realization of such a scheme are the construction of a comprehensive model of the earth's climatic system and the development of a computational facility capable of simulating

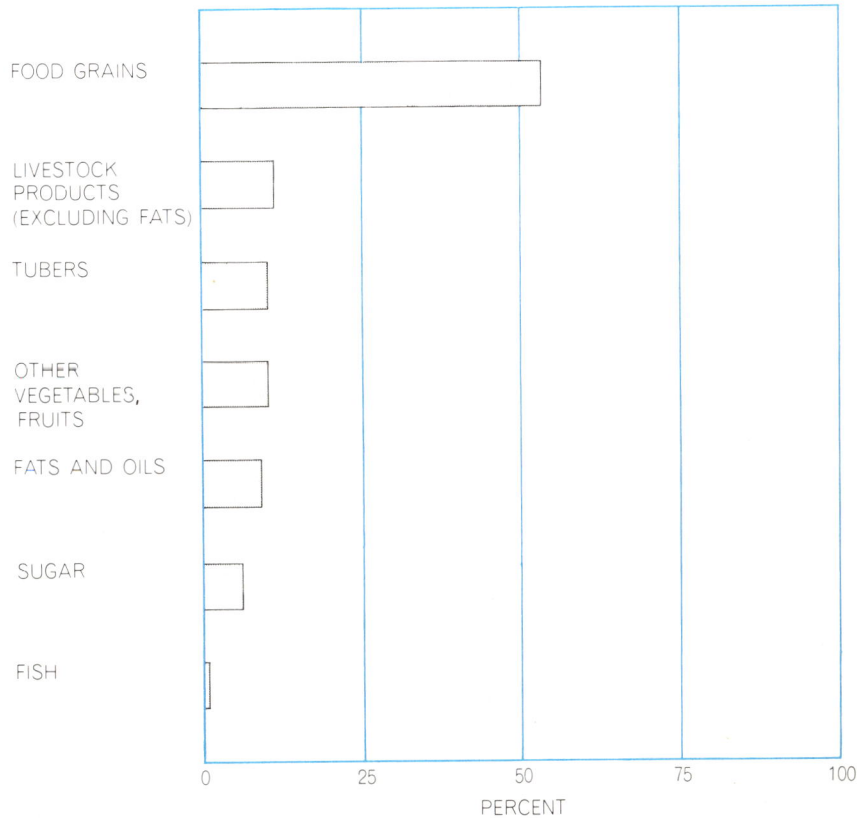

WORLDWIDE FOOD ENERGY comes in different amounts from different products. Cereals outstrip other foodstuffs; wheat and rice each supply a fifth of mankind's food energy.

and manipulating the model. The required information includes data on temperatures, humidity, precipitation, the movement of air masses, ocean currents and many other factors that enter into the weather. Earth-orbiting satellites will doubtless be able to collect much of this information, and the present generation of advanced computers appears to be capable of carrying out the necessary experiments on the model. For the implementation of the findings, that is, for the useful control of rainfall, there will of course be a further requirement: the project will have to be managed by a global and supranational agency if it is not to lead to weather wars among nations working at cross purposes. Some commercial firms are already in the business of rainmaking, and they are operating on an international basis.

The third great technology that man has introduced to increase food production is the use of chemical fertilizers. We owe the foundation for this development to Justus von Liebig of Germany, who early in the 19th century determined the specific requirements of nitrogen, phosphorus, potassium and other nutrients for plant growth. Chemical fertilizers did not come into widespread use, however, until this century, when the pressure of population and the disappearance of new frontiers compelled farmers to substitute fertilizer for the expansion of cropland to meet growing food needs. One of the first countries to intensify its agriculture, largely by the use of fertilizers, was Japan, whose output of food per acre has steadily risen (except for wartime interruptions) since the turn of the century. The output per acre of a few other countries, including the Netherlands, Denmark and Sweden, began to rise at about the same time. The U.S., richly endowed with vast farmlands, did not turn to the heavy use of fertilizer and other intensive measures until about 1940. Since then its yields per acre, assisted by new varieties of grain highly responsive to fertilizer, have also shown remarkable gains. Yields of corn, the production of which exceeds that of all other cereals combined in the U.S., have nearly tripled over the past three decades.

Experience has demonstrated that in areas of high rainfall the application of chemical fertilizers in conjunction with other inputs and practices can double, triple or even quadruple the productivity of intensively farmed soils. Such levels of productivity are achieved in Japan and the Netherlands, where farmers apply up to 300 pounds of plant nutrients per acre per year. The use of chemical fertilizers is estimated to account for at least a fourth of man's total food supply. The world's farmers are currently applying 60 million metric tons of plant nutrients per year, an average of nearly 45 pounds per acre for the three billion acres of cropland. Such application, however, is unevenly distributed. Some poor countries do not yet benefit from the use of fertilizer in any significant amounts. If global projections of population and income growth materialize, the production of fertilizer over the remaining three decades of this century must almost triple to satisfy food demands.

Can the projected demand for fertilizer be met? The key ingredient is nitrogen, and fortunately man has learned how to speed up the fixation phase of the nitrogen cycle [see "The Nitrogen Cycle," by C. C. Delwiche, SCIENTIFIC AMERICAN Offprint 1194]. In nature the nitrogen of the air is fixed in the soil by certain microorganisms, such as those present in the root nodules of leguminous plants. Chemists have now devised various ways of incorporating nitrogen from the air into inorganic compounds and making it available in the form of nitrogen fertilizers. These chemical processes produce the fertilizer much more rapidly and economically than the growing of leguminous-plant sources such as clover, alfalfa or soybeans. More than 25 million tons of nitrogen fertilizer is now being synthesized and added to the earth's soil annually.

The other principal ingredients of chemical fertilizer are the minerals potassium and phosphorus. Unlike nitrogen, these elements are not replenished by comparatively fast natural cycles. Potassium presents no immediate problem; the rich potash fields of Canada alone are estimated to contain enough potassium to supply mankind's needs for centuries to come. The reserves of phosphorus, however, are not nearly so plentiful as those of potassium. Every year 3.5 million tons of phosphorus washes into the sea, where it remains as sediment on the ocean floor. Eventually it will be thrust above the ocean surface again by geologic uplift, but man cannot wait that long. Phosphorus may be one of the first necessities that will prompt man to begin to mine the ocean bed.

The great expansion of the use of fertilizers in this century has benefited mankind enormously, but the benefits are not unalloyed. The runoff of chemical fertilizers into rivers, lakes and underground waters creates two important hazards. One is the chemical pollution

EXPERIMENTAL PLANTINGS at the International Rice Research Institute in the Philippine Republic are seen in an aerial photograph. IR-8, a high-yield rice, was bred here.

RUINED FARM in the "dust bowl" area of the U.S. in the 1930's is seen in an aerial photograph. The farm is near Union in Terry County, Tex. The wind has eroded the powdery, drought-parched topsoil and formed drifts among the buildings and across the fields.

of drinking water. In certain areas in Illinois and California the nitrate content of well water has risen to a toxic level. Excessive nitrate can cause the physiological disorder methemoglobinemia, which reduces the blood's oxygen-carrying capacity and can be particularly dangerous to children under five. This hazard is of only local dimensions and can be countered by finding alternative sources of drinking water. A much more extensive hazard, profound in its effects on the biosphere, is the now well-known phenomenon called eutrophication.

Inorganic nitrates and phosphates discharged into lakes and other bodies of fresh water provide a rich medium for the growth of algae; the massive growth of the algae in turn depletes the water of oxygen and thus kills off the fish life. In the end the eutrophication, or overfertilization, of the lake slowly brings about its death as a body of fresh water, converting it into a swamp. Lake Erie is a prime example of this process now under way.

How much of the now widespread eutrophication of fresh waters is attributable to agricultural fertilization and how much to other causes remains an open question. Undoubtedly the runoff of nitrates and phosphates from farmlands plays a large part. There are also other important contributors, however. Considerable amounts of phosphate, coming mainly from detergents, are discharged into rivers and lakes from sewers carrying municipal and industrial wastes. And there is reason to believe that in some rivers and lakes most of the nitrate may come not from fertilizers but from the internal-combustion engine. It is estimated that in the state of New Jersey, which has heavy automobile traffic, nitrous oxide products of gasoline combustion, picked up and deposited by rainfall, contribute as much as 20 pounds of nitrogen per acre per year to the land. Some of this nitrogen washes into the many rivers and lakes of New Jersey and its adjoining states. A way must be found to deal with the eutrophication problem because even in the short run it can have damaging effects, affecting as it does the supply of potable water, the cycles of aquatic life and consequently man's food supply.

Recent findings have presented us with a related problem in connection with the fourth technology supporting man's present high level of food production: the chemical control of diseases, insects and weeds. It is now clear that the use of DDT and other chlorinated hydrocarbons as pesticides and herbicides is beginning to threaten many species of animal life, possibly including man. DDT today is found in the tissues of animals over a global range of life forms and geography from penguins in Antarctica to children in the villages of Thailand. There is strong evidence that it is actually on the way to extinguishing some animal species, notably predatory birds such as the bald eagle and the peregrine falcon, whose capacity for using calcium is so impaired by DDT that the shells of their eggs are too thin to avoid breakage in the nest before the fledglings hatch. Carnivores are particularly likely to concentrate DDT in their tissues because they feed on herbivores that have already concentrated it from large quantities of vegetation. Concentrations of DDT in mothers' milk in the U.S. now exceed the tolerance levels established for foodstuffs by the Food and Drug Administration.

It is ironic that less than a generation after 1948, when Paul Hermann Müller of Switzerland received a Nobel prize for the discovery of DDT, the use of the insecticide is being banned by law in many countries. This illustrates how little man knows about the effects of his intervening in the biosphere. Up to now he has been using the biosphere as a laboratory, sometimes with unhappy results.

Several new approaches to the problem of controlling pests are now being explored. Chemists are searching for pesticides that will be degradable, instead of long-lasting, after being deposited on vegetation or in the soil, and that will be aimed at specific pests rather than acting as broad-spectrum poisons for many forms of life. Much hope is placed in techniques of biological control, such as are exemplified in the mass sterilization (by irradiation) of male screwworm flies, a pest of cattle that used to cost U.S. livestock producers $100 million per year. The release of 125 million irradiated male screwworm flies weekly in the U.S. and in adjoining areas of Mexico (in a cooperative effort with the Mexican government) is holding the fly population to a negligible level. Efforts are now under way to get rid of the Mexican fruit fly and the pink cotton bollworm in California by the same method.

Successes are also being achieved in breeding resistance to insect pests in various crops. A strain of wheat has been developed that is resistant to the Hessian fly; resistance to the corn borer and the corn earworm has been bred into strains of corn, and work is in progress on a strain of alfalfa that resists aphids and leafhoppers. Another promising approach, which already has a considerable history, is the development of insect parasites, ranging from bacteria and viruses to wasps that lay their eggs in other insects. The fact remains, however, that the biological control of pests is still in its infancy.

I have here briefly reviewed the major agricultural technologies evolved to meet man's increasing food needs, the problems arising from them and some possible solutions. What is the present balance sheet on the satisfaction of human food needs? Although man's food supply has expanded several hundredfold since the invention of agriculture, two-thirds of mankind is still hungry and malnourished much of the time. On the credit side a third of mankind, living largely in North America, Europe, Australia and Japan, has achieved an adequate food supply, and for the remaining two-thirds the threat of large-scale famine has recently been removed, at least for the immediate future. In spite of rapid population growth in the developing countries since World War II, their peoples have been spared from massive famine (except in Biafra in 1969–1970) by huge exports of food from the developed countries. As a result of two consecutive monsoon failures in India, a fifth of the total U.S. wheat crop was shipped to India in both 1966 and 1967, feeding 60 million Indians for two years.

Although the threat of outright famine has been more or less eliminated for the time being, human nutrition on the global scale is still in a sorry state. Malnutrition, particularly protein deficiency, exacts an enormous toll from the physical and mental development of the young in the poorer countries. This was dramatically illustrated when India held tryouts in 1968 to select a team to represent it in the Olympic games that year. Not a single Indian athlete, male or female, met the minimum standards for qualifying to compete in any of the 36 track and field events in Mexico City. No doubt this was partly due to the lack of support for athletics in India, but poor nutrition was certainly also a large factor. The young people of Japan today are visible examples of what a change can be brought about by improvement in nutrition. Well-nourished from infancy, Japanese teen-agers are on the average some two inches taller than their elders.

Protein is as crucial for children's mental development as for their physical development. This was strikingly shown in a recent study extending over several years in Mexico: children who had been severely undernourished before the age of five were found to average 13 points lower in I.Q. than a carefully selected control group. Unfortunately no amount of feeding or education in later life can repair the setbacks to development caused by undernourishment in the early years. Protein shortages in the poor countries today are depreciating human resources for at least a generation to come.

Protein constitutes the main key to human health and vigor, and the key to the protein diet at present is held by grain consumed either directly or indirectly (in the form of meat, milk and eggs). Cereals, occupying more than 70 percent of the world's cropland, provide 52 percent of man's direct energy intake. Eleven percent is supplied by livestock products such as meat, milk and eggs, 10 percent by potatoes and other tubers, 10 percent by fruits and vegetables, 9 percent by animal fats and vegetable oils, 7 percent by sugar and 1 percent by fish. As in the case of the total quantity of the individual diet, however, the composition of the diet varies greatly around the world. The difference is most marked in the per capita use of grain consumed directly and indirectly.

The two billion people living in the poor countries consume an average of about 360 pounds of grain per year, or about a pound per day. With only one pound per day, nearly all must be consumed directly to meet minimal energy requirements; little remains for feeding to livestock, which may convert only a tenth of their feed intake into meat or other edible human food. The average American, in contrast, consumes more than 1,600 pounds of grain per year. He eats only about 150 pounds of this directly in the form of bread, breakfast cereal and so on; the rest is consumed indirectly in the form of meat, milk and eggs. In short, he enjoys the luxury of the highly inefficient animal conversion of grain into tastier and somewhat more nutritious proteins.

Thus the average North American currently makes about four times as great a demand on the earth's agricultural ecosystem as someone living in one of the poor countries. As the income levels in these countries rise, so will their demand for a richer diet of animal products. For the increasing world population at the end of the century, which is expected to be twice the 3.5 billion of today, the world production of grain would have to be doubled merely to maintain present consumption levels. This increase, combined with the projected improvement in diet associated with gains in income over the next three decades, could nearly triple the demand for grain, requiring that the food supply increase more over the next three decades than it has in the 10,000 years since agriculture began.

There are ways in which this pressure can be eased somewhat. One is the breeding of higher protein content in grains and other crops, making them nutritionally more acceptable as alternatives to livestock products. Another is the development of vegetable substitutes for animal products, such as are already available in the form of oleomargarine, soybean oil, imitation meats and other replacements (about 65 percent of the whipped toppings and 35 percent of the coffee whiteners now sold in U.S. supermarkets are nondairy products). Pressures on the agricultural ecosystem would thus drive high-income man one step down in the food chain to a level of more efficient consumption of what could be produced by agriculture.

What is clearly needed today is a cooperative effort—more specifically, a world environmental agency—to monitor, investigate and regulate man's interventions in the environment, including those made in his quest for more food. Since many of his efforts to enlarge his food supply have a global impact, they can only be dealt with in the context of a global institution. The health of the biosphere can no longer be separated from our modes of political organization. Whatever measures are taken, there is growing doubt that the agricultural ecosystem will be able to accommodate both the anticipated increase of the human population to seven billion by the end of the century and the universal desire of the world's hungry for a better diet. The central question is no longer "Can we produce enough food?" but "What are the environmental consequences of attempting to do so?"

An Early Energy Crisis and Its Consequences

by John U. Nef
November 1977

In the 16th century Britain ran out of wood and resorted to coal. The adoption of the new fuel set in motion a chain of events that culminated some two centuries later in the Industrial Revolution

In medieval Europe wood was utilized not only in many types of construction but also in most domestic and industrial heating. Then in Britain in the second half of the 16th century coal came into widespread use as a substitute for wood as fuel. The earliest coal-burning economy the world has known was established first in England and then in Scotland between about 1550 and 1700. This transition from woodcutting to coal mining as the main source of heat was part of an early British economic revolution. The first energy crisis, which has much to do with the crisis we now face, was a crisis of deforestation. The adoption of coal changed the economic history of Britain, then of the rest of Europe and finally of the world. It led to the Industrial Revolution, which got under way in Britain in the last two decades of the 18th century. The substitution of coal for wood between 1550 and 1700 led to new methods of manufacturing, to the expansion of existing industries and to the exploitation of untapped natural resources.

To make these assertions is not to belittle the role of other changes during the Middle Ages and the Renaissance in the coming of our industrialized world. The century before Britain's wood crisis—the 100 years from about 1450 to 1550—was characterized by a new spirit of expansion. Voyages of discovery were launched, carrying explorers to the ends of the earth. The art of printing with movable type spread across Europe, and the production of paper expanded; millions of books were printed and put in circulation. In central Europe, where the major centers of mining and metallurgy were to be found, the output of ores, particularly silver-bearing copper ores, multiplied severalfold. The years between 1494 and 1529 have been described as bringing about a "revolution in the art of war." With the help of the new firearms Spain conquered Mexico and Peru.

These and other innovations increased, directly or indirectly, the need for all existing kinds of energy: the heat provided by wood and the power provided by wind, animals and running water. The need for larger amounts of wood for construction and for heating, particularly for the smelting and refining of ores, called for a substantial increase in the felling of trees.

All Europe felt these pressures, and yet the first large area to experience an acute shortage of wood was Britain. Why did the fuel revolution that led to new uses of heat energy begin in that particular place? Was wood particularly scarce there? It seems to be true that the most populous parts of Scotland (the areas surrounding the Firth of Forth) were barren of trees; a wit from England is said to have observed in the reign of James I that if Judas had repented in the king's native land (Scotland), he would have been hard put to find a tree on which to hang himself! Such an explanation does not fit England. The wood crisis there has to be attributed to the requirements of expanding agriculture, industry and commerce, all stimulated by a growing, shifting population.

It appears that Sweden and the Netherlands were the only other European countries to experience anything comparable to the growth and resettlement of the British population in the period from 1550 to 1700. The population of England and Wales, about three million in the early 1530's, had nearly doubled by the 1690's. The resulting demand for wood for various purposes was further increased by changes in the distribution of the population. In this period the inhabitants of London multiplied at least eightfold, from some 60,000 in 1534 to some 530,000 in 1696.

According to Gregory King's estimate for the latter year, the British capital had by then become the largest city in Europe and perhaps the world. King estimates that England's other "cities and... market towns" had a total population of about 870,000. This means that although only one person in 10 was a "townsman" in the 1530's, one person in four was a townsman in the 1690's. Larger towns meant heavier demands on nearby wood supplies. Moreover, outside the towns there was much migration of the unemployed across the country in search of work. Wherever they found employment, shelter had to be provided, putting still another strain on the forests.

During the reigns of Elizabeth I (1558–1603) and James I (1603–25) this pressure on the supply of trees was reflected in the soaring cost of firewood and lumber for construction. The period from 1550 to 1640 was a time of inflation throughout Europe, but the price of wood in England rose very much faster than that of any other commodity in general use anywhere. Complaints of deforestation came from all parts of the kingdom.

Wherever coal seams outcropped in Europe, coal had been burned in small quantities since the 12th century. (It had been more extensively burned in China earlier than that and also to some degree in Roman Britain.) In Europe during the later Middle Ages peasants had occasionally warmed their homes or stoked their lime kilns and smithies with these "black stones." Why then was coal not widely adopted as a fuel on the Continent and in Britain before the forests were seriously depleted?

In societies earlier than the one that arose in western Europe in medieval times mining was looked on with disfavor. It was often regarded as robbery, even as a kind of rape. Unlike the plow, which made the earth fertile, the pick and shovel removed what seemed to be irreplaceable soil and subsoil.

By the early 16th century a different attitude toward the exploitation of the more valuable underground resources found expression in two books. In *De re metallica* (1556) Georgius Agricola (1494–1555) ranked the miner's calling higher than "that of the merchant trading for lucre." And in *Pirotechnia* (1540) Vannoccio Biringuccio (1480–1539) advocated an all-out assault on these underground riches. He advised "whoever mines ores...to bore into the center of the mountains...as if by the work of necromancy or giants. They should not only crack the mountains asunder but also turn their very marrow upside down in order that what is inside may be seen and the sweetness of the fruit despoiled as soon as possible."

The new dignity attached to mining was reserved for metallic ores. It did not extend to coal. The medieval craftsmen who needed fuel wanted their work to be beautiful, whether it was for their church or for rich laymen. The unpleasant smoke and fumes of coal therefore limited the market for it. There was little incentive before the mid-16th century to dig deep into the soil in search of this dirty fuel as long as wood was available, and there seemed to be an abundance of that. Biringuccio himself believed the forests of Europe could fill all conceivable future demands for fuel. In *Pirotechnia* he wrote: "Miners are more likely to exhaust the supply of ores than foresters the supply of the wood needed to smelt them. Very great forests are found everywhere, which makes one think that the ages of man would never consume them...especially since Nature, so very liberal, produces new ones every day." Coal is mentioned only once in his long treatise and then just to dismiss it: "Besides trees, black stones, that occur in many places, have the nature of true charcoal, [but] the abundance of trees makes [it] unnecessary...to think of that faraway fuel."

Less than a generation later the English turned to coal under pressure from the high price of wood. By the early 17th century efforts by the government to stop deforestation were felt to be imperative because the shortage of lumber for shipbuilding seemed to threaten Britain's existence. A royal proclamation of 1615 laments the former wealth of "Wood and Timber," the kind of wood that is "not only great and large in height and bulk, but hath also that toughness and heart, as it is not subject to rive or cleave, and thereby of excellent use for shipping, as if God Almightie, which had ordained this Nation to be mighty by Sea and navigation, had in his providence indued the same with the principall materiall conducing thereunto." By the middle of the 17th century coal had proved so useful and was already so widely burned that the British had come to make necessity a virtue. They reconciled themselves to the disappointing failure of their explorers to locate sources of precious metal and of their miners to find much of it in Britain itself. In spite of the smoke and fumes of coal and in spite of a widespread distaste for it, by the time of the civil war in the 1640's Londoners were dependent on the coastwise shipment of coal to keep warm. In 1651 the anonymous author of *News from Newcastle* wrote verses in praise of the new fuel. "England's a perfect World! Has Indies too! / Correct your Maps; New-castle is Peru!... / Let th' naughty Spaniard triumph, 'til 'tis told / Our sooty mineral purifies his gold."

Even earlier, as is made clear by William Harrison's *Description of Britain* (1577) and by a petition London brew-

COAL WAS BRITAIN'S PRINCIPAL FUEL by the end of the 17th century. Coal heavers, such as the ones shown in this print from 1805, handled coal destined for homes and industries across Britain and for many foreign countries as well. In background are coal barges.

ers addressed to Sir Francis Walsingham, Queen Elizabeth's secretary of state (1578), coal was acquiring a new and important place in domestic and industrial heating. The surviving records of customs officials at Newcastle-on-Tyne (and later records of other towns) reveal a continuous and rapid growth in the shipments of coal between 1550 and 1700, first from Newcastle-on-Tyne and then from other ports. These records suggest that the coastwise shipments increased at least twentyfold between 1550 and 1700. Coastwise imports to London grew even faster, probably more than thirtyfold, which is not surprising in view of the multiplication of the city's population in that period. Lord Buckhurst, who became Queen Elizabeth's lord treasurer at the end of the 16th century, required the customs officials during the 1590's to determine the "rate of growth" in coal shipments from Newcastle, thereby introducing a new concept into human affairs. The calculations on which Buckhurst insisted indicated that taxes on coal shipments could be counted on to provide a continually increasing source of revenue, and so taxes on coal shipments were imposed in 1599 and 1600.

The most impressive rises in the growth rate of coal production occurred in the second half of the 16th century and at the beginning of the 17th. In fact, the growth rate in the volume of coal mined between 1556 and 1606 may even exceed the growth rate (computed from less incomplete statistics) in the volume mined during the first part of the 19th century, that is, at the height of Britain's Industrial Revolution. The actual quantities involved in the rapid growth of coal production in the earlier period may seem insignificant today, but it is the viewpoint of the Elizabethans and their immediate successors that needs to be recaptured. To them the expansion in the output of coal must have seemed extraordinarily rapid.

Coal was not only a source of energy but also a spur to technological development. Most products that could be manufactured with open wood fires were damaged by contact with coal fumes. John R. Harris has commented that as a result "coal was hardly ever adopted without significant alteration of industrial processes." Indeed, the technological advances of the Industrial Revolution were largely the culmination of the innovative period associated with the conversion to coal.

New methods of firing had to be developed in which the materials to be heated were protected from direct contact with the burning coals and the gases evolved in their combustion. Otherwise the coal would have had to be reduced to coke and so purged of its noxious properties. After about 1610 glass began to be manufactured with mineral fuel in a variant of the reverberatory furnace, a system that later played an important role in the growth of other major industries. In this type of furnace an arched roof reflects the heat of the burning coal onto the material to be heated, thereby preventing the contamination of the material by substances originating with the fuel. The potash and sand to be melted down to form glass were enclosed in a clay crucible to further protect them from the fumes. Like the reverberatory furnace, the crucible was later employed in many other manufacturing processes.

Over the decades following 1610 new technology brought coal into many kinds of manufacturing. The cementation process for converting wrought iron into steel with coal was introduced between 1612 and 1620. By 1618 a method of baking bricks in coal fires near London was described by the Venetian ambassador in words showing that Italians were no longer disposed to ignore this "faraway fuel" as Biringuccio had recommended. Before the British civil war of the 1640's coke was introduced for the drying of malt in connection with the brewing industry, which had expanded rapidly during most of the 16th century with the spread of hop gardening from the Netherlands.

One of the most important applications of coal following the restoration of the British monarchy in 1660 was in the adaptation of the reverberatory furnace for smelting nonferrous metals. This innovation of the 1680's made it possible to smelt the lead, copper and tin ores of Britain with coal. By the end of the 17th century only the production of pig and bar iron remained dependent on wood. Although the problem was not completely solved until the 1780's, an important step toward its solution was taken in 1709, when coke was introduced by Abraham Darby the elder at his blast furnace in Shropshire. In this kind of furnace the fuel and the ore are in contact. The trouble with Darby's process was that it yielded a kind of pig iron that, unlike the pig iron produced with wood, could not be converted to wrought iron, the form of iron then most in demand. In 1784 Henry Cort invented the puddling process, in which pig iron (even pig iron from a blast furnace) is remelted and manipulated in a

BEFORE THE ADVENT OF COAL wood was the main source of heat energy in Europe. Industrial power was provided by wind, animals and running water. It was often necessary to convert the wood to charcoal by partially burning it in furnaces such as the ones shown here. The wood was piled in stacks, covered with earth and powdered charcoal dust and then burned. The covering kept combustion at a minimum so that the end product was charcoal rather than ashes. For some manufacturing processes charcoal was preferred to wood because it is mostly pure carbon and so yields a greater amount of heat per unit volume of fuel. Illustration is from Diderot's *Encyclopédie, ou Dictionnaire Raisonné des Sciences, des Art et des Métiers*.

coal-fired reverberatory furnace to produce wrought iron. Until Cort's invention the making of iron remained largely dependent on charcoal. Thus although iron production in England had increased several times between 1540 and about 1620, this growth had been arrested by the shortage of wood for making charcoal in the 1620's. Beginning in that decade, however, an increase in iron imports, notably from Sweden, made possible a continuous slow growth in the output of finished iron wares, which were already produced by processes utilizing mineral fuel.

Samuel Eliot Morison has observed about innovations in shipbuilding and navigation that there is always "a gap between the invention of a device and persuading owners to supply it or sailors to use it." The same can be said about the spread of inventions connected with the introduction of coal in Britain after 1550. It took a substantial period of experimentation to make the new coal-based methods efficient. For example, in brickmaking (as also in the baking of clay tobacco pipes) there was much waste through breakage when coal-burning furnaces were introduced. Before the end of the 17th century, however, few bricks were lost in the course of coal firing.

As it became clear that coal could mean cheaper and more efficient production more industries turned to it as a fuel. Before the end of the 17th century in Britain's growing textile industry, where processes such as steaming and dyeing called for large quantities of fuel, that fuel was usually coal. Before 1700 the expanding manufactures of salt, alum, copperas (vitriol, or ferrous sulfate), saltpeter, gunpowder, starch and candles depended on coal. Coal was then also being employed extensively in the preparation of preserved foods, vinegar and Scotch whisky, and in brewing, soap boiling and sugar refining. A French visitor studying English technology in the Midlands in 1738–39 reported that the new coal-burning kilns (made of coal-baked bricks) had produced such a superior lime fertilizer that the yield of arable land had tripled. He considered coal "the soul of English manufactures."

The spread of coal into British homes that began early in Elizabethan times was continuous throughout the 17th century. This was not the only residential change brought about by the conversion of Britain to mineral fuel. The kingdom was extensively rebuilt under Queen Elizabeth and her Stuart successors. Brick and stone structures (with mortar made from coal-burned limestone) were replacing wood ones. Windows made of glass (produced in coal furnaces) were installed in buildings to retain the heat from the new coal-burning fireplaces (which had iron grates and brick chimneys manufactured with coal). In spite of its grime and stench coal had brought a new comfort to Britain's damp, chilly climate. Already in 1651 the author of *News from Newcastle* observed that the sacks of coal had heightened the joys of intimacy!

Coal had been so successfully incorporated into the British technology and economy that during the last four decades of the 17th century wood prices stopped rising. Some years ago I ventured a rough estimate of three million tons for Britain's annual coal produc-

THE WOOD CRISIS of the 16th century coincided with the expression of a changed attitude toward mining. Until the Middle Ages mining had been widely considered an affront to nature. In *De re metallica*, published in 1556, however, Georgius Agricola expressed a new respect for mining. This careful account of metallurgy and mining gives a good picture of those industries at about the time when it was first necessary to increase coal production. In this illustration from *De re metallica* a tunnel, *D*, has been cut into a hill and three shafts have been dug from above. Although the mining was facilitated when a shaft connected with the tunnel, not all the shafts were meant to do so. In this case the shaft at *A* will be mined only from the surface; the shaft at *B* connects with the tunnel, and the tunnel will soon connect with the shaft at *C*. Material was hauled vertically out of a shaft with a windlass, which was usually covered with a shed to keep rain out of the shaft. Agricola pointed out that it was desirable to construct a separate building as a dwelling because "sometimes boys and other living things fall into the shafts."

tion in the 1690's. In Harris' opinion that figure "may eventually prove conservative rather than excessive." It appears that at least as much as four times more heating was done at that time with coal than was done with wood. Never before had a major country come to depend on underground resources for the bulk of its fuel.

Although the exploitation of coal had largely solved the fuel shortage before 1700, there was still a wood shortage because other demands for wood had increased. In 1618 a traveler from London described his time as a "rattling, rowling, rumbling age" and remarked that "the World runnes on [wood] Wheeles." Great quantities of lumber were required for the construction of the growing number of ships and horse-drawn vehicles needed to transport people and goods across water and land. Moreover, although there was some reforestation during the 17th century, more and more forest was being cleared for farms and pastures. In addition smaller areas were being cleared for the growing metallurgical industries and for the expansion of mining, particularly of coal mining. Britain's forests simply could not keep up with the island's demand for wood.

The British were forced to supplement their domestic supply with imports, mostly from the American colonies and from the Baltic region. (In his *Wealth of Nations,* published in 1776, Adam Smith remarked that in his native Edinburgh "there [was] not perhaps a single stick of Scotch timber.") The imports of wood were paid for in part by the mounting exports of coal and probably in greater part by the mounting exports of textiles manufactured in varying degrees with coal fuel. This foreign trade, and even more the rapidly expanding coastwise trade, had already resulted in the 17th century in the development of a large British merchant marine. New colliers, or coal ships, were designed to carry more coal with a smaller crew, and the coastwise coal trade was considered the chief training ground for seamen, a major factor in Britain's emergence as a sea power.

Yet in some instances coal made Britain less dependent on imported commodities, for example salt. As Robert Multhauf explains in his forthcoming book *Neptune's Gift: A History of Common Salt,* this commodity was an essential one in Europe during the 16th and 17th centuries. In Britain, where food from the sea was coming to occupy a more important place in an increasingly abundant diet, salt was indispensable for preserving fish. In southern and western France salt was obtained by allowing the sun to evaporate seawater in shallow pans, or ponds, but this method was impractical in Britain's climate. In the early 16th century two-thirds of the salt consumed in England had to be imported, mostly from France. Britain's almost total conversion to coal changed the situation. At the end of the 17th century some 300,000 tons, or nearly 10 percent of the coal mined annually in Britain, was burned to evaporate water for the production of salt in England and Scotland. As a result the country had become virtually self-sufficient in terms of salt.

The conversion to a new kind of fuel might have had less effect on the British economy if Britain had been poorly, or even only moderately, endowed with coal. Before the end of the 17th century, however, it had become clear that Britain possessed enormous coal reserves. A piece of coal-inspired technology provided new and reassuring information. The device, called a boring rod, was introduced at the beginning of the 17th century. Early boring-rod surveys were inaccurate, but before the 17th century had ended mining experts were able to determine the thickness and quality of coal seams without sinking shafts. Boring rods had become reliable tools and had revealed a newfound land of plenty under the soil and even under the surrounding seas. Much of the island was seen to be underlain with coal. This trove of energy resources began to exert a pull in the direction of a quantity production that had not been equaled in previous history.

REVERBERATORY FURNACE made possible the utilization of coal in spite of the fuel's reactive smoke and flames. The arched roof of a reverberatory furnace reflects the heat of combustion onto the material to be heated. When the fuel being burned is coal, the arrangement prevents contamination of the product by the substances in the coal fumes. This view of a reverberatory annealing furnace is from the section on coinmaking in Diderot's *Encyclopédie.* Blanks, such as one shown in furnace, had to be annealed before coins could be struck.

It was not until the middle of the 19th century, after an unprecedented acceleration in the rate of growth of production had begun, not until the publication in 1865 of William Stanley Jevons' *The Coal Question,* that some became aware that the coal deposits were exhaustible. By this time resources of petroleum and natural gas were known outside Britain, although neither were much exploited until later in the 19th century. It was not until the 1920's that a few people began to realize the supplies of all fossil fuels had distinct limits.

The shift to fossil fuel in the 17th century led on after 1785 to the aggressive exploitation of the world's vast stores of iron ore. Without the coming of the first coal-burning economy the age of iron and steel might never have developed. The conversion to coal that began in Elizabethan England had further consequences in bringing into being the modern mechanized age. The utilization of steam power and of travel by rail were also vital to the coming of that age. Attempts to build steam engines and to introduce railed ways with horse-drawn wagons in Britain go back at least to the reign of James I, but it was not until 1712 that Thomas Newcomen installed at a colliery in Staffordshire a steam en-

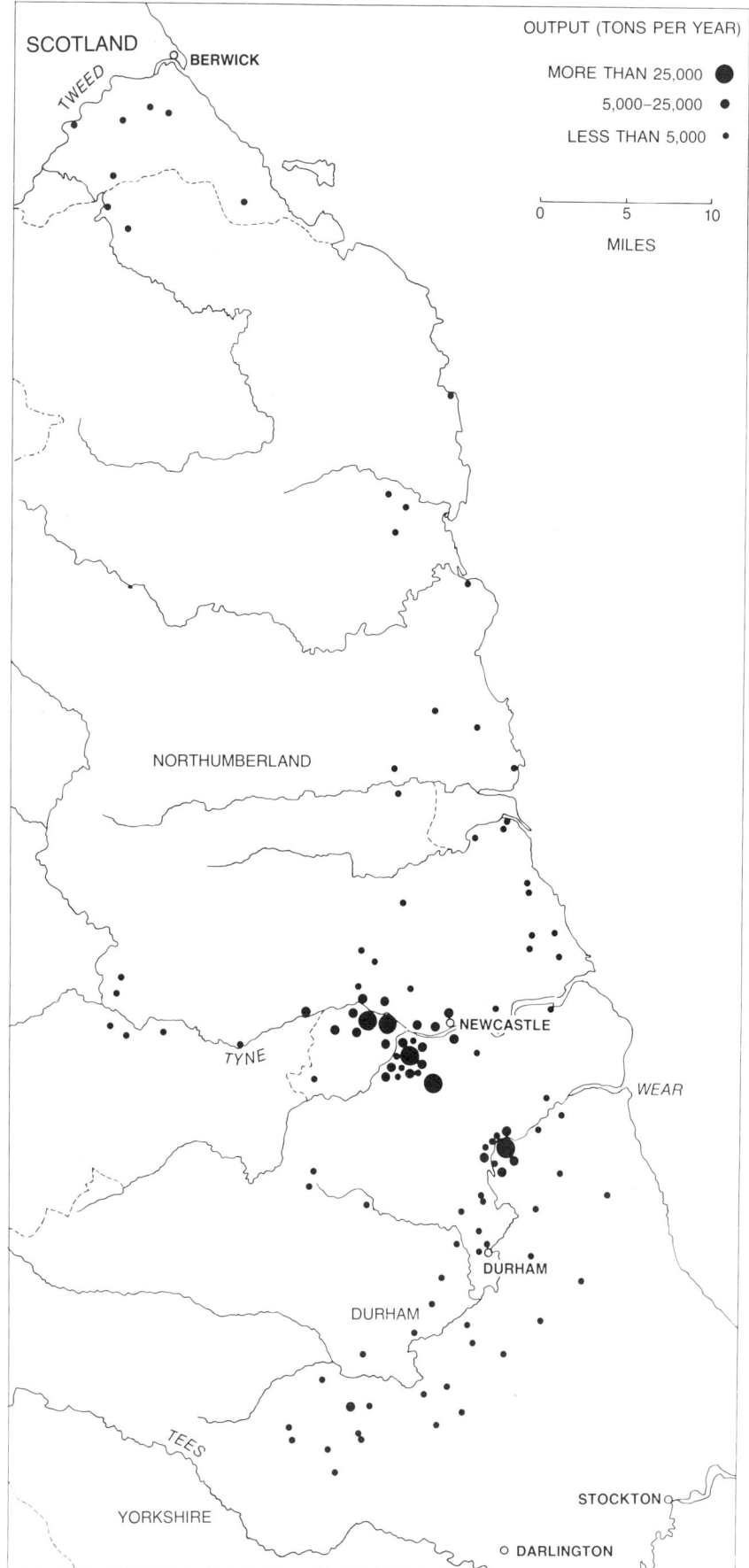

MAP OF DURHAM AND NORTHUMBERLAND COUNTIES in England shows the approximate locations of collieries in 1635. There were probably more collieries than are shown on the map. Illustration is adapted from map in author's *The Rise of the British Coal Industry.*

gine that actually worked. It was to no small extent the needs of coal mining and coal transport that led to the steam engine and the railroad. Britain's damp climate made the damage of water in the multiplying coal mines a serious problem. Power from horses (which ate costly fodder) and from running water (which required capital for dams and overshot wheels) was diminishing the profits from coal mining throughout the 17th century. The compelling need for more efficient drainage systems in the British coal mines in that early age played an important part in the development of the Newcomen engine. Once these "fire engines" were invented, as John S. Allen and Alan Smith have shown, they spread rapidly across Britain between 1712 and about 1730.

It should be mentioned that coal appears to have been burned for many industrial purposes in China in the Sung era, in the 10th and 11th centuries. The episode was largely forgotten. It clearly did not lead, as it did in Europe much later, to an industrial revolution.

Studies made over the past 50 years, since I published my own two volumes on coal, have shown that the period of Britain's energy crisis—the late 16th and 17th centuries—was also the period of what has come to be called the scientific revolution. The revolution in thinking that brought modern science into being was an even more important factor than coal in the establishment of the mechanized age. By the 1620's and 1630's Europeans were becoming aware of the immense growth in production promised by the development of the new fuel. It was in those two decades that Francis Bacon wrote *The New Atlantis* (1627) and René Descartes his *Discourse on Method* (1637). Bacon's imaginary island over the seas was provided with a great institution of scientific research presiding over human destiny, and he was confident that a new abundance, made possible by the growth of scientific knowledge, would solve intellectual and moral problems as well as economic ones. And Descartes in his *Discourse* was no less confident. Even more specifically than Bacon he foresaw greater output, lighter labor and longer life for human beings everywhere. Even at that time there was talk of airships, submarines, devastating explosives and journeys to the moon. It was the scientific revolution in the late 16th and 17th centuries, together with the economic transformations brought about by the introduction of coal, that gave birth to the industrial world in which we live.

In Britain the period of the onset and resolution of the energy crisis (1550–1700) was characterized by increased returns from labor in all kinds of production. The British statesman and historian Lord Clarendon (1609–1674) was referring to this prosperity when he wrote that during the period before the 1640's the English "enjoyed... the fullest measure of felicity, that any people in any age for so long time together have been blessed with; to the wonder and envy of all the parts of Christendom." Clarendon did not base his assertion on what would today be considered reliable statistics, and indeed it is not possible to provide such statistics. Yet the new information on English economic growth contained in recent books of Eric Kerridge's and of mine supports Clarendon's statement. Britain, which lagged behind the rest of Europe in many economic areas during the later Middle Ages, was probably ahead of the other European countries in per capita agricultural and industrial output by 1700.

Kerridge has shown that whereas it has been thought that British agriculture was transformed in the 18th and early 19th centuries, the transformation actually took place between the late Middle Ages and the end of the 17th century. In this period, he writes, "the improvement of yields [from farming] must have been enormous. Corn [that is, grain] and grass yields rose about fourfold, and the yields of the fallows [the land not previously tilled] increased out of recognition. All told it is difficult to resist the conclusion that yields rose up to tenfold and fivefold on the average."

In the 1920's and 1930's most students of the coming of industrialism (myself included) accepted the explanations of Karl Marx, Sir William Ashley, Max Weber, Henri Hauser and others. The works of these scholars suggested that the advent of capitalism and of the "capitalist spirit" was the main factor leading to the overwhelming increase in the output of goods and services in the 19th century. I now think that an even more important factor was a growing faith in quantitative progress, in the multiplication of output.

Late in the 16th century a new attention came to be focused on concepts of quantity. The effects of this new concern could be seen in the more exact measurements employed in the developing natural sciences and in the replacement of the Julian calendar by the far more accurate Gregorian calendar. It was also reflected in a series of inventions designed to speed up numerical calculations, one made by Galileo (1564–1642), another made by the Dutch mathematician Simon Stevin (1548–1620) and two more by the Scottish laird John Napier (1550–1617), the originator of logarithms. A sophisticated mathematics—the calculus—was developed first in France after 1620 and more fully later in the 17th century by Newton and Leibniz. The idea of rates of growth introduced during the Elizabethan age brought a fresh precision to economic studies. The new point of view emphasized the probable value of quantitative goals to humanity. The transformation of industrial aims constituted a major advance toward an industrialized world.

In 1697 an Englishman named James Puckle wrote: "Our artisans [are] universally allow'd the best upon Earth for Improvements." This was certainly true in manufacturing that called for efficiency and quantity production. Yet a different evaluation needs to be made of the state of the arts and the luxury crafts in Britain following the conversion to coal. At the juncture of the 17th and 18th centuries Europe was eager to learn more efficient production methods from the British, but the British were equally eager to learn ways of fashioning beautiful products and environments from the Italians, the French and the Dutch. (Nowhere in 17th-century Europe was the quest for beauty and harmony in buildings and furnishings as remarkable as it was in the Netherlands of Rembrandt and Vermeer.) Harris has shown that in the 18th century the British, in spite of their aspirations to high fashion, had great difficulty copying the methods of making high-quality glass that were employed by the French at Saint-Gobain. In Britain the rise of the coal industry had weakened the position of craftsmanship and art as the heart and soul of production.

Moreover, the rise of coal mining had cast a shadow over the laborers connected with coal. Coal miners and coal carriers, stained by the black mineral, were often outcasts. They were seen as black men, and in the 17th century, when real black men were being shipped as slaves from Africa to America, coal laborers were being subjected to a new form of slavery in Scottish collieries and coal-burning salt pans.

As coal spread from Britain to the rest of Europe in the late 18th century and afterward the concern for beauty in manufactures and in the human environment weakened. Throughout history this kind of dedication to beauty has been important in setting reasonable limits to economic growth. The advent of coal seems to have diminished such dedication. The exploitation of the earth's resources has often violated the bounds of good taste. To make the most of these resources calls not only for ingenuity but also for restraint. At present man's dependence on fossil fuels is as problematic as his dependence on wood was some 400 years ago. The best hope for the fruitful exploitation of fuel resources may lie in a renewal and an amplification of the standards of beauty. If humanity is to advance, the making of history must become an art, that is, a search for beauty.

The Migrations of Human Populations

by Kingsley Davis
September 1974

Ancient migrations carried man to almost every corner of the earth; modern ones are an ebb and flow that results from technological and economic inequality. The migrations of today are the largest of all

Human beings have always been migratory. Sometime between 100,000 and 400,000 years ago man's predecessor *Homo erectus* had spread from China and Java to Britain and southern Africa. Later, Neanderthal types spanned Europe, North Africa and the Near East; modern *Homo sapiens*, originating probably in Africa, reached Sarawak at least 40,000 years ago, Australia some 30,000 years ago and North and South America more than 20,000 years ago. Excluding Antarctica, Paleolithic man made his way to every major part of the globe. Except for species dependent on him, he achieved a wider distribution than any other terrestrial animal.

Since this propensity to migrate has persisted in every epoch, its explanation requires a theory independent of any particular epoch. My own view is that the abiding cause is the same trait that explains man's uniqueness in many other ways: his sociocultural mode of adaptation. As culture advanced and diversified, a profound and distinctly human stimulus to migration developed, namely technological inequality between one territorial group and another. At the same time the possibility of migration was increased by man's capacity to adjust culturally to new environments without the slow process of organic evolution.

Although the particular conditions of each epoch shaped migration, the underlying cause remained the same. Paleolithic man, for example, was a hunter and gatherer who naturally followed his prey and forage. Urging him on was the contrast between exploited territory and virgin territory. This tendency, inherent in any predatory animal, was augmented by the unique advantages his technology gave him in hunting itself and in adapting to environments into which his prey took him. With weapons and cooperation he could quickly skim the big game from an area and move on, and with fire, skins, shelters and tools he could adjust readily to the new climatic and dietary conditions he encountered. Soon, however, most areas (and eventually all of them) would be skimmed and occupied by humans. The thrill and above all the advantage of moving into an empty land would be gone; instead migration would involve confrontation between newcomers and earlier inhabitants. At that point the difference in technology between one group and another would replace the difference between exploited territory and virgin territory as the stimulus to migration. Men with superior techniques could invade and use more fully an area occupied by others.

Whatever the specific factors, the worldwide dispersion of Paleolithic man had significant consequences. By enlarging the resource base it enabled the human population to expand to a size otherwise impossible. Men remained sparse, to be sure, but they roamed everywhere. Migration also stimulated sociocultural evolution both by making environmental adjustments necessary and by diffusing innovations. Finally, since migration also involved interbreeding, it caused man, in spite of his worldwide dispersion and his adaptation to diverse environments, to remain a single species.

Offhand one might think that the coming of agriculture and animal husbandry some 10,000 to 12,000 years ago would have reduced migration by making people "sedentary." The evidence is to the contrary. Not only did some Neolithic practices, such as slash-and-burn agri-

LONE DOG'S "WINTER COUNT," a pictographic historical chart painted a century ago on the inside of a buffalo robe (*opposite page*), chronicles 71 turbulent years in the migratory life of the Yankton tribe of the Dakota, or Sioux, Indians. The chart, in which each successive year (or winter, as the Plains Indians counted) is represented by a symbol recalling some memorable event of that interval, is dominated by encounters between the Dakotas, themselves comparative newcomers to the northern Great Plains, and other westward-migrating people, both Indian and white. This particular specimen, part of the Heye Foundation collection at the Museum of the American Indian in New York, is a copy made by the Indians for their own use from the original chart by Lone Dog, the Yankton whose task it was to record the years from the winter of 1800–1801 to that of 1870–1871 (or, according to the Dakota system, from the "Crow killed 30 Sioux" winter to the "Crow war-party surrounded and killed" winter). The record begins near the center of the robe and spirals outward in a counterclockwise fashion. The first symbol, for the winter of 1800–1801, consists of 30 black lines (representing the Sioux dead) arrayed in three rows of 10 lines each, the outside lines being joined. The last symbol, for the winter of 1870–1871, consists of a large circle (a fort) that encloses a number of smaller arcs (the Crow dead) and is in turn surrounded by figures representing the attacking Sioux; the short streaks radiating to and from the enclosure denote bullets and mark the first time on the Dakota charts that Indians are shown using firearms in battle. Other noteworthy events depicted include the outbreak of various diseases among the Indians (smallpox in 1801–1802, whooping cough in 1813–1814, cholera or measles in 1818–1819); the first appearance in their region of horses wearing shoes (1802–1803), of trading posts (1817–1818, 1819–1820, 1822–1823), of Spanish blankets (1853–1854) and of beef cattle from Texas (1868–1869). Celestial events recorded include a single bright meteor (1821–1822), a meteor shower (1833–1834) and an eclipse of the sun (1869–1870). The symbolism of the entire chart was interpreted by Col. Garrick Mallery in the Fourth Annual Report of the Bureau of American Ethnology (1882–1883).

culture and nomadic pastoralism, necessitate movement through a sizable territory but also the Neolithic transition as a whole created a gulf between peoples who had made the transition and those who had not. Furthermore, the Neolithic complex did not arise fully developed anywhere, nor did it ever cease developing; rather, technological improvements in production, weaponry and transport kept appearing, and that created inequality and hence migratory potential between one territory and another. Pastoralists or shifting cultivators could evict hunters and gatherers, because hunters and gatherers required more land per man and therefore could mobilize less manpower at any one spot. For the same reason permanent cultivators could evict migratory cultivators and herders, but they might be evicted in turn by pastoralists with superior weapons and greater mobility.

Stuart Piggott of the University of Edinburgh describes the process of domestication (sheep and goats) and agriculture (barley and wheat) starting in the Near East about 11,000 years ago and gradually spreading across Europe as the climate modified. "By 2500 B.C.," he writes, "stone-using peasant economies had been established over the whole of Europe, side by side with [hunters and fishermen]." This wave of change was still in progress in Europe long after a new one had begun, starting with the smelting of copper in the Near East about 3000 B.C. The use of rare metals set afoot a perennial search for natural deposits and created routes between mines and trading centers. In Spain metalworking enclaves, apparently manned by foreigners, were established as early as 2500 B.C. The Near Eastern centers where the metals accumulated, however, became the foci of invasions by "barbarians." About 2200 B.C., according to Piggott, hundreds of sites in Palestine, Anatolia and Greece were sacked and pillaged. Among the invaders were Indo-European speakers originating somewhere northeast of the Black Sea. As Hittites they reached Anatolia by 2000 B.C., and as Aryans they reached India by 1500 B.C. They pushed into the Balkans and even into northern and central Europe.

Other migration streams moved in a west-east direction. There is the famous case of the bell-beaker potters, who, starting before 2000 B.C. from coastal settlements in Portugal, journeyed north and east, carrying not only their metallurgy in copper and gold but also their highly standardized pottery—so standardized that, as Piggott notes, "bell-beakers made in Britain or Bohemia might almost be mistaken for those of Spanish manufacture." Bell-beaker settlements were established in many parts of Europe, as far away as the River Vistula [see illustration on this page]. In contrast to other Europeans at the time, the bell-beaker people were round-headed and strongly built.

Somewhat later than in Europe people of Neolithic culture (Melanesians and Polynesians) settled the tiny islands of the vast Pacific. By the fourth century even Easter Island, the world's most isolated piece of land, some 1,200 miles from the nearest inhabitable spot, was reached. The lateness of settlement in the Pacific islands suggests that great stretches of water were the main barrier to migration. Long before those islands were settled man had reached and had traveled throughout the Americas, where he evolved new Neolithic cultures.

With the rise of town-based and quasi-literate civilizations new kinds of inequality between one territory and another arose, generating migration. The civilized centers operated as magnets, drawing both peasants and artisans from the immediate hinterland and barbarians from beyond. The barbarians frequently came not as peaceful newcomers but as marauders or invaders. In eastern Europe and central Asia the vast steppes evidently allowed pastoralism and an increase in population but not much agriculture. From this region nomads (the word is Greek for pasturing) began their invasions, each tribe pushing the one before it. When the tribesmen learned to ride horses, by at least 1500 B.C., their rapid movement made possible the creation of empires stretching for thousands of miles. Each wave tended eventually to become sedentary itself, a target for a fresh wave of nomadic invaders.

The list of invaders from central Asia is bewildering. Among the best-remembered are the Hittites, who reached the Anatolian plateau by 2000 B.C., were masters of iron metallurgy by 1500 B.C. and succumbed to the Phrygians and others about 1200 B.C.; the Scythians, who drove and followed the Cimmerians into central Europe and raided Egypt in 611 B.C.; the Huns, who emerged in Mongolia and from the second century B.C. were the scourge of China and moved steadily westward, reaching the Volga around A.D. 250, Gaul and Italy the following century, and stopping in 453 with the death of Attila. The Roman Empire was finally subjugated by two sets of nomadic invaders: those from eastern Europe and central Asia (Goths,

EXTENSIVE CHARACTER of prehistoric migrations is evident from this map, which shows the generalized distribution and movements of the bell-beaker potters, who, starting from coastal enclaves in Portugal, established settlements in many parts of Europe about 2000 B.C. Colored and gray areas on the map represent four different subgroups of bell-beaker culture. The map is based on the work of Stuart Piggott of the University of Edinburgh.

Vandals, Alani, Franks and Burgundians) and those from the Arabian peninsula. The latter expanded rapidly after A.D. 630, until by 750 the Islamic world extended from Spain to the Punjab. Much of the expansion was accomplished not by Arabs, however, but by nomads from central Asia. The Seljuk Turks, forced out by the resurgent Chinese of the Sung dynasty, overran Persia, Armenia, Anatolia and Syria in the 11th century. Two centuries later Mongol tribes under Genghis Khan conquered northern China, eastern Turkestan, Afghanistan, Persia, Russia, a large part of eastern Europe, Asia Minor, Mesopotamia, Syria and finally southern China. As a result the Ottoman Turks were pushed into Asia Minor in the 14th century and then to the Balkans, culminating with the conquest of Constantinople in 1453. The Turks ruled India from the 11th to the 16th century, when the Moguls (offshoots of Genghis Khan's people) took over and ruled until the British arrived.

How much actual migration was involved in these conquests it is impossible to say, but it was clearly from sparsely settled territory to thickly settled and from less advanced societies to more advanced. If it had been the only form of movement into civilized centers, the centers could not have existed. A more normal type was the movement of peasants and artisans into the city to sell their wares or earn a wage. This, however, did not suffice. The rulers and entrepreneurs of the civilized world needed manpower under direct control, and they took it by force, mainly from the barbarian world.

"The old Sumerian ideograph for slave," the historian William Linn Westermann wrote, "means 'male of foreign land,' indicating that the source of slavery was war and its prisoners." Although slavery was not a major institution in Egypt, it was indispensable in most of the ancient world. At the time of Pericles, Athens had between 75,000 and 150,000 slaves, representing between 25 and 35 percent of the population. They were the non-Greeks who were captured wherever the Athenians were fighting. The slaves practiced nearly all occupations; a large contingent (approximately 20,000) worked in the silver mines at Laureion, and a significant number were used in handicrafts that gave the city something to trade for foodstuffs and materials from distant lands.

In Athens the free immigrants called *metics*, who were permanent residents rather than passing traders, may have outnumbered the slaves. Most of them were Greeks, some being rural-urban mi-

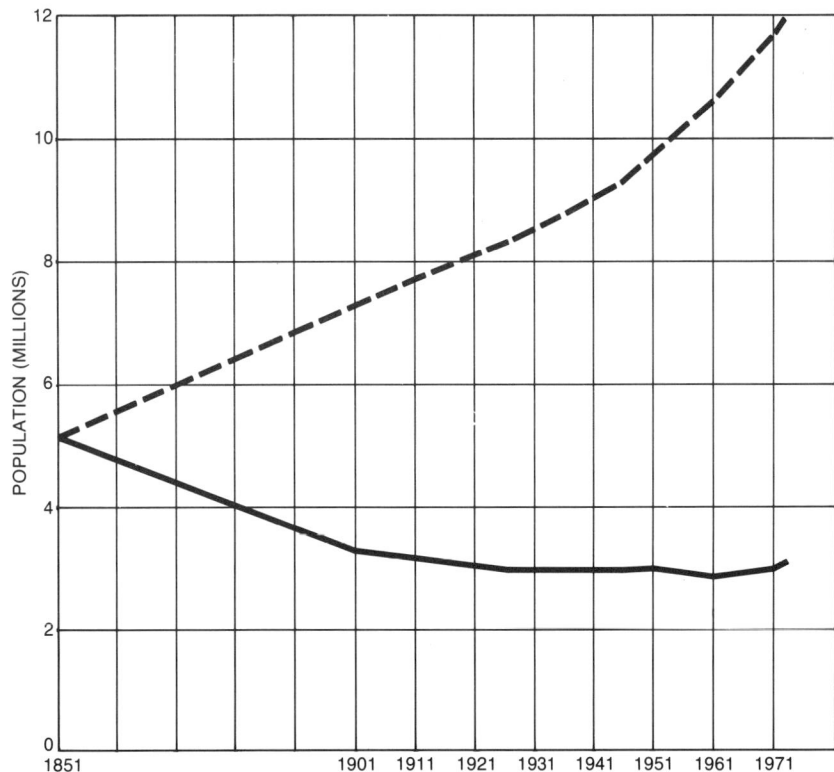

IMPACT OF EMIGRATION on the population of Ireland since 1851 is exceptional in that Ireland was the only European country whose population declined as a result of emigration. Solid black curve shows the actual population of Ireland during this period; broken black curve shows the projected population without emigration but with the birth and death rates that actually prevailed. (It seems unlikely, however, that the actual rates would have been maintained if there had been no emigration; emigration enabled the country to keep its marital fertility higher than that of other northwestern European countries.)

grants in the sense familiar today. Counting them with the slaves, at least half of the population in the time of Pericles consisted of migrants.

Rome was even more dependent on slaves than Athens, but the number at any one time hardly measures their importance, because many were freed. Doubtless there would have been more free migrants if there had been fewer slaves. In Rome, where a single military campaign might bring in 50,000 prisoners, the influx of slaves appears to have overshadowed free migration. Tenney Frank long ago calculated from inscriptions that at least 80 percent of the population born in Imperial Rome were of slave extraction. Since the Romans, like all urban populations until recently, failed to replace themselves, the large population of Rome (perhaps a million at its zenith) was generated entirely by migration, much of it slave.

A milder form of migration, but still one controlled by the civilized centers, was colonization. Beginning before 750 B.C., the Greeks spread settlements from Spain to the eastern shore of the Black Sea. Whereas the Phoenicians, with the exception of Carthage, had founded mere trading stations, the Greeks installed full-fledged towns to serve as trading centers and to provide opportunities for poor Greek citizens. With the Athenian navy as the link, these towns remained attached to Greece and were colonies in that sense; instead of expanding territorially, however, they remained only urban outposts. When Alexander tried to settle Greeks in large territories, he failed. The Romans came closer to reaching Alexander's ideal, because they gradually Romanized entire regions of Europe, but they did so more by installing Roman institutions than by sending out Roman settlers. Although administrators and army veterans did go to the provinces, the Roman population was not large enough to supply many migrants.

Clearly, by the close of the Roman Empire virtually all forms of migration were known. In all of them an inequality between areas led either to voluntary movement or to compulsory movement controlled by the sending or receiving area. The modern age did not so much invent new forms of migration as alter drastically the means and conditions of the old forms. The general cause was

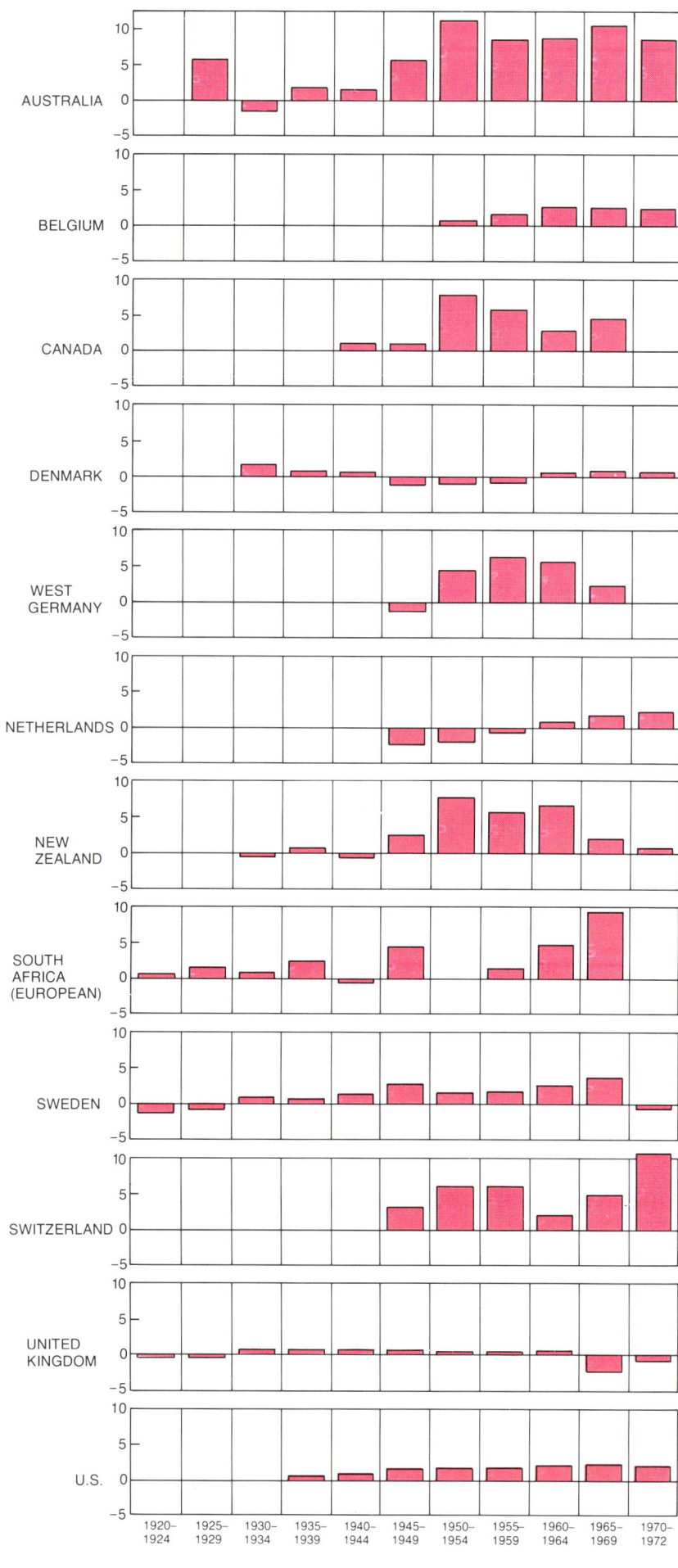

still the same: the difference between technologically advanced and less advanced. What was new was the depth of the difference, its world scope and its capacity for change.

Since Europeans initiated the technological transformation, the key to modern migration is to be found in their relation to other peoples. In the 16th and 17th centuries, for the first time, the world as a whole began to be one migratory network dominated by a single group of technologically advanced and culturally similar states. Largely as a result of the European countries' use of this network, they eventually were able to start the Industrial Revolution and thus enormously enhance their world dominance. The subsequent spread of industrialism to other parts of the world made industrialism per se, not European culture, the main basis of technological inequality.

How did the Europeans, their armies, navies and economies honed by incessant warfare among themselves, deal with the world they had discovered? Their first impulse was to skim the cream, to obtain luxuries and precious metals by confiscation, all the while preventing their European rivals from doing the same, but this could not last. Soon they followed the ancient world's example by setting up trading posts and coastal fortifications, but they needed more control over indigenous production and therefore claimed entire territories. Their handling of each territory depended on its climate, accessibility and inhabitants. In these terms four types of territory can be distinguished.

The first type, inaccessible and sparsely inhabited (such as Tibet, central Africa and the eastern Andes), was left in abeyance and need not detain us. A second type, tropical or subtropical, sparsely inhabited and accessible by sea, was immediately exploited; a third type, also accessible and lightly populated but temperate, was eventually exploited; a fourth type, accessible but thickly populated, was handled more indirectly. Let us discuss the last three types.

Warm and accessible territories were of immense potential value, because their products complemented those of Europe. When sparsely peopled by ab-

NET MIGRATION RATES per 1,000 population per year are presented in the bar charts at left for 12 developed countries in the period from 1920 to 1972. The absence of bars signifies the unavailability of data.

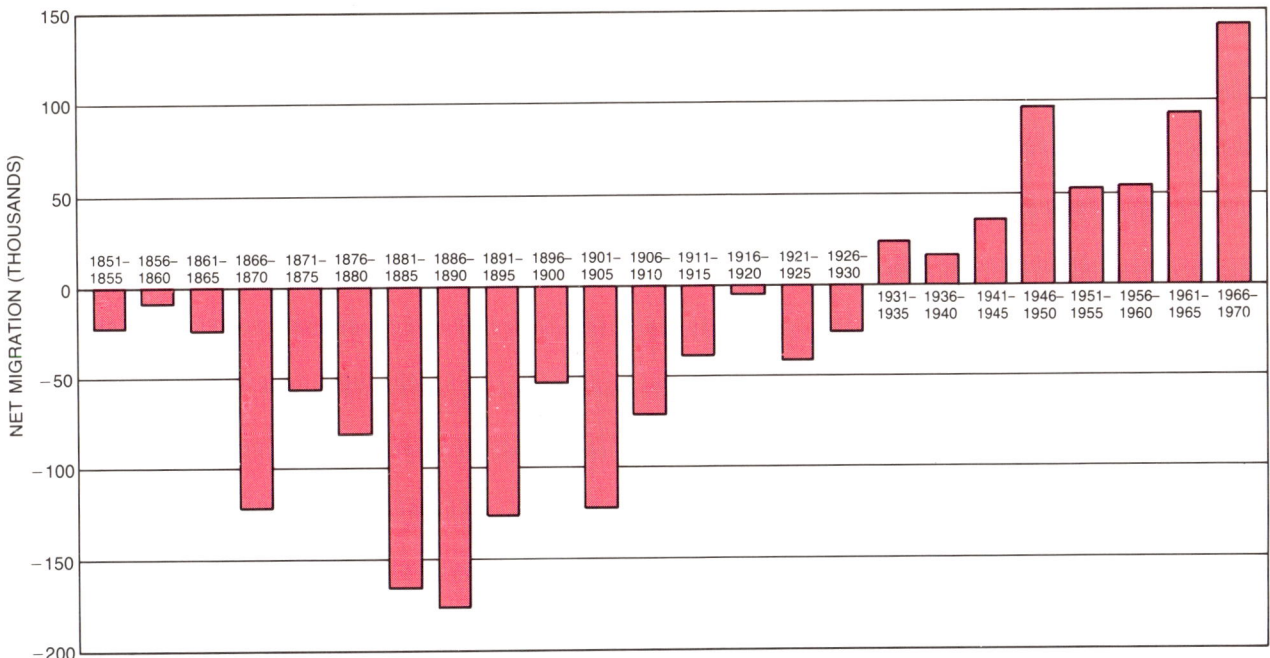

REVERSAL in the historic tide of migration in the case of a typical European industrial country is seen clearly in this bar chart, which records net migration in and out of Sweden since the middle of the 19th century. Before 1930 Sweden was a land of emigration; since then it has been a land of immigration. Other advanced European countries have exhibited a similar migratory reversal.

origines, the land required only clearing. Hence in the region closest to Europe—the Caribbean and the Gulf of Mexico and the warm coasts of North and South America—the Europeans undertook the production of indigo, rice, cotton, spices, sugar, tobacco, coffee, tea and other tropical crops. For this they needed huge inputs of cheap labor, but Europeans themselves were too expensive and too ill-adapted to such work in a hot climate, and the original inhabitants were too few and too recalcitrant. To obtain the needed labor the European managers resorted to the same device the Greeks and Romans had used: slavery. According to estimates recently evaluated and summarized by the historian Philip D. Curtin, 9.6 million slaves were imported into slave-using areas between 1451 and 1870. Since mortality during the voyages was great—normally 10 to 25 percent for slaves—the total number enslaved probably exceeded 11 million, virtually all from Africa. In distance and number this movement transcended any other slave migration in history.

When slavery was abolished in the British Empire in 1833, the British, who controlled a large share of the world's tropical lands, substituted indentured labor, and the Dutch did the same. Instead of coming from Africa, however, indentured plantation labor came overwhelmingly from densely settled areas such as southern China, Java and India, which not only were closer to new zones of plantation agriculture in Malaya, Sumatra, Burma, Ceylon and Fiji but also were societies in which thousands of illiterate and landless workers could be induced to risk their fate in unknown places. Usually the indentured contract guaranteed the return fare after three to five years of service, but plantation managers often escaped this clause by paying a bonus for reenlistment. Migrants coming under a short-term *kangani* agreement (group recruitment under a leader, a form used for areas near the place of origin) were normally free to leave employment after a month if they paid back the cost of their journey. In some cases labor recruitment, ostensibly by contract, was achieved by force. In the latter half of the 19th century the practice of kidnapping Melanesians to work in Queensland and Fiji was notorious under the name of "blackbirding," and the impressment of Chinese coolies for naval duty gave rise to the verb "shanghai." Abusive or not, the contract system fueled plantation agriculture in tropical areas around the world. I have estimated that 16.8 million Indians left India, of whom 4.4 million stayed away permanently. It seems probable that several million Chinese left China and hundreds of thousands left Java. Although the coolie migration was historically brief, its total volume probably exceeded that of slave migration.

The third type of region, usually tropical but in any case densely settled and civilized (such as China, India, Java and Japan), fell either under the direct control of Europeans or under their indirect influence. When the Europeans did gain control, they tended to set up estate agriculture in less populated areas, causing currents of internal migration similar to the international movement of contract labor. Europeans themselves did not migrate to these countries in any number, because they could not compete with the natives except as managers and officials, and not many of these were needed. The maximum number of Europeans ever in India was about 200,000 in 1911, representing one European for every 1,515 Indians. The centers of population in Asia were major exporters of people, not importers.

It was the fourth type of area, Temperate Zone lands with sparse and backward native populations, that attracted European migrants. These regions, comprising about a fourth of the earth's inhabitable area, were suited to European technology and temperament and offered an unparalleled opportunity for settlement. At first, however, Europeans showed amazingly little interest. Spain and Portugal, the earliest colonial powers, deliberately discouraged permanent migration. The Dutch and the French sent out few settlers. The trouble was that Europe's population was growing slowly and few people were so poor or so persecuted that they wanted to transfer to a wild area to live under subsistence conditions and battle savages. Such places were good for soldiers, criminals, adventurers and derelicts but not for ordinary citizens. For three centuries only a trickle of Europeans settled in these territories, and once there they clung to the coasts where contact with Europe could be maintained. Since the original inhabitants were decimated by even slight contact, the total population of the Temperate Zone colonies grew slowly, more by the natural increase of the Europeans already there than by further immigration. By 1800, almost 200 years after the founding of the first permanent colony at Jamestown, the white population of the U.S. was only 4.3 million. As late as 1840, 52 years after the start of the first penal colony in Sydney, there were only 190,000 Europeans in Australia and 2,000 in New Zealand. Similarly, Canada, Argentina, Chile and South Africa all had few white people in the early 19th century.

Only with the introduction of a new and greater technological gap produced by the Industrial Revolution did European emigration take off. Although the continent was already crowded, the death rate began to drop and the population began to expand rapidly. Simultaneously urbanization, new occupations, financial panics and unrestrained competition gave rise to status instability on a scale never known before. Many a bruised or disappointed European was ready to seek his fortune abroad, particularly since the new lands, tamed by the pioneers, no longer seemed wild and remote but rather like paradises where one could own land and start a new life. The invention of the steamship (the first one crossed the Atlantic in 1827) made the decision less irrevocable.

Little wonder that the great period of voluntary overseas European migration was from 1840 to 1930, and that the mania moved across Europe along with industrialism. At least 52 million people emigrated during that period. This equaled a fifth of the population of Europe at the start and exceeded the number of Europeans already abroad after more than three centuries of settlement.

The prime destination was the nearest Temperate Zone land, North America, but the wave spilled over to Australia, southern South America, southern Africa and central Asia. The movement fed on itself, not only because the migrants wrote back to friends and relatives but also because the new lands underwent rapid development. They turned out crops and products that competed with those of Europe, worsening the plight of many Europeans and improving the prospects for migrants. By World War I, 65 years after the big wave had started, the New World countries already rivaled northwestern Europe economically.

The new lands were so vast that not all parts could be settled simultaneously. In Russia settlement began beyond the Urals, but elsewhere it hit the seacoasts first and worked its way inland. The moving frontier became a part of life and folklore.

What were the consequences of the migrations of slaves, indentured laborers and free migrants in the four centuries preceding the Great Depression? One was a steep rise in world population

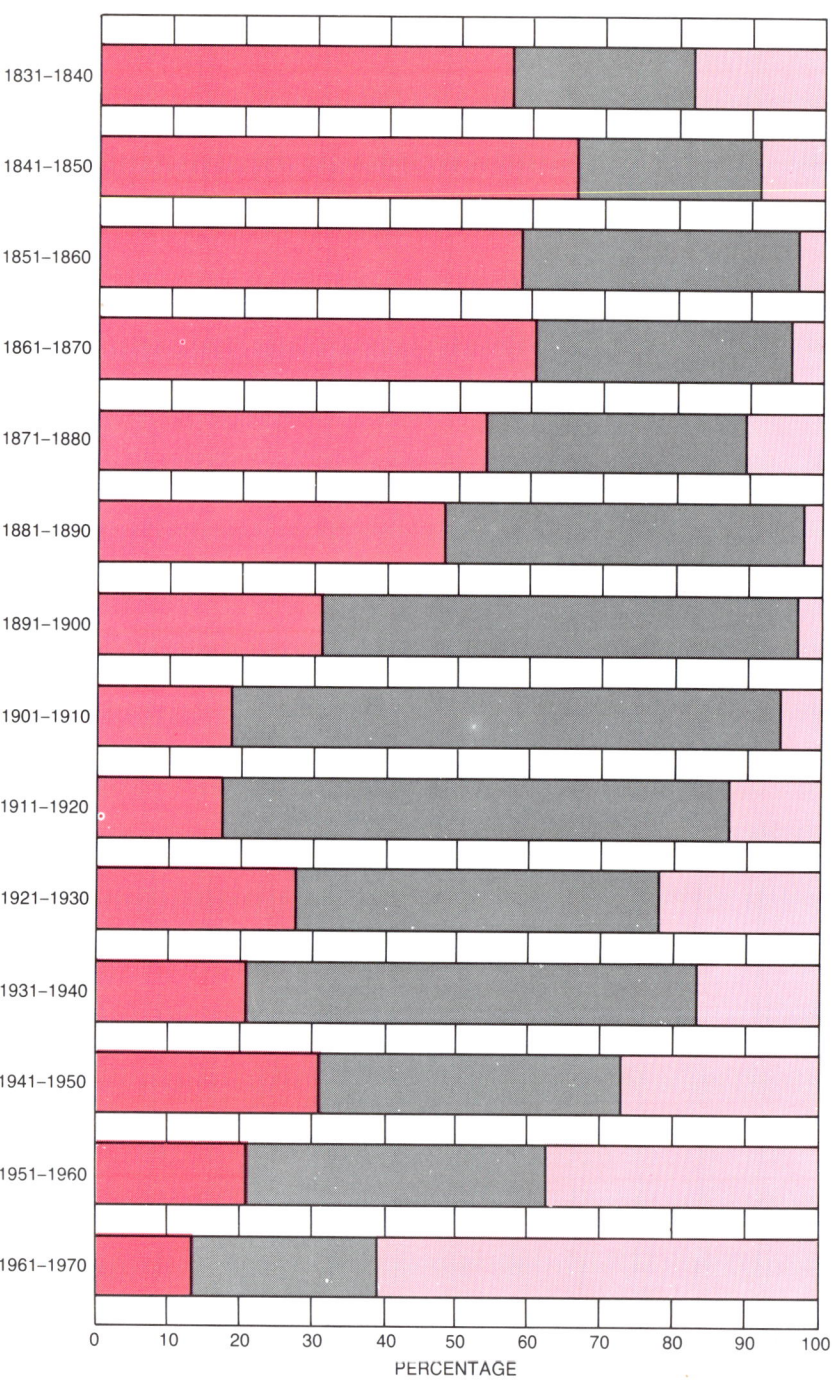

CHANGING COMPOSITION OF IMMIGRANTS to the U.S. is evident in these bars, which break down the immigration totals for each decade from the 1830's through the 1960's according to whether the area of origin was northwestern Europe (*dark color*), the rest of Europe (*gray*) or the rest of the world except Canada (*light color*). The bars reflect how eastern and southern Europe gradually replaced northwestern Europe as the main source of immigration to the U.S. and how these regions were in turn displaced by Latin America and Asia. (Immigrants from Canada are omitted from the chart because a substantial number of them were not originally Canadians but recent migrants to that country.)

growth after 1750, because in the regions of origin (except in Ireland) the migrations did little to damp population increase, whereas in the regions of destination, after initial setbacks, they greatly stimulated it. The sending areas, by the standards of the time, were densely settled. Emigration therefore enabled them to postpone an inevitable change in birth or death rates. Comparative data show that in Europe the countries with the highest rates of emigration postponed longest the reduction in their birth rate. France, with little emigration, had the lowest birth rate; Ireland and Italy, with much emigration, had high birth rates. Ireland was the only country whose population declined; if it had had no migration but had exhibited the birth and death rates that actually existed, its population today would be nearly 12 million instead of about three million [see illustration on page 139]. In Europe as a whole emigration did little to hold down population growth; the population rose from 194 million in 1840 to 463 million in 1930—about double the rate for the world as a whole. Emigration had even less effect in Asia and Africa.

In contrast, in the areas of destination the effect was electric. Even the primitive peoples after initial decimation generally made a strong comeback, and the descendants of African, Asian and European immigrants multiplied so fast that they were widely cited as being an illustration of the biological maximum of human increase. The reason for the growth was that entire new continents were being transformed overnight from stone-age technology to modern technology. This was a much greater transition than what was happening in Europe itself; in fact, it was the most fantastic jump in cultural evolution ever known, and it took the lid off population growth. Between 1750 and 1930 the population of the main areas of destination increased 14 times, while the rest of the world increased only 2.5 times.

Another consequence of the migrations was a geographic redistribution of the world's population. In 1750 the new regions, which accounted for half of the world's land area, held fewer than 3 percent of its people; by 1930 they held 16 percent.

At the same time the world's racial balance was altered. Certain groups became extinct, others disappeared by hybridization and still others made great gains. Caucasians increased 5.4 times between 1750 and 1930, Asians 2.3 times and blacks less than two times.

Even more dramatic was the geographic displacement of races. By 1930

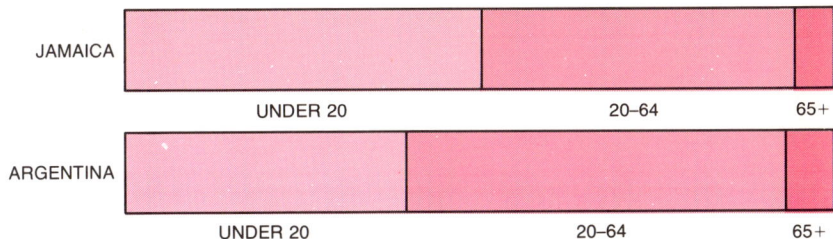

AGE STRUCTURE of a typical country of emigration (Jamaica) is contrasted with that of a typical country of immigration (Argentina). Migrants tend to be in the middle age range.

approximately a third of all Caucasians (and by 1970 more than half) did not live in Europe and more than a fifth of all blacks did not live in Africa. If all Europeans had stayed in Europe and had had the same natural increase that Europeans exhibited everywhere, there would have been 1.08 billion people in Europe in 1970 instead of 650 million. The earliest immigrants exercised a disproportionate influence on subsequent racial distribution because their natural increase lasted longer than that of later immigrants. Although the immigration of blacks into the U.S. was minuscule after 1850 compared with European immigration, they almost held their own by sheer excess of births over deaths. Blacks represented 15.7 percent of the American population in 1850 and 11.1 percent by 1970.

Although most of the migrations involved no drastic shift in climate, some of them did. In the U.S. there are now 11 million blacks outside the South and 50 million whites (mostly northwestern Europeans) in the South. In Queensland in Australia there are about 1.7 million whites and in sultry Panama about half a million.

As a result of the displacement and mixing of races there are more racial problems in the world today than at any time in the past. In nearly all immigrant countries, in the Americas, Southeast Asia and southern Africa, race is one of the most important bases of political division. In some countries particular hybrids have become separate groups, for example the "Coloureds" who comprise 9.4 percent of the population of South Africa and the "Creoles" who make up 35 percent of the population of Surinam. Among immigrant countries Australia has been most effective in excluding racial minorities. Australia's freedom from racial strife compares with that of Sweden or Denmark.

It is often thought that with two world wars, a Great Depression and restrictive

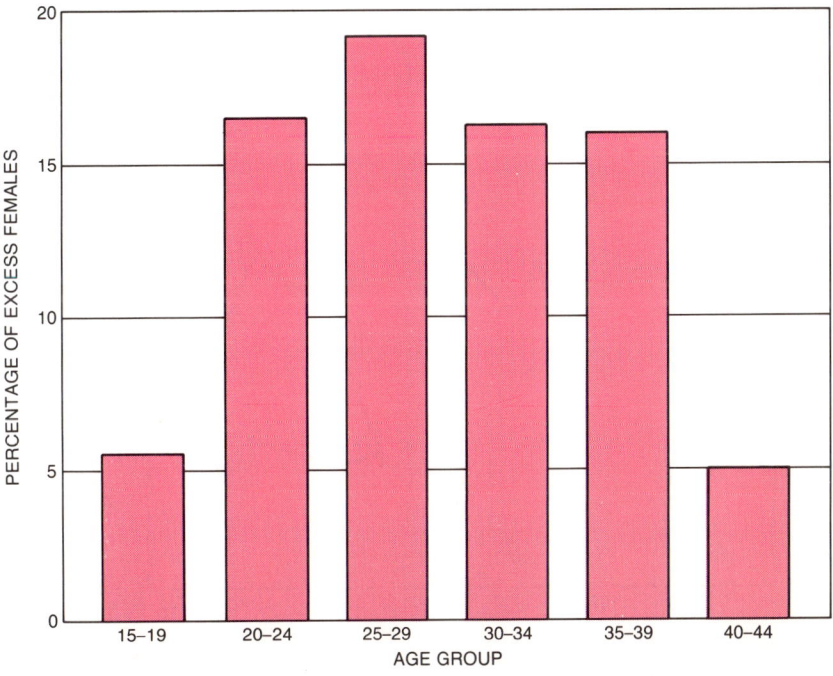

SEX RATIO in a country of emigration such as Jamaica also tends to be unbalanced, since men (particularly young men) participate in international migration more than women.

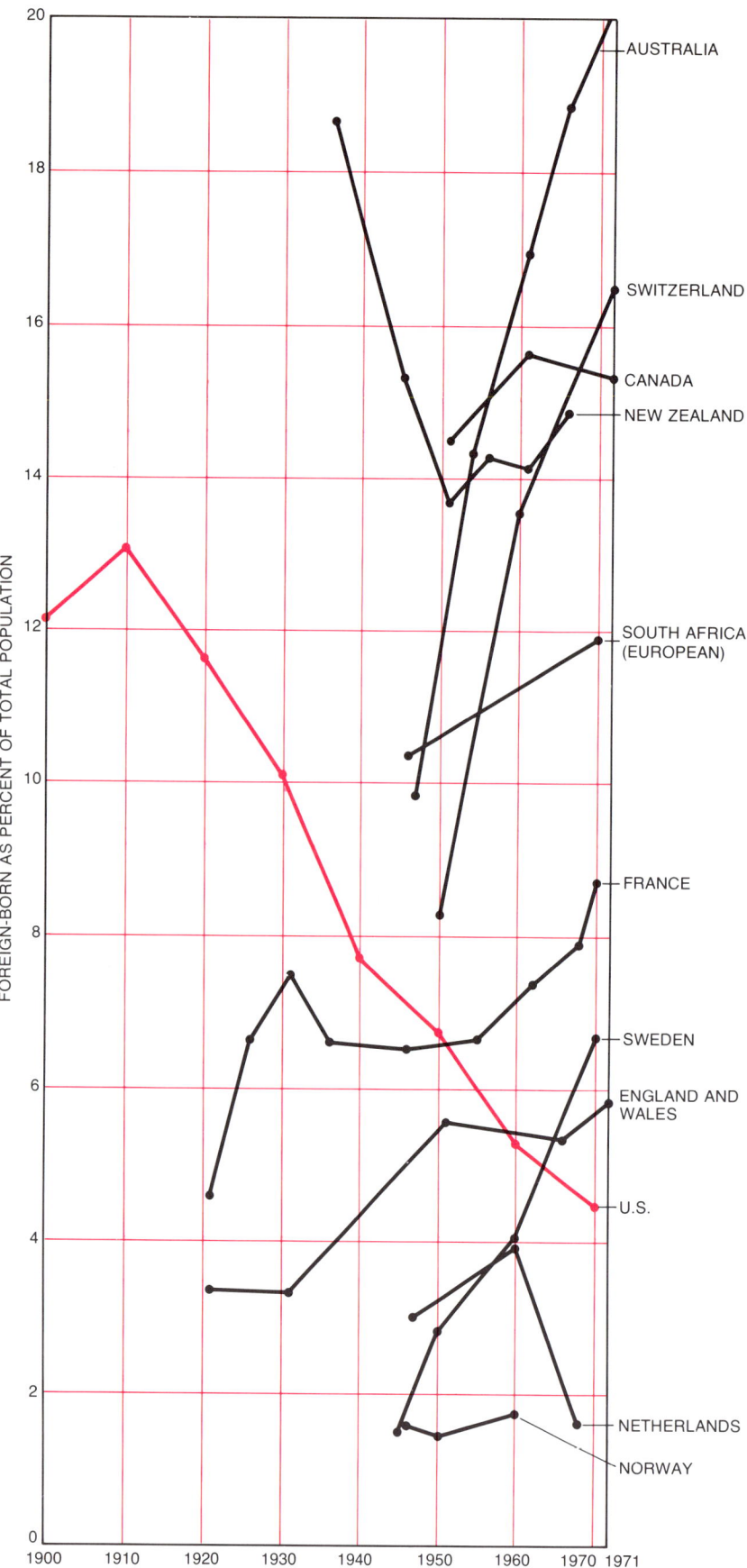

FOREIGN-BORN POPULATIONS of a selection of countries are plotted as a percentage of each country's total population. In most developed countries proportion has been rising, and in some of older industrial countries of Europe it now exceeds proportion in U.S.

legislation the volume of international migration has declined. This illusion appears to be born of the preoccupation with free migration from Europe to the New World. In 1942 an Australian, W. D. Forsyth, pointed out in *The Myth of Open Spaces* that desirable lands sparsely occupied by primitives no longer existed, that Europe's population had virtually ceased to grow and that therefore the traditional flow of migration from the Old World to the New World was over. He was right, but he did not foresee the magnitude of two developments then already under way: the rebirth of forced migration in the world and a massive reversal of migration between the developed countries and the underdeveloped ones.

To understand these two developments one must recall the principle that migration is generated by significant differences between one area and another. In the 20th century some of these differences have been political and ethnic. Two world wars ignited by a nation obsessed with the separateness and solidarity of its own folk were ironically ended by a legitimation of that obsession for nations in general. Under the Wilsonian banner of "national self-determination" it was all peoples, not only the Germans, who could claim folk sovereignty. Carried to its extreme, this ideal, which justified the dismemberment of the defeated German, Turkish and Austro-Hungarian empires, encouraged every minority to seek a territory of its own and every colony to seek "independence." In a world where most states had minorities and many had colonies the result was to frighten them into seeking ethnic purity and to release former colonial areas. Between 1900 and 1970 independent nations multiplied 2.5 times, from 56 to 142. The combination of political independence and economic weakness made the greatly expanded phalanx of underdeveloped states receptive to systems of government that promised shortcuts to Utopia in exchange for political freedom. The wars, revolutions and ideological struggles that accompanied these changes not only uprooted people against their will but also made migration a political instrument. Unlike slavery or kidnapping, the force was usually applied by the sending region rather than the receiving one, and in the name of ethnic purity or ideological correctness rather than personal gain.

Ethnic purity was easiest to attain when two countries had minorities that "belonged" to each other and could therefore be "exchanged." Thus the

Treaty of Neuilly (1919) sanctioned an exchange of some 46,000 Greeks for about 120,000 Bulgarians; the Treaty of Lausanne (1923) provided for the transfer of 190,000 Greeks from Turkey to Greece and 388,000 Muslims from Greece to Turkey. In 1945 and 1946 population-exchange agreements were made between Czechoslovakia and the U.S.S.R. and between Hungary and Yugoslavia. Some of the exchanges were more like panics and less like trades than the treaties imply. In the Czechoslovak-Russian exchanges migration was virtually all one way—out of the U.S.S.R.

Cases of exchangeable minorities are rare, however, because many minorities have no state to which they belong, and when they do, they are seldom paired there with a reciprocal minority. Minorities were more often expelled than exchanged. After World War II some 2.7 million Sudeten Germans were transferred to Germany and 415,000 Karelian Finns were moved to Finland. Even if a group had nowhere to go, it might still be expelled or forced to flee, as were 250,000 Armenians who survived Turkish massacres, a million White Russians, 2.5 million Chinese and 200,000 Hungarians.

In the effort to provide a separate territory for each ethnic or ideological camp, nations have been carved up, as in the partition of India, Korea, Vietnam and Palestine, often creating two minority problems where one existed before, but in any case setting in motion a forced migration. Following the partition of India some 15 million people survived the flight to or from Pakistan, yet there are still Muslims in India and Hindus in Pakistan. A difficult minority problem was created in Palestine by legal and illegal immigration of Jews from other countries where, in nearly all cases, a Jewish minority remained. In 1946 there were approximately 650,000 Jews and 1,044,000 Arabs in Palestine. In the war following the proclamation of the state of Israel in 1948, more than 500,000 Arabs fled, leaving an Arab minority of almost 200,000 in the four-fifths of Palestine that became Israel. After the "six-day war" in 1967 the entire territory controlled by Israel contained about 2.4 million Jews and more than a million Arabs. The original Palestinian refugees and their descendants, now approaching a million, were scattered as minorities in several surrounding countries.

The noted authority on European migration Eugene Kulischer compiled a table of population displacements in Europe from World War II to 1948. Omit-

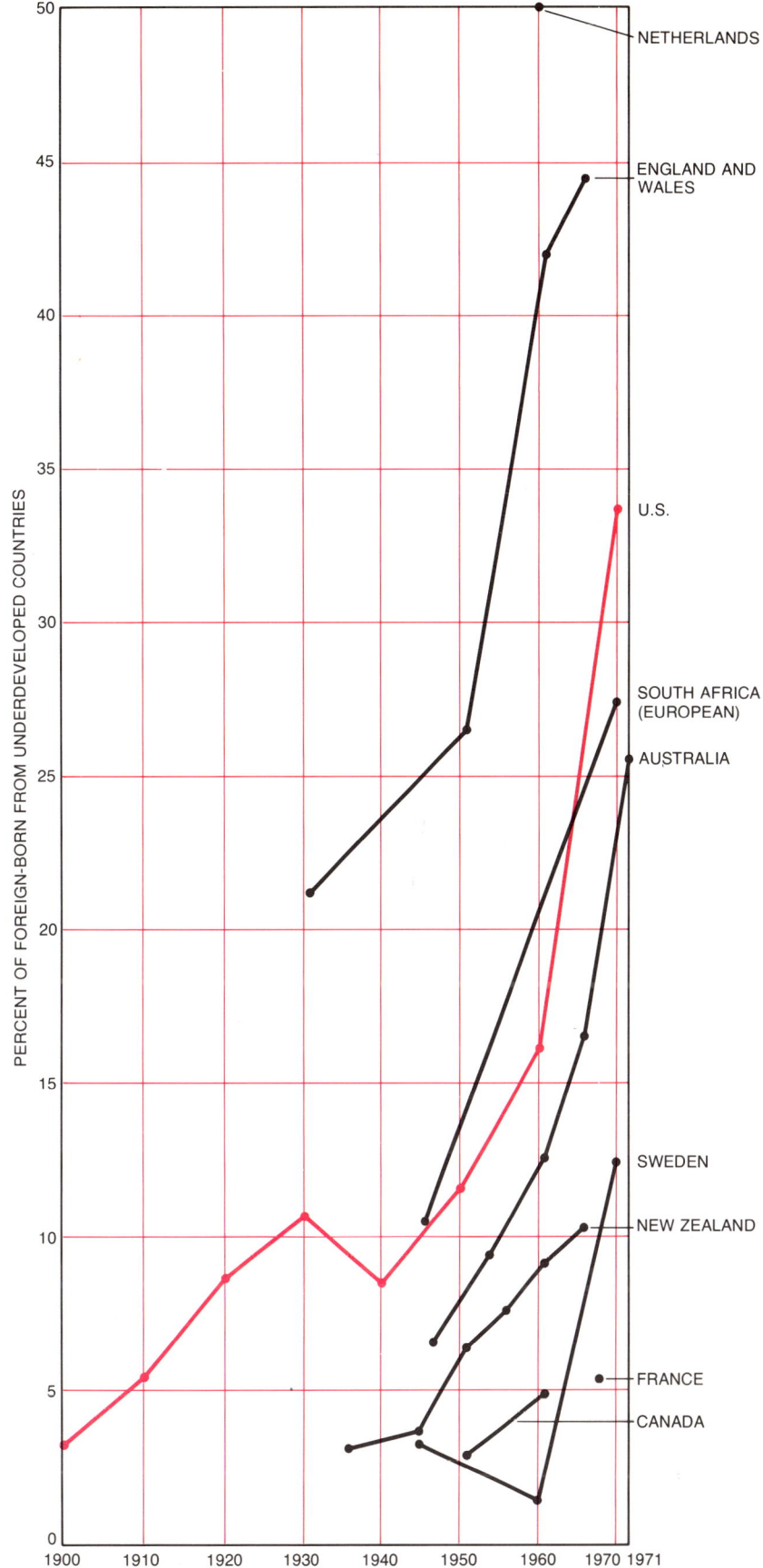

FOREIGN-BORN FROM UNDERDEVELOPED COUNTRIES make up an increasing proportion of the total foreign-born populations of most developed countries, as this graph demonstrates. The U.S. totals for 1940 and 1950 count white foreign-born population only.

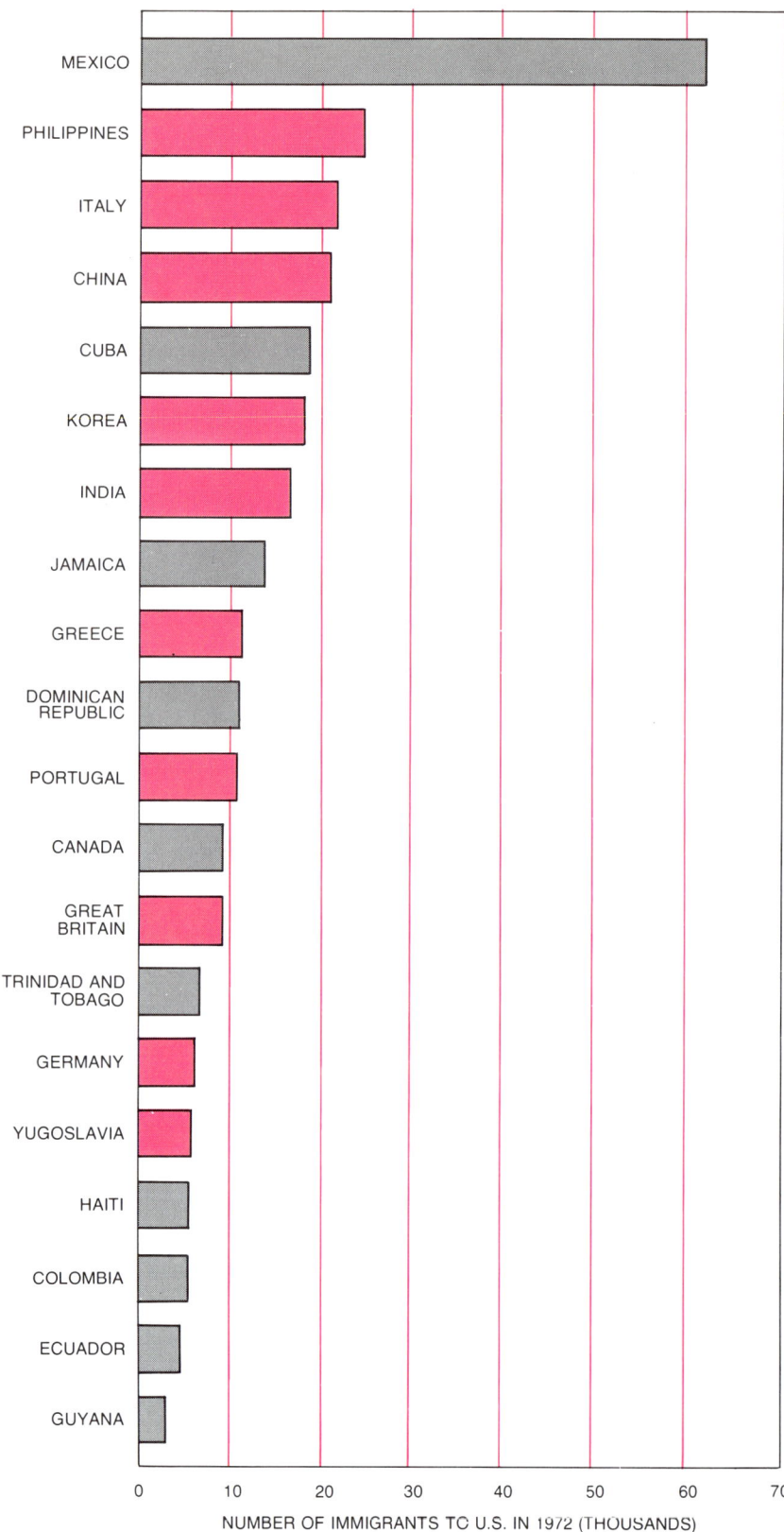

SOURCES OF CURRENT IMMIGRATION TO U.S. are ranked here in descending order, with the top 10 countries of origin in the Western Hemisphere in black and the top 10 in the Eastern Hemisphere in color. The figures for each country in the Western Hemisphere (except for Cuba) represent the number of visas issued in fiscal year 1972; the figure for Cuba includes 16,380 "adjustments of status" granted by the Immigration and Naturalization Service to aliens subject to numerical limitations. The figures for the Eastern Hemisphere represent the number of visas issued in fiscal year 1972 (excluding recaptured visas) together with the number of adjustments of status and conditional entries granted to aliens subject to numerical limitation. Chart is based on 1973 data from U.S. Department of State.

ting internal displacements, some of which were enormous, the total comes to 18.3 million. For the periods from 1913 to World War II and from 1948 to 1968 I have tallied exchanges and refugee movements totaling 28.7 million. If we add similar displacements in Asia, Africa and the Western Hemisphere, the grand total for the world during the period from 1913 to 1968 comes to 71.1 million. This number of migrants is considerably higher than the estimated 52 million who left Europe of their own free will in the heyday of the transatlantic movement from 1840 to 1930, in spite of the fact that the period is shorter (55 years compared with 90).

Clearly the amount of forced migration since 1913 belies predictions that world migration would diminish. But what about free migration? The answer is that it has not diminished either, but it has changed direction. Instead of flowing from the crowded industrial countries of Europe to open spaces in the New World, it has gradually shifted until it is now flowing toward developed countries everywhere. The nations of northwestern and central Europe, exporters of people for so long, are now net importers. The New World industrial countries, still relatively uncrowded, receive professional and highly qualified immigrants from industrial Europe, but increasingly their migration is from less developed countries in southern and eastern Europe, Asia, Latin America and Africa.

Evidence of the surge into developed nations is abundant. Four New World countries—Australia, Canada, New Zealand and the U.S.—received a net total of 13.9 million migrants between World War II and 1972. The U.S. alone, still admitting more foreigners than any other nation in the world, received 9.2 million during that period. More surprising is the tide of migrants into industrial Europe; for example, Sweden, for centuries a country of emigration, became a country of immigration after 1930 [see illustration on page 141]. Other advanced countries in Europe have shown a similar reversal, some more sharply than Sweden. Data on seven such countries, including Sweden, reveal a net migration of 6.3 million between 1950 and 1972. Adding this figure to the one for the four New World countries gives a total of 20.2 million net migrants to 11 industrial countries during the period.

What explains the reversed migration into industrial Europe and the continued migration into New World industrial nations? In my view the driving force is the widening technological and demographic gap between the developed nations and the underdeveloped three-fourths of the world. The gap differs in several important respects from the former differences between Europe and the rest of the world. First, the developed nations are now scattered over the entire world instead of being concentrated in Europe. Second, the underdeveloped countries are no longer overwhelmingly colonies but rather are independent nations. Third, the technological gap has widened in absolute terms while commercial and intellectual communication has drawn the two classes of nations closer together. Fourth, the demographic contrast between the two groups has been reversed. Formerly the technologically advanced nations had the most rapid population growth; now it is the technologically backward nations, and their rates of growth are without precedent. The population of the 176 countries I classify as underdeveloped in 1950 increased by 1.04 billion from 1950 to 1972, while the population of the 47 developed countries increased by only 200 million. Originally more sparsely populated, the underdeveloped countries as a whole were already more densely settled than the developed ones in 1950. Their comparative density was still greater by 1970: 36.3 persons per square kilometer compared with 17.2 in the developed countries.

As a consequence of the gap as it is now constituted the advanced countries have on the average more resources per person, more workers in relation to dependents, more capital generated from savings and more investment and trade. They therefore have more jobs and offer higher wages. Their native populations have become so educated, comfortable and upwardly mobile that in times of labor shortage they refuse to fill low-paying, low-status or disagreeable jobs. Millions of workers in the bulging underdeveloped countries are eager to take those jobs, and employers are anxious to hire them. Hence legally or illegally the migrants come, their transit facilitated by modern means of travel and communication and even by government and international assistance.

The dichotomy between developed and underdeveloped is, of course, arbitrary. Special geographic and political circumstances aside, the general principle is that a nation tends to gain migrants from countries less developed than itself and to send migrants to countries more developed. When an underdeveloped nation is close to a developed one (as Mexico is to the U.S. or Greece is to Germany) or has special ties with a developed one (as Britain's ex-colonies have with her), the migratory pressure is very strong. In the U.S. the 1970 census counted 4.53 million people of Mexican origin, more than the number from the rest of Latin America combined but equivalent to only two years of current population increase in Mexico. In Germany the number of foreign workers, 167,000 in 1959, rose to 2,345,000 in 1973, 82 percent of whom came from six countries (Greece, Italy, Portugal, Spain, Turkey and Yugoslavia).

That the immigrant stream is being increasingly drawn from underdeveloped countries is easy to see. In the U.S. the current shifted from northwestern and central Europe to southeastern Europe, and then to Asia and Latin America. In European countries Africa and Asia are playing an increasing role in immigration.

What are the effects of this new free migration? Let us look first at the receiving nations. A few of these are "churners," nations in which immigration and emigration are nearly balanced, leaving only a small net migration. In their case the main effect is not on the population's growth but rather on its composition. Since the immigrants increasingly come from the underdeveloped countries and the natives go to the developed ones, the churners are on the whole taking in untrained people at the bottom of the social hierarchy and sending out trained people at the top. Britain provides an example. Since 1930 she has had a small net intake but large movements in and out. The inward migration has given the country a large foreign-born population (2.5 million in England and Wales by 1966, representing 5.4 percent of the total population). The outward movement has in turn caused a comparable loss of natives: about 3.1 million people born in Britain now live elsewhere. More than a million of the foreign-born are from Africa, Asia and the Caribbean. Although some of them are well educated, the majority are not. On the other hand, 97 percent of Britain's exiles live in five advanced countries: Australia, Canada, New Zealand, South Africa and the U.S. They are mainly well qualified. Evidently Britain is importing relatively unskilled foreigners from the underdeveloped world and sending out her own professional and skilled citizens to more prosperous nations. To a lesser extent the Netherlands is doing the same.

The most prosperous countries are the ones that have the largest net immigration. The influx not only gives them a large foreign population but also adds to their population growth. The growth comes in two ways: directly as a result of the net migration itself and indirectly as a result of the immigrants' natural increase after they arrive. The indirect effect is greater the longer the period of time under consideration is. (The entire population of the U.S. is the result of immigration at some time in the past.) For a period less than a generation the indirect effect is a function of the migrants' fertility and age-sex structure. Normally, since young adults are more numerous among immigrants than among natives, their crude birth rate is higher. On the other hand, international migration ordinarily includes more males than females, thus depressing the crude birth rate. In recent years this rule has not held for the U.S., but in the receiving countries of Europe contemporary free migration, often called "labor migration," is largely composed of young males. In West Germany in 1970–1972, for example, foreign workers were 71 percent male. Finally, the indirect effect of immigration on population growth depends on the fertility of the immigrant women. Insofar as they come from underdeveloped countries, their fertility is high compared with that of native women. In the U.S. in 1970 the number of children ever born to women aged 40 to 44 was 4.4 per woman for those of Mexican origin and 2.9 for all women. In Sweden the fertility of foreign women in 1970 was 28.3 percent higher, age for age, than that of native women. An approximate calculation indicates that about 42 percent of Sweden's increase in population (1.04 million) between 1950 and 1970 was contributed by net immigration: 33 percent by the entry of immigrants themselves and 9 percent by their natural increase during the period. Hence direct immigration accounts for a large share of the growth of the major industrial nations.

Where the economy is concerned net immigration should have a stimulating effect because it adds more workers than dependents, but this benefit is more or less canceled by several factors, including the lower average skills of immigrant workers compared with those of native workers. Since it is the sheer availability of jobs (jobs unacceptable to native workers) rather than wages or conditions that attracts workers from underdeveloped countries, the question is: What would happen if immigrants did not come? One possibility is that certain jobs would be eliminated, jobs too unproductive to justify making them attractive to native labor. More immigrant workers come to the U.S. as live-in maids than as anything else; it would be no great loss to the economy if this category of employment were reduced. Other jobs characteristic of immigrants would be improved with respect to wages and conditions to make them attractive to natives. In other words, immigration enables employers to fill unproductive jobs or to forgo capital improvements, thus slowing the rate of technological progress. These effects are minimized but not eliminated by countries that select their immigrants carefully, such as Australia. For example, a large immigration of physicians and other professionals from underdeveloped countries not only deprives natives of opportunities for upward mobility but also allows inadequacies in the system of professional training to persist.

The assertion that natives will not take the jobs that immigrants fill is curious in view of the considerable unemployment in the industrial countries. Comparisons are misleading because of unstandardized definitions, but unemployment appears to have been rising. It is particularly high in precisely those groups—the least skilled, youths just entering the labor market and poorly educated minorities—that most directly compete with immigrants. In addition, if the industrial countries actually have a labor shortage, there is a reserve labor force that could be tapped to a much greater extent, namely women. In view of the low birth rates prevailing since the late 1950's, there would seem little hindrance to using this reserve and obtaining workers more competent than those from the underdeveloped countries.

Even if the labor shortage is real, immigration is a clumsy way of meeting it. Labor shortages come and go, but whether the migrant workers intend to stay or not, their move is often permanent. Moreover, immigrants do not stay in their first occupation. It is estimated that 57 percent of immigrants certified for a job on entering the U.S. change occupations within two years. Thus extremely short-run problems in labor supply are met by means that incur long-run population growth, the effect of which is to reduce the ratio of resources to people and to make the industrial level of living

EXTREME URBANIZATION of the eastern half of the U.S. is evident in this night infrared photograph made recently by an Air Force weather satellite. The patterns of heat concentration recorded by the infrared film reflect the distribution of population.

still more dependent on draining the rest of the world. There is also the difficulty of assimilation. Immigrants give rise to school problems, health risks, welfare burdens, race prejudice, religious conflicts and linguistic differences.

So dubious are the advantages of immigration that one wonders why the governments of industrial nations favor it. Why do they use such devices as advance job placement, housing aid, bilateral agreements on visas and work permits, and (in countries of origin) official propaganda, recruiting offices and preparatory training programs? Strictly speaking, except where former colonies are involved, their efforts are not directed to the most backward countries but to quasi-developed ones. Still, why invite immigrants at all?

One will find few clarifications, but official statements hint that the goals are to fill essential jobs and to stimulate population growth. One suspects that the actual causes are government inertia and pressure by employers to obtain cheap labor. Given strong employer demand and a limitless supply of job-hungry people in the underdeveloped countries, migration will occur whether it is encouraged or not. To stop it requires a great effort; to permit it requires none. Estimates of all illegal aliens in the U.S. run as high as two million. The tendency to reward illegal entry is illustrated by the announcement in San Francisco on June 4 of this year that the immigration service had resumed its "confession" program. According to the *San Francisco Chronicle*, "aliens who gained entry illegally may confess and have their status adjusted to permanent residency." "Have no fear," the immigration official reportedly said, "we are not out to deport anyone."

Special interests favoring immigration seem better able to influence the government than those opposing it. In a 1951 poll in France 93 percent of the respondents said there were enough foreigners in France. Nevertheless, the French government thereafter pursued one of the most active proimmigration policies in Europe, increasing the proportion of foreign-born from 6.5 percent to 8.7 percent by 1970. Polls in 1965 and 1971 still found the public more than 90 percent opposed to immigration, but French officials were evidently not listening. The respondents in 1971 felt that immigrants from countries closest to France adjust best to French life, yet in 1970–1971, as nearly as can be determined from French data, the government admitted at least 200,000 people from groups considered as being the least assimilable. In Germany 51 percent of those polled in 1965 opposed bringing foreign workers into the country and only 27 percent favored it. Most of those opposed (30 percent) mentioned difficulty of employment as the reason. In Switzerland in 1965, 47 percent of native Swiss employees said they would be willing to work overtime in order to decrease the number of foreign workers in Switzerland. Shortly after some 200,000 Cuban refugees were admitted to the U.S. a poll in Minnesota found 51 percent opposed to admitting them and only 36 percent favorable. In Britain, after a Labor government earlier than the current one had come to power, a poll asked what matters the respondents would like to see the government concentrate on. The third most frequently mentioned item on a list of 13 was "Keep strict controls on immigration." Governments in Europe's industrial countries are now having second thoughts about immigration; although free movement is a basic principle of economic union, it seems likely that the recent volume will be reduced.

Contemporary migration has drawbacks for the sending countries as well as the receiving ones. They derive chiefly from the fact that migration is inevitably selective. Although the quality of migrants may be lower on the average than that of natives in the developed countries, it is higher than that of natives in the underdeveloped nations. Since the developed countries cannot admit all who wish to come, they can pick and choose as the interests of their employers dictate. This means that the underdeveloped country does not simply lose untrained manpower but often loses trained manpower that is scarce and costly to produce. In the U.S. in 1972, of the immigrants admitted who had an occupation 31.1 percent were classified as "professional, technical and kindred workers," compared with only 14 percent in this category in the U.S. labor force. In 1971 there were 8,919 medical degrees conferred in the U.S.; in the same year 5,748 immigrant physicians were admitted and in the next year 7,143 were admitted. At the same time many thousands of American youths failed to gain admission to medical school. Even when, by the standards of the receiving country, the foreign workers are relatively unskilled, they are often on the average better trained than the ones who do not move. In any case emigration removes people of productive age and leaves children and old people, thereby raising the underdeveloped country's already high dependency ratio. The value of remittances sent back home may partly compensate for those losses, but the remittances are uncertain and subject to stoppage or control in times of crisis. Indeed, migration itself may be cut off and migrants may be returned precisely when the sending country is in its worst condition. How ominous that prospect can be is suggested by the fact that in Germany alone the number of Greek workers is equivalent to 8.4 percent of Greece's entire labor force and the number of Portuguese workers is equivalent to 4.7 percent of Portugal's labor force.

For the underdeveloped country emigration appears to be a stopgap allowing postponement of internal economic and demographic changes that would make emigration unnecessary. It is like borrowing money at high interest to pay off debts that one's income could not support in the first place. As the underdeveloped countries become still more crowded, there will be increasing pressure for greater admission to developed countries, on humanitarian grounds if for no other reason. By and large, however, the problems of underdeveloped countries are beyond solution by emigration. If developed nations tried to accept as migrants the excess population growth of the underdeveloped ones, they would currently have to receive about 53 million immigrants per year. This would give them a population growth of 5.2 percent per year, which added to their own natural increase of 1.1 percent per year would double their population every 11 years.

In the future the failure of international migration to solve problems will not necessarily prevent its happening. The present wave of voluntary movement from underdeveloped nations to developed ones may reach a maximum and be reduced, but if so, it will be replaced by other waves. Although particular migratory streams are temporary, migratory pressure is perpetual because it is inherent in technological inequality. In the past migration has helped to fill the world with people. That the world is now full is a new condition that complicates prediction. Another new condition is the degree to which nations can, if they wish, control their borders. Nations strong enough to prevent voluntary migration, however, are also strong enough to engender forced migration. Whether migration is controlled by those who send, by those who go or by those who receive, it mirrors the world as it is at the time.

BIBLIOGRAPHIES

I EARLY CIVILIZATION

1. The Origins of Cities

THE EVOLUTION OF URBAN SOCIETY. Robert M. Adams. Aldine Publishing Company, 1966. (Reviews Adams's hypothesis.)

WHAT HAPPENED IN HISTORY. V. Gordon Childe. Penguin Books, 1946. (Summarizes Childe's basic hypotheses.)

2. The Sumerians

ANCIENT NEAR EASTERN TEXTS RELATING TO THE OLD TESTAMENT. Edited by James B. Pritchard. Princeton University Press, 1950.

THE ART AND ARCHITECTURE OF THE ANCIENT ORIENT. Henri Frankfort. Penguin Books, 1954.

THE BIRTH OF CIVILIZATION IN THE NEAR EAST. Henri Frankfort. Indiana University Press, 1951.

THE INTELLECTUAL ADVENTURE OF ANCIENT MAN. H. and H. A. Frankfort, John A. Wilson, Thorkild Jacobsen and William A. Irwin. The University of Chicago Press, 1946.

SUMERIAN MYTHOLOGY: A STUDY OF SPIRITUAL AND LITERARY ACHIEVEMENT IN THE THIRD MILLENNIUM B.C. S. N. Kramer. The American Philosophical Society, 1944.

FROM THE TABLETS OF SUMER: TWENTY-FIVE FIRSTS IN MAN'S RECORDED HISTORY. Samuel Noah Kramer. The Falcon's Wing Press, 1956.

3. An Early City in Iran

THE SUMERIANS: THEIR HISTORY, CULTURE, AND CHARACTER. Samuel Noah Kramer. The University of Chicago Press, 1963. (The classic work.)

EXCAVATIONS AT TEPE YAHYA, SOUTHEASTERN IRAN, 1967–1969. C. C. Lamberg-Karlovsky in *Bulletin of the American Journal of Prehistoric Research*, No. 27; 1970. (Describes the excavations mentioned here.)

THE INDUS CIVILIZATION. Sir Mortimer Wheeler. Cambridge University Press, 1968. (Another classic.)

4. Teotihuacán

MEXICO. Michael Coe. Praeger Publications, 1962. (A succinct summary of Mexican prehistory including Teotihuacán.)

URBANIZATION AT TEOTIHUACÁN, MEXICO. Edited by René Millon. University of Texas Press, 1974. (The multivolume report on Millon's project, which will appear over a number of years.)

II INVENTIONS AND THE URBAN TRADITION

5. How the Iron Age Began

THE DARK AGE OF GREECE. A. M. Snodgrass. Edinburgh University Press, 1971.

A STEEL TOOL OF THE FOURTH CENTURY B.C. FROM AL MINA IN SYRIA. Tamara S. Wheeler, James D. Muhly and Robert Maddin in *Levant*, Vol. VIII, pages 107–112; 1976.

AN IRON ADZE OF THE FIFTH-FOURTH CENTURIES B.C. FROM AL MINA. James D. Muhly, Tamara S. Wheeler and Robert Maddin in *Levant*, Vol. IX, pages 156–161; 1977.

6. The Beginnings of Wheeled Transport

THE FIRST WAGONS AND CARTS: FROM THE TIGRIS TO THE SEVERN. V. Gordon Childe in *Proceedings of the Prehistoric Society*, Vol. 17, Part 2, pages 177–194. (A useful, if a little outdated, survey article.)

ANCIENT EUROPE. Stuart Piggott. Edinburgh University Press, 1965. (Rapidly becoming a classic source on European prehistory. A thoroughly literate and well-researched study.)

BEFORE CIVILIZATION. Colin Renfrew. Alfred A. Knopf, 1973. (Assesses the impact of new radiocarbon dates on the prehistory of Europe. Complements Piggott.)

7. Roman Carthage

EXCAVATIONS AT CARTHAGE, 1974: FIRST INTERIM REPORT. Henry Hurst in *Antiquaries Journal*, Vol. 55, pages 11–40; 1975.

EXCAVATIONS AT CARTHAGE CONDUCTED BY THE UNIVERSITY OF MICHIGAN, 1975: I. Edited by John H. Humphrey. Tunisian National Institute of Archaeology and Art, 1976.

CARTHAGE 1977: THE PUNIC AND ROMAN HARBORS. L. Stager in *Archaeology*, Vol. 30, pages 198–200; 1977.

EXCAVATIONS AT CARTHAGE, 1975: SECOND INTERIM REPORT. Henry Hurst in *Antiquaries Journal*, Vol. 56, Part 2, pages 177–197; 1977.

8. The Archaeology of Winchester

The Winchester excavations have been summarized in a series of preliminary reports written by Martin Biddle in *The Antiquarian Journal*, Vol. 44–54; 1964–1974. The articles appear annually except for 1971, 1972, and 1973.

WINCHESTER: THE BROOKS. Andrew and Wendy Selkirk in *Current Archaeology*, No. 20, pages 250–255. (A brief account of one part of the excavations. Reprinted in *Corriders in Time*. Edited by Brian M. Fagan. Little, Brown and Company, 1974.)

9. The Planning of a Maya Ceremonial Center

EXCAVATIONS AT LUBAATUN, 1970. Norman Hammond in *Antiquity*, Vol. 44, pages 216–223; 1970.

THE AZTECS, THE MAYA, AND THEIR PREDECESSORS. Muriel Porter Weaver. Seminar Press, 1972. (A useful summary of the field.)

III CONSEQUENCES

10. The Origin and Evolution of Cities

THE CULTURAL EVOLUTION OF CIVILIZATIONS. Kent V. Flannery in *Annual Review of Ecology and Systematics*, Vol. 3, pages 399–426; 1972. (A fascinating essay on the mechanics of urban life.)

THE EMERGENCE OF CIVILIZATION. Colin Renfrew. Methuen & Company, Ltd., 1972. (Another study of mechanisms, this time in an Aegean context.)

THE PREINDUSTRIAL CITY: PAST AND PRESENT. Gideon Sjoberg. The Free Press, 1960.

11. Human Food Production as a Process in the Biosphere

MALNUTRITION AND NATIONAL DEVELOPMENT. Alan D. Berg in *Foreign Affairs*, Vol. 46, No. 1, pages 126–136; October, 1967.

ON THE SHRED OF A CLOUD. Rolf Edberg. Translated by Sven Ahmån. The University of Alabama Press, 1969.

POLITICS AND ENVIRONMENT: A READER IN ECOLOGICAL CRISIS. Edited by Walt Anderson. Goodyear Publishing Company, Inc., 1970.

POPULATION, RESOURCES, ENVIRONMENT: ISSUES IN HUMAN ECOLOGY. Paul R. Ehrlich and Anne H. Ehrlich. W. H. Freeman and Company, 1970.

SEEDS OF CHANGE: THE GREEN REVOLUTION AND DEVELOPMENT IN THE 1970's. Lester R. Brown. Praeger Publishers, 1970.

12. An Early Energy Crisis and Its Consequences

THE RISE OF THE BRITISH COAL INDUSTRY: VOLS. I AND II. John U. Nef. George Routledge & Sons, Ltd, 1932.

NOTE ON THE PROGRESS OF IRON PRODUCTION IN ENGLAND, 1540–1640. John U. Nef in *The Journal of Political Economy*, Vol. 44, No. 3, pages 398–403; June, 1936.

SILVER PRODUCTION IN CENTRAL EUROPE, 1450–1618. John U. Nef in *The Journal of Political Economy*, Vol. 49, No. 4, pages 575–591; August, 1941.

THE AGRICULTURAL REVOLUTION. Eric Kerridge. Allen & Unwin Ltd, 1967.

WAR AND HUMAN PROGRESS: AN ESSAY ON THE RISE OF INDUSTRIAL CIVILIZATION. John U. Nef. W. W. Norton & Co., 1968.

13. The Migrations of Human Populations

EMIGRANT COMMUNITIES IN SOUTH CHINA. Ta Chen. Institute of Pacific Relations, 1940.

THE MYTH OF OPEN SPACES. W. D. Forsyth. Melbourne University Press in association with Oxford University Press, 1942.

EUROPE ON THE MOVE: WAR AND POPULATION CHANGES, 1917–1947. Eugene M. Kulischer. Columbia University Press, 1948.

THE REFUGEE IN THE WORLD: DISPLACEMENT AND INTEGRATION. Joseph B. Schechtman. A. S. Barnes and Company, 1963.

BRITAIN AND THE LABOR TRADE IN THE SOUTHWEST PACIFIC. Owen W. Parnaby. Duke University Press, 1964.

THE ATLANTIC SLAVE TRADE: A CENSUS. Philip D. Curtin. University of Wisconsin Press, 1969.

REFUGEES SOUTH OF THE SAHARA: AN AFRICAN DILEMMA. Edited by Hugh C. Brooks and Yassin El-Ayouty. Negro Universities Press, 1970.

THE UN AND THE PALESTINIAN REFUGEES. Edward H. Buehrig. Indiana University Press, 1971.

INTERNATIONAL MIGRATION LAW. Richard Plender. Humanities Press, Inc., 1972.

MIGRATION AND ECONOMIC GROWTH: A STUDY OF GREAT BRITAIN AND THE ATLANTIC ECONOMY. Brinley Thomas. Cambridge University Press, 1972.

THE MIGRATION OF WORKERS IN THE UNITED KINGDOM AND THE EUROPEAN COMMUNITY. W. R. Böhning. Oxford University Press, 1972.

INTERNATIONAL MIGRATION in *The Determinants and Consequences of Population Trends: Vol. I*. United Nations, 1973.

INDEX

Accessibility index, 99–101
Adab, 27, 40
Adams, Robert M., 7, 11–17
Agade, 27
Age and migration of peoples, 143, 147
Agricola, Georgius, 130, 132
Agriculture
  advances in, 120, 121
  biosphere and food production, 119–128
  colonization and, 139–142
  England, 135
  erosion of soil, 123
  fertilizer, consumption of, 122–124, 126, 127
  genetics, 120
  hybrid crops, 120, 121
  Lubaantún, 102
  Mayans, 95
  mechanization of, 122, 123
  Mesopotamia, 11–17, 119
  overpopulation and, 107
  slavery and, 140, 141
  soil erosion, 123
  Teotihuacán, 41, 51
  See also Irrigation
Ah, Basilio, 96
Akkad, 19, 110
Allen, John S., 134
Al Mina, 61, 62, 64
Al Ubaid, 40
Andean peoples, 112, 113
Animal husbandry. *See* Domestication of animals
Animal remains
  Carthage ruins, 81
  Lubaantún, 97, 98
Anyang, 112
Arab empires, 115, 118
Aratta, 20
Architecture, 7
  Carthage, 78, 80, 81
  Elizabethan England, 132
  Lubaantún, 95–104
  Mesopotamia, 12, 14, 15
  Sumerian cities, 23
  Teotihuacán, 41–51
  Tepe Yahyā, 32–40
  Winchester, 83–94
  See also Houses
Armenian discovery of wheeled transport, 65–67
Arsenical copper ores, 57, 58
Ashley, Sir William, 135
Asmar, 20
Assyrian cities, 19, 39
Athens, 114, 139
Autonomy of cities, 118
Aztecs, 41–51, 54, 95, 112

Babelon, E. C. F., 75
Bacon, Francis, 134
Baden culture and wheeled transport, 69, 171
Bakun, 33
Ball courts of Lubaantún, 95, 101, 102
Bampur, 31, 35, 40
Barbarians, migrations of, 138, 139
Behistun, Rock of, 19
Bell-beaker potters, 138
Benares, 113
Bernal, Ignacio, 41, 50
Beschaouch, Azedine, 75
Biddle, Martin, 55, 83–94
Biosphere and food production, 119–128
Biringuccio, Vannoccio, 130
Blacksmithing, 57–64
Braidwood, Robert J., 12
Britain. *See* England
Brno (Czechoslovakia), 70
Bronze, smelting of, 57–64
Bronze Age sites, 57, 114
  Tepe Yahyā, 2–40
Brooks, Robert R., 123
Brown, Lester R., 107, 119–128
Bullard, Reuben G., 80, 82
Burial
  Baden culture, 69–71
  Elista, 68
  Kura-Araxes culture, 68
  Lake Sevan, 68, 69
  Sumerians, 23
  Tepe Yahyā, 32
  Trialeti, 68, 70
  Ur excavations, 18
  See also Cemeteries

Buttrey, T. V., 77
Byzantine empire, 114–116, 118

Cacao trees, beans of, 102
Caldwell, Joseph R., 31
Carandini, A., 75, 76
Carbon-14. *See* Dating
Carburization of iron, 57–64
Carthage, 3, 55, 56, 75–82
Carts, invention of, 65–73
Cemeteries
  grave offerings, 12, 15, 16
  Roman Winchester, 84, 85
  Ur excavations, 15
  Winchester, 85, 89, 90
  See also Burial
Chalcopyrite, 57
Charioteer of the Blues mosaic, 74
Chariots, invention of, 65–73
Chemical fertilizers, 126, 127
Chichén Itzá, 100
Childe, V. Gordon, 2, 6, 7, 113
Chinese civilization, 1, 111
  chariot, pictographs of, 68
  iron smelting, 59
  trade routes, 113, 114
  urban centers of, 8
Cholula, 41, 49
Churches
  Carthage ruins, 80, 81
  Winchester, 83–94
Clarendon, Lord, 134, 135
Climate
  alteration of, 125, 126
  origin of cities and, 109
  Teotihuacán, 51
Coal, use of, 107, 129–135
Coe, William R., 50
Coitburi, 89
Colonization, 108, 139, 142
Contenau, G., 38
Copper-smelting sites, 57
Cort, Henry, 131, 132
Crafts, 6, 7
  17th century England, 135
  Sumerians, 23
  Teotihuacanos, 49
Cuicuilco, 41, 49

Cuneiform tablets, 19, 20, 26, 27
    evolution of Sumerian writing, 24, 25
    pictures of, 22
    signs, 24, 25
Curtin, Philip D., 141

Darby, Abraham, 131
Dark Ages, 115
Dating
    calendar years and, 72
    corroboration in written records, 12
    Sumerian civilization, 20
    Tepe Yahyā tablets, 31–33
    wheels, 67–69
Dávalos, Eusebio, 41
Davis, Kingsley, 108, 118, 137–149
Davis, Nathan, 76
DDT, use of, 119, 127
de Cardi, Beatrice, 31
Decision-making, 7
Definition of civilization, 1
Denmark, discovery of wheels, 69–72
Descartes, René, 134
Diadem of Queen Shub-Ad of Sumer, 29
Dietz, S., 76
Dilmun, 34, 35, 39
Domestication of animals, 12
    biosphere and food production, 119–128
    horses, 55
    Mesoamerica, 112
    migration of peoples, 137, 138
    productivity, 120, 121
    Tepe Yahyā, 32
    wheeled transports and, 55, 65
Dunbabin, Katherine, 80
Dura Europos, picture of, 115
Dwellings. See Houses
Dzibilchaltun, 111

Early Bronze Age, 32–34
Early Dynastic period of Mesopotamia, 15, 17
Egyptian civilization, 12, 110
Elamite culture, 19, 31–40
Elista burials, 68
Energy sources, 8, 107, 121, 123
    Britain in 16th century, 129–135
    preindustrial cities and, 109
    scarcity of, 122, 123
England
    agriculture in, 135
    attitudes on immigration, 149
    colonization, 139–142
    energy sources in 16th century, 129–135
    migrations of people, 147
    population of, 129
    social structure of, 118
    Winchester, history of, 83–94
Erbil, aerial view of, 14
Erech, 20, 27, 110
Eridu, 110
Ethnic purity, 144, 145
Eunatti, Abdelinajid, 75
Euphrates and Tigris Rivers. See Mesopotamia
Eutrophication of fresh waters, 127
Ewig, E., 115

Falbe, C. T., 76
Famine, 128
Fayalite, 58
Fertile Crescent. See Mesopotamia
Fertility and migration, 147
Fertilizer, consumption of, 122–124, 126, 127
Feudal society, 109
Figurines
    Pusilhà, discoveries, 102
    Tepe Yahyā, 34, 39
Flannery, Kent, 7
Folk societies, 1, 2, 109
Food
    biosphere and production of, 119–128
    Carthaginian diet, 81
    chart of food energy, 125
    feudal societies, 109
    folk societies, 109
    Lubaantún, 101
    malnutrition, 128
    Mesopotamia, 12, 113
    See also Agriculture
Ford, Richard I., 81
Foreign born populations, chart of, 144
Form of civilization, 1
Forsyth, W. D., 144
France and immigration, 149
Frank, Tenney, 139
Frankfort, Henri, 1
Fuel supplies. See Energy sources

Games of Maya, 95, 101, 102
Germany and immigration, 149
Gilgamesh, 16, 27
Gordion, 61
Government, 106
    Mesopotamia, 15, 16
    Sumerian cities, 23
    theocracy, 113
Grave offerings, 12, 15, 16
Gurgan River, city on, 109

Hammond, Norman, 56, 95–104
Hammurabi
    code of, 22
    Sumerians and, 30
Harrappan culture, 35, 37–40, 110
Harris, John R., 131, 135
Harrison, William, 130
Hasanlu, 61
Hattusha, 39
Hauser, Henri, 135
Hayes, John W., 77
Hazelden, John, 96
Hematite, 58
Hittites, 39, 138
Homo erectus, migration of, 137
Homo politicus, 2
Honduras, Maya ceremonial center, 95–104
Horse, domestication of, 55
Houses
    Carthage ruins, 78, 80
    Lubaantún, 99
    Mesopotamia, 17
    Roman Winchester, 84
    Sumerians, 23
    Teotihuacán, 45, 47

Winchester, 84, 89–91
Humphrey, John H., 55, 75–82
Hurst, Henry, 75
Hybrid crops, 121, 122

Idalion, 61
Incas, 54, 95, 112
Industrial Age, 3, 55
Industrial Revolution, 106–108, 118
    coal as new source of energy, 129–135
    migrations of people and, 140, 142–146
Ireland
    emigration and, 139
    potato introduced in, 119
Iron
    electron micrograph of, 58
    implements of, 54, 57–64
    quenching process, 62, 63
    smelting of, 57–64
Iron Age, 114
    Tepe Yahyā, 37
Irrigation, 122, 124, 125
    diverting of rivers, 125
    feudal societies, 109
    Mesopotamia, 12–14
    Sumerians, 19, 20
    Teotihuacanos and, 41
    See also Agriculture
Isin, 30

Jacobsen, Thorkild, 15
Jamaica and migration of people, 143
Jerusalem, 113
Jevons, William Stanley, 133

Kaminaljuyu, 50
Kelsey, Francis W., 76
Kerridge, Eric, 135
Khafaje, 40
King, Gregory, 129
Kish, 20, 27, 39, 40, 67, 68, 110
Kluckhohn, Clyde, 7
Kramer, Samuel Noah, 8, 19–30
Kulischer, Eugene, 145
Kulli-Damb, 40
Kültepe, 39
Kura-Araxes culture, 68, 72

Labor shortages and migration, 147–149
Lagash, 20, 27, 110
Lake Sevan, 66, 68
Lake Urmia and wheeled transports, 65–73
Lake Van and wheeled transports, 65–73
Lamberg-Karlovsky, C. C., 31–40
Lamberg-Karlovsky, Martha, 31–40
Lancel, S., 75
Landsberger, Benno, 20
Larsa, 30
Lattimore, Richard, 62
Law code
    Hammurabi, 22
    Sumerians, 19, 30
Lchashen carts, 68, 69
Literacy. See Writing
Lubaantún, 56, 95–104
Lucca, picture of, 116

McKerrell, H., 32, 34
McLuhan, Marshall, 65
Maddin, Robert, 54, 57–64
Magan, 34
Magnetite, 58
Mallery, Col. Garrick, 137
Mallowan, Max, 61
Malnutrition, 128
Maluhha, 35
Mari, 34, 40
Marx, Karl, 135
Mathematics, 135
    Arabs, 115
    Mayans, 111
Maurya empire, 113
Maya civilization, 12, 50, 51, 112
    agriculture of, 95
    ball games, 100
    cities of, 112
    domestication of animals, 113
    Lubaantún, 56, 95–104
    stelae of, 95, 103, 104
    writing, 112
Mechanization, 121, 123
Medical science, 118
    Sumerians, 23
Mesoamerica
    crops of, 113
    development of urban centers, 8
    origin of cities in, 111
    Teotihuacán, 8, 9, 41–51, 95, 107, 112
    See also Maya civilization
Mesopotamia, 11–17, 111
    agriculture, 119
    archeological periods of, 15, 16
    architecture of, 12, 14, 15
    chariots, 69
    forms of cities, 17
    fortification of cities in, 17
    grave offerings, 15, 16
    irrigation in, 12–14
    literacy, 110
    map of, 13, 37
    militarism in, 16, 17
    population of, 17, 111
    pre-urban, 12, 13
    religious institutions in, 15
    social stratification, 16, 17
    technological development, 16, 17
    Tepe Yahyā, 8, 31–40
    trade and, 8
    wheeled transport, 55, 65, 67
    written records of, 17
    See also Sumerians
Metals
    Mesopotamia, 16, 17
    Tepe Yahyā, 32–40
    See also Iron
Metalworking, 138
Mexico, maps of early civilizations, 42, 44
Migrations of people, 107, 108, 137–149
Militarism
    Mesopotamia, 16, 17
    Teotihuacán, 50
    See also Warfare
Miller, Naomi, 81
Millon, René, 9, 41–51, 112
Mining, 129, 130

Minorities and migration, 144, 145
Mixtecs, 112
Mohenjo-Daro, 34, 40, 110
Monte Alban, 51
Monuments. See Architecture
Morison, Samuel Eliot, 132
Morley, Sylvanus Griswold, 104
Mosaics of Carthage, 76, 78, 80
Mount Adir, 61
Muhly, James D., 57–64
Müller, Paul Hermann, 127
Multhauf, Robert, 133
Murals of Teotihuacán, 51
Music of Sumerians, 23
Myths
    Aztec, 51
    Sumerian, 15

Nef, John U., 107, 129–135
Neolithic man, 137, 138
    Tepe Yahyā, 32, 33
Netherlands, discovery of wheels, 69–72
Newcomen, Thomas, 133, 134
Nigeria, Yoruba tribe of, 14
Nimrud, 61–63
Nineveh, 19, 114
Nippur, 20, 23, 40
    destruction of, 27
    excavation of, 28
    map of, 11
Numbers. See Mathematics

Oaxaca, Valley of, 47, 49
Obsidian mining, 41
    Lubaantún, 101
    Teotihuacán, 47
Olmecs, 41
Oppert, Jules, 19, 20
Overijssel, 72

Pacific Islands, settlement of, 138
Paddock, John, 49
Paleolithic man, 137
Pearlite, electron micrograph of, 60
Pedley, John Griffiths, 55, 75–82
Persian empire, 113
Pesticides, 119, 127, 128
Petén lowlands, maps of, 96
Phoenicians, expansion of, 114
Pictographs
    Lone Dog's "Winter Count," 136
    Sumerians, 24
    wheeled transport, 68
Piedras Negras, 95
Piggott, Stuart, 54, 65–73, 138
Pit Grave culture, 68, 73
Pivoted axles, 68
Plow, invention of, 20
Pompeii, 114
Population, 106, 107
    biosphere and food production, 119–128
    criteria for civilization, 7
    emigration and, 142, 143
    England in 16th century, 129
    Lubaantún, 101
    Mesopotamia, 17, 110

    migrations of, 137–149
    Rome, 115
    Sumerian cities, 23
    Teotihuacán, 45, 48, 49
    Tikal, 48–50, 112
    written records of, 17
Potato introduced in Ireland, 119
Pottery
    bell-beaker potters, 138
    Carthage ruins, 77, 78, 80
    Mesopotamian tombs, 12
    Roman Winchester, 85
    Tepe Yahyā, 32–40
    wheels, 69, 70
Preindustrial civilization, 3
Protein deficiency, 128
Protoliterate period of Mesopotamia, 15, 17
Puckle, James, 135
Punic wars, 75
Pusilhà, 102, 104
Pyramid of the Moon, 41–51
Pyramid of the Sun, 41–51

Quarries
    Carthage ruins, 82
    Lubaantún, 97
Quetzalcoatl, Temple of, 41–51
Quiriguá, 95

Race and migrations of people, 143
Radiocarbon dating. See Dating
Rakob, F., 75
Redfield, Robert, 1, 2, 4
Reese, David, 81
Religion, 6, 7, 106
    Lubaantún, accessibility at, 99–101
    Mesopotamia, 15
    Sumerians, 24–26
Residences. See Houses
Revelle, Roger, 125
Riley, J. A., 77
Rock of Behistun, 19
Roman empire, 3, 114, 115
    Carthage, 3, 55, 56, 75–82
    collapse of, 9
    invaders and, 138, 139
    slavery, 139
    Winchester, history of, 55, 56, 83–94

Sailboat, invention of, 20
St. Catharine's Hill, 83, 85
Salt trade, 133
Sanders, William T., 42
Sargon the Great, 27
Sassanian occupation of Tepe Yahyā, 37, 38
Scanning electron microscope, 58, 60, 61
Schistosomiasis, 125
Schmidt, Erich F., 109
Schools of Sumerians, 26, 27
Science, advancement of, 106, 118
Seals
    Mesopotamia, 16, 17
    Sumerian cylinder, 23, 24
    Tepe Yahyā, 33–40
Seleucia, 114
Sénay, P., 75
Settlement patterns, 95, 96, 106

Sex and migration, 143, 147
Shahdāb, 33, 40
Shahr-i-Sokhta, 40
Shuruppak, 20
Sialk, 33
Sioux Indians, 136, 137
Sjoberg, Gideon, 106, 109–118
Slavery, 23, 108, 139, 141
Smelting, 57–64
Smith, Adam, 133
Smith, Alan, 134
Snail fever, 125
Snodgrass, A., 57
Soapstone trade, 31, 34–40
Social organization, 7, 112, 113
    Teotihuacán, 47, 49
Soil erosion, 123, 124
Spearheads from Ur, 15
Specialists, 109, 112, 113
Statuettes of Sumerians, 26, 27
Steeled iron, 57–64
Stein, Sir Aurel, 31
Stelae of Maya, 95, 103, 104
Stone weights of Sumerians, 29
Streets
    Teotihuacán, 42, 43
    Winchester, 90, 91
Stross, Fred H., 101
Sumerians, 7, 8, 18–30
    accomplishments of, 19
    agriculture, 12
    crafts, 23
    education and, 26, 27
    history of, 27, 30
    horse, domestication of, 55
    inventions of, 20, 23
    law code of, 19, 30
    life of, 20–23
    map of Sumer, 20, 21
    myths of, 15
    religion of, 24–26
    settlement patterns, 106
    vehicles, pictograph of, 68
    warfare, 27
    writing, evolution of, 24
    See also Cuneiform tablets
Surveying instruments, development of, 20, 23
Susa, 33, 35, 67, 114
Sweden
    fertility of foreign born women in, 147
    migration in, 141, 146
Systems models, 7

Tal-i-Iblis, 31–40
Technology
    coal, use of, 131
    migrations of people and, 137
    modern agriculture, 121, 123
    origins of cities, 113
Tell Aqrab, 40
Tell Asmar, 39, 40
Telloh, 40
Temple of Quetzalcoatl, 41–51
Temples. See Architecture
Tenochtitlán, 41
Teotihuacán, 8, 9, 41–51, 95, 107, 112
Tepe Yahyā, 8, 31–40
Theocracy, 112
Tigris and Euphrates Rivers. See Mesopotamia
Tikal, 48, 50, 111
Timber
    Carthage ruins, 81, 82
    coal to replace, 129–135
    shortage of, 107
    wheels, 65, 72, 73
Tools
    iron implements, 57–64
    Mesopotamia, 16, 17
    Teotihuacán, 49
    Tepe Yahyā, 32–40
Toynbee, Arnold, 1
Trade, 8
    Elamite trading, 31
    Italian city-states, 115
    Lubaantún, 101, 102
    Teotihuacanos, 41
    Tepe Yahyā, 32–40
    Winchester, 83
Traffic plans, 99–101
Transcaucasia and wheeled vehicles, 65–73
Trialeti burials, 68, 70
Troy, 55
Tunis, 75
Turkestan empire, 114
Tylecote, R. F., 32, 34

Ubaid period of Mesopotamia, 15–17
Umma, 38
Umm-an-Nai, 35
Underdeveloped countries, migration from, 145, 146, 149
Unemployment and migration, 147–149
United States, immigration to, 142, 146

Ur, 15, 16, 18, 20, 24, 27, 39, 40, 67, 68, 110
Ur-of-the-Chaldees, 55
Uruk, 16, 17, 65, 72
Usumacinta River, 95

Venice, 115, 118
Venta Belgarum, 84
Vesalius, Andreas, 118
Vijayanagar, 114
von Liebig, Justus, 126

Wagons, invention of, 20, 65–73
Walton, Michael, 96
Warfare
    Mesopotamia, fortification of cities in, 17
    migrations of people, 138, 139
    Rome and Carthage, 75
    Sumerians, 27
    See also Militarism
Warka period of Mesopotamia, 15
Weapons, 57
Weber, Max, 135
Wells, C., 75
Westermann, William Linn, 139
Wheeled transport, 54, 65–73
Wheeler, Sir Mortimer, 40
Wheeler, Tamara S., 57–64
Wheels, 54, 65–73
Wightman, E., 75
Winchester, 55, 56, 83–94
Wing, Elizabeth S., 96
Wood. See Timber
Woolley, Sir Leonard, 110
Writing, 6, 7, 109, 110
    Elamite tablets, 19, 31, 33–40
    Incas, 112
    Mesoamerica, 111
    Mesopotamia, records of, 17
    proto-Elamite tablets, 31, 33–40
    Sumerians and, 7, 8, 24
    Tepe Yahyā, 31, 34–40
    See also Cuneiform tablets

Yaxchilán, 95
Yoruba tribe of Nigeria, 14

Zapotecs, 112
Zelenyy, 68